EVEN AS WE SPEAK

CLIVE JAMES is the author of more than twenty books. As well as three volumes of autobiography, *Unreliable Memoirs*, *Falling Towards England* and *May Week Was in June*, he has published collections of literary criticism, television criticism, verse and travel writing. His most recent novel was *The Silver Castle*. As a television performer he has appeared regularly for both the BBC and ITV, most notably as writer and presenter of the *Postcard* series of travel documentaries. He helped to found the independent television company Watchmaker, and is currently chairman of the Internet enterprise *Welcome Stranger*. In 1992 he was made a member of the Order of Australia.

BY THE SAME AUTHOR

CLIVE JAMES
EVEN AS WE SPEAK

NEW ESSAYS 1993–2000

PICADOR

To Christopher Hitchens

in affectionate disagreement

First published 2001 by Picador
an imprint of Macmillan Publishers Ltd
25 Eccleston Place, London SW1W 9NF
Basingstoke and Oxford
Associated companies throughout the world
www.macmillan.com

ISBN 0 330 48176 2

Typeset by Intype London Ltd
Printed and bound in Great Britain by
Mackays of Chatham plc, Chatham, Kent

Mankind is conservative. When this tendency weakens, however, revolutions devote themselves to its renewal.

Ernesto Sabato, *Uno y el universo*

The generations work within each other in the most amazing way, and it doesn't need the Kingdom of Death to bring people of profoundly different times together in speech.

Golo Mann, *Friedrich von Gentz*

Just as to the eyes of the emigrant who goes home after a long exile the familiar appears stripped clean, so the assimilated man possesses a particular acuity of gaze: the cultural manifestations with which he lacks an intimacy become the frozen material of his absorption, and thus reveal their structures all the more clearly.

Jürgen Habermas, *Philosophische-Politische Profile*

Contents

Introduction

'A man either has a picture of the world, or he lives in a world of pictures. In the first case, he has only to report the facts, and his report will have style. In the second case, he may strive for a style all he likes, but he will never have one.'

Anton Kuh, *Luftlinien*

Finally, it is a writer's way of putting things that gives unity to his work. There is no other unity that the fugitive pieces in this book can claim, but I don't need telling that it is a large claim to make. It is like saying that fragments can add up to an edifice. None of the pieces here collected, however, felt like a fragment at the time. They all felt like something to which I was giving everything I had, even when the subject seemed trivial. And some of the subjects, alas, didn't seem trivial at all.

They never have. Six decades after I was born into its years of triumph, the Nazi era is still here, still at the centre of intellectual discussion, still demanding, insatiably, to be dealt with. The same applies to the Soviet Union, which is gone but not forgotten – a lot less forgotten, in fact, than it was when it was still in business. In the year of my birth, Stalin's terror was at its frenzied height: in the year I turn sixty, scholars are still trying to find out exactly what went on. The scholars who finally figure it all out will almost certainly have come into the world long after those particular horrors happened. My only claim to expertise is that I was *there*, when all those innocent people were being obliterated. It was clever of me to be less than four feet tall and to have chosen Australia as my birthplace, a good way away from the nearest mass graves, but I still got a solid dose of the insecurity that radiates from historical disaster and works its most arresting mental distortions on minds of a tender age. (Nor, indeed, were the nearest mass graves all *that* far away: while I was running in baggy shorts around the back garden, blasting the sugar-ants with my wooden machine-gun, the Imperial Japanese Army was still busy reminding the Asian and Pacific countries it had promised to liberate from colonialism that they had been wrong to suppose there could be nothing worse than European arrogance.) When you grow up in an epoch seemingly dedicated to extermination, it influences your world view for life. Opinions can change – they are on the surface of the mind – but a world view is part of the soul, as fundamental as your sense of what is fair or funny. When we shy from a man who tells tasteless jokes, it isn't his wit that we don't like, it's his *Weltanschauung*. Hitler, after all, could be quite a card.

Throughout my six collections of non-fiction, it is thus no mystery that there is a consistency of outlook: nobody else would be unable to say the same. The only mystery is why I should have bothered to express it. I could say that for anyone who earns his living by being unrelentingly *allegro* it is hard to resist the temptation of proving himself *penseroso* as well: we all like to be thought deep. But there has always been more to it than that, or anyway it has always felt to me as if there has. If I had wanted to be thought deep, I would have spent the last thirty years proposing something a lot less scrutable than the elementary proposition that democracy is even more important for what it prevents than for what it provides. Some quite complicated issues grow out of that proposition – the most troublesome being that a free nation is bound to provide opportunities for incitement to the very kind of suffocating orthodoxies whose hegemony it exists to prevent – but there is nothing complicated about the proposition itself, beyond the consideration that historic circumstances drilled it into my head almost before I could spell the words in which it is written. The best justification for plugging away at the self-evident, it seems to me, arises from the lurking fear that for too many people who should know better it doesn't seem to be self-evident at all. My first book of essays, *The Metropolitan Critic*, was assembled in 1974 in the immediate aftermath of the counter-culture, which some of its *illuminati* fancied as the Cultural Revolution of the West. (Their notions of what the Cultural Revolution of the East had really been like, it must be said in mitigation, were of the haziest.) Many of the pieces in the book had been written when the idea was still in vogue that youthful values represented some kind of political vision all by themselves. Still feeling quite youthful myself at the time, I thought there was something to it, and said so: there *was* a new generosity in the air, and American foreign policy, with the disaster in Vietnam as its stellar achievement, *did* need opposing – the patent decency of some of its American opponents was sufficient evidence of that.

But here already the difference between mere opinions and a world view showed up with awkward clarity. The undoubted fact that democracy was currently making a murderous fool of itself couldn't make me forget that totalitarianism was still the enduring and implacable antagonist. I had opinions about what a democratic state should do in the circumstances – pull out of Vietnam, decommission the CIA, put Henry Kissinger on trial for sedition, stop subsidizing the kind of dictators who exported their own economies to Switzerland – but it was part of my world view that a totalitarian state was unjustifiable in any circumstances. The boat people hadn't yet set sail, but I was already with them in spirit. It bothered me that there were so many of our bright young people eager to buy the whole radical package, up to and including the potentially lethal notion that if the representative political structure could be reduced to a state of nature, paradise would ensue. *We've got to get ourselves back to the garden.* The universities, in particular, were stiff with young enthusiasts who plainly had no idea of what could be lying in wait for them at the bottom of the garden, especially at night. Even worse, some of the loudest enthusiasts were on the faculty, actually *teaching* that the tenure they themselves had safely attained was not worth having, that the modern democratic state was the repressive mechanism of late Capitalism, that – but there was no end to it.

There never would be an end to it. Such was the realization that completed my battle with the eggshell. To find ourselves, we all have to fight our way out of isolation, because it is only in the community outside that individuality is to be had. The role of the freelance man of letters (the personage on whom I so blithely conferred the title of Metropolitan Critic) is to accept – and to act on the acceptance – that he is engaged in a perpetual discussion, an interminable exchange of views in which he cannot, and should not, prevail. If he could prevail, and the discussion did terminate, he would have become his enemy, the dogmatist whose only answer to opposition is annihilation – a response which, for a mercy, he is usually allowed only to dream of, but which he would put into practice if he could.

Not even Orwell ever dared to suggest that the reason why so
many professional intellectuals sympathized with totalitarian regimes
was that they themselves were born totalitarians, but looking back
from the end of the century there seems reason to think that the
state of mind all too often goes with the territory. In 1936 Stefan
Zweig, characteristically employing his wide cultural range to focus
an acute political perception, traced the tendency back to sixteenth-
century Geneva. In his book *Castellio gegen Calvin, oder Ein Gewissen
gegen die Gewalt* ('Castellio against Calvin, or A Conscience against
Power') he convincingly demonstrated why Calvin's natural mode of
argument against a preacher of religious tolerance was to burn him.
Clearly Zweig had aimed his book at Hitler, although it would also
have fitted Stalin, whose own mode of assertive philosophical discourse was already well in train, with the death toll running far into
the millions. More disturbing, in the long term – more disturbing
because less immediately obvious – is the way it fits generations of
modern thinkers. Comfortably domiciled in academic institutions or
on the heights of literary prestige, they never actually killed anyone
but didn't seem to mind much when other people did. It is perhaps
not my place to make too much of this (there is always a chance that
my view of twentieth-century history is not only dark, it is neurotic-
ally so), but I do sometimes wonder why, in the continuing discussion
about, say, Heidegger, the possibility is not more often entertained
that he actually *liked* the idea of helpless people being kicked in the
mouth. As I go on reading deeper into our era's mental background,
more and more often I find myself needled by the unsettling suspicion
that there is an intellectuals' version of 'If only the Führer knew' and
'Someone must tell Stalin'. It is the consoling assumption that if
Sartre, for example, could have been brought to *imagine* what the
Gulag system was really like, he would never have granted the Soviet
Union the prestige of his loftily withheld condemnation. But what
(whisper it) if he *did* imagine it?

It's a dreadful thought, and I wouldn't want to try erecting it
into a principle. For one thing, as Raymond Aron suggested in his
calling-card booklet *Le Spectateur engagé*, it is always a mistake to
underestimate the role of sheer obtuseness in human affairs. You
don't need to have malice aforethought to make a travesty of the
history happening around you. Benevolence aforethought can work
the same trick. The mountainous accumulation of progressive theorizing that we nowadays characterize as *gauchiste* grew out of the most

generous side of the human character. Even Karl Popper, the great deconstructor of Karl Marx's scientific pretensions, took care to acknowledge his stature as an inspirational visionary. For a hundred and fifty years, left-wing analysis retained the impetus of Christian revelation. Even after the Soviet Union, its holy land, showed clear signs of coming to pieces, the Marxist heritage retained its prestige. In the Soviet bloc nobody with any sense believed any of it – direct experience had done its work – but in the West there was still a reputation for frivolity to be earned by not paying it sufficient respect. By 1979, when I published my second collection of critical pieces, *At the Pillars of Hercules*, the dissident movement in the USSR had built up an impressive body of achievement, but it is possible to guess, by the tone of what I wrote on the subject, that I thought there were intelligent readers in the West who might still need persuading that some of their dearest beliefs were in the process of being not just questioned peripherally but discredited utterly. The same was still true in 1982, when I published *From the Land of Shadows*. In retrospect, 1982 was the year when the eventual collapse of the Soviet Union became inevitable. The tanks of the Red Army should have come to Poland: when they didn't it was a sign that they would never come again. But in a piece about Osip Mandelstam, I can still be found speaking as if the historical forces that did for him might yet do for us.

A paranoid reflex? Possibly. A reactionary view, certainly: but the question remains of what I was reacting against. I wish it had been a figment of my imagination, but all the evidence that has accumulated since suggests that I was right to start asking myself a new question. In cancer research, it was the asking of a new question that revolutionized the field. The old question, which had had the merit of seeming reasonable but the drawback of being unanswerable, was: why do some people get cancer? The new question was: why doesn't everyone get it? The answer turned out to be that everyone does, all the time, but a mechanism called apoptosis ensures that in most people the disease makes no progress. In politics and culture, my old question, prompted by the seemingly anachronistic savagery of the times I had been born into, had been about totalitarianism: why does it sometimes happen, what starts it? My new question was: what if it always happens, and it takes something to stop it? The implications of this line of thought were unsettling, but they had the merit of opening up to interpretation a vast array of phenomena that I had previously found baffling. The most immediately alarming of these was constituted by the successive waves of pseudo-scientific dogma that had taken over humane studies in the universities, most damagingly in the English faculty. Most of this busy but essentially vacuous theorizing could be traced back to the obscurantism of the French left, an obscurantism whose origins could in turn be traced back to the period of the Occupation, when there had been shamefully good reasons for intellectuals to hatch an impersonal language by which history would take responsibility for what they said. What was startling, however, was the way that these Laputan doctrines, all dedicated to the dismantling of humane culture rather than its protection, continued to flourish as belief in the prospect of an egalitarian utopia declined. Indeed they burgeoned, with constantly self-renewing supplies of virulent energy.

Capped by its masterpiece, political correctness, the irrationality in the universities clearly had its provenance in the classic Left. Other rampaging viruses just as clearly had their provenance in the classic Right: specialization, atomization, niche-marketing, the transformation of tabloid journalism into a sort of plain-clothes police state – they all worked the sadly recognizable trick of erecting opportunism to the status of a principle. Whatever their origins, it seemed more realistic to treat these developments as malignant strains bursting with their own vitality, rather than as mere symptoms of a benign system grown weary. As a corollary, the main discussion from now on would have to be about what values would prevail in bourgeois democracy, and not about how bourgeois democracy would be replaced. But by now everyone was acting that way, even if they could not yet bring themselves to declare it. The tendency was well established by the time I published *Snakecharmers in Texas* in 1989. The Soviet Union was on its last legs and the End of History was already being proclaimed. (For the quarter of the world's population who were still up to their necks in history, this was one more insult than they needed, but by some trick of the mind the Chinese as individuals have never mattered much more to us than they did to Mao.) It was at last being generally accepted that the only struggle for power that counted would take place within the society we already had. In the eye of eternity, such an acceptance had only ever been a matter of time. What Lassalle tried to tell Marx was always going to be true: the free-market economy, as an economic system, had a much greater potential for development than Marx ascribed to it, whereas the command economy had much less. Despite the perennial suspicion of the totalitarian Left that the totalitarian Right was capitalism's logical offshoot and natural ally, the bourgeois democracy so despised by both extremes inexorably proved, by its power to defend itself, that it was capitalism's natural host; and, by its power to go on developing a supervening structure of liberal institutions, that it was the only political system with a plausible claim to the future, because it alone could accommodate the unexpected. Bourgeois democracy has never been susceptible to exhaustive analysis: it has always grown beyond the limitations ascribed to it by its critics because it is capable of listening to them. It doesn't always listen, and scarcely ever at the right time: but the possibility of listening is not ruled out, and that's enough.

It would have gone beyond conceit, and far into megalomania, to suppose that it was my business to speak in a way which would ensure that bourgeois democracy would listen to me. In *The Dreaming Swimmer* (1992), my last book of collected pieces before this one, the only section of the Establishment I specifically targeted as an audience was the television executives, whom I took every opportunity to lecture on their duty to sustain public service broadcasting. They greeted my passionate sentiments with deafening applause and altered their conduct not one iota. I would have been surprised had it been otherwise. Really, in all these books, I have had no other audience in mind except people like myself: generalists repelled by an age of increasing specialization, misfits caught between the active and the contemplative life, hustlers too hard at work to examine at leisure the way the world is going yet incurably athirst for the totality of knowledge – the true, the eternal students. If I am right, and all the forces which made life an out-and-out nightmare in the totalitarian societies are likely, albeit in less toxic form, to go on spoiling the daydream of the democratic ones, then such non-utilitarian concepts as humanity and individuality will always have to be fought for. They will be best fought for by those of us who know something about what life is like when they are absent, and by those young people to whom we succeed in passing on our historic memories. It is all talk, but this is a job that can be done only by people talking. Even as we speak, so shall our children live. For someone who gives his time and effort to this kind of writing, a proud view is always handy to give him courage: he can think of himself as the people's champion. For the humble view that he needs to stay sane, he can always console himself with the realization that to be ignored by the state is his proper destiny. Were things otherwise, the state would be in a worse condition than he is. Anton Kuh, from whose writings I took the epigraph at the head of this introduction, was one of the Viennese coffee-house wits whose mastery of the brief critical essay reached its apotheosis in the last nervous years before the *Anschluss*. He did bits and pieces: a parody here, a *feuilleton* there, a cabaret act around the next corner. Among his little triumphs was a prosodic analysis of Hitler's oratorical style that would have earned him the reward of death by torture if the Nazis had ever caught him.

If I had the audacity and the sparkling talent of Anton Kuh, I would call him my kind of writer. Yet along with his moral and verbal gifts went a gift which among writers is even rarer – a sure sense of the complex, mutually sustaining relationship between society and the arts, between politics and civilization. Even as disaster loomed, Kuh, like so many of his fellow Jewish men of letters, found himself desperately conjuring up bright ideas about how it might be staved off. Kuh's brightest notion was for the government to attract a last-minute majority among the people by springing one of the most popular Socialist leaders from gaol. Kuh shared this idea with Mahler's widow, the famous and famously influential Alma. To Kuh's astonishment and gratification, Alma arranged a meeting between Kuh and a top-echelon government official. The official listened to Kuh's proposal in detail, promised to do something about it, and left for his ministry. Kuh left for the railway station, where he caught the last train for Prague that was not boarded by Stormtroopers at the frontier. With the solid realism that lay at the foundation of his brilliant facility, he had correctly deduced that any administration with time to consider his ideas was doomed.

Anton Kuh died forgotten in New York in 1940, from one of those heart attacks which among his generation were the polite way of saying heartbreak. But like his acidly lyrical voice, the message of his precisely calculated getaway is still transparent across time: if we would speak to each other, we must speak first of all for ourselves, with no other end in view save to speak well. My usual thanks go to the editors who helped me try to do this: they had a lot to put up with, but I like to think it was mainly because I was trying to get a lot said.

London, 2001

WHICH NEVER SLEEPS OR DIES

THE ALL OF ORWELL

Who wrote this? 'Political language – and with variations this is true of all political parties, from Conservatives to Anarchists – is designed to make lies sound truthful and murder respectable, and to give an appearance of solidity to pure wind.' But you guessed straight away: George Orwell. The subject stated up front, the sudden acceleration from the scope-widening parenthesis into the piercing argument that follows, the way the obvious opposition between 'lies' and 'truthful' leads into the shockingly abrupt coupling of 'murder' and 'respectable', the elegant, reverse-written coda clinched with a dirt-common epithet, the whole easy-seeming poise and compact drive of it, a world view compressed to the size of a motto from a fortune cookie, demanding to be read out and sayable in a single breath – it's the Orwell style. But you can't call it Orwellian, because that means Big Brother, Newspeak, The Ministry of Love, Room 101, the Lubyanka, Vorkuta, the NKVD, the MVD, the KGB, KZ Dachau, KZ Buchenwald, the *Reichsschrifttumskammer*, Gestapo HQ in the Prinz-Albrecht-Strasse. *Arbeit macht frei, Giovinezza, Je suis partout,* the compound at Drancy, the Kempei Tai, Let A Hundred Flowers Bloom, *The Red Detachment of Women,* the Stasi, the Securitate, cro-magnon Latino death squad goons decked out in Ray-bans after dark, that Khmer Rouge torture factory whose inmates were forbidden to scream, Idi Amin's Committee of Instant Happiness or whatever his secret police were called, and any other totalitarian obscenity that has ever reared its head or ever will.

The word 'Orwellian' is a daunting example of the fate that a distinguished writer can suffer at the hands of journalists. When, as almost invariably happens, a totalitarian set-up, whether in fact or in fantasy – in Brazil or in *Brazil* – is called Orwellian, it is as if George Orwell had conceived the nightmare instead of analysed it, helped to create it instead of helping to dispel its euphemistic thrall.

(Similarly Kafka, through the word Kafkaesque, gets the dubious credit for having somehow wished into existence the same sort of bureaucratic labyrinth that convulsed him to the heart.) Such distortions would be enough to make us give up on journalism altogether if we happened to forget that Orwell himself was a journalist. Here, to help us remember, are the twenty volumes of the new complete edition, cared for with awe-inspiring industry, dedication and judgement by Peter Davison, a scholar based in Leicester, who has spent the last two decades chasing down every single piece of paper his subject ever wrote on and then battling with publishers to persuade them that the accumulated result would supply a demand. The All of Orwell arrives in a cardboard box the size of a piece of check-in luggage: a man in a suitcase. As I write, the books are stacked on my desk, on a chair, on a side table, on the floor. A full, fat eleven of the twenty volumes consist largely of his collected journalism, reproduced in strict chronology along with his broadcasts, letters, memos, diaries, jottings, *et* exhaustively and fascinatingly *al*. The nine other volumes, over there near the stereo, were issued previously, in 1986–87, and comprise the individual works he published during his lifetime, including at least two books that directly and undeniably affected history. But, lest we run away with the idea that *Animal Farm* and *Nineteen Eighty-Four* are the core of his achievement, here, finally, is all the incidental writing, to remind us that they were only the outer layer, and could not have existed without what lay inside. Those famous, world-changing novels are just the bark. The journalism is the tree.

A four-volume edition of the journalism, essays, and letters, which was published in 1968 (co-edited by Ian Angus and Orwell's widow, Sonia), had already given us a good idea of how the tree grew, but now we get an even better chance to watch its roots suck up the nutrients of contemporary political experience and— But it's time to abandon that metaphor. Orwell never liked it when the writing drove the meaning. One of his precepts for composition was 'Let the meaning choose the word, and not the other way around.' For him prose style was a matter in which the ethics determined the aesthetics. As a writer, he was his own close reader. Reading others, he was open to persuasion, but he would not be lulled, least of all by mellifluous rhetoric. Anyone's prose style, even his, sets out to seduce. Orwell's, superficially the plainest of the plain, was of a rhythm and a shapeliness to seduce the angels. Even at this distance, he needs watching, and would have been the first to admit it.

*

Orwell was born into the impoverished upper class – traditionally, for its brighter children, a potent incubator of awareness about how the social system works. Either they acquire an acute hunger to climb back up the system – often taking the backstairs route through the arts, *à la* John Betjeman – or they go the other way, seeking an exit from the whole fandango and wishing it to damnation. Orwell, by his own later accounts, went the other way from his school days onward. In one of his last great essays, 'Such, Such Were the Joys', he painted his years at prep school (where he nicknamed the head-master's gorgon of a wife Flip) as a set of panels by Hieronymus Bosch:

> 'Here is a little boy,' said Flip, indicating me to the strange lady, 'who wets his bed every night. Do you know what I am going to do if you wet your bed again?' she added, turning to me. 'I am going to get the Sixth Form to beat you.'

Orwell had a better time at Eton – it sounds as if he would have had a better time in Siberia – but twenty years later, after he left it, reviewing his friend Cyril Connolly's partly autobiographical *Enemies of Promise*, he poured scorn on Connolly's fond recollections of the place. When Connolly proclaimed himself fearful that after his climactic years of glory at Eton nothing in the rest of his life could ever be so intense, Orwell reacted as if Flip had just threatened to deliver him to the Sixth Form all over again: ' "Cultured" middle-class life has reached a depth of softness at which a public-school education – five years in a luke-warm bath of snobbery – can actually be looked back upon as an eventful period.'

Orwell often reviewed his friends like that. With his enemies, he got tough. But it should be said at the outset that even with his enemies he rarely took an inhuman tone. Even Hitler and Stalin he treated as men rather than as machines, and his famous characterization of the dogma-driven hack as 'the gramophone mind' would have lost half its force if he had not believed that there was always a human being within the fanatic. His comprehension, though, did not incline him to be forgiving: quite the reverse. Society might have made the powerful what they were as surely as it had made the powerless what they were, but the mere fact that the powerful were free to express whatever individuality they possessed was all the more reason to hold them personally responsible for crushing the freedom of others. When they beat you, you can join them or you can join the fight on behalf of those they beat. It seems a fair guess that Orwell had already made his choice by the time Flip threatened him with a visit from the Sixth Form.

*

In the early part of his adult life, he was a man of action. He wrote journalism when he could – for him it was more natural than breathing, which, thanks to a lurking tubercular condition, eventually became a strain – but he wanted to be where the action was. Already questioning his own privileged, if penny-pinching, upbringing and education, he went out to Burma at the age of nineteen and for the next five years served as a colonial policeman – an experience from which he reached the conclusion (incorporated later into his novel *Burmese Days* and his essays 'Shooting an Elephant' and 'A Hanging') that the British Empire was a capitalist mechanism to exploit the subjugated poor. Back in Europe, he found out what it was like to be a proletarian by becoming one himself – *Down and Out in Paris and London, The Road to Wigan Pier* – and expanded his belief about the exploitative nature of the Empire to embrace the whole of capitalist society, anywhere. He volunteered for service in Spain in the fight against Franco, and the selfless comradeship of ordinary Spaniards risking their lives to get justice – *Homage to Catalonia* – confirmed his belief that an egalitarian socialist society was the only fair and decent alternative to the capitalist boondoggle, of which Franco's Fascism, like Hitler's and Mussolini's, was merely the brute expression.

So here, already formed, were two of his three main political beliefs – about the awfulness of capitalism and the need for an egalitarian alternative. There was nothing uncommon about them except their intensity: plenty of intellectuals from his middle-class background had reached the same conclusions, although few of them as a result of direct experience. The third belief was the original one. It was more than a belief, it was an insight. Again, he was not the only one to have it, or at any rate part of it: though such illustrious invitees to the Soviet Union as Bernard Shaw, H. G. Wells and the Webbs had been fooled into admiration by the standard tricks of Potemkin Village set-dressing, Bertrand Russell, André Gide, E. E. Cummings, Malcolm Muggeridge and several other visiting commentators had already spotted that the vaunted socialist utopia was a put-up job, and in 1938 the Italian-born Croatian ex-Communist Anton Ciliga, in his book *Au pays du grande mensonge* (In the Land of the Big Lie), gave a detailed account of the Gulag system, which he knew from the inside. But nobody ever expressed his revulsion better or more lastingly than Orwell, who got it right without ever having to go there.

He went somewhere else instead. Discovering in Spain, from the behaviour of the Russian representatives and their Communist adherents, that the Soviet Union was as implacable an enemy of his egalitarian aspirations as Nazi Germany or Fascist Italy, he developed the idea that it wasn't enough to be against Mussolini and Hitler: you had to be against Stalin as well, because the enemy was totalitarianism itself. That was as far as he got before his career as a man of action came to an end. Shot in the throat by a sniper, he recuperated, but if he had stayed in Spain any longer he would have almost certainly been murdered. The anarchist group in whose ranks he had fought, the POUM, was being liquidated on Soviet orders, and his name was on the list. (The evidence is all here, in Volume XI, and it is enough to bring on a cold sweat: losing Orwell to the NKVD would have had the same devastating effect on our intellectual patrimony that the loss of the historian Marc Bloch and the literary critic Jean Prévost to the Gestapo had on the French.)

Back in England with his three main beliefs – capitalism was a disease, socialism was the cure, and Communism would kill the patient – the erstwhile man of action carried on his cause as a man of letters. For part of the Second World War, he was a member of the Home Guard, and for a further part he was with the BBC, preparing broadcasts for India, but as far as the main action went he was an onlooker. No onlooker ever looked on more acutely. The journalism he wrote at the close of the thirties and in the forties would have been more than enough by itself to establish him as having fulfilled his life's purpose, which he made explicit in his last years: 'What I have most wanted to do is to make political writing into an art.' The whole heavy atmosphere of the prelude to the war, the exhausting war itself, and its baleful aftermath: it's all there, reported with a vividness that eschews the consciously poetic but never lapses from the truly dramatic, because he had the talent and the humility to assess even a V-1 in terms of its effect on his own character, using his soliloquy to explain the play:

> Every weapon seems unfair until you have adopted it yourself. But I would not deny that the pilotless plane, flying bomb, or whatever its correct name may be, is an exceptionally unpleasant thing, because, unlike most other projectiles, it gives you time to think. What is your first reaction when you hear that droning, zooming noise? Inevitably, it is a hope that the noise *won't stop.* You want to hear the bomb pass safely overhead and die away into the distance before the engine cuts out. In other words, you are hoping that it will fall on somebody else.

Along with the exterior drama, however, an interior drama is now, at long last, fully revealed. Tracking his mind from note to memo, from letter to book review, from article to essay, we can see what happened to those early beliefs – which two of them were modified, and which one of them was elaborated into a social, political, ethical and even philosophical concept whose incorporation into *Animal Farm* and *Nineteen Eighty-Four* would make him into a man of action all over again, a writer whose books helped to bring down an empire, even if it wasn't the same empire he originally had in mind.

First, though, with the Spanish war over and the full European war not yet begun, he had another battle on his hands, bloodless this time but almost as noisy: the battle against Britain's left-wing intellectuals. He realized that they had wilfully declined to get the point about Spain: they still saw Communism as the only bulwark against Fascism. Worse, they thought that the Moscow trials were justified or otherwise to be condoned – a price worth paying to Build Socialism. Orwell's conviction that no socialism worth having could be built that way set him at odds with the progressive illuminati of his generation, and that altercation was made sharper by how much he and they had in common. He, too, had had the generosity to declare his own privileges meaningless if they were bought at the expense of the downtrodden. He, too, believed that the civilization that had given birth to him was a confidence trick. And, although

he had already concluded that free speech was the one liberal institution no putative future society could abolish if it was to remain
just, he still thought that the plutocratic oligarchy allowed liberal
institutions to continue only as part of the charade that favoured the
exploitation of the poor. (In the sixties, the same notion lived again,
as 'repressive tolerance'.) Fascism, he proclaimed, was just bourgeois
democracy without the lip service to liberal values, the iron fist
without the velvet glove. In 1937, he twice ventured the opinion that
democracy and Fascism 'are Tweedledum and Tweedledee'. In the
same year, he warned that 'the moneyed classes' might trick Britain
into 'another imperialist war' with Germany: language hard to
distinguish from Party-line boilerplate.

Orwell could always see the self-serving fallacy of pacifism, but
he had a soft spot for Bertrand Russell's version of it, which should
have been detectable as pure wind even at the time, when Hitler had
already spent more than five years abundantly demonstrating that
the chances of the non-violent to temper his activities by their moral
example were exactly zero. But Orwell gave the philosopher's well-
intended homilies a sympathetic review. Orwell was thus in line
with the Labour Party, which, from the opposition benches, railed
against the threat of Fascism but simultaneously condemned as
warmongering any moves towards rearmament. It was the despised
reactionaries, with Chamberlain at the head of the Conservative
government and Churchill growling encouragment from the back
benches, who actively prepared for war against Hitler. Distancing
himself from the Communists and their fellow travellers in his attitude to the USSR, Orwell was dangerously close to them in supposing
bourgeois democracy to be teetering on the rim of history's dustbin,
into which more realistic forces would combine to shove it beyond
retrieval. In Germany, the same aloof attitude on the part of the social
democrat intellectuals had fatally led them to high-hat the Weimar
Republic while the Communists and the Nazis combined to strangle
it, but Orwell had not yet fully learned the lesson. On the Continent,
or already fleeing from it, there were plenty of veteran political
commentators who had learned it all too well at the hands of one
or the other of the two extremist movements and sometimes both,
but apart from Franz Borkenau, Arthur Koestler and perhaps Boris
Souvarine it is remarkable how few of them influenced Orwell's views.
By international standards he was a late developer.

Pre-war, Orwell was in a false position, and his journalistic output during the war is largely the story of how he came to admit it. But before he started getting round to that, he had one more, even more glaring, false position still to go. When the war began he said that Britain was bound to be defeated unless it had a social revolution, which might even require an armed uprising. Possibly he had been carried away by the rifles issued to the Home Guard, and had visions of an English POUM taking pot shots at the oppressor. (Orwell rose to the rank of sergeant in the Home Guard, but Davison should have found room to say, in a footnote, that his hero was notoriously more enthusiastic than competent: a Court of Inquiry was conducted after he supervised a mortar drill that almost resulted in the decapitation of one of his men.) Even in 1941, well after the Battle of Britain demonstrated that this bourgeois democracy might well hope to withstand Hitler, we can still hear Orwell promising that 'England is on the road to revolution' and that to bring the revolution about a 'real English socialist movement' would be 'perfectly willing to use violence if necessary'.

But if a pious wish helped to sustain him, the facts were simultaneously hard at work on a mind whose salient virtue was its willingness to let them in. He had noticed that Poland, whatever the condition of its liberal institutions under the pre-war regime, was immeasurably worse off now that the Nazis and the Soviets (following the letter of the Molotov-Ribbentrop Pact's secret protocols, although he had no means of knowing that yet beyond guesswork) had combined to expunge all traces of its civilization, including as many of its intelligentsia as they could round up. There were steadily accumulating written indications that he was becoming more and more impressed by the one fact about his country he had never been able to argue away. A state against which he could say out loud that he 'was perfectly willing to use violence if necessary' might have something to be said for it – something central, and not just peripheral – if it was not perfectly willing to use violence against him.

Probably armed more by his ability to interpret news than by solid reading of social theorists, Orwell can be seen elaborating his own theory of society towards the point where he would begin to abandon some of its postulates, which had come from classical Marxism and its dubious historiographic heritage. Reviewing, in that same year, 1941, a book of essays about the English Revolution of 1640 edited by the Marxist historian Christopher Hill, Orwell pinpointed 'the main weakness of Marxism', its inflexible determination to attribute to 'the superstructure' (his inverted commas as well as mine) even the most powerful human motives, such as patriotism. Orwell asked the Marxist contributors an awkward question: 'If no man is ever motivated by anything except class interests, why does every man constantly pretend that he is motivated by something else?'

Orwell had spent a lot of time before the war saying that class interests were indeed predominant – especially the interest of the ruling class in sacrificing the interests of every other class in order to stay on top – but now he had discovered his own patriotism, and typically he followed up on the climb-down. Even before the war, he had been impressed by how the English people in general had managed to preserve and develop civilized values despite the cynicism of their rulers. Now he became less inclined to argue that all those things had happened merely because the sweated labour of colonial coolies had paid for them, and were invalidated as a result. He was even capable, from time to time, of giving some of the cynical rulers a nod of respect: Orwell's praise of Churchill was never better than grudging, but nobody else's was ever more moving, because nobody else would have so much preferred to damn Churchill and all his works. From the early war years until the end of his life, Orwell wrote more and more about British civilization. He wrote less and less about the irredeemable obsolescence of bourgeois democracy. He had come to suspect that the democratic part might depend on the bourgeois part.

Most of the left-wing intellectuals hadn't. After Hitler clamorously repudiated his non-aggression pact with Stalin by launching Operation Barbarossa, they were once again able to laud the virtues of the Soviet Union at the tops of their voices. Even on the right, keeping Uncle Joe sweet was regarded as mandatory. In this matter, Orwell showed what can only be described as intellectual heroism. Though his unpalatable opinions restricted his access to mainstream publications – most of his commentaries were written for *Tribune*, an influential but small-circulation weekly newspaper backed by the Labour Party's star heavyweight, Aneurin Bevan – Orwell went on insisting that the Soviet regime was a tyranny, even as the Red Army battled the Panzers to a standstill on the outskirts of Moscow. At this distance, it is hard to imagine what a lonely line this was to take. But when it came to a principle Orwell was the sort of man who would rather shiver in solitude than hold his tongue.

Solitude fitted his character. Though he was sociable, and even amorous, in his everyday life, he didn't look it: he looked as gauntly ascetic as John Carradine, and in his mental life he was a natural loner. Collectivist theories could appeal to his temperament for only so long, and in this strictly chronological arrangement of his writings we can watch him gradually deconstructing his own ideology in deference to a set of principles. Even with this degree of document-ation, it is not easy to see quite when he shifted aside a neat notion in order to let an awkward fact take over, because for a crucial period of the war he metaphorically went off the air. Literally, he had gone on it. For a two-year slog, from 1941 to late 1943, he expended most of his time and energy broadcasting to India for the BBC. Belated market research on the BBC's part revealed that not many Indians were listening (you guessed it: no radios), but the few who did manage to tune in heard some remarkable stuff from a man who had expended so much ink on insisting that the British would have to quit India. Orwell told them the truth: that they had a better chance with the British than with the Japanese. He also scripted weekly summaries of the war's progress. Writing on the tenth of January, 1942, he remarked on a tonal shift in Germany's official pronouncements:

> Until a week or two ago, the German military spokesmen were explaining that the attack on Moscow would have to be postponed until the spring, but that the German armies could quite easily remain on the line they now occupied. Already, however, they are admitting that a further retreat – or, as they prefer to call it, a rectification of the line – will be necessary . . . Before the end of February, the Germans may well be faced with the alterna-tive of abandoning nearly all their conquests in the northern part of the Russian front, or of seeing hundreds of thousands of soldiers freeze to death.

It was an optimistic forecast for 1942, but it all came true in 1943, and it showed two of Orwell's best attributes operating at once: he had a global grasp, and he was able to guess the truth by the way the other side told lies. The broadcasts make such good reading today that you almost feel sorry he ever stopped. From these indirect sources, you can surmise something of what was going on deep within his mind, and when he started writing journalism again he retroactively filled in some of the gaps. From the realization that the violent socialist revolution would not take place, he was apparently moving towards the conclusion that it should not. Reviewing a collection of Thomas Mann's essays published in English translation in 1943, he praised Mann in terms that would have been impossible for him before the war: 'He never pretends to be other than he is, a middle-class Liberal, a believer in the freedom of the intellect, in human brotherhood; above all, in the existence of objective truth.' While careful to point out that Mann was pro-socialist, and even excessively trustful of the USSR, Orwell went on to note, approvingly, that 'he never budges from his "bourgeois" contention that the individual is important, that freedom is worth having, that European culture is worth preserving, and that truth is not the exclusive possession of one race or class.' For Orwell, who had once preached that bourgeois democracy existed solely in order to bamboozle the proletariat into accepting its ineluctable servitude, this was quite a switch.

At no time did Orwell come quite clean about having rearranged the playing field. Near the end of 1943 he conceded that he had been 'grossly wrong' about the necessity of a revolution in order to stave off defeat. But to concede that he had been 'grossly wrong' about his view of society was beyond even him, and no wonder. It would have been to give away too much. By now he was always careful to say that he wanted a *democratic* socialism, and was even ready to contemplate that reconciling a command economy with individual liberty might be a problem: but he still clung tenaciously to the socialist part of his vision, in his view the only chance of decent treatment for everyone. Piece by piece, however, he was giving up on any notion that his socialist vision could be brought about by coercion, since that would yield liberty for no one. If he had lived long enough, his fundamental honesty might have given us an autobiography which would have described what must have been a mighty conflict in his soul. As things are, we have to infer it.

His socialist beliefs fought a long rearguard action. In that same year, 1943, he gave *The Road to Serfdom* a review tolerant of Hayek's warnings about collectivism, but there was no sign of Orwell's endorsing the desirability of free market economics. Orwell was still for the centralized, planned economy. He never did quite give up on that one, and indeed, at the time, there must have seemed no necessity to. To stave off defeat, Britain had mobilised its industry under state control – had done so, it turned out, rather more thoroughly than the Nazis – and, with the war won and the country broke, even the Royal Family carried ration books without protest. So a measure of justice had been achieved.

In hindsight, the postwar British society that began with the foundation of the National Health Service *was* the socialist revolution – or, to put it less dramatically, the social-democratic reformation which Orwell had gradually come to accept as the only workable formula that would further justice without destroying liberty. The Welfare State began with shortages of almost everything, but at least the deprivations were shared, and for all its faults, British society, ever since World War II, has continuously been one of the more interesting experiments in the attempt to reconcile social justice with personal freedom. (The Scandinavian societies might be more successful experiments, but not even they find themselves interesting.) If Orwell had lived to a full span, he would have been able, if not necessarily delighted, to deal with the increasing likelihood that his dreams were coming true. Even as things were, with only a few years of life left to him, he might have given a far more positive account, in his post-war journalism, of how the British of all classes, including the dreaded ruling class, were at long last combining to bring about, at least in some measure, the more decent society that had haunted his imagination since childhood. But he was distracted by a prior requirement. His own war wasn't over. It had begun all over again. There was still one prominent social group who had learned nothing: the left-wing intellectuals.

The last and most acrimonious phase of Orwell's battle with the left-wing intelligentsia began not long after D-Day. As the Allied forces fought their way out of Normandy, a piece by Orwell landed on a desk in America. *Partisan Review* would publish a London Letter in which Orwell complained about the Western Russophile intellectuals who refused to accept the truth about Stalinist terror. Clearly, what frightened him was that, even if they did accept it, Soviet prestige would lose little of its allure for them. For Orwell, the Cold War was already on, with the progressive intellectuals in the front rank of the foe. Orwell was the first to use the term 'cold war', in an essay published in October 1945 about the atomic bomb – the very device that would ensure, in the long run, that the Cold War never became a hot one. At the time, however, he saw no cause for complacency.

But unreconstructed *gauchiste* pundits who would still like to dismiss Orwell as a 'classic' Cold Warrior can find out here that he didn't fit the frame. For one thing, Orwell remained all too willing to accuse the West of structural deficiencies that were really much more contingent than he made out. When he argued, in the pages of *Tribune*, that the mass-circulation newspapers forced slop on their readership, he preferred to ignore the advice from a correspondent that it was really a case of the readership forcing slop on the news-papers. He should have given far more attention to such criticisms, because they allowed for the possibility – as his own assumptions did not – that if ordinary people were freed from exploitation they would demand more frivolity, not less.

To the end, Orwell's tendency was to overestimate the potential of the people he supposed to be in the grip of the capitalist system, while simultaneously underestimating the individuality they were showing already. In his remarks on the moral turpitude of the scien-tists who had cravenly not 'refused' to work on the atomic bomb – clearly he thought they should have all turned the job down – there was no mention (perhaps because he didn't yet know, although he might have guessed) of the fact that many of them were European refugees from totalitarianism and had worked on the bomb not just willingly but with anxious fervour, convinced, with excellent reasons, that Hitler might get there first.

On the other hand, he was still inclined to regard Stalin's regime as a perversion of the Bolshevik revolution instead of as its essence: as late as 1946, it took the eminent émigré Russian scholar Gleb Struve (the future editor of Mandelstam and Akhmatova) to tell him that Zamyatin's *We*, written in 1920 but never published in Russia, might well have been, as Orwell thought, a projection of a possible totalita-rian future, but had drawn much of its inspiration from the Leninist present. If Orwell took this admonition in, he made little use of it. (He made great use of *We*, however: if the English translation of Zamyatin's little classic had been as good as the French one, a lot more of *Nineteen Eighty-Four*'s reviewers might have spotted that

Orwell's phantasmagoria was a bit less *sui generis* than it seemed.) Already in 1941, reviewing *Russia Under Soviet Rule* by the émigré liberal de Basily, Orwell had taken on board the possibility that Lenin's callous behaviour made Stalin inevitable – after all, Lenin had actually *said* that the Party should rule by terror – but neither then nor later did Orwell push this point very hard. It flickers in the background of his anti-Soviet polemics and can be thought of as the informing assumption of *Animal Farm* and *Nineteen Eighty-Four*, but in his journalism he was always slow to concede that the Bolshevik revolution itself might have been the culprit. Perhaps he thought he had enough trouble on his hands already, just trying to convince his starry-eyed Stalinist contemporaries that they had placed their faith in a cynic who left their own cynicism for dead, and would do the same to them if he got the chance. 'The direct, conscious attack on intellectual decency comes from the intellectuals themselves.'

*

As a journalist, Orwell had laboured long and hard for small financial reward, and overwork had never been good for his delicate health. Life was pinched, not to say deprived, especially after his wife and faithful helpmeet Eileen (he was an unfaithful spouse and she may have been as well, but they depended on each other) died as a result of a medical blunder. The success of *Animal Farm*, in 1945, could have bought him a reprieve. He upped stakes to a small farmhouse on the island of Jura, in the Hebrides, and cultivated his garden. Though he overestimated the strength he still had available for the hard life he lived there – he could grow vegetables to supplement his ration, but it took hard work in tough soil – the place was a welcome break from the treadmill of London. Mentally, however, he found no peace. A heightened anguish can be traced right through his last journalism until he gave it up to work on *Nineteen Eighty-Four*. The left-wing intellectuals, already promoting the revisionism that continues into our own day, not only were giving Stalin the sole credit for having won the war but were contriving not to notice that he had rescinded the few liberties he had been forced to concede in order to fight it; that his rule by terror had resumed; and that in the Eastern European countries supposedly liberated by the Red Army any vestige of liberty left by the Nazis was being stamped flat. Once again, crimes on a colossal scale were being camouflaged with perverted language, and once again the intellectuals, whose professional instinct should have been to sick it up, were happily swallowing the lot. It took a great deal to persuade him that reasoned argument wasn't enough. But it wasn't, so he wrote *Nineteen Eighty-Four*.

There are still diehards who would like to think that *Nineteen Eighty-Four* is not about the Soviet Union at all. Their argument runs: *Animal Farm* is a satire about what happened in Russia once upon a time, but *Nineteen Eighty-Four* is a minatory fantasy about something far bigger – the prospect of a world divided up into a few huge centres of absolute power, of which a Soviet-style hegemony would be only one, and the United States, of course, would be another. It is just possible that Orwell thought the Marshall Plan was meant to have the same imperialist effect in Europe as the Red Army's tanks. He never actually said so, but people as intelligent as Gore Vidal believe much the same thing today. The late Anthony Burgess sincerely believed that *Nineteen Eighty-Four*, because the Ministry of Truth bore such a strong resemblance to the BBC canteen, had been inspired by the condition of postwar Britain under rationing. As Orwell said so resonantly in his essay 'Notes on Nationalism', 'One has to belong to the intelligentsia to believe things like that: no ordinary man could be such a fool.'

He didn't mean that all intellectuals are *ipso facto* fools – he himself was an intellectual if anybody was – but he did mean that verbal cleverness, unless its limitations are clearly and continuously seen by its possessor, is an unbeatable way of blurring reality until nothing can be seen at all. The main drive of all Orwell's writings since Spain had been to point out that the Soviet Union, nominally the hope of mankind, had systematically perverted language in order to cover up the wholesale destruction of human values, and that the Western left-wing intellectuals had gone along with this by perverting their own language in its turn. To go on denying that *Nineteen Eighty-Four* was the culmination of this large part of Orwell's effort is to defy reason. At the time, denying it was still not a wholly unreasonable reaction. After all, the democracies couldn't have won the war without the Soviet Union, and the book was so bleak and hopeless. Maybe it was about something else.

If they didn't get it in the West, they got it in the East. From the day of the book's publication until far into the Thaw, it meant big trouble for any Soviet citizen who had a copy in his possession. In the years to come, now that the Soviet archives are opening up, there will be a fruitful area of study in trying to decide which were the Western cultural influences that did most to help the Evil Empire melt down. For all we know, the jokes were always right, and it was the Beatles albums and the bootleg blue jeans that did the trick. But it is a fair guess that of all the imported artefacts it was the books that sapped the repressive will of the people who ran the empire or who were next in line to do so. Robert Conquest's *The Great Terror* might well turn out to be the key factor in the unprecedented turn-around by which those state organizations with a solid track record of pre-emptive slaughter somehow began to spare the very lives they would previously have been careful to snuff out: it is said that even the KGB read it, perhaps as the quickest way of finding out what their predecessors had been up to. (There is no doubt at all, by the way, that they eventually read *Nineteen Eighty-Four*. When head of the KGB, Andropov had a special edition printed and circulated.)

But for all we know they might have been just as much subverted by *samizdat* translations of *The Carpetbaggers* and *Valley of the Dolls*. Nor, of course, can the effect of the dissident literature, whether written in exile or home-grown, be dismissed as merely unsettling, although for the books written at home there will always be the consideration of whether they could have even been conceived of if the set-up were not already crumbling in the first place. What we are talking about is a contrary weather-system of opinion that event-ually took over a whole climate, and to trace its course will be like following the dust of Ariadne's crumbled thread back into a ruined labyrinth. But it will be a big surprise if *Nineteen Eighty-Four*, even more than *The Gulag Archipelago*, does not turn out to be the book that did most, weight for weight, to clear thousands of living brains of the miasma sent up through the soil by millions upon millions of dead bodies. It was a portable little slab of spiritual *plastique*, a mind-blower.

But if the part played by Orwell's dystopian novels in the dismant-ling of the Sovietized monolith will always be hard to assess, there is less difficulty about measuring the effect of his last period of jour-nalism on his own country. Self-immured on Jura, he was a Prospero running on the reserve tank of his magic. Orwell was only forty-two, but he had little physical strength left, and although many friends and colleagues sent him letters and books, and presents of rice and chocolate, and some even made the slow and tricky journey to visit him, he was short of love. A widower of some fame and no longer without means, he offered his affections to a succession of young women and found himself in the humiliating position of being respected and refused. When it emerged recently that he handed a list of fellow-travellers to a government propaganda unit, suggestions that he had conspired in a witch-hunt carried little force. McCarthyism was a nonstarter in Britain, and most of those named on the list were already glad to have it known that they had aligned their prayer mats in the direction of the Kremlin. But if he lapsed from his own standards by tittle-tattling in school the most likely reason was that his Foreign Office contact was a noted beauty. He was sending her a bouquet.

The young woman who finally accepted him, Sonia Brownell (renowned in literary London as the Venus of Euston Road), married him practically on his deathbed: cold comfort. He kept a diary of what was happening in his garden – small things growing as the great man withered. For us, the only consolation is that he could speak so clearly even as the walls of his lungs were giving way against the tide of blood.

'Britain has lost an empire but has not found a role', said Dean Acheson. Raymond Aron said something better: '*L'Angleterre a perdu son empire, sans perdre sa civilization morale.*' In helping Britain to maintain and extend its moral civilization, Orwell's voice was surely crucial. The succession of magnificent essays he wrote as the harsh war wound down into an austere peace add up to a political event in themselves, the culmination of his journalism as a textbook example of how a sufficiently informed commentary on events can feed back into history and help to shape its course.

It takes nothing from Davison's achievement to say that these last essays are probably best encountered in the *Collected Essays*, or even in a single small volume, such as *Inside the Whale*, where they will be found to have the effect of poems, as the paragraphs succeed one another with the inevitability of perfectly wrought stanzas, with every sentence in the right place yet begging to be remembered on its own, like a line from a magisterial elegy. 'Notes on Nationalism', 'The Prevention of Literature', 'Politics and the English Language', 'Why I Write', 'Politics vs. Literature: An Examination of "Gulliver's Travels" ' – read for and by themselves, they tell you all you need to know about Orwell except the one fact so poignantly revealed here: that they were the work of a man who was not only dying but dying young. Very few writers about politics have said much in their forties that is lastingly true; and even Orwell undoubtedly would have continued to deepen, enrich, modulate, and modify his opinions.

But he had come a long way, and, by coming as far as the great last essays, he left a precious heritage to the country that he loved in spite of itself. Though the appeal to a totalitarian model of a just society (and the corresponding contempt for piecemeal solutions) was to remain possible in the academy, it became much more difficult in everyday political journalism, simply because Orwell had discredited the idea in a plain style that nobody could forget and everybody felt obliged to echo. The theoretical work that disenfranchised all total transformations was done by others, such as Karl Popper, Raymond Aron, Leszek Kolokowski and Isaiah Berlin. Orwell never got around to figuring all that out in detail. But he felt it, and the language of his last essays is the language of feeling made as clear and bright as it can ever get.

*

How clear is that? Finally, it comes down to a question of language, which is only appropriate, because, finally, Orwell was a literary man. Politics inspired Orwell the way the arts had always inspired the great critics, which gives us the clue to where he got the plainly passionate style that we are so ready to call unique. It is unique, in its flexibility of speech rhythms and its irresistible force of assertion, but he didn't invent it; he invented its use. George Saintsbury had something of Orwell's schooled knack for speaking right out of the page, and Shaw had almost all of it: Orwell isn't often outright funny, but Shaw, in his six volumes of critical writings about music and theatre, deployed the full range of Orwell's debunking weapons with a generous humour to drive them home. Orwell called Shaw a windbag, but had obviously taken in every word the old man wrote. And there are many other critics who could be named, all the way up to the young F. R. Leavis, whom Orwell read with interest, if not without a certain distaste for his joyless zeal.

Orwell was a superb literary critic himself: he is the first person to read on Swift, on Dickens, and on Gissing, and if he had lived to finish his essay on Evelyn Waugh it would have been the best thing on the subject, the essay that really opens up Waugh's corrosively snobbish view of life without violating his creative achievement. Had Orwell lived to a full term, he might well have gone on to become the greatest modern literary critic in the language. But he lived more than long enough to make writing about politics a branch of the humanities, setting a standard of civilized response to the intractably complex texture of life. No previous political writer had brought so much of life's lesser detail into the frame, and other countries were unlucky not to have him as a model. Sartre, for example, would have been incapable of an essay about the contents of a junk shop, or about how to make the ideal cup of tea – the very reason he was incapable of talking real sense about politics.

In one of the very last, and best, of his essays, 'Lear, Tolstoy, and the Fool', Orwell paid his tribute to Shakespeare. He was too modest to say that he was paying a debt as well, but he was:

Shakespeare was not a philosopher or a scientist, but he did have curiosity: he loved the surface of the earth and the process of life – which, it should be repeated, is *not* the same thing as wanting to have a good time and stay alive as long as possible. Of course, it is not because of the quality of his thought that Shakespeare has survived, and he might not even be remembered as a dramatist if he had not also been a poet. His main hold on us is through language.

A writer has to know a lot about the rhythms of natural speech before he can stretch them over the distance covered by those first two sentences. Each of them is perfectly balanced in itself, and the second is perfectly balanced against the first – the first turning back on itself with a strict qualification, and the second running away in relaxed enjoyment of its own fluency. They could stand on their own, but it turns out that both of them are there to pile their combined weight behind the third sentence – the short one – and propel it into your memory. It hits home with the force of an axiom.

And it isn't true – or, anyway, it isn't true enough. Elsewhere in the essay, Orwell shows signs of being aware that the relationship of Shakespeare's language to the quality of his thought can never be fully resolved in favour of either term. But not even Orwell could resist a resonant statement that fudged the facts – a clarity that is really an opacity. Yes, Orwell did write like an angel, and that's the very reason we have to watch him like a hawk. Luckily for us, he was pretty good at watching himself. He was blessed with a way of putting things that made anything he said seem so, but that was only a gift. His intellectual honesty was a virtue.

Orwell's standards of plain speaking always were and still are a mile too high for politicians. What finally counts with politicians is what they do, not how they say it. But for journalists how they say it counts for everything. Orwell's style shows us why a style is worth working at: not just because it gets us a byline and makes a splash but because it compresses and refines thought and feeling without ceasing to sound like speech – which is to say, without ceasing to sound human. At a time when ideological politics still exercised such an appeal that hundreds of purportedly civilized voices *had* ceased to sound human, Orwell's style stood out. The remarkable thing is that it still does. Ideologues are thin on the ground nowadays, while any substantial publication has a would-be George Orwell rippling the keys in every second cubicle, but the daddy of modern truthtellers still sounds fresh. So it wasn't just the amount of truth he told but the way he told it, in prose transmuted to poetry by the pressure of his dedication. This great edition, by revealing fully for the first time what that dedication was like, makes his easy-seeming written speech more impressive than ever, and even harder to emulate. To write like him, you need a life like his, but times have changed, and he changed them.

New Yorker, 18 January, 1999

Postscript

Even if our intention is the most abject homage, we can't write in praise of heroes without taking their limitations into account, because unless we had noticed their limitations we wouldn't be writing at all: they would have silenced us. While you are reading them, the great stylists make you want to give up, and in the case of Orwell, the stylist with the anti-style, the effect can last a long time after you have finished reading. I was in bed with a convenient nervous breakdown when I read the four volumes of his collected journalism that came out in 1969. I already knew the standard essays quite well, but the accumulated impact of reading them again, along with all the other material which had become generally available for the first time, would have kept me away from the typewriter for years if I hadn't noticed something fundamentally wrong amongst everything that he got right.

He was wrong about the British Empire. He never gave up on the idea that it was a fraud, designed with no other end in view except to stave off rebellion at home by eking out the miseries of capitalism with the exploited fruits of coolie labour in the colonies. Born under the Empire myself, with few coolies in sight, I knew it to be a more equivocal thing. Orwell's procrustean notions on the subject might have served as a useful reservoir of polemical force, but their heritage was all too obvious. In 1902 G. A. Hobson's book *Imperialism* promoted the idea that colonial possessions were critical for advanced, or 'finance', capitalism. In 1916 Lenin took the idea over for his *Imperialism, the Highest State of Capitalism*, and after the Revolution it became a standard item of Comintern dogma, working its worldwide influence even on those Left-inclined intellectuals who refused to swallow the party programme hook, line and sinker. They spat out the line and sinker, but they stayed hooked.

I was thus being as kind as I could to suggest, in my *laudatio*, that Orwell inherited some of his theoretical precepts from classic Marxism. He got at least one of them, and perhaps the most misleading one, from classic Leninism – a still more dubious patrimony. Even in Orwell's own time, it should have been evident that the idea was a misconception. The mere existence of Sweden, for example, was enough to refute it. Sweden had a capitalist system, advanced social welfare, and no imperial dreams that had not died with Gustavus Adolphus. After Orwell's death, when the last of the British Empire was given up and the final accounts came in, it became easy to question whether colonialism had ever yielded a dividend, let alone supported Britain as a capitalist economy. But Orwell, who justly prided himself on his capacity to puncture received notions, should have questioned the assumption when questioning was hard. Had he done so, however, it might have made him a less effective speaker for the independent Left. It might have sapped the confidence that energized his style. Any successful style is a spell whose first victim is the wizard. Unless he is alert to the trickery of his own magic, he will project an air of Delphic infallibility that can do a lot of damage before the inevitable collapse into abracadabra. The obvious example is Shaw, but no master stylist has ever been exempt from the danger. It follows that there is always something useful to say, even about the man who appears to say everything. Orwell said what mattered, and will always matter, about totalitarianism. But he never got far with saying what mattered about democracy. He thought it was a capitalist trick. It's a lot trickier than that.

2001

HITLER'S UNWITTING EXCULPATOR

Hitler's Willing Executioners **by Daniel Jonah Goldhagen, Alfred A. Knopf**

There was a hair-raising catchphrase going around in Germany just before the Nazis came to power: *Besser ein Ende mit Schrecken als ein Schrecken ohne Ende.* Better an end with terror than terror without end. Along with Nazi sympathizers who had been backing Hitler's chances for years, ordinary citizens with no taste for ideological politics had reached the point of insecurity where they were ready to let the Nazis in. The Nazis had caused such havoc in the streets that it was thought that only they could put a stop to it. They did, but the order they restored was theirs. When it was over, after twelve short years of the promised thousand, the memory lingered, a long nightmare about what once was real. It lingers still, causing night sweats. A cool head is hard to keep. Proof of that is Daniel Jonah Goldhagen's new book *Hitler's Willing Executioners*, provocatively subtitled 'Ordinary Germans and the Holocaust'. Hailed in the publisher's preliminary hype by no less an authority than the redoubtable Simon Schama as 'the fruit of phenomenal scholarship and absolute integrity', it is a book to be welcomed, but hard to welcome warmly. It advances knowledge while subtracting from wisdom, and whether the one step forward is worth the two steps back is a nice question. Does pinning the Holocaust on what amounts to a German 'national character' make sense? I don't think it does, and in the light of the disturbingly favourable press endorsement that Goldhagen has already been getting, it becomes a matter of some urgency to say why.

The phenomenal scholarship can be safely conceded: Schama and comparable authorities are unlikely to be wrong about that. Tunnelling long and deep into hitherto only loosely disturbed archives,

Goldhagen has surfaced with persuasive evidence that the Holocaust, far from being, as we have been encouraged to think, characteristically the work of cold-blooded technocrats dispassionately organizing mass disappearance on an industrial basis, was on the contrary the enthusiastically pursued contact sport of otherwise ordinary citizens, drawn from all walks of life, who were united in the unflagging enjoyment with which they inflicted every possible form of suffering on their powerless victims. In a constellation of more than ten thousand camps, the typical camp was not an impersonally efficient death factory: it was a torture garden, with its administrative personnel delightedly indulging themselves in a holiday packaged by Hieronymous Bosch. Our post-Hannah Arendt imaginations are haunted by the wrong figure: for every owl-eyed, mild-mannered penpusher clinically shuffling the euphemistic paperwork of oblivion, there were a hundred noisily dedicated louts revelling in the bloodbath. The gas chambers, our enduring shared symbol of the catastrophe, were in fact anomalous: most of those annihilated did not die suddenly and surprised as the result of a deception, but only after protracted humiliations and torments to whose devising their persecutors devoted inexhaustible creative zeal. Far from needing to have their scruples overcome by distancing mechanisms that would alienate them from their task, the killers were happily married to the job from the first day to the last. The more grotesque the cruelty, the more they liked it. They couldn't get enough of it. Right up until the last lights went out on the Third Reich, long after the destruction made any sense at all even by their demented standards, they went on having the time of their lives through dispensing hideous deaths to the helpless.

The book concludes, in short, that there is no point making a mystery of how a few Germans were talked into it when there were so many of them who could scarcely be talked out of it. Since we have undoubtedly spent too much time wrestling with the supposedly complex metaphysics of how an industrious drone like Eichmann could be induced to despatch millions to their deaths sight unseen, and not half enough time figuring out how thousands of otherwise healthy men and women were mad keen to work extra hours hands-on just for the pleasure of hounding their fellow human beings beyond the point of despair, this conclusion, though it is nowhere near as new and revolutionary as Goldhagen and his supporters think it is, is undoubtedly a useful one to reach.

Unfortunately Goldhagen reaches it in a style disfigured by rampant sociologese and with a retributive impetus that carries him far beyond his proper objective. It would have been enough to prove that what he calls 'eliminationist anti-Semitism' was far more widespread among the German people than it has suited their heirs, or us, to believe. But he wants to blame the whole population, and not just for prejudice but for their participation, actual or potential, in mass murder. He is ready to concede that there were exceptions, but doesn't think they count. He thinks it would be more informative, and more just, to stop fooling ourselves by holding the Nazis responsible for the slaughter, and simply call the perpetrators 'the Germans'. Didn't we call the soldiers who fought in Vietnam 'the Americans'?

Well, yes – but we didn't blame 'the Americans' for the atrocities committed there, or, if we did, we knew that we were talking shorthand, and that the reality was more complicated. No doubt many of the soldiers involved had a ready-to-go prejudice against the Vietnamese, but without the ill-judged, and even criminal, initiatives of their government it would have remained a prejudice. What needed examining was not simply the soldiers' contempt for alien life-forms but the government policies that had put the troops in a position which allowed their contempt to express itself as mass murder. Much of the examining was done by Americans at the time, sometimes in the face of persecution by their own government, but never without the hope of getting a hearing from the American people. So it would make little sense, except as an *ad hoc* rhetorical device, to say that it was the natural outcome of the American cultural heritage to burn down peasant huts in Vietnam. Putting up Pizza Huts would have been just as natural. And it makes no sense whatsoever to call the perpetrators of the Holocaust 'the Germans' if by that is meant that the German victims of Nazism – including many Jews who went on regarding themselves as Germans to the end of the line – somehow weren't Germans at all. That's what the Nazis thought, and to echo their hare-brained typology is to concede them their victory. Nothing, of course, could be further from Goldhagen's intention, but his loose language has led him into it.

The Nazis didn't just allow a lethal expression of vengeful fantasy; they rewarded it. They deprived a readily identifiable minority of

German citizens of their citizenship, declared open season on them, honoured anyone who attacked them, punished anyone who helped them, and educated a generation to believe that its long-harboured family prejudices had the status of a sacred mission. To puzzle over the extent of the cruelty that was thus unleashed is essentially naïve. To marvel at it, however, is inevitable, and pity help us if we ever become blasé about the diabolical landscape whose contours not even Goldhagen's prose can obscure, for all his unintentional mastery of verbal camouflage. In a passage like the following – by no means atypical – it would be nice to think that anger had deflected him from a natural style, but all the evidence suggests that this *is* his natural style.

> Because there were other peoples who did not treat Jews as Germans did and because, as I have shown, it is clear that the actions of the German perpetrators cannot be explained by non-cognitive structural features, when investigating different (national) groups of perpetrators, it is necessary to eschew explanations that in a reductionist fashion attribute complex and highly variable actions to structural factors or allegedly universalistic social psychological processes; the task, then, is to specify what combination of cognitive and situational factors brought the perpetrators, whatever their identities were, to contribute to the Holocaust in all the ways that they did.

A sentence like that can just about be unscrambled in the context of the author's attention-losing terminology, but the context is no picnic to be caught up in for 500-plus pages, and the general effect is to make a vital dose of medicine almost impossible to swallow. This book has all the signs of having begun as a dissertation and it makes you wonder what America's brighter young historians are reading in a general way about their subject before they are issued with their miner's lamps and lowered into the archives. Clearly they aren't reading much in high school, but isn't there some spare time on campus to get acquainted with the works of, say, Lewis Namier and find out what an English sentence is supposed to do? If only jargon were Goldhagen's sole affliction, things would not be so bad, because what he must mean can quite often be arrived at by sanforizing the verbiage. A 'cognitive model of ontology' is probably your view of the world, or what you believe to be true; an 'ideational formation' is almost certainly an idea; when people 'conceptualize' we can guess he means that they think; when they 'enunciate' we can guess he means that they say; and if something 'was immanent in the structure of cognition' we can guess it was something that everybody thought.

But along with the jargon come the solecisms, and some of those leave guesswork limping. Goldhagen employs the verb 'brutalize' many times, and gets it wrong every time except once. Until recently, when the wrong meaning took over, no respectable writer employed that verb to mean anything else except to turn someone into a brute. Nobody except the semi-literate supposed that it meant to be brutal to someone. Our author does suppose that on all occasions, except when, to show that he is aware the word is being used incorrectly, he employs inverted commas on the only occasion when he uses it correctly. But a modern historian can possibly get away with inadvertently suggesting that he has never read a book written by a historian with a classical education. It is harder to get away with providing evidence that he has never read a book of history emanating from, or merely written about, the classical world. Throughout his treatise, Goldhagen copies the increasingly popular misuse of the verb 'decimate' to mean kill nearly everybody. Julius Caesar was not the only author in ancient times to make it clear that the word means kill one in ten. When Goldhagen repeatedly talks about some group of Jews being decimated, all the reader can think is: if only the death-toll had been as small as that.

Still, we know what he must mean, and no disapproval of Goldhagen's style can stave off discussion of the story he has to tell with it. In the long run he mines his own narrative for implications that are not always warranted and are sometimes tendentious, but there is no way round some of his initial propositions. From the archives he brings back three main narrative strands that will make anyone think again who ever thought that the men in the black uniforms did all the dirty work and that any culpability accruing to anyone else was through not wanting to know. The mobile police battalions who conducted so many of the mass shootings in the East were drawn from run-of-the-pavement *Ordnungspolizei* (Order Police) and many of them were not even Nazi Party members, just ordinary Joes who had been drafted into the police because they didn't meet the physical requirements for the army, let alone the SS elite formations.

So far we have tended, in the always sketchy mental pictures we make of these things, to put most of the mass shootings down to the *Einsatzgruppen*, SS outfits detailed by Himmler specifically for the task of pursuing Hitler's cherished new type of war, the war of biological extermination. Goldhagen is right to insist that this common misapprehension badly needs to be modified. (Here, as elsewhere, he could have gone further with his own case: the *Einsatzgruppen* themselves were a fairly motley crew, as Gitta Sereny, in her recent biography of Albert Speer, has incidentally pointed out while pursuing the subject of just how one of the best-informed men in Germany managed to maintain his vaunted ignorance for so long: if, indeed, he did.) The police battalions tortured and killed with an enthusisasm outstripping even the *Einsatzgruppen*, whose leaders reported many instances of nervous breakdown and alcoholism in the ranks, whereas the police seem to have thrived physically and mentally from the whole business, sometimes even bringing their wives in by train to share the sport. The few that did request to be relieved of their duties were granted a dispensation without penalty. Goldhagen draws the fair inference that all who stayed on the job were effectively volunteers. Very few among the innocent people they shot into mass graves were spared the most vile imaginable preliminary tortures. The standard scenario in a mass shooting was to assemble the victims first in the town centre, keep them there for a long time, terrorize them with beatings and arbitrarily selective individual deaths, and thus make sure the survivors were already half dead with thirst and fear before flogging them all the way to the disposal site, where they often had to dig their own pit before being shot into it. It was thought normal to kill children in front of their desperate mothers before granting the mothers the release of a bullet. The cruelty knew no limits but it didn't put new recruits off. If anything, it turned them on: granted, which the author does not grant, they needed any turning on in the first place.

Had these operations been truly mechanical, there would have been none of this perverted creativity. If Goldhagen's limitations as a writer mercifully ensure that he can't evoke the wilful cruelty in its full vividness, he is right to emphasize it, although wrong to suppose that it has not been emphasized before. The cruelties are everywhere described in the best book yet written on the subject, Martin Gilbert's *The Holocaust*, which strangely is nowhere referred to or even mentioned in Goldhagen's effort. Raoul Hilberg's monumental *The Destruction of the European Jews* is elbowed out of the way with the assurance that though it deals well with the victims it says little about the perpetrators, but Gilbert, who says a lot about the perpetrators, doesn't get a look in even as an unacknowledged crib, as far as I can tell. (For a work of this importance, the absence of a bibliography is a truly sensational publishing development. What next: an index on request?) It is a lot to ask of a young historian who has spent a good proportion of his reading life submerged in the primary sources that he should keep up with the secondary sources too, but Gilbert's book, with its wealth of personal accounts, *is* a primary source, quite apart from doing a lot to presage Goldhagen's boldly declared intention of showing that the detached modern industrial mentality had little to do with the matter, and that most of those who died were killed in a frenzy. But Goldhagen's well backed-up insistence that a good number of the perpetrators were not Nazi ideologues but common or garden German citizens is a genuine contribution, although whether it leads to a genuine historical insight is the question that lingers.

The second main story is about the 'work' that the Jews who were not granted the mercy of a comparatively quick death were forced to do until they succumbed to its rigours. It is Goldhagen who puts the inverted commas around the word 'work' and this time he is right, because it was the wrong word. Real work produces something. 'Work' produced little except death in agony. Non-Jewish slave labourers from the occupied countries were all held in varying degrees of deprivation but at least they had some chance of survival. For the Jewish slaves, 'work' really meant murder, slow but sure. Here is further confirmation, if it were needed (he overestimates the need, because the sad fact is already well established throughout the literature of the subject) that the Nazi policy on the exploitation of Jewish labour was too irrational even to be ruthless. A ruthless policy would have employed the Jews for their talents and qualifications, concentrated their assigned tasks on the war effort, kept them healthy while they laboured, and killed them afterwards. Nazi policy was to starve, beat and torture them up to and including the point of death even in those comparatively few cases when the job they had been assigned to might have helped win the war, or anyway stave off defeat for a little longer. The Krupp armaments factories in Essen were typical in that the Jewish workers were given hell (Alfried Krupp, who might have faced the rope if he had ever admitted knowledge of the workers tortured in the basement of his own office block, lived to be measured for a new Porsche every year), but atypical in that the Jews were actually employed in doing something useful. The more usual scenario involved lifting something heavy, carrying it somewhere else, putting it down, and carrying back something just like it, with beatings all the way if you dropped it. What the something was was immaterial: a big rock would do fine. These were Sisyphean tasks, except that not even Sisyphus had to run the gauntlet. Tracing well the long-standing strain in German anti-Semitism which held that Jews were parasites and had never done any labour, Goldhagen argues persuasively that this form of punishment was meant to remind them of this supposed fact before they died: to make them die of the realization. Here is a hint of what his book might have been – he is really getting somewhere when he traces this kind of self-defeating irrationality on the Nazis' part to an ideal: perhaps their only ideal. It was a mad ideal, but its sincerity was proved by the price they paid for it. At all costs, even at the cost of their losing the war, they pursued their self-imposed 'task' of massacring people who had not only done them no harm but might well have done them some good – of wasting them.

Many of the top Nazis were opportunists. In the end, Goering would probably have forgotten all about the Jews if he could have done a deal; Himmler did try to do a deal on that very basis; and Goebbels, though he was a raving anti-Semite until the very end, was nothing like that at the beginning. During his student career he respected his Jewish professors, and seems to have taken up anti-Semitism with an eye to the main chance. He got into it the way Himmler and Goering were ready to get out of it, because even his fanatacism was a power-play. But for Hitler it was not so. According to him, Jews had never done anything useful for Germany and never could. It was a belief bound to result in his eventual military defeat, even if he had conquered all Europe and Britain with it; because in the long run he would have come up against the atomic bomb, developed in America mainly by the very scientists he had driven out of Europe. On the vital part played in German science by Jews he could never listen to reason. Max Planck protested in 1933 about what the new exclusion laws would do to the universities. In view of his great prestige he was granted an audience with the Führer. Planck hardly got a chance to open his mouth. Hitler regaled him with a three-quarters-of-an-hour lecture about mathematics, which Planck later called one of the stupidest things he had ever heard in his life. The pure uselessness of all Jews, the expiation they owed for their parasitism, was at the centre of Hitler's purposes until the last hour, and the same was true of all who shared his lethal convictions.

This bleak truth is brought out sharply by the third and main strand in Goldhagen's book, which deals with the death marches in the closing stage of the war, when the camps in the East were threatened with being overrun. The war was all but lost, yet the Nazis went on diverting scarce resources into tormenting helpless civilians. The survivors were already starving when they set out from the Eastern camps, and as they were herded on foot towards camps in the Third Reich their guards, who might conceivably have gained credit after the imminent capitulation by behaving mercifully, behaved worse than ever. They starved their charges until they could hardly walk and then tortured them for not walking faster. This behaviour seems beyond comprehension, and, indeed, it is – but it does make a horrible sort of sense if we accept that for the Nazis the war against the Jews was the one that really mattered.

Goldhagen's account of the death marches gives too much weight to the fact that these horrors continued even after Himmler issued instructions that the Jews should be kept alive. ('Perhaps it's time,' he famously said to a Jewish representative in 1945, 'for us Germans and you Jews to bury the hatchet.') Goldhagen doesn't consider that the guards, both men and women, were facing a return to powerlessness and were thus unlikely to relinquish their shred of omnipotence while they still had it. He prefers to contend that the killings went on because the people in general were in the grip of a force more powerful than Nazi orders: eliminationist anti-Semitism. To him, nothing but a theory in the perpetrator's mind – in this case, the Germans' view that the Jews were subhuman and thus beyond compassion – can explain gratuitous cruelty. But recent history has shown that people can become addicted to torturing their fellow human beings while feeling no sense of racial superiority to them, or even while feeling that no particular purpose is being served by the torture. In some of the Latin-American dictatorships, torturers who had quickly extracted all the relevant information often went on with the treatment, simply to see what the victim could be reduced to, especially if the victim was a woman. To construct a political theory that explains such behaviour is tempting, but finally you are faced with the possibility that the capacity to do these things has no necessary connection with politics – and the truly dreadful possibility that it might have some connection with sexual desire, in which case we had better hope that we are talking about nurture rather than nature. A genetic propensity would put us all in it: Original Sin with a vengeance.

The price for holding to the conviction about the all-pervasiveness of murderous anti-Semitism among the Germans is the obligation to account for every instance of those who showed mercy. In his discussion of *Kristallnacht*, Goldhagen quotes a Gestapo report (obviously composed by a factotum not yet fully in synch with the Führer's vision) as saying that by far the greater part of the German population 'does not understand the senseless individual acts of violence and terror.' Why shouldn't the people have understood, if their anti-Semitism was as eliminationist as Goldhagen says it was? Later, talking about one of Police Battalion 309's operations in Bialystok, he mentions a 'German army officer appalled by the licentious killing of unarmed civilians,' and he dismisses a conscience-stricken Major Trapp, who, having been ordered to carry out a mass killing, was heard to exclaim, 'My God! Why must I do this?' Were these men eliminationist anti-Semites, too? We could afford to consider their cases without any danger of lapsing into the by now discredited notion that the *Wehrmacht* was not implicated. Finally, during a reflection on the Helmbrechts death march, Goldhagen mentions that some of the guards behaved with a touch of humanity. He doesn't make enough of his own observation that they were the older guards – 'Germans . . . old enough to have been bred not only on Nazi culture.'

For Goldhagen, prejudice is the sole enemy. Other scholars, such as Raul Hilberg in his *Perpetrators, Victims, Bystanders*, have tried to show how Germans overcame their inhibitions to kill Jews. Goldhagen's monolithic thesis is that there were no inhibitions in the first place. But we need to make a distinction between Germany's undeniably noxious anti-Semitic inheritance – an age-old dream of purity, prurient as all such dreams – and the way the Nazi government, using every means of bribery, propaganda, social pressure and violent coercion in its power, turned that dream into a living night-mare. Goldhagen slides past the point, and the result is a crippling injury to the otherwise considerable worth of his book. He could, in fact, have gone further in establishing how early the Final Solution got rolling. Gilbert does a better job of showing that it was, in effect, under way after the invasion of Poland, where thousands of Jews were murdered and the rest herded into the ghettos. Goldhagen quotes some of Heydrich's September 21, 1939, order about forming the ghettos but omits the most revealing clause, in which Heydrich ordered that the ghettos be established near railheads. That can have meant only one thing. In May of 1941, Goering sent a memo from the Central Office of Emigration in Berlin ordering that no more Jews be allowed to leave the occupied territories. That, too, can have meant only one thing. Hannah Arendt was not wrong when she said about Nazi Germany in its early stages that only a madman could guess what would happen next. In 1936, Heinrich Mann (Thomas's older brother) published an essay predicting the whole event, simply on the basis of the Nuremberg laws and what had already happened in the first concentration camps. But his was a very rare case, perhaps made possible by artistic insight. It needed sympathy with the Devil to take the Nazis at their word; good people rarely know that much about evil. But well in advance of the Holocaust's official starting date there were plenty of bad people who didn't need to be told about mass extermination before they got the picture.

Here Goldhagen, in his unquenchable ire, provides a useful cor-rective to those commentators who persist in extending the benefit of the doubt to opportunists like Albert Speer. Gitta Sereny's book is a masterpiece of wide-ranging sympathy, but she wanders too near naïveté when she worries at the non-subject of when Speer knew about what his terrible friends had in mind and whether he had actually read *Mein Kampf.* In 1936, a popular album about Hitler carried an article under Speer's name which quoted *Mein Kampf* by the chunk: of course Speer had read it, and of course he knew about the Final Solution from the hour it got under way. The top Nazis didn't conceal these things from one another. They did, however, conceal these things from the German people. Why was that? There is something to Goldhagen's contention that the people found out anyway – that eventually everyone knew at least something. But why, if they were so receptive to the idea, weren't the people immediately told everything? Surely the answer is that Hitler shared the Gestapo's suspicion about the ability of the people to think 'correctly' on the subject.

He certainly had his doubts before he came to power. In the election of 1930, which won the Nazis their entrée into the political system, the Jewish issue was scarcely mentioned. And later, when the Third Reich began its expansion into other countries, in all too many cases a significant part of the local populations could be relied on to do the very thing that Goldhagen accuses the Germans of – to start translating their anti-Semitism into a roundup the moment the whistle blew. In the Baltic countries, in the Ukraine, and in Romania and Yugoslavia, the results were horrendous from the outset. A more civilized-sounding but even more sinister case was France, where the Vichy regime exceeded the SS's requirements for lists of Jewish men, and handed over lists of women and children as well – the preliminary to the mass deportations from Drancy, which proceeded with no opposition to speak of. Why weren't the Germans themselves seen by the Nazis as being thoroughly biddable from the start?

Goldhagen leaves the question untouched because he has no answer. He is so certain of the entire German population's active collaboration – or, at the very least, its approving compliance – in the Holocaust that he underplays the Nazi state's powers of coercion through violence, something that no previous authority on the subject has managed to do. He overemphasizes the idea that the German people weren't completely powerless to shape Nazi policies; he cites, for example, the widespread public condemnation of the policy that resulted in the euthanizing of physically and mentally handicapped Germans. The practice was stopped, but in that case people were protesting the treatment of their own loved ones, and the Jews were not their loved ones. There could easily have been more protests on behalf of the Jews if the penalty for protesting had not been severe and well known.

Goldhagen qualifies the bravery of the Protestant minister and Nazi opponent Martin Niemöller by pointing out – correctly, alas – that he was an anti-Semite. But he doesn't mention the case of a Swabian pastor who after *Kristallnacht* told his congregation that the Nazi assault on the Jews would bring divine punishment. The Nazis beat him to a pulp, threw him onto the roof of a shed, smashed up his vicarage, and sent him to prison. And what about the Catholic priest Bernhard Lichtenberg, who, after the burning of the synagogues, closed each of his evening services with a prayer for the Jews? When he protested the deportations, he was put on a train himself – to Dachau. These men were made examples of to discourage others. They were made to pay for their crime.

Because it *was* a crime – the biggest one a non-Jewish German could commit. In Berlin (always the city whose population Hitler most distrusted), some non-Jewish German wives managed to secure the release of their Jewish husbands from concentration camps, but that scarcely proves that a mass protest would have been successful, or even, in the long run, tolerated without reprisal. The penalties for helping Jews got worse in direct proportion to the sanctions imposed against them, and everyone knew what the supreme penalty was: forms of capital punishment under the Nazis included the axe and the guillotine. (The axe was brought back from the museum *because* it was medieval.) Both the Protestant and the Catholic Church knuckled under to the Nazis with a suspicious alacrity in which rampant anti-Semitism was undoubtedly a factor, but the general failure of rank-and-file priests and ministers to bear individual witness has to be put down at least partly to the risks they would have run if they had done so. (Later on, when the Germans occupied Italy after the Badoglio government signed an armistice with the Allies, and the extreme anti-Jewish measures that Mussolini had stopped short of were put into effect, the roundup was a comparative failure, partly because the priests and nuns behaved so well. But they had not spent years with the threat of the concentration camp and the axe hanging over them.) In Germany, everyone knew that hiding or helping Jews was an unpardonable crime, which would be punished as severely as an attack on Hitler's life – because it *was* an attack on Hitler's life. Why, Goldhagen asks, did the population not rise up? The answer is obvious: because you had to be a hero to do so.

*

Eventually, of course, a small but significant segment of the German people did rise up, because they *were* heroes. About the various resistance groups of the pre-war years Goldhagen has little to say, and about the participants in the attempt on Hitler's life of July 20, 1944, he concludes that they were mostly anti-Semitic and that their rebellion against the Nazi regime was not motivated chiefly by its treatment of the Jews. But from Joachim Fest's 1994 *Staatsstreich* (Coup d'État) we know that Axel von dem Bussche-Streithorst, who was twenty-four at the time of the plot, turned against Hitler after witnessing a mass shooting of thousands of Jews at the Dubno airfield, in the Ukraine, and that Ulrich-Wilhelm Graf Schwerin von Schwanenfeld was turned towards resistance after seeing what the *Einsatzgruppen* were up to in Poland. There are further such examples in the *Lexikon des Widerstandes 1933–1945*, an honour roll of those who rebelled, and in a 1986 collection of essays by various historians entitled *Der Widerstand Gegen den Nationalsozialismus* (The Resistance Against National Socialism). The latter volume includes a list of the twenty July plotters who, after the plot failed, told the Gestapo during their interrogation that the reason for their rebellion was the treatment of the Jews. There are several names you would expect: Julius Leber, Dietrich Bonhöffer, Adolf Reichwein, and Carl Goerdeler – men who had been scheming to get rid of Hitler even during the years of his success. But then there are names that smack of the *Almanach de Gotha*: Alexander and Berthold Graf Schenk von Stauffenberg, Hans von Dohnanyi, Heinrich Graf von Lehndorff, Helmuth James Graf von Moltke . . . There is no reason to think that these *Hochadel* sons were necessarily liberal. Some of them came from archconservative families, and no doubt a good number had grown up with anti-Semitism hanging around the house like heavy curtains. Most of them were career officers who had relished the chance to rebuild the German Army; some even nursed the hopelessly romantic idea that after Hitler was killed *Grossdeutschland* might remain intact to go on fighting beside the Western Allies against the Soviet Union. But about the sincerity of their disgust at what happened to the Jews there can be no doubt. Though it could scarcely have made things easier for them, they told the Gestapo about it, thereby testifying to the sacrificial element in an enterprise that may have failed as a plot but succeeded as a ceremony – the ceremony of innocence which the Nazis had always been so keen to drown.

The plot was already a ceremony before it was launched. The experienced Henning von Tresckow, who had been in on several attempts before, was well aware that it might fail but told his fellow conspirators that it should go ahead anyway, *coute que coute*. Claus Graf von Stauffenberg's famous last words *Es lebe das geheime Deutschland* have turned out to be not quite so romantically foolish as they sounded at the time. If there never was a secret Germany, the July plotters at least provided a sacred moment, and the Germans of today are right to cherish it. As for the aristocracy, though even the bravery of its flower could not offset the way that it helped to sabotage the Weimar Republic, at least it regained its honour, in preparation for its retirement from the political stage. Since then the aristocracy has served Germany well in all walks of life – the Gräfin Dornhoff, active proprietress of *Die Zeit*, one of the great newspapers of the world, would be an asset to any nation – but it has paid democracy the belated compliment of a decent reticence. Churchill, the instinctive opponent of Hitler and all his works, always thought that Prussia was the nerve centre of German bestiality. He was wrong about that. Hans Frank, outstanding even among Gauleiters for his epic savagery, was closer to the truth. Many of the July plotters had a background in the famously snobbish Prussian Ninth Infantry regiment, of which Frank himself was a reservist. Just before his own hanging at Nuremberg, Frank said that the Ninth's officers had never understood *Antisemitismus der spezifisches Nazi-Art* (anti-Semitism of the specific Nazi type). They had been unsound on the Jewish question.

How many of the German population were unsound on the Jewish question we can never now know. Probably there were fewer than we would like to think, but almost certainly there were more than Goldhagen allows. However many there were, there was not a lot they could do if they didn't want to get hurt. After the Nazis finally came to absolute power, the build-up to the annihilation of the Jews moved stage by stage, always with the occasional lull that allowed people to think the madness might be over. Certainly there were a lot of Jews who wanted to think that, and who can blame them? Seizing the chance to emigrate meant leaving behind everything they had. Some of them – especially the baptized and those who no longer practised their faith – never stopped thinking of themselves as Germans, believing, correctly, that the regime which criminalized them was a criminal regime. They thought Germany would get its senses back. They would scarcely have done so if they had thought that there were no non-Jewish Germans who thought the same.

From the year the Nazis took power right up until *Kristallnacht* in November 1938, the legal deprivations and persecutions looked selective, as if there might be some viable limit beyond which they would not go. After *Kristallnacht*, it became clearer that an all-inclusive, no-holds-barred pogrom was under way, but by then it was too late. It was too late for everyone, non-Jewish Germans included. But really it had always been too late, ever since the Nazis rewrote the laws so that their full apparatus of terror could be legally directed against anyone who disagreed with them. Is it any wonder that so many of those who retained their citizenship turned their backs on the pariahs from whom it had been stripped? When one Communist shot a stormtrooper, eleven Communists were immediately decapitated in reprisal. Everyone knew things like that. Those were the first things that every German in the Nazi era ever knew – a fact worth remembering when we confidently assume that they all must have known about the last thing, the Holocaust. It can be remarkable what you don't find out when you are afraid for just yourself, let alone for your family. All you have to do is look away. And the Nazis made very sure, even when Hitler was tumultuously popular in the flush of his diplomatic and military successes, that failure to join in the exultant unanimity would not pass unnoticed. Even if you lay low, you still had to stick your right hand in the air. Max Weber defined the state as that organization holding the monopoly of legalized violence. The Nazi state overfulfilled his definition by finding new forms of violence to make legal. Probably Goldhagen realizes all that. But he doesn't say much about it, because he has a bigger, better idea that leaves the Nazis looking like last minute walk-ons in the closing scene of *Götterdammerung*: spear-carriers in Valhalla.

Here we have to turn to his account of the growth of German anti-Semitism, which means that we have to turn back to the beginning of the book. His thesis would have gone better at the end, as a speculative afterthought, but he puts it at the front because it contains the premise that for him explains everything. Since most of it is written in the brain-curdling jargon which he later partly lets drop when he gets to the Holocaust itself, this glutinous treatise would make for a slow start even if it were consistent. But the reader is continually stymied by what is left out or glossed over. An artist in the firm grip of his own brush, Goldhagen slap-happily paints a picture of anti-Semitism pervading all levels of society, without explaining how it failed to pervade the members of the political class who contrived to grant citizenship to the Jews. Beginning early in the nineteenth century, the process of emancipation moved through the German States, culminating, in 1869, with citizenship for every Jew in the North German Confederation. (The laws were carried over into the *Kaiserreich* after German unification, in 1871.) Even in the tolerant Austria-Hungary of Emperor Franz Josef, citizenship for Jews had some strings attached, whereas in Germany civil rights for Jews remained on the books until the Nazis rewrote them. Not even in the reign of Kaiser Wilhelm II, a choleric anti-Semite by the end, were people of Jewish background deprived of their rights. They undoubtedly had trouble exercising them – prejudice was indeed everywhere, in varying degrees – but that doesn't alter the fact that they were granted them.

Perhaps those nineteenth-century politicians were thorough anti-Semites, and merely stopped short of trying to put their prejudice into law. President Truman freely used the word 'nigger' among his Southern friends, but when some returning black GIs were beaten up he made the first move in the chain of legislation that eventually led (under President Johnson, who was not without prejudice, either) to voter registration by blacks in the South. There have always been people with prejudice who have nevertheless served justice, whether out of a supervening idealism, out of expediency, or out of a simple wish not to be thought provincial by more sophisticated peers. In other words, there is prejudice and there is prejudice. But Goldhagen wants all the grades of anti-Semitism, from the enthusiasm of nutty pamphleteers down to the stultifying, self-protective distaste of the *Kleinbürgertum* at their pokey dinner tables, to add up to just one thing: the eliminationist fervour that led to extermination as soon as it got its chance.

Until recent times, one of Germany's recurring troubles was that it was more integrated culturally than it was politically. A case can be made for the Jews not having been integrated at all into the political structure, although you would have to eliminate a towering figure like Walther Rathenau – which is exactly what some of the Nazi Party's forerunners did. But from the time of Goethe up until the Anschluss the Jews were, at least in part, integrated into the culture; they made a contribution whose like had not been seen in Europe since Alfonso IX founded the University of Salamanca. Though they often aroused envy and spite among non-Jewish rivals, they aroused admiration in at least equal measure. Kant said that if the Muse of Philosophy could choose an ideal language, it would choose the language of Moses Mendelssohn. Goethe said that the Jewish contribution was vital. Nietzsche ranked the Jew Heine as the most important German poet after Goethe. The novelist Theodor Fontane, who started out as an anti-Semite, gave up on the idea when he realized that the Jewish bourgeoisie was a more cultivated audience than the aristocracy, which he had tried in vain to enlighten. Even the dreadful Wagner was ambivalent on the subject: when Thomas Mann's Jewish father-in-law left Germany after the Nazis came to power, all he took with him were Wagner's letters of thanks for his having helped to build the *Festspielhaus* in Bayreuth.

Which brings us to Thomas Mann. Here one is forced to wonder if whoever gave Goldhagen high marks for his thesis ever showed it to a literary colleague. As evidence of the all-pervading nature of eliminationist anti-Semitism, Goldhagen has the audacity to rope in, without qualification or explanation, a remark by Thomas Mann. Well, there is a grain of truth in it. In 1933, when Mann had already begun his long exile, he did indeed confide to his diary that it was a pity the new regime should include him along with some of the undesirable Jewish elements it was dealing with. But against this grain of truth there is a whole silo of contrary evidence. Thomas Mann had always disliked what he saw as the rootless Jewish cosmo-politanism (shades of his beloved Wagner there) that criticized because it couldn't create, and thus gave rise to a bugbear like Alfred Kerr. Mann the Nobel Prize-winning eminence, the new Goethe, the walking cultural icon, had a bad tendency, quite normal among writers even at their most successful, to take praise as his due and anything less as sabotage. He thought, with some justification, that the annoyingly clever Kerr was on his case. But for Jews who, in his opinion, *did* create, Mann had nothing but admiration. He had it in the first years of the century, when his conservatism was still as hide-bound as the snobbery he was never to overcome: his two early encomiums for Arthur Schnitzler are models of generosity. He had scores of friendships among the Jewish cultural figures of the emi-gration and maintained them throughout the Nazi era, often at the expense of his time, effort and exchequer. For Bruno Walter, it was always open house *chez* Mann, because Mann honoured Walter as the incarnation of the Germany that mattered, just as he despised Hitler as its exterminating angel. Even to allow the possibility of our inferring that Mann might have thought otherwise is to perpetrate a truly stunning libel, and one can only hope that the excuse for it is ignorance.

Nowadays it has become fashionable to mock Mann's supposed equivocation *vis-à-vis* the Nazi regime in its first years, because of the time that passed before he publicly condemned it. At the time, his own children were angry with him for the same reason. We have to remember that his prestige, worldly goods and most appreciative reading public were all locked up in Germany; that he was deeply rooted in its complex society; and that at his age he did not fancy leading the very kind of rootless cosmopolitan life for which he had condemned men like Kerr. But his 1933–34 diaries (which one can safely recommend Goldhagen to read whole so that he will not in future run the risk of quoting a misleading fragment from a secondary source) reveal unmistakably, and over and over, that he loathed the bestiality of the new regime from its first hour. All Mann's *Tagebüche*, through the Thirties and the war years – and hurry the day when the whole fascinating corpus is properly translated – show that he never wavered in his utter disgust at what the Nazis had done to his country. As for his opinion of what they were doing to the most defenceless people in it, he went public about that in his 1936 essay on anti-Semitism, in which he definitively penetrated, and devastatingly parodied, the unconscious logic of the Nazi mentality: 'I might be nothing, but at least I am not a Jew.'

*

Historical research has by now established beyond question that the Nazi Party was principally financed not by the great capitalists of Brecht's imagination but by the *Kleinleute* – the little people. Reduced to despair by inflation and by the Depression, they assigned their hopes and their few spare pennies to the cause of the man they thought might rescue them from nothingness. He did, too – so triumphantly that they didn't suspect until the eleventh hour that he was leading them into a nothingness even more complete than the one they had come from. The Holocaust would have been unimaginable without the Nazi Party; the Nazi Party would have been unimaginable without Hitler; and Hitler's rise to power would have been unimaginable without the unique circumstances that brought the Weimar Republic to ruin. To hear Goldhagen tell it, mass murder was all set to go: a century-long buildup of eliminationist anti-Semitism simply had to express itself. But the moment when a historian says that something had to happen is the moment when he stops writing history and starts predicting the past.

After the Second World War, the British historian A. J. P. Taylor began publishing a series of books and articles which added up to the contention that Hitler's regime was the inevitable consequence of Germany's border problem, and that his depredations in the East were just a harsh version of what any German in his position would have been obliged to do anyway. Hitler's war, Taylor argued, brought Europe back to 'reality', out of its liberal illusions. Then, in 1951, the German historian Golo Mann – one of Thomas Mann's three sons – made a survey of Taylor's historical writings, and took them apart. He accused Taylor of predicting the past. The Weimar Republic, Mann pointed out, had been no liberal illusion and might have survived if extraordinary circumstances hadn't conspired to undermine it. German nationalism was not a demon that always strode armed through the land – it was in the minds of men, and could have stayed there. This confrontation between the frivolously clever Taylor and the deeply engaged Golo Mann was a portent of the intellectual conflict that blew up in Germany more than thirty years later, when the learned historian Ernst Nolte foolishly went to print with an opinion that sounded like one of Taylor's brainwaves cast in more turgid prose: he stated that Nazi Germany, by attacking Russia, had simply got into the Cold War early, and that Nazi extermination camps had been the inevitable consequence of tangling with an enemy who was up to the same sort of thing. This time, there were plenty of German historians and commentators ready to oppose such views, because by now the perverse urge to marginalize the Nazis had penetrated the academic world, and had been identified as a trend that needed to be stopped. Younger historians who had looked up to Nolte hastened to distance themselves from him; the glamorous Michael Stürmer, in his virtuoso summary of modern German history *Die Grenzen der Macht* (The Limits of Power), consigned Nolte's theory to a dismissive passing reference. Stürmer also wrote a sentence about Hitler that is unfortunately likely to remain all too true: 'Even today, the history of Hitler is largely the history of how he has been underestimated.'

Why is this so? Strangely, anti-Semitism has probably played a part. We tend to think of him as an idiot because the central tenet of his ideology was idiotic – and idiotic, of course, it transparently is. Anti-Semitism is a world view through a pinhole: as scientists say about a bad theory, it is not even wrong. Nietzsche tried to tell Wagner that it was beneath contempt. Sartre was right for once when he said that through anti-Semitism any halfwit could become a member of an élite. But, as the case of Wagner proves, a man can have this poisonous bee in his bonnet and still be a creative genius. Hitler was a destructive genius, whose evil gifts not only beggar description but invite denial, because we find it more comfortable to believe that their consequences were produced by historical forces than to believe that he *was* a historical force. Or perhaps we just lack the vocabulary. Not many of us, in a secular age, are willing to concede that, in the form of Hitler, Satan visited the Earth, recruited an army of sinners, and fought and won a battle against God. We would rather talk the language of pseudoscience, which at least seems to bring such cataclysmic events to order. But all that such language can do is shift the focus of attention down to the broad mass of the German people, which is what Goldhagen has done, in a way that, at least in part, lets Hitler off the hook – and unintentionally reinforces his central belief that it was the destiny of the Jewish race to be expelled from the *Volk* as an inimical presence.

Hannah Arendt, in her long, courageous, and much misunderstood career, had her weak moments. In her popular *Eichmann in Jerusalem* (first published serially in this magazine) she undoubtedly pushed her useful notion of the detached desk worker too far. But she was resoundingly right when she refused to grant the Nazis the power of their *fait accompli*. She declined to suppose, as Hitler had supposed, that there really was some international collectivity called the Jews. Echoing the fourth count of the Nuremberg indictment, she called the Holocaust a crime against humanity.

The Jews were the overwhelming majority among Hitler's victims, but he also killed all the Gypsies and homosexuals he could find. He let two and a half million Russian POWs perish, most of them from the gradually applied technique of deprivation. The novelist Joseph Roth, drinking himself to death in Paris before the war, said that Hitler probably had the Christians in his sights, too. We can never now trace the source of Hitler's passion for revenge, but we can be reasonably certain that there would have been no satisfying it had he lived. Sooner or later, he would have got around to everybody. Hitler was the culprit who gave all the other culprits their chance. To concentrate exclusively on the prejudice called anti-Semitism – to concentrate even on *his* anti-Semitism – is another way of underestimating him.

*

At the end of this bloodstained century, which has topped by ten times Tamburlaine's wall of skulls, lime, and living men, the last thing we want to believe is that it all happened on a whim. In the Soviet Union, the liquidation of bourgeois elements began under Lenin. By the time Stalin took power, there were no bourgeois elements left. He went on finding them. He found them even within the Communist Party. They didn't exist. They never had existed. He killed them anyway. Eventually, he killed more people than Hitler, and it was all for nothing. Far from building socialism, he ensured its ruin. His onslaught had nothing to do with social analysis, about which he knew no more than he did about biology. Unless you believe in Original Sin, there is almost no meaning that can be attached to his behaviour, except to say that he was working out his personal problems.

In China, Mao Zedong went to war against the evil landlords and the imperialist spies. Neither group actually existed. The death toll of his countrymen exceeded the totals achieved by Hitler and Stalin combined. They all died for nothing. Dying innocent, they have their eternal dignity, but there are no profundities to be plumbed in their collective extinction except the adamantine fact of human evil. In Cambodia, Pol Pot encouraged the persecution, torture, and murder of everyone who wore glasses – but enough. A country, no matter how cultured, either respects the rights of all its citizens or is not civilized. The answer to the nagging conundrum of how a civilized country like Germany could produce the Holocaust is that Germany ceased to be civilized from the moment Hitler came to power. It had been before, and it has been since – a fact that might secure for Goldhagen's book, when it is published there, a considered reception, despite its contents. I look forward to reading the German critical press, especially if one of the reviewers is Marcel Reich-Ranicki. Of Jewish background (his book about his upbringing in the Warsaw ghetto is a minor masterpiece), Reich-Ranicki is one of the most brilliant critical writers in the world. I know just where I want to read his piece: in my favourite café on the Oranienburger Strasse, just along from the meticulously restored synagogue, whose golden dome is a landmark for the district. Two armed guards stand at the door, but this time in its defence – a reminder of what Germany once did not only to others but to itself, and need not have done if democracy had held together.

A shorter version first appeared in the *New Yorker*, 22 April, 1996

POSTSCRIPT TO GOLDHAGEN

The preceding review is reprinted in a form substantially different from the way it first appeared in the *New Yorker*. The way it looks here is much closer to the way I first wrote it. Goldhagen's book was big news at the time, so Tina Brown very properly decided that my notice should be promoted from the 'back of the book' reviews department to 'Critic at Large' status in the middle of the magazine. This unlooked-for elevation, however, proved to be a mixed blessing, because in a position of such prominence the *soi-disant* Critic at Large often finds himself not as at large as he would like. Suddenly he is held to be speaking for the magazine as much as for himself, and inevitably it is decided that his personal quirks should be suppressed, in the interests of objectivity. My animadversions on Goldhagen's prose style were held to be a potentially embarrassing irrelevance: to dispute his interpretation of factual events was going to be contentious enough, without getting into the subjective area of how he wrote his interpretation down. I didn't think that it was a subjective area; I thought the callow over-confidence of his jargon-ridden style was a clear index of how he had been simply bound to get his pretended overview of the subject out of shape from the start; but I knuckled under or we would have all been stymied.

It wasn't, after all, as if the editors wanted to change the main thrust of the piece. There is a fine line between being asked to say something differently and being required to say something different, but it is a clear one. When they do want you to say something different, of course, it's time to take the kill fee and quit. But this piece was guaranteed to give me trouble whatever the circumstances. Goldhagen's book aspires to be wide-ranging over both the political and cultural background to the Holocaust, and if you hope to show that his reach exceeds his grasp, you have to be pretty wide-ranging yourself, over a literature that it takes half a lifetime to absorb. It was

probably as much a blessing as a curse that I had to write the piece
against a deadline, and that I had to do much of the work on it
while I was filming in Mexico City, away from my own library and
any other library that held the relevant books. To a great extent I
had to rely on what was in my memory. In retrospect, the restriction
feels like a lucky break. Otherwise I would have ended up writing a
review longer than the book, and it would have had footnotes hanging
off it in festoons.

There is something to be said for being forced into ellipsis. Skimp-
iness, however, is inevitably part of the result. You wouldn't know,
from Goldhagen's book, that the question of the Jewish contribution
to German-speaking culture was far more complicated than he makes
out. Unfortunately you wouldn't know from my review just how
complicated it was. It was elementary work to rebut his line with a
few simple examples. The editing process reduced them to even fewer,
but the obvious point was made. It was also fudged. Goldhagen is
clamorously wrong on that particular topic, but the evidence by
which he might think himself right is stronger than I had the time,
the room or – less forgivably – the inclination to make out. As my
admired Marcel Reich-Ranicki explains in his *Der Doppelte Boden*
(augmented edition, Fischer, 1992), some of the Jewish writers, though
they enjoyed huge public acclaim, had ample motive for feeling
rejected. The novelist Jakob Wasserman, for all his success as a
best-seller, despaired of social acceptance. Among Jewish artists in
Germany after World War I that state of mind was not rare, and
in Austria it was common. Its epicentre had been registered by Arthur
Schnitzler at the turn of the century, in a key passage of his great
novel *Der Weg ins Freie* (The Path into the Clear), where a leading
character spells out the impossibility of true assimilation with a
mordant clarity not very different from the polemical Zionism of
Theodor Herzl. There can be no doubt that Schnitzler was speaking
from the heart.

The question abides, however, of whether he was speaking from
a whole heart or only a part of it. Though insecurity was ever-present
and outright abuse always a threat, the Jewish artists and thinkers, if
assimilation to the German-speaking culture was what they wanted,
had good reasons to think it was being achieved in those last years
before 1933. Their influence, even their dominance, in the various
fields of culture was widely acknowledged. On playbills, in concert

programmes and on publishers' lists there were Jewish names that attracted an audience totalling millions. The career of Stefan Zweig, alone, would be enough to make Goldhagen's cultural theory look fantastic. Zweig's books were customarily translated into about thirty languages but his sales in the German-speaking countries would have been enough on their own to make him wealthy. It shouldn't need pointing out that his sales couldn't have been that big if they had been confined to an audience of Jewish background, a qualification which applied to only 300,000 people in the whole of Germany. Zweig was part of the German literary landscape, together with the liberal values he professed. Hans Scholl, the master spirit of the White Rose resistance group in Munich, had already turned against his Hitler Youth upbringing, but his trajectory towards outright subversion was accelerated after one of Zweig's books was taken away from him by a Nazi official. Scholl thought that if the Nazis were against *that*, they were against the Germany he cared about. (Goldhagen's failure to so much as mention the White Rose, incidentally, is the kind of omission that makes a mockery of his scientific vocabulary. In science, the fact that doesn't fit the theory eliminates the theory, not the other way about. Hans and Sophie Scholl were gentiles born into a household formed by liberal German culture, were well aware that Jews had helped to form that culture, and were ready to die for it rather than betray it. If Goldhagen wants to go on asking why the German population did not rise up, he might consider the manner in which those two brave young people perished. The guillotine is a big price to pay for a conviction.)

A necessary conclusion, about the large and well-informed German-speaking audience for the arts, would be that if they were all eliminationist anti-Semites, they must have been strangely ready to sideline their otherwise overmastering prejudice when it came to matters of aesthetic enjoyment. It's not a conclusion that Goldhagen feels bound to draw, because he doesn't even consider the matter. Nor does he consider that the abuse heaped on Jewish artists by the Nazi propaganda machine before the *Machtergreifung* was a measure of the success they had achieved in becoming a part of the landscape. Finally and fatally, he doesn't consider that the massive and irreversible damage done to German-speaking culture by the repression, expulsion and murder of the Jews was the full, exact and tragic measure of how they had been vital to it. Once again it is an awful thing to find oneself saying, but it has to be said: the *Reichskültur-kammer*, if it were still in business, couldn't have done a better job of treating the Jewish contributors to German culture as if they had been an irrelevance, simply begging to be swept away.

But a young historian can be forgiven for lacking the kind of cultural information that would bring such questions to the forefront. The richness of what the German-speaking Jews achieved before the Nazi era takes time to assess. Harder to understand is Goldhagen's apparent supposition that nothing much has happened in Germany *since* the Nazi era when it comes to his own field – history. You would never know, from his book, that whole teams of German historians, in the full knowledge that they are trying to make bricks from rubble, have dedicated themselves to the study of the catastrophe that distorted their intellectual inheritance. As in any other country at any time, there have been a few historians who have devoted prodigious resources to missing the point. Of the star revisionists mixed up in the *Historikerstreit*, Ernst Nolte and Andreas Hillgruber at least had the merit of being too blatant to be plausible: they pretty well blamed the Holocaust on the Soviet Union. Klaus Hildebrand and Michael Stürmer were more insidious because there was nothing wrong with their facts: after the Red Army crossed the German border, the retreating *Wehrmacht* really *was* fighting heroically for its country's heritage. Unfortunately their suggestion that post-war German patriotism might thus claim a solid base was hopelessly compromised by the consideration that part of the heritage was the Holocaust. In his various essays and open letters about the *Historikerstreit*, Jürgen Habermas (who, it is only fair to concede, admires Goldhagen's book) was marvellous on the equivocations and the delusions of the revisionists, but on the main point he didn't need to be marvellous: it was too obviously true. The revisionist historian can't reasonably hope to have a Germany that is not obsessed with the past. There can be no putting off shame to achieve maturity. The shame *is* the maturity.

Most of the German historians are well aware of this. The revisionists did not prevail, and the work entailed in rebutting them had already become part of the accumulated glory of Germany's indigenous historical studies as the terrible twentieth century neared its end. But if German culture really had been nourished at its root by eliminationist anti-Semitism, as Goldhagen argues, it is hard to see why so many of today's German historians should now be so concerned about the Holocaust. Very few of them are Jews, for sadly obvious reasons. Surely they, too, are 'the Germans', as Goldhagen would like to put it. It can only follow that their culture has other continuities apart from the one that Goldhagen picks out. Their urge to comprehend, their respect for the facts – these things could not have started up all by themselves, out of nowhere.

There are plenty of Germans, naturally enough, who would like to think that their country as they know it today *has* started up out of nowhere. For those who would like to throw off the burden of history and move on, Goldhagen's book has been a welcome gift. Purporting to bring the past home to the unsuspecting present, he has had the opposite effect. If he has not yet asked himself why his book has received such an enthusiastic reception in Germany, he might ponder why 'the Germans' should be so glad to be supplied with the argument that their parents and grandparents were all equally to blame because they inhabited a culture blameworthy in itself: we're different now. But nobody is that different now, because nobody was that different then. It will always suit the current generation of any country to blame the turpitude of their ancestors on the culture then prevailing, as if people had no choice how to act. It saves us from the anguish of asking ourselves how we might have acted had we been there, at a time when plenty of people knew there was a choice, but couldn't face the consequences of making it, and when those who did choose virtue were volunteers for torture and death.

No wonder Goldhagen is so popular. On top of leaving out the large numbers of German citizens who declined to vote for the Nazis even when there was almost no other party remaining with credible means to stop the chaos in the streets, he doesn't even mention the Germans who were so suicidally brave as to defy the Nazis after they came to power. Sacrificial witnesses to human decency, they died at the rate of about twenty-five people per day for every day that the Third Reich was in existence. They might seem to add up to a drop in the bucket, and it was terribly true that they had no real hope of having any effect, but Goldhagen is keeping questionable company when he treats a handful of powerless lives as if their deaths meant nothing in the eye of history. Some of the questionable company he is keeping is alive now. We would all find life a lot easier if we didn't have to ask ourselves how we would have measured up to the same test. Hence the temptation to suppose that nobody ever did. The challenge to one's compassion is tough enough, without compounding it by the challenge to one's conscience.

In our time and privileged surroundings there has been no such examination to pass or fail, but what makes the difference is political circumstances. The new Germany is a democracy. So was the old Germany, or it tried to be: but then the Nazis got in, and Hell broke loose. It can break loose anywhere, in any people: all peoples have hellish propensities. When Daniel J Goldhagen has lived long enough to value democracy for what it prevents, he will be less ready to be astonished by what his fellow human beings are capable of when they are allowed. And the Germans really are his fellow human beings. To assert otherwise is to further the kind of argument which the Nazis, thereby achieving their sole lasting value, contrived to discredit beyond redemption.

2001

WRITERS IN THEIR TIME

MARK TWAIN, JOURNALIST

Two volumes of the Library of America containing all that matters of Mark Twain's journalism – *Tales, Sketches, Speeches, & Essays* is the title – came out last autumn, and have kept at least one reader going ever since, with the occasional pause to consult the two volumes of Twain's major writings which were published in the same format a decade or so ago. There is an almost audible clicking into place: this covetable quartet of books gangs up like gauge blocks, those machine-shop measures that don't need anything except their trueness to keep them together. At least two more Twain volumes are yet to come, but for now it's hard to imagine a set more satisfactory than this – four volumes just as neat as all the others in the Library of America, and even more solid, energetic, genial and creative: it makes a good gift suggestion for the new Administration. If President Clinton is a better speechmaker than President Bush, it is mainly because he steals better stuff. He should steal from the best: Mark Twain, who could rock the room for an hour while talking nothing except sense, and would have staved off Arsenio Hall without needing a saxophone.

For some years, it has been becoming clearer that the Library of America is the symbol for itself that the United States has long been in search of. Colonial Williamsburg is too Disneyfied to stand for tradition, Disneyland too childish to stand for innovation, Mt Rushmore too big to stand in your living room. You can line up the Library of America on a few shelves. Of course, the French could do the same sort of thing earlier. The Pléiade was the library that Edmund Wilson had in mind when he caned the Modern Language Association for burying the country's intellectual heritage while pretending to preserve it, sponsoring volumes that owed too much to pedantry, not enough to readability, weighed a ton, and looked like hell. Wilson kept up the campaign for a long time but seemed to stand no better chance of winning it than of beating his income-tax rap. Then the Library of America made Wilson's dream happen. From its first few volumes it was obvious that the Library of America had struck the ideal balance between authority and portability. Its volumes begged irresistibly to be picked up, like brilliant children.

Remarkably, they didn't lose this unthreatening quality even as they multiplied. If you own more than about thirty of the sixty-five volumes so far, monumentality becomes a present danger: the massed black jackets loom like midnight, and it starts to look as if the Pléiade had chosen better – first, to wear white, and then, when that started looking like a cliff of snow, to let the horizontally striped gold-blocked spines show through a transparent jacket, like scaling ladders to a Fabergé Bastille of imprisoned wisdom. But you can always alleviate the pangs of gazing at a wall of uniformity by taking one of the Library of America volumes down and letting it fall open in the hand. If this is dignity, it is user-friendly. And with these two volumes of Twain's minor writings here is the original, unashamed vitality that lies at the heart of the whole enterprise. You could just about convince yourself that *Huckleberry Finn* was a work of literature in the Old World style, aimed at a refined public – after all, it certainly has the rank, if not the manner. But Twain's journalism is a daunting reminder that he was ready to lavish everything he had on everybody, every time. He was democratic all the way down to his metabolism. For Twain, there was no division between democracy and creativity. They were versions of the same thing: exuberance.

Twain's fugitive pieces have been collected before; but now we have, with just the right amount of critical apparatus, the authoritative texts, and all arranged chronologically, so that we can watch him grow. He grew like bamboo in the rain. His first hit was a newspaper sketch called 'Jim Smiley and His Jumping Frog'. Twain wasn't the first American journalist to write tall tales under a pen name; Petroleum V. Nasby, whom Twain knew and admired, was one of several practitioners already in the field. Nor was Twain the first to combine the high style with the low, squandering highfalutin resources on a shaggy-dog story. What was new, attention-getting, and instantly popular was the quality of the evocation when he worked the switch out of mandarin diction into the concrete vernacular.

The story of the Jumping Frog is told to Twain by a yarn-spinner

– 'good-natured, garrulous old Simon Wheeler' – who isn't afraid to be boring: 'Simon Wheeler backed me into a corner and blockaded me there with his chair – and then sat down and reeled off the monotonous narrative which follows this paragraph.' Twain is true to his word: Wheeler is what the British would call a crasher. His story of Jim Smiley and the Jumping Frog goes on for pages before it even gets to the frog. Much more of it would put the reader to sleep, even though Twain the narrator makes it clear that the verbosity belongs to his interlocutor, not to him. But Wheeler's drone goes on just long enough to ensure that we are given the set-up for the story without suspecting how funny it's going to get. We hear that Jim Smiley, who owns the champion jumping frog, suckers himself into a bet with a hustler who appears to know nothing about frogs. But while Smiley is out of the room (Twain rather muffs this bit: we don't find out Smiley has left the room until *after* we are told about how the stranger works his trick) the stranger fills Jim's precious frog with a meal of lead shot. At just the moment when the champion frog gets the cue to unleash its usual stunning jump, Wheeler's long-winded vocabulary snaps into focus. The champion frog 'give a heave, and hysted up his shoulders – so – like a Frenchman, but it wasn't no use – he couldn't budge; he was planted as solid as an anvil.' The anvil is good, but Twain's mentor, Artemus Ward, might have done it. The Frenchman's shrug is what makes it Twain. You can see it happening.

The Jumping Frog story was reprinted in periodicals all over the United States following its publication in 1865, and two years later it was the keynote piece of Twain's first collection, *The Celebrated Jumping Frog of Calaveras County, and Other Sketches*. Twain was disappointed with the way the book's publication was handled, and was further miffed to find that it didn't sell very well, but the Jumping Frog had already done its job in the periodicals. The young Mark Twain was made, and so was a tradition. It was a comic tradition, but now more than ever that shouldn't be taken to mean that it was merely humorous. Every subsequent American humour writer writes in the range of tones established by Twain. When Thurber says of his fellow economics student the football player Bolenciecwcz that 'while he was not dumber than an ox he was not any smarter,' he is in touch with Twain. Even so cosmopolitan a *pasticheur* as S. J. Perelman, whose macaronic vocabulary seems bent on superseding provincialism as its first impulse, sounds, when he has a picture to evoke, like Twain talking. There is a Perelman story that begins with the narrator waiting for his date to show up. The story goes off somewhere else, and long after we have forgotten about the date she finally appears, 'sobbing drunk with a Marine on either arm'.

That instant of clarity, with all the baroque vocabulary suddenly forgotten, wouldn't have been the same if Twain hadn't first written such pieces as his tour-de-force diatribe of 1882, 'The McWilliamses and the Burglar Alarm', in which the new burglar-alarm system makes the house so attractive to burglars that they come to live there, until there is 'not a spare bed in the house; all occupied by burglars'. The burglars take the alarm system, along with everything else. You could be watching the characters accumulate in the New Old Lompoc House, W. C. Fields' favoured hostel in 'The Bank Dick', or – to go beyond America, as Twain's influence almost immediately did – you could be listening to Stephen Leacock talking about his first bank account, or Henry Lawson telling his story about the Loaded Dog, the dog that got its teeth fastened into a bomb and terrorized a mining camp. Leacock was active in Canada and Lawson was an Australian determined to free the natural speech of his countrymen from the thralldom of literary preciosity. Twain's style had reached both of them, and in America it was all-pervasive almost from the start.

Unfortunately, American humour, like every other American product, has long since paid the inevitable penalty attached to any consumable in a society of abundance. There are so many choices that they all seem the same. It isn't really like that – nobody sane has to watch the comedy channel all the time it's on the air – but it seems like that. There is a humour glut, as if being funny were an escape from reality. Twain never thought so. For him, humour was a way – and just one of the ways – to escape from unreality. He wanted to get the whole of life into his most casual work. He was a comic writer in the classic sense: Dante's divinely inspired cosmos was a comedy because it mixed low speech with high, the profane with the sacred. In that sense, even Shakespeare's tragedies were comedies. Twain was in the recognizable position of the storyteller who emerges during the formative history of his country and helps to provide its characteristic voice, thereby incidentally reinforcing the general rule that genius arrives early. Twain and Dickens, in their public position so similar – best-selling authors who electrified audiences when they read aloud – were different in this: Dickens was only metaphorically creating a world, whereas Twain was literally creating a nation.

*

Perhaps re-creating would be a better word. Like Shakespeare arriving after Bloody Mary left, Twain was lucky in his timing. The new nation looked as if it had just finished destroying itself, in the Civil War. The young Twain had managed to stay out of the war's way. In 'The Private History of a Campaign That Failed', a piece written in 1885, he looks back twenty-five years to the young man he was when history suddenly boiled up all around him. As slaveowners went, Twain's family had been liberal and even enlightened, but when the war started Twain didn't hesitate to join a small volunteer group of Confederate riders hiding out in the woods. He just hesitated about what to do next. So did they all. One night, a strange rider materialized from the direction of the Union camp. Twain had a sixth share in shooting him down – or, anyway, he remembered it that way. That was enough for him. He faded away to the West. If President Clinton gets this set of books as a birthday gift from his wife, he will find consolation here, because if Twain didn't know what to do about a war that split the nation's heart he did know what to do about healing the wound. When that war was over and he started to publish in earnest, he treated the two sides as if they belonged together. Not that he spread any soft soap. He was fierce on the liberal issues. Mrs Clinton will find her spirit here, too: perhaps the President should give her the gift.

Twain's journalism is full of contempt for racism in all its forms. Like Swift, he had a low opinion of the human race in general, reserving his admiration for individuals. He was not much given to admiring ethnic authenticity, but he condescended on a cultural basis rather than a racial one. For any creed or colour that was being persecuted he was a vocal champion. Chinese immigrants given a bad time by the locals could count on one kind voice, at least. His initial sympathy for America's Cuba adventure was based on his contempt for Spain's horrific colonial record, which was almost as bad as its domestic record. When the United States began to show Spanish tendencies in the Philippines, Twain soon started

condemning American colonialism, too. As with the Spanish, so with
any other European nation: he was always ready to point out that
the Old World had dirty hands. Belgium's depredations in the Congo
survived the invective of Roger Casement, but King Leopold II's
reputation was settled forever by Twain's 'King Leopold's Soliloquy',
which had Leopold performing absurd mental gymnastics to disown
the atrocities committed in his name.

Twain knew that the brute facts of imperialism undid all pretensions to civilization on the part of the old countries. But he never
lost sight of the great crime at home. In view of recent suggestions,
inspired by the dubious spirit of political correctness, that *Huckleberry
Finn* and other major works of Twain should be swept from the
library shelves because of the picture they paint of black people, it is
useful to read through Twain's journalism and see just how much
time and effort he put into fighting Jim Crow. When the first lynch-
ings occurred in Missouri, he wept for his home state in a plangent
threnody called 'The United States of Lyncherdom'. It is all written
in one long sob: 'And so Missouri has fallen, that great state! Certain
of her children have joined the lynchers, and the smirch is upon the
rest of us.' In another essay, Twain reminded the evangelists that their
fathers had thumped the same Bibles while perpetrating the same
blasphemy, 'closing their doors against the hunted slave'.

There is enough said outright in the journalism to remind us, if
we needed reminding, that Twain speaking in story form was and
remains the great post-bellum writer about the condition of whites
and blacks in the America they share. Only his vocabulary can blur
the point, and it is a nice question whether the fault is his rather
than ours. In the fictional South inhabited by Tom Sawyer and Huck
Finn and Pudd'nhead Wilson, even the blacks call blacks niggers. It
was the way things were. But if you can see past what you hear, the
great message of those books is about human equality, and how
racism violates it, reducing everyone to servitude, and no one more
than the supposed master. The emotional centre of *Huckleberry Finn*
is Jim's story of how he escaped. Huck listens silently, as well he
might, because it is only by grace that Jim is not including him in
the vast system rigged against a slave's bid for freedom – the whole
white civilization.

In 'Pudd'nhead Wilson', the sixteenth-black Roxy is an invention
that Toni Morrison might have been proud of: indeed, it is hard to

read *Beloved* without wondering whether Roxy might have been one of the models for its heroine. Roxy has a boy baby – only a thirty-second black, but that's enough. Twain shirks the probability, which the modern reader instantly suspects, that Roxy's owner must have been the father, but he doesn't shirk anything else. Roxy's boy, black even though he doesn't look it, is doomed to be a chattel. So she swaps him for the owner's all-white baby of the same age. What happens to the changelings gives no comfort to the sentimental, for whom a more satisfactory story would have centered on the white boy turned into a black, in the way that Kipling's 'Captains Courageous' made the rich boy poor, and so revealed the actual world to him. Twain concentrates on the black boy turned into a white. He grows up as a wastrel, thief, liar and cheat. We are at liberty to suppose that he got the seeds of these characteristics from his white father, but we would have to ignore what Twain spells out: Twain is saying that a slave-owning household is a bad one to grow up in – even worse for the personality than the shack where the slaves live, with the fear of being sold down the river.

Reading 'Pudd'nhead Wilson', we would like to rewrite it so that the slave boy's natural goodness reforms the whole system by example. But one of Twain's points – and the point that, apart from his vocabulary, is most likely to irritate the politically correct – is that natural goodness doesn't come any more easily to the oppressed than it does to the oppressor. The only person of noble character in the book is Roxy, and she is no genius: she can't tell that the bank she puts her hard-earned money into will fold; she doesn't know how to avoid being whipped until her back looks 'like a washboard'. (Toni Morrison's terrifying descriptions of Sethe's wounds from whipping in *Beloved* deserve their high reputation, but as a climactic passage in a horror story they can't hope to have the unexpected impact of Twain's quiet phrase slipped into a light narrative, like a bite in a kiss.)

Twain thought that the Negro question was the biggest issue facing America both past and present, and he gave it his best efforts, in his private life as in his public work. His personal conduct on the issue was impeccable. It is well known that Twain helped finance the education of Helen Keller. Less well known is that he supported one of the first black students to attend Yale all the way through college without meeting him more than once. Twain thought that to do such a thing was a white man's plain duty and shouldn't depend on the personal qualities of the beneficiary. Twain thought that the white man's debt was endless. He didn't come out on the side of the Union just because it won. The Southern cause had depended on repressing a minority, and that made the cause irredeemable.

Twain had the same sympathy for all oppressed minorities, including (this would have got him into trouble if he had lived later) the workers. Harbouring no illusions about the benevolence of unrestrained capital or the innate wisdom of the free market, Twain guessed that there would have to be an organized union movement to secure elementary rights for those who had to sweat. But he allowed no crude prejudice against those who made money from them. Accepting human villainy to be even more fundamental than human decency, Twain didn't believe you needed a conspiracy theory to explain piracy. He deplored anti-Semitism, and pointed out that the Jews were good at making money because so many of them were honest. He was one of the most vocal Dreyfusards after Zola.

Twain's sympathy for American Indians might not be apparent in an early piece like 'The Noble Red Man', of 1870, which would not please Marlon Brando, but really Twain was just mocking the idea that the Noble Red Man had lived in a civil order that made modern American civilization look barbaric by comparison. Twain didn't believe that you could set about dealing with the deficiencies of modern America unless you first stopped dreaming of Arcadia. He was as optimistic as one could be about modern life without seeing it through pink glasses.

Twain's sympathy for women might similarly seem questionable by modern standards – on the whole, he preferred to joke about the issue of women's suffrage rather than face it – but he was a long way ahead of his time. His work is full of flirtation that now seems like condescension. 'There may be prettier women in Europe, but I doubt it,' he writes about the women of Genoa in *The Innocents Abroad*. 'The population of Genoa is 120,000; two-thirds of these are women, I think, and at least two-thirds of the women are beautiful. They are as dressy, and as tasteful and as graceful as they could possibly be without being angels,' etc. Andrea Dworkin probably wouldn't like that much. Twain suffered from gallantry, chivalry, and all the other virtues that we have since been instructed are vices in disguise. But he always spoke against the exploitation of women as servants and married chattels, regretted the conditions that doomed them to do less than they could, and never doubted that they could do anything. His article reflecting on Joan of Arc's trial is a clarion call that could fill an issue of *Ms*. In private, he was famously tender to his sick daughters and lived in a state of controlled despair about his invalid wife: he was so devoted to her that he was thought saintly by powerful men of his acquaintance, some of whom weren't saintly at all and had been, by implication, flayed in his regular philippics against the great crime of seduction. (When it turned out that Maxim Gorky, during his tour of America, was sharing his hotel suite with a mistress, Twain ceased to call on him, not because he had broken the law but because he had violated custom.)

In fact, Twain was so blameless that he is likely to make us uncomfortable. Nowadays, the press – the cultural press, which is no less implacable than the doorstep reporters, only a bit slower – would try to get something on him. In his last years, he compensated for the loss of his dearest daughter by cultivating the friendship of pre-teen young ladies he called 'angelfish'. Shades of Lewis Carroll and Ernest Dowson, not to neglect Roman Polanski and the Mia Farrow version of Woody Allen! A promising field of inquiry. On second thoughts, it seems more likely that as he neared the end of his great long life the prospect of new life became incandescent to him. Inviting his young friends to tea, corresponding with them as they grew up, he was passing on his love of the world, which he loved even more than his country, although he could see the world's faults more clearly than anyone else. But he didn't despair about correcting them. Having despaired of the human race in the first instance, he was free to cheer any of its achievements, and he thought America among the greatest. His journalism shows, in a more readily detected form than his books, that he cherished and relished America's entire creativity in a way far beyond the literary – or, at any rate, in a literary way that didn't leave out the political but brought his country's every institution and custom under scrutiny, whether to be celebrated or castigated. William Dean Howells was right to call him the Abraham Lincoln of American literature.

Howells was one of the few American men of letters and cultural figures who saw Twain's literary stature from the beginning. Most of them, even when they revelled in his work, missed the point initially. In a country nominally dedicated to a new start and equal rights, there was still a nervous tendency to keep high art and popular entertainment rigidly separate: the urge to build a first-rate culture came to the aid of snobbery. In the European countries, high culture was self-assured enough to acknowledge the possibility of art up from nowhere. Twain the entertainer won his first celebrity at home, but the first solid admiration for Twain the great artist happened elsewhere. The Jumping Frog made him famous all over America. *The Innocents Abroad* made him famous all over the world, and, paradoxically, it was in the old countries, to which America was supposed to be the democratic alternative, that the artist found himself at home. His first internationally famous book was a product of his tentative initiation into foreign travel, and after that he was almost always on the move, clocking up thousands of miles like a modern frequent flier, but with one big difference: he was never blasé about it. The thrill of discovery that he transmitted made him irresistible even to those inhabitants of exotic lands who might otherwise have felt patronized by being discovered.

The Innocents Abroad is a weak book by Twain's later standards. Even his gift for parody, one of the basic weapons in his comic armoury, was a blunt instrument before he learned that if it was to stay sharp it would have to spend most of the time in its scabbard. In *Huckleberry Finn*, the duke's all-purpose Hamlet soliloquy is the paradigm case of all bardic spoofs. In *The Innocents Abroad*, the parodic instant history of Abelard and Héloïse could have been the product of Twain's first pseudonym, W. Epaminondas Adrastus Perkins: 'She lived with her uncle Fulbert, a canon of the cathedral of Paris. I do not know what a canon of a cathedral is, but that is what he was. He was nothing more than a sort of a mountain howitzer, likely, because they had no heavy artillery in those days. Suffice it, then, that Heloise lived with her uncle the howitzer, and was happy.' And so on.

But if Twain's comic fantasy had a long way to go before it would be infallibly funny, his gusto for the reality in front of him was fully developed right from the start. He saw everything, relished everything, and without playing the yokel as much as you might think. Rereading the book now, you can see what he had that all of us have lost. He was first in on the new mobility – the first great writer to be a traveller without having had to be an explorer. He is discovering the world as a world citizen: a true *Weltbürger* is speaking to the people he is travelling among just as much as to those at home – to them and for them.

They loved him for it. In the twentieth century, foreign nations that have been defeated by American power – or, even harder to forgive, saved by it – have comforted themselves with the reassuring caricature of the know-nothing American traveller, who might as well not have left home. In the nineteenth century, Twain was the know-everything traveller, who made his homeland seem doubly attractive by so engagingly representing its energy and creativity. His natural ear for the melody of his own language applied to other languages, too. He could read French well enough to make a good job of pretending to misunderstand it. Late in his life, spending a lot of time in Italy, he acquired enough of its language to write a wildly inventive piece concerning a story in an Italian newspaper about some fatal imbroglio. His German was good enough to enable him to read easily.

He was no scholar in any language but an easily nourished dabbler in anything he took up. The mistake is to mark him low for being unsystematic. He was, but genius often is. His opinions on literature were pragmatic, not to say erratic. He could praise Cervantes' romanticism and not say a word for Jane Austen's realism, although her keen appreciation of the power of money in human affairs lies far closer to his cast of mind than any amount of tilting at windmills. But really Twain was not interested in literature as such. He was interested in it as a part of everything else. When pointing out what he didn't know about art, one is always wise to remember what he did know about, say, science. His was a wide-ranging mind. He was American global expansionism before the fact.

In England, he was lionized by royalty, the literary establishment, the whole flattering system. Oxford gave him an honorary degree. (Saint-Saëns and Rodin got their degrees at the same ceremony as Twain: cue music and fade up the sound of chisel on marble.) Shaw was only one of the big names who called him a great master of the English language. More remarkably, his magic survived translation – indirect proof that it was his point of view that drove his style, and not vice versa. His work was translated into all the major languages. The Kaiser requested an audience. Nor was the encounter one of those ill-advised diplomatic gestures called for on a whim and arranged by equerries, of the type in which Irving Berlin was called into the

presence of Winston Churchill, where he was surprised to find that
the conversation had little to do with popular music, a puzzle later
resolved when it turned out that Churchill had thought he was
consulting Isaiah Berlin on matters of diplomacy. The Kaiser had
read Twain's books and thought *Life on the Mississippi* to be the best.
(The porter at Twain's hotel in Vienna held the same opinion.) At
least when Twain was abroad, he didn't suffer from being unappreci-
ated. He could have easily suffered from the opposite.

At home, he became accustomed to a high standard of living:
even during his recurrent periods of financial embarrassment, there
was usually a millionaire friend to provide a private railroad car or
a trip on a yacht. But that was nothing to how he lived it up in less
democratic lands. The grand hotels of the European spas routinely
offered him a reduced tariff, or no tariff at all, just to have his fame
on the premises. In Tuscany, he lived in a villa, like Bernard Berenson.
He could make himself at home no matter how high the ceiling and
exalted the company. Countesses plumed like birds of paradise ate
out of his hand. Yet he was never corrupted. The Innocent Abroad
stayed innocent. How was that?

Surely the main reason was America itself. He had a pride in his
country all the more robust for his loathing of patriotism, which
he thought the enemy of common brotherhood. It follows that he
thought America was its friend – a contention he could propound
without sounding naïve, because he never blinked his country's follies
while praising its virtues. The Henry James option – to go abroad
and set up shop where artists were more coddled – had no appeal
for Twain. For one thing, he was much loved in his homeland, even
when he wasn't fully understood. For another, and more important,
he would have regarded exile as patronizing, a betrayal of the enterprise that was his burgeoning nation, a flight from adventure into
safety, and a craven endorsement of those who looked down from
what they imagined were the heights of civilization on a land that
he refused to believe was anything less than history's great opportunity for human fulfilment.

This explains the touch of anger that creeps in when he dismantles
Matthew Arnold's snooty observations on Grant's use of the English
language. There is no evidence that Twain disliked Arnold personally.
When they met they seem to have got on like two sets of facial hair
on fire. But in print Twain took obvious glee, masquerading as regret,

in picking Arnold's prose style apart to show that it wasn't as classical, or even as grammatical, as its perpetrator thought. Arnold, according to Twain, had no call to speak *de haut en bas:* the *haut* just wasn't all that high. As a corollary, and without having to say so, Twain demonstrated that the *bas* wasn't all that low: his homespun demotic was more economical than Arnold's solemn rodomontade, and in prose the economical *is* the classical.

Twain's celebrated demolition of James Fenimore Cooper is based on the conviction that American English is a classical style that has to be protected against the impurities of posturing humbug. Twain traced Cooper's exfoliating verbiage to its roots in the besetting sin of inaccurate observation. 'Fenimore Cooper's Literary Offenses' and 'Fenimore Cooper's Further Literary Offenses', both collected here, are killingly funny – funnier, even, than Macaulay's pitiless inspection of the poetry of Robert Montgomery. Poor Montgomery was celebrated at the time, but obviously, to anyone with literary taste, doomed to oblivion, a destination to which Macaulay could only help him along. Cooper is still with us, but Twain did his best to make sure that Cooper's mystery-mongering flimflam wouldn't be allowed to pass itself off as a model of American prose style. By implication, his own prose style got the job.

What he did to Cooper was only a closer-to-home version of the treatment he habitually handed out to foreign critics of the Arnoldian stamp. The guardian of clear speech at home, Twain didn't have to bend the knee when pundits abroad curled their lip. Arnold's idea of a high culture increasingly and necessarily out of reach of a brutalized populace – an idea destined to generate a whole library of its own in the age to come – got its most penetrating answer from an American. Arnold should have stayed on his own turf, where pity for the emerging proletariat was a more plausible attitude. 'Wragg is in custody,' a four-word sentence in a newspaper, inspired Arnold to a long lament on the predestined cultural impoverishment of the workers – a feat of prescience based mainly on Arnold's confident assumption that Wragg was inherently a more wretched surname than, say, Arnold. Such sensitivity, however commendable, entailed presuppositions about civilization which Twain, speaking as an American, wasn't inclined to buy. He just didn't think that civilization had been all that civilized. 'Hard,' he called it, 'and glittering, and bloodless, and unattainable.'

Twain provided the same enlightening information for the French pundit Paul Bourget, and for any other Old World panjandrum who tried to high-hat the new nation. He went at them as if they were imperialists, which, in a way, they were: cultural imperialists. What he couldn't guess was that he was himself one of the pioneers of a cultural imperialism fated to have a large share in determining the history of the twentieth century.

He couldn't guess it because he was a nineteenth-century figure – the hardest thing to remember when you are caught up in reading him. He seems so close in time that you wouldn't be surprised to look up from the book and see him talking to Larry King on television. But he can seem so familiar only because the America we like best sounds like him, not because he sounds like it. He was there first. Even his personal weaknesses presaged the America we have come to know and like from its infinitely exportable popular culture. Twain had a weakness for profitable schemes. The first of them did make a profit: when Twain personally published Grant's memoirs, the deal worked out so well that he thought he had revolutionized the publishing industry. 'The prosperity of the venture,' as Howells pointed out, 'was the beginning of Clemens' adversity, for it led to excesses of enterprise which were forms of dissipation.' Twain's further ventures into private enterprise oscillated between a waste of time and a waste of money, not always his own. The typesetting machine he thought would revolutionize printing eventually did so, but not his version of it. He went broke in a big way. Like Sir Walter Scott, he heroically wrote himself out of debt, but as soon as enough money accumulated he was back into another scheme. For years, he maintained his faith in a much-publicized energy food, which in his time performed the same function as the vitamin pills that the British bodice-ripper author Barbara Cartland so enthusiastically favours now – that of helping naturally energetic people convince themselves that they are medically savvy beyond the ken of doctors.

Yet Twain, for all his susceptibility to plausible wheezes, was no crank. He was crazy about know-how. He was a can-do merchant, a prototype for Gyro Gearloose and all those nutty inventors who go on building weird machines in the back-yard sheds of American popular culture, even in the space age. And after all, some of the machines work. Twain's typesetting machine almost did. Twain was in tune with the mechanical efflorescence of the new nation. For him, there was no separation between machinery and poetry. You couldn't even call him a proto-Futurist, because for him art and machinery had never grown apart to the point of needing to be reunited. He had been brought up to the practical. The printing house was his high school and the riverboat his university. He could make things work. It was one of the qualities that the women of Paris loved about the liberating American troops of 1944 – all those Tom Sawyers and Huck Finns who rode six to a jeep. It wasn't just that they could get you chocolate and sheer stockings: when they had finished kissing you, they could fix your bicycle.

*

If that sounds like sentimentality now, it is only because of the devastating effect on America's image, and especially its self-image, wrought by the Vietnam War. Since then, instead of a jeep full of smiling boys with girls jumping in to join them we think first of scowling men tumbling out of a helicopter to torch a village. We think of some fat-bottomed sergeant checking crates of ice-cream-making equipment off a C-130 at Cam Ranh Bay while the local girls are being sold into prostitution outside the wire, of the CIA super-vising torture sessions in which the questions and the answers are both in a language they don't understand except for the screams. America cast itself as the villain and agreed when the rest of the world hissed. Actually, there was reason even at the time to believe that the average grunt was more remarkable for his kindness than for his insensitivity to an alien culture. Later on, even the Italian journalist Oriana Fallaci – whose articles (especially her interview with Kissinger, the granting of which he subsequently called the most stupid mistake he ever made) did so much to put America in the bad light that many Americans conceded was deserved – changed her tune. Interviewed in her turn by the Italian magazine *King*, she said that her abiding memory of Vietnam was of how well-mannered the American boys had been, even when they didn't have the slightest idea of where they were or what they were supposed to be doing there.

Vietnam was only part of a postwar pattern in which the United States, whether by accident or design, propped up the kind of authoritarian regimes whose sinister luminaries wore dark glasses indoors. All too often, especially in Latin America, it was by design. *Realpolitik* was held to be mandatory. But the real trouble with *realpolitik* was that it wasn't real. In foreign policy, ruthlessness undid the best thing America had going for it: benevolence. In the Western countries, it handed the Marxist intellectuals an opportunity – ultimately fatal to them, since it encouraged them to stay Marxist long after their opposite numbers in the East had given up – to misinterpret twentieth-century history. It became temptingly easy to argue that the machinations of American foreign policy were what had stopped the Western European countries from going fully socialist after the Second World War. But American Machiavellianism wasn't what did that. What did it was American generosity: the Marshall Plan. The same applied to the occupation of Japan. The Japanese economic superstate that we are now all so concerned about was made possible by America. If that was Machiavellianism, it was of a strangely self-defeating kind.

Diehard opponents of the American Empire – on this subject Gore Vidal remains determined to be only half as clever as he is – insist that America rebuilt the defeated nations only to secure markets, and so forth. This seductive notion first took off along with the economies of the rebuilt nations. Quite often, it was noised abroad in newspapers and magazines that owed their editorial freedom to guarantees insisted upon by the victorious allies, with America in the forefront. Suspicion of American power became harder to quell as American power went on increasing. Perhaps that was a good thing: about power, suspicious is the way we should always be. But to focus on America's misuse of its economic and military strength was to abdicate the obligation, and the opportunity, to talk about the aspect of American power that actually worked – its cultural influence, the thing that made America irresistibly attractive even after it had just finished dropping bombs on you.

The Japanese had been told that the American GIs would rape their women. The threat was easy to believe, since the right to rape civilians was an unofficial but commonly granted reward for conquest in the Imperial Japanese Army. But in the American Army of Occupation the penalty for rape was imprisonment or death. When the GIs handed out gum instead, the Japanese got the point in the first five minutes. The Germans had got the point while the war was still on. German civilians threatened with liberation by the Russians headed in the opposite direction. Surrendering to the

Americans became the rule in the *Wehrmacht* when the SS or the military police weren't watching. Any defeated nation had something with which to compare America – itself as it had previously been. America's allied nations, their gratitude either tinged by jealousy or annulled by it, were less inclined to admire but just as bound to compare: America was their measure, whether as a challenge or as a threat. America's problem was that it had no standard of comparison except its own ideal of itself.

The problem got worse, and by now it is acute. This is where America's congenital insulation from the less fortunate contemporary world, and its isolation from the needy past brought about by abundance in the present, has played the Devil. Both from the right and from the left, America attacks itself for lapsing from its supposedly normal condition as the ideal state. But the ideal state is a platonic concept destined to be even more frustrating than platonic love. For the Right, modern America is a disappointing lapse from godliness, purity, and order. For the Left, modern America is a disappointing lapse from social justice. Increasingly, the argument between them is about language and its legalistic interpretation, with the Constitution as the unquestioned yet ineffable ur-document, as if God's will were literally a will, leaving everything he ever owned to America, but on certain conditions, all of which conflict.

In sober moments, we know that the Constitution of the United States would mean nothing without the laws that grow out of it and back it up. Without them, the rights it promulgates would be no better guaranteed than those enshrined in the old Soviet Constitution, a document that, as the dissident sociologist Alexander Zinoviev suggested, was published only in order to find out who agreed with it, so that they could be dealt with.

Americans, however, are less inclined to realize that the laws would mean nothing without the spirit that gave rise to them, and that this spirit was first made manifest in the country's classic literature. To see the problem, it helps to be outside America looking in. Angst at falling short of its dreams for itself has sapped the country's initial confidence that it could alter circumstances in its own favour: the lure of the ideal has stymied the practical. It is a dream to imagine that even the most comprehensive laundering of language would expunge racism from human consciousness. The realistic alternative is to deny racist consciousness practical expression. It won't be easy,

but to disarm the population would be a good start. A start can't
be made, though, because the gun lobby has too much power. On
this point, as on so many others, left-wing idealists and right-wing
idealists work in a fearful synergy to undo the possibility of practical
government. Seemingly conflicting interests have combined to erode
an institution.

*

As a more recent institution, one that is actually still growing rather
than falling apart, the Library of America provides a heartening
example of what can be done. Perhaps it will give courage to people
who would like to see public television properly funded. In the United
States, public-service institutions, unless they are operating in a field
where private enterprise has no urge to compete, are in the position
of a heresy against an orthodoxy. But in matters of the mind they
are essential to the nation's health. Twain was in no doubt on the
point. In 1898, having grown old in the new country, he warned
against the consequences of a free-market culture. Thirty years before,
he said, Edwin Booth had played Hamlet a hundred nights in New
York. Now Hamlet was lucky to get a look-in. Comparing the Burg
Theatre, in Vienna, with Broadway, he thought Broadway was
nowhere. 'You are eating too much mental sugar; you will bring on
Bright's disease of the intellect.'
    As we now know, Broadway was to be the *fons et origo* of
twentieth-century popular culture in its most sophisticated form: the
musical show. But Twain still had a right to speak, because the popular
culture that was on its way wouldn't have been the same without
him. What he couldn't guess – because he was only a genius, not a
clairvoyant – was that it would go so far, that entertainment would
become, on such a scale, mere entertainment. Modern America is a
society of abundance in almost every aspect, even when it comes to
quality. The visitor who prides himself on his sophistication is first
startled, then benumbed, to find that everything he thought treasur-
able where he came from is present in America, only more so. If he
is interested in the Books of Hours of the early Renaissance, he will
find the world's greatest collection in the Pierpont Morgan Library.
He can be a world expert on Ming vases and still not survive the
shock of turning a corner on Melrose Avenue in Los Angeles to find
a glass-fronted warehouse chock-full of them. There are classical-

music lovers in London who pay for a return plane trip from New York with what they save buying a suitcaseful of CDs at American prices. A few years ago, in a music shop on Broadway, I reached into a discount bin and fished out a boxed set of cassettes of the Mahler First and Second Symphonies in the touchstone performances conducted by Bruno Walter. Five bucks. It made me annoyed that I had previously paid so much, and then afraid that I was not paying enough. The precious was practically free. It was value without price.

But that doesn't offset the menace of price without value. The abundance isn't intelligently distributed, and never could be by a free market, whose famous invisible hand is incurably short of a brain. Unless public-service institutions are made robust, the art will go to the élite that knows what it wants, while those who might have wanted it but never found out about it are stuck with the junk. Twain was an élitist: when he punished Cooper for supposing that 'more preferable' was a more impressive way to say 'preferable' he was saying that literary expression isn't just self-expression. But he would have been appalled to be told in advance that the enlightenment of the American people was going to be a matter of niche marketing. He would have regarded that, surely correctly, as a boondoggle.

Though beset by remorse for his own failings, Twain had a sure sense of his rank, but he didn't imagine that he had attained it by his own unaided efforts. He had an institution to help him – the world literary heritage, which he regarded as belonging to America by right, because America was the world's country. Twain's own contribution, daring in every way, was most daring in its dedication to the principle that the institution belonged to the people, and not to its adepts. He was a man so superior he needed no support from self-esteem. One wonders whether the Kaiser, for once in his life face to face with a real aristocrat, realized the implications.

They weren't revolutionary – not politically, anyway. Though a devout republican at home, Twain abroad had a soft spot for monarchs. But culturally he was a bigger revolutionary than Karl Marx, and, in the long run, more successful, because what Marx started went backward in the end, while the popular culture to which Twain gave such a boost has gone on expanding. Doing that, it has necessarily left him behind. The precocious modernity that makes him seem so close to us can only obscure, not obviate, the dependence of his inspiration on a more immediate world than any we know –

or anyone will ever know again, unless the industrialized world dismantles itself. The young Twain rode on stagecoaches and talked to strangers. He saw people murdered. Death and disease struck his family at a time when such things didn't happen just to other people; they happened to everybody. Life has improved, but in improving it has grown less real, and there is no going back except through a disaster.

Huckleberry Finn may survive the misguided clean-up of the library shelves. Unless I lost count, there are forty-two instances of the word 'nigger' in the first fifteen chapters of the book, but its heart is so obviously in the right place that it may weather the intentions of the politically correct, whose salient folly is to arouse false expectations of the past. Even if Huck makes it, however, he won't ever again be read by everybody. Professional admiration for the book will remain intense. (In *Green Hills of Africa*, when Hemingway names *Huckleberry Finn* as the book that made American literature, for a moment the campfire fabulist is speaking the truth.) Amateur enjoyment must remain restricted to those who actually read books instead of just hearing about them or watching the video of the movie. Twain was marginalized by the popular culture he helped to create. It had to happen.

Where these four beautiful books will have their effect, along with the Library of America as a whole, is in the academy. With a few exceptions (which have been punished ferociously by qualified reviewers who realize that this project, above all others, is too important to permit lapses from its own standards) every volume in the collection is a model of scholarship in service to literature. By now the damage reports are in and we know that a whole generation of students have had literature killed for them by the way they have been obliged to study it. Instead of the books, they have had to study theories about the books, always on the assumption that the theorists are wiser than the authors. And finally scholasticism, as always, has reduced itself to absurdity, with the discovery by the theorists that there were no authors. There weren't even any books, only texts, and there wasn't any history for the texts to emerge from, because history was just a set of signs, too.

Well, here are the books, with not a text in sight except as a reasoned agreement on what the author actually wrote. Every volume in the Library has a chronology to help you follow the life of the author (who actually existed), with pertinent notes to place him in the context of history (which exists, too). Armed with this subsidiary information, the student will be able to give a book the only 'reading' that counts – the one by which the book brings something to him, without his bringing a load of hastily acquired pseudoscience to it. The authors will emerge as the living human beings who made the larger Constitution, the one behind the document. And one author will emerge as even more alive than the rest, stricken by tragedy but unquenchable in his delight, shaking his head as if he had seen everything – even the future that is our frightening present – and not given up.

New Yorker, 14 June, 1993

CASANOVA COMES AGAIN

Casanova, outed long ago as a flagrant heterosexual, is out again. This time he's out in paperback – the whole of his memoirs, in six hefty double volumes (Johns Hopkins). What a pity he couldn't be here for a launch party at, say, the Algonquin. He always said that his literary career was the one that really mattered. In his small talk for the assembled *prominenti* he would have said it again, even as he put the moves on the younger and more personable females at the thrash: the editors, the journalists, the PR hacks, the bimboid wannabes toting the canapés. Feeling his age but galvanized by the attention, he would have taken on the biggest challenge in the room: the drenchingly beautiful, impeccably refined junior editor on the point of marrying the tortoise-necked publishing tycoon jealously quavering in the background. As the lights dim for a screened montage of his big moments on film, Casanova talks his target out the double doors, down the stairs and into a cab. Most weekends, like the modest, well-brought-up girl she is, she takes the jitney home to East Hampton, but when Cas explains that he gambled away the last of his *per diem* stash the previous night she immediately offers to cover the cab fare with her spare change. Step on it! The publisher's heavies are already on the sidewalk and scoping the street through their dark glasses. Back upstairs, the indignant publisher has personally lifted the phone to consign the entire print run of Casanova's great book to a garbage scow, but our hero's authorial ambitions never did stand a chance against his primal urge.

Lesser writings aside, *History of My Life* is Casanova's main claim to the literary importance that he always dreamed of in the intervals – sometimes lasting for days on end – between chasing skirt. The claim has to be called successful, if with some reluctance. When the first instalment of the hardback edition came out, in 1966, bigwigs of the literary world united to rain hosannas on its editor and translator, Willard R. Trask, for restoring a masterpiece to just pre-eminence after its long history of being bowdlerized, rewritten by interfering hacks, truncated, mistranslated, and attacked from the air. (A Second World War bomb through the roof of the Brockhaus office, in Leipzig, almost did to the manuscript what the bomb through the roof of the Eremitani church in Padua did to Mantegna's frescoes.) Since then, there has been time to think, and wonder whether many of the mandarins who heaped Casanova's *capolavoro* with praise ever read it again, or even read in it. For one thing, it isn't a book for a literal-minded age in which the authenticity of a quotation has to be guaranteed by marking supplied words with square brackets. What about all that dialogue, remembered in detail over the stretch of decades? Did he carry a tape recorder? A limiting judgement would have plenty to go on.

But that's just it: plenty is what the book has – plenty of every-thing, even without the sex. There are swindles and scandals, pretensions and inventions, clerics, lyrics and bubbling alembics, sword fights at midnight and complots at the palace, bugs in the bed and bedlam in the tavern, masked balls, balls-ups and shinnying up drainpipes, flummery, mummery and summary executions. All that, as the journalists say, plus a pullulating plankton field of biddable, beddable broads, through which Casanova moves with the single-minded hunger of a straining whale, yet somehow brings the whole populated ocean of eighteenth-century society to phosphorescent life. The book teems. It flows. It does everything but end. Written in his old age, the memoirs, recounting his picaresque manoeuvres almost day by day, could get only so far before he croaked, leaving uncovered his most fascinating and possibly most edifying years – the declining years, when the old magic had finally and forever ceased to work. But the memoirs got far enough to establish a pattern that becomes as predictable to the reader as a flimflam man's tent show on tour. Casanova checks into the inn, checks out the upmarket talent, screws the pick of the bunch, screws up a business deal, and moves on. Roaming the whole of Europe, he penetrates the local high society in each new place, penetrates all the attractive females up to and including the nobility, works some scam to raise funds, blows it, and blows town. (The two previous sentences say the same thing with the words changed. Casanova's prose works the same effect for thousands of pages, the miracle being that it isn't worked to death.)

To call Casanova's *chef d'oeuvre* repetitive is like calling Saint-Simon snobbish or de Sade sadistic. Repetition is what he lived for, especially with beautiful women. Variety had to be serial, or it wasn't variety. After he had done all the different things with the same woman, he wanted to do all the same things with different women. He could never get enough of them, and there were more of them than even he could envision. Think of it: there was one born every minute! Every second! But the eternal problem with which he faces us is that he didn't feel like that at the time. He dealt wholesale but he thought retail. Each love affair was the only one that counted for as long as it lasted. Sometimes it lasted only a matter of minutes, but the liaison got the whole of his attention, even if the Inquisition was waiting for him down on the street. He never had one eye on the clock. He had both eyes on his beloved's face, utterly caught up in the moment when her crisis of ecstasy made her soul his. Anxiety that such a revelation might never come again, as it were, conferred the precious gift of delay. He writes, 'I have all my life been dominated by the fear that my steed would flinch from beginning another race; and I never found this restraint painful, for the visible pleasure which I gave always made up four fifths of mine.' Four-fifths is eighty per cent whichever way you slice it: a lot to give away. But then it was by giving that he took. Even in – especially in – bed, he could convince them that it wasn't about him, it was about them. This was, and remains, a winning formula.

*

There were serving maids whom he routinely leaped on just because he bumped into them on the stairs, and there was the occasional faded *grande dame* he more or less had to satisfy because it was easier than talking his way out of it, but on the whole he never got it on with a woman who he didn't think, while she lay in his arms, was the woman of his dreams, the one designed to appeal to his imagination by the qualities of her mind and soul as well as the beauty of her body. Women knew that about him just by the way he looked at them. He was a great lover because they knew in advance that he would love them greatly – that he cherished each one's unique individuality even though he adored them holus-bolus, as a sex, as a race, as an angelic species. The question remains whether Casanova's infinitely replicated experience of once-in-a-lifetime love has anything to do with love at all. If you believe it hasn't, he and his book are easily dismissed: they have the same significance as JFK jumping a secretary in the White House elevator and telling a crony a few minutes afterwards that he got into the blonde. If you believe it has, then Casanova is still here, now more than ever haunting the civilized world's collective consciousness, and the book of his life, for all its mephitic undertow, has the reverberating ring of an awkward truth: this man is the man you would be if you were free to act.

One of the things you would have to be free from, of course, is sexual morality. But to call Casanova free from sexual morality invites a rejoinder: sexual morality was the only kind of morality he had. About sex, he had at least a few principles, which are best examined after one notes the thoroughness with which he lacked them in all other departments. Living always beyond his means and forever running to escape the consequences, in his life as an adventurer, even more than in his loves, he was ready for anything. He made it up as he went along, and it all came true. Even his name was a fabrication: he really was Giacomo Girolamo Casanova, but his title, Chevalier de Seingalt, was one he gave himself. He was born in 1725, into a theatrical family in Venice, and on the social scale of the time show folk ranked not far above gravediggers. Casanova's self-election to noble status was in itself a theatrical coup, and his career is best regarded as a succession of vaudeville numbers with nothing to link them except a rapidly falling and rising curtain.

As a boy, he bled easily and was thought mentally backward, but his father was astute enough to secure the patronage of the Grimani family, who staked Casanova to a course at the University of Padua, the idea being that he would have a career in the Church. Casanova graduated – one of the few examples of his properly finishing anything he began – but his entry into Holy Orders was occluded by his entry into the sister of the priest who was giving him instruction. Back in Venice and into bed with two sisters, he started attracting patrons on his own account – a talent that remained with him until the end, although the even more useful talent of keeping his patrons sweet was one he sadly lacked. Offered an ecclesiastical post in the Calabrian province of Martorano, Casanova took one look at the place and called off the deal. He knew he was meant for higher things. In Rome, he met the Pope – big game. Unfortunately, there was some fuss over a woman, and he had to skip town. After a spell in

Constantinople brought him nothing but more women, he moved
on to Corfu and there added to his handicaps by acquiring a taste
for gambling unmatched by any concomitant ability: as a general
rule, applicable to his entire lifetime, he could quit gambling only
when he was in debt, and dealt with the debt by blowing the scene.

In Venice once more, he scraped a living with a violin, mastered
at high speed so that he could join a theatre orchestra. A new patron
was so impressed by Casanova's knowledge of the occult sciences that
he considered legally adopting the prodigy into his noble family.
Since Casanova's knowledge of the occult sciences was largely
imaginary, there was no reason he could not have gone on expanding
it until the deal was clinched, but once again scandal intervened. The
tribunal in charge of religion and morals wanted to question him
about possible offences in both fields. Even worse, Casanova had
reason to believe that the Inquisition wanted to hear about those
occult sciences. Time to take a powder.

It was 1749, Casanova was twenty-four, and he was on his way,
which is to say on the run, seemingly forever. In Lyons, he was a
Freemason; in Paris, he wrote plays; in Vienna, he met intolerance
of his amatory success. Back to Venice yet again, where he was
charged with sorcery and imprisoned in the notorious Leads. His
daring escape was the basis of a subsequent book, which earned him
some measure of the authorial prestige he always craved. Returning
to Paris, he founded a lottery, the proceeds of which he neglected to
abscond with – a rare lapse. He later established a silk manufactory
there with hopes of success, which his success at getting a titled
mistress pregnant soon translated into failure. In Geneva, he met
Voltaire. In London, he was presented at court, presented a false bill
of exchange, got busted, and left with little to show for his stay except
a fourth dose of the clap. In Berlin, Frederick the Great thought
highly of him, and offered him a post as tutor to the Pomeranian
Cadet Corps, but, typically, he aimed higher still, and headed for
St Petersburg and fortune. Catherine the Great offered him nothing.

In Warsaw, he fought a duel. An accusation – it was false, but it
jibed with his billing – that he had embezzled the Paris lottery funds
caught up with him there. Banished from Poland, he moved on to
be expelled from Vienna, mainly because Maria Theresa had heard
that he had been expelled from Poland. So on to Paris, in order to
be expelled from France. It was as if his mug shot had been put out

by Interpol. During a stretch in a Spanish slammer, he wrote a three-volume opus about Venice, probably designed as a sop to the Venetian State Inquisition. If that was his idea, it worked: in 1774, at the age of forty-nine, he got a pardon. The Inquisition got him all the same – not as a victim but as a fink. In this role, as a paid informer, he had regular employment at last. How could he screw it up? He wrote a satire that satirized the wrong patrician, and was banished all over again.

In Vienna, he finally got lucky by ingratiating himself with Count Waldstein, who, in 1785, appointed him librarian of his castle in Bohemia. There, growing old and bored, Casanova began writing his memoirs in 1789, the year of the French Revolution – an event whose significance almost entirely escaped him. He had never been that kind of revolutionary, and by now he wasn't even a rebel: he had gone legit at long last. But even while he lived out his days in provincial isolation he always dreamed of Venice, where, had he ever returned, he would undoubtedly have accomplished his own ruin all over again. In his last summer alive, two years before the century ended, the Inquisition pardoned him, but it was too late.

It was always too late, or too early, or too something. In a life of opportunism, he took every opportunity to make a shambles of anything he had managed to achieve. Confusion was a compulsion, as if everything had to be tested to the point of destruction, to prove that it wasn't real. And, in fact, nothing *was* real, except women. Women were something he could grasp, however briefly, and if you seek the rhythm of Casanova's mind working – instead of just his feet running away from trouble – it is to what he says about women that you must turn. And one of the first things he says, in the preface to his *magnum opus*, is proved by the rest of it to be true: 'Feeling that I was born for the sex opposite to mine, I have always loved it and done all that I could to make myself loved by it.' Feminists should not seize too quickly on the generalized term 'the sex opposite to mine'. The operative words are 'to make myself loved'. That's what he really wanted to do, and that's what he really did. Women really existed for him. Everything else was a fantasy, even his literary ambitions – except in the case of this one great book, whose greatness, for all the sordid detail of unwashed linen and down-at-heel shoes, depends on making reality fantastic, a dream world like *The Thousand and One Nights.*

*

In the last act of *Don Giovanni*, Mozart consigns the great lover to Hell. Even today – in fact, today more than ever – this is a conclusion morally satisfactory for the audience, even though some of its members will be committing adultery that very night, and a few of them may have committed it during the intermission. But all of them respect the conventions. The rat had it coming to him. That's the way we are supposed to feel about the Don and all his confrères in libertinage, with Casanova as the arch exemplar: that for their crime of callously pillaging the emotional life of their helpless victims they deserve punishment, and might even have been visited with it ahead of time, through their never having properly lived. But Lorenzo Da Ponte was not the sole author of the opera's libretto. His collaborator-cum-technical adviser was Casanova himself, who knew better – or, at any rate, knew that that's not all we feel. We also feel envy. When Woody Allen said that he wanted to be reincarnated as Warren Beatty's fingertips, he was articulating a longing widely felt among men. The moral consensus of today would like to pretend that a Lothario's deadly charm is no less reprehensible than a paedophile's sack of candy. But nobody except a pervert envies a pervert. There are few men, no matter how virtuous, who do not envy the seducer.

If the seducer really were a rapist in disguise, he would be easier to condemn. But all too obviously his success depends at least as much on co-operation as on coercion. The virtuous man's envy is made worse by the consideration that if the virtuous woman takes a holiday from the straight and narrow the seducer is the very man she is likely to choose as an accomplice, just because he is irresponsible, passing through, and won't be coming back. Among the recently bereaved, the faithful but bored, and the businesswomen whose poetry has been insufficiently appreciated, the seducer cruises for his easiest prey: the woman of substance who wants an amorous encounter that doesn't mean anything. Later on, she can tell us that it didn't mean anything. But we know very well that at the time it meant everything. The louse got the best of her; he gets the best of all of them.

By the standards of the great lovers in our own century, Casanova didn't run up all that big a total. (Richard Burton scored at the rate of a *Luftwaffe* fighter pilot on the Russian front.) But today's dedicated stick man has the advantage of modern communications. For Casanova, the hunting grounds were days apart by slow coach. Factor that in and you have to marvel at what he achieved. A statistical check of the complete book turns up a figure of a hundred and thirty-two full-scale conquests. The breakdown by nationality reveals him as sowing the seed of a united Europe. Forty-seven Italian women said *si*. Nineteen French women said *oui*. Ten Swiss women said *si*, *oui*, or *ja*. There were eight German, five English, and ten women from sundry other countries. The total has to be reduced somewhat if you count the twelve sets of doubles as single victories, but doubtless it could be restored and even extended by the tussles that he thought weren't worth a mention, having taken place too low on the social scale. Nevertheless, twenty-four servant girls are registered as having succumbed, along with, at the top of the range, eighteen gentlewomen and fifteen members of royalty. There were only two nuns, which must have meant that the convents were hard to crack, because nothing inflamed him like spiritual refinement. Nor was he put off by brains ('The older I grew,' he writes in Volume XI, 'the more what attached me to women was intelligence'), although he endorsed the assumption, standard in his time, that men were naturally smarter than women and therefore he would never have to face the difficulty of dealing with a woman who mentally outstripped him. Even the divine Henriette, the greatest love of his life, he admired for her accomplishments without ever considering that they might shame him into inferiority. Though disarmingly ready to admit his occasional foolishness, he was confident about his superior mind. In that respect, his mind was commonplace, a point seized on by Arthur Schnitzler in the most interesting work ever inspired by Casanova, the novella *Casanovas Heimfahrt* (*Casanova's Homecoming*).

In Schnitzler's novella, Casanova, over the hill and under the weather, is heading home to Venice for one last crack at straightening out his business affairs, getting himself off the hook with the authorities, etc. – the usual unfounded hopes exacerbating the same old permanent imbroglio, but by now the energy that made it all into an adventure is almost gone. Nevertheless, this time he is determined that nothing can halt him on his homeward path – except, of course, one thing. An old friend, now enviably well set up in life, tells him about his house guest, a girl of unusual intelligence and grace. Casanova, stopping off just to clap eyes on this paragon, resolves to stay and win her. So far, so blah: but Schnitzler gives the story a twist that makes it unlike anything in Casanova's memoirs. This time, the girl really is Casanova's mental superior. She has a gift for mathematics that shows up his vaunted capacity in that field as a cabalistic mishmash. To top off that humiliation, she is, *mirabile dictu*, not attracted to him physically. He is too old for her, and she has a young lover. To nail her, Casanova must resort to a trick. The brilliance of Schnitzler's story lies in what kind of trick it is. Casanova has to pretend to be the young lover. In the darkness, she doesn't realize that the man making great love to her is the great lover himself. Casanova's identity counts for nothing. For treating her as an object whose emotions do not count, he is treated as an object in his turn: the rapist is raped.

As a hanging judge, Schnitzler was sitting behind a shaky bench. He himself pursued brilliant young females more ardently the older he became, and his series of wonderful, untranslatable plays concerning that very subject of intergenerational affections was based on a private life that would get him pilloried today. But before saying that Schnitzler was unwarrantedly tough on Casanova, one must admit that there is plenty to be tough about. Casanova did indeed rape at least one servant girl. ('I resolved to have her by using a little violence.') And he was indeed a cradle snatcher, on a career basis: Roman Polanski was threatened with a stretch in Chino for a lot less. Of Casanova's registered victories, twenty-two were between eleven and fifteen years of age, twenty-nine between sixteen and twenty, only five were over thirty, and only one was over fifty. That he loved women for their individuality should not be doubted – his sketchy prose condenses into lyricism when evoking a woman's character – but the point needs to be qualified by the consideration that he preferred their individuality to be in its formative stage, so that he could, as it were, get in on it. He had an automatic, full-throttle response to anything, seen from any angle, that might conceivably turn out to be a beautiful young woman – a shadow in the alley, a light footstep on the stairs. His incandescent love affair with Henriette began when he had seen nothing of her except a bump under the coverlet. But, with all that admitted, when we read what he has to say about his love for, and with, Henriette it is hard to remain suitably censorious. When, to cap the effect on him of her beauty and her gift for philosophy, she unexpectedly reveals her prowess on the violin, he is not just further delighted with her, he is delighted for her – a crucial plus.

> She did not thank the company for having applauded her; but turning to the professor she told him, with an air of gracious and noble courtesy, that she had never played a better instrument. After thus complimenting him, she smilingly told the audience that they must forgive the vanity which had induced her to increase the length of the concert by half an hour.
> This compliment having put the finishing touch to my astonishment, I vanished to go and weep in the garden, where no one could see me. Who can this Henriette be? What is this treasure whose master I have become? I thought it impossible that I should be the fortunate mortal who possessed her.

In moments like this – and his enormous book is abundantly peppered with them – Casanova's prose is energized by the sort of spiritual generosity made possible to a man only through the recognition that the woman he adores has a life separate from his, and can be 'possessed' only in the metaphorical sense. Casanova, cuckolding honest husbands right and left, never more than one step ahead of the law and continually dogged by inopportune doses of the clap, might seem an unlikely candidate to be a moralist. But, given the times, he was. He had scruples about passing the clap on, and not just because it would have got him into trouble. For reasons too complicated to repeat here but fully recorded in convincing detail, he nobly refrained from seducing a desperate young beauty who had escaped from her troubles by flinging herself into his practised arms:

> To restore her courage and to give her blood a chance to flow freely, I persuaded her to undress and get under the covers. Since she had not the strength, I had to undress her and carry her to the bed myself. In so doing, I performed a new experiment on myself. It was a discovery. I resisted the sight of all her charms without any difficulty. She went to sleep, and so did I, lying beside her, but fully dressed. A quarter of an hour before dawn I woke her and, finding her strength restored, she did not need me to help her dress.

He also admitted, in cold print, if with a hot flush, to sixteen separate instances of having his attentions rejected. Since no mere rake ever admits to anything except progress, this statistic alone should be enough to prove that Casanova was something other and better than a heartless monster. For the rake, the woman is not really alive. For Casanova, nothing could be more alive: that was his problem, and it lies at the heart of the problem he presents us with today. His success as a philanderer was dependent in part on his acuity as a psychologist. Conventional behaviour, without which civilization cannot exist, closes out possibilities. The faithful, while no doubt attaining satisfactions that the faithless can never know, must doom themselves to realizing some of our most haunting dreams only as fantasies. Casanova, by living those fantasies, knew their force.

What are these dreams of unbridled bliss doing in our poor minds? Casanova didn't know, either, but he did know that they are as intense for women as for men. In that regard, he was a kind of genius, and his book remains a ground-breaking work of modern psychology. Freud was a back number beside him. Freud thought that the fine women of Vienna who didn't want to sleep with their husbands were mentally disturbed. Casanova would have solved their problems in an hour on the couch.

Casanova's pretensions to morality are absurd not because his moral sense doesn't exist but because it is based on his desires. As if life were art, he deduced his rules of conduct from the pursuit of beauty. What made him irresistible, apart from his looks and his charm, was the poetic power of his *visione amorosa*; his women thought, correctly, that they were his inspiration. What made him reprehensible was his conviction that love could justify any and all conduct. But no less reprehensible is it for us, today, to deny that desire, with an awkward frequency, can be felt with all the force of love, and with enough of love's poetry to convince the person feeling it that he is in a state of grace – which is always a flying start towards convincing the person at whom he directs it that she might as well join him. Giving in to desire is not the only, or even the best, method of dealing with it, but failing to admit its power and all-pervasiveness is a sure formula for being swept away by it when it floods its banks, as sooner or later it always does. Casanova, by contriving, against all the odds posed by his chaotic personality, to transfer his awareness of that perennial conundrum from life to print, attained his literary ambitions after all, and lives on in his magnificently ridiculous book as some kind of great man – the most awkward kind, the man we call a force of nature because he reminds us of nature's force.

New Yorker, 25 August and 1 September, 1997

BERTRAND RUSSELL STRUGGLES AFTER HEAVEN

Two twentieth-century philosophers whose names are inseparable, Ludwig Wittgenstein and Bertrand Russell, were such a great double act that there simply has to be a buddy movie sooner or later. At last, the material is all set to be licked into a script. Ray Monk has now matched his justly lauded biography of Wittgenstein with a fat and equally enthralling first volume wrapping up the earlier half of Bertrand Russell's long life – *Bertrand Russell: The Spirit of Solitude 1872–1921* (Free Press) – and is sitting on the hottest Hollywood prospect since Paul Newman and Robert Redford signed on for *Butch Cassidy and the Sundance Kid*. Every A-list male star will want to play Wittgenstein – the philosopher who blew away all the other philosophers, including Russell – so, although Lyle Lovett looks the part and Arnie has the accent, Tom Cruise will probably get the job, armed with a Tatlin-tower lopsided bouffant coiffure personally teased out by the great José. ('Mmm! You look like *beeg theenker* now!') Nobody bankable – not even Steve Martin, a philosophy wonk who can actually explicate *Principia Mathematica* while wearing a plastic arrow through his head – will want to play the physically unappealing Russell, so the way should be clear for the perfect choice: Gene Wilder. Fluctuating uncontrollably between idealism and disillusion, forever persuaded that sexual fulfilment is at hand in the form of a luscious girl in a red dress, Wilder's persona, like his appearance, exactly fits a part that should revive his career. The only strike against Wilder is that even he has a bit too much gravitas for the role. On the evidence of Monk's book, Russell, for all his clipped speech and pipe-sucking air of cerebral precision, was a zany, a pantaloon, a fourth Stooge. Monk does his best to lend Russell dignity and stature, but that's the way it comes out, like a fanfare from a whoopee cushion.

It took Russell a long time to get to here. While he was alive, he was a sage. Even in his last phase, when he recklessly allowed himself to be set up as the star turn in various World Peace tent shows that had little to do with any known world and nothing to do with peace, he was regarded as, at worst, a supermind whose bonnet had been unaccountably penetrated by fashionable bees. In his early life, he was universally assumed to be a genius. For all most of us know, he was. Most of us, when we give our opinion on such subjects as analytical philosophy and symbolic logic, are only grazing, the way we are with relativity theory, quantum mechanics and how a mobile telephone works: the best we can hope to do is talk a good game, backed by the consensus of those who really know. Ray Monk, who really knows, says that the young Bertrand Russell's brilliantly original thinking in mathematics and symbolic logic laid the foundations of analytical philosophy and helped open up the field of theory which made our modern computerized world possible. Glad to take all this on trust, I will add it to the store of dinner-table science talk by which I contrive to maintain some kind of communication with my molecular biologist daughter.

The difference between me and the molecular biologists, of course, is that they know what they're talking about, whereas I know only how to talk. It is a difference basic to the life of the mind in our time – a time that can usefully be thought of as going back to Goethe, who didn't like Newton's theories about colour. Goethe had good humanist reasons for his dislike but didn't have the maths to back them up. Science was already off on its own; there were already two cultures. It could be said – it should be said, in my view – that only one of these, the unscientific one, is really a culture, since the mark of culture is to accumulate quality, whereas science merely advances knowledge. But my view is part of the unscientific culture, and has no weight in the scientific one, which settles its questions within itself, marshalling evidence powerful enough to flatten cities and bore holes in steel with drills of light. If Russell the philosopher had been content to keep his philosophy sounding scientific, his reputation would have remained unassailable, even though, or perhaps because, its published basis was unintelligible. There would never have been any way for the lay critic to get at him.

But, to give Russell his due, he was reluctant to confine his philosophical writings to the safely abstruse. Like most of the great philosophers before him – and unlike many of his successors – he strove to instruct the general reading public in ordinary language. Commendably, and sometimes heroically, he sought the most transparent possible exposition of his ideas, thereby proselytizing for the scientific, critical spirit that would liberate mankind from its perennial irrationality and offer the only hope for reforming a cruel world. Reason was Russell's religion: he believed in it passionately. The question now is not whether this is a self-contradictory position – surely it isn't, unless passion becomes zeal – but whether Russell was equipped by nature to promote it. The evidence provided by this book overwhelmingly suggests that he wasn't. His natural use of language was hopelessly in thrall to high-flown, over-decorated rhetoric. When he wrote passionately, he wrote dreadfully, and he could eschew the ornate only by leaving the passion out. Much of his workaday prose was plain to a fault. The principles he promoted in his voluminous writings on human affairs were unexceptionable – it would be better if people were persuaded by facts instead of myths, loved each other, and sought peace – but the language in which he set them down defeats memory. His heart wasn't in it, even if his mind was. His professional philosophy, the hard stuff, all sprang, we are told and must accept, from his conviction that our complex knowledge of the world could be analyzed down to its ultimately simple conceptual foundations. But his popular philosophy, the easy stuff that you and I are meant to understand, all too clearly proves that a prose bereft of nuances leaves out the texture of real life. Qualities that Russell entirely lacked were the stylistic density and precision of a writer capable of judging common life in the light of his own most intimate failures and defeats – the density and precision by which a great writer clarifies complexity without simplifying it and intensifies the clarity into incandescence. The last thing Russell could write from was personal experience.

*

By Monk's account, it isn't any wonder. Russell's personal experience was awful, first of all for himself and later on, crucially, for the women he was involved with. Paradoxically surrounded by the complete apparatus of wealth and comfort, his childhood was all bereavement.

In what must have seemed a conspiracy to leave him alone, his parents and everyone else he might have loved departed prematurely, stricken by diphtheria and other then incurable diseases with no respect for rank: in adult life, he would say that he always felt he was a ghost. Nowadays, armed with the knowledge distilled into John Bowlby's great trilogy *Attachment and Loss*, those interested in such things would be able to identify Russell's situation as a casebook example of detachment: undermined from the start by childhood separations of such violent intensity, the victim's relationships in adult life tend to be more controlling than cooperative and much more eloquent than felt. Russell filled the bill to what would be hilarious effect if you could forget that the women who made the mistake of getting involved with him were real, and really suffered. Russell could forget it, but then he had the advantage of having never fully realized it in the first place. In matters of emotion, he was an almost perfect solipsist: a woman could exist for him not as a separate personality but only as an extension of his own personality. Like conscientious objection, free love was a cause he was ready to suffer for, but the freedom was all for him, and the suffering, it turned out, was all for those he loved.

The pattern was set from the start, when he wooed and won Alys Pearsall Smith as his first wife. Russell, a suitor not to be denied, or even interrupted, talked for hours and covered square miles of paper explaining to her that the great thing about marriage would be sex. Alys, by her own admission, distrusted the whole idea, proclaiming for women in general and for herself in particular what Russell described as 'an aversion to sexual intercourse and a shrinking from it only to be overcome by the desire for children'. Undaunted, the budding ratiocinative genius pursued the courtship with a heat from him that increased with every glint of ice from her. He attempted to persuade her that sex would be the ideal *spiritual* expression of their mutual love. When, in a rare moment of abandon, she allowed him to kiss her glacial breasts, he soared into the stratosphere of prose, declaring in a letter to her that the event was 'far and away the most spiritual thing there has yet been in my life'. Russell then attempted to convince her that, once the knot had been tied, the proper approach to conjugal bliss would be a plenitude of indulgence, thus to tame in his otherwise elevated soul the disruptive element of testicular agitation. Using the Quakerish 'thee' and 'thou' familiar

form with which the two betrothed conspired to elevate their discourse to the empyrean plane, Russell declared:

> It would be a good plan, for me at any rate, to indulge physical
> feelings a good deal *quite* at first till they no longer have that
> maddening excitement to the imagination which they now have.
> I lie in bed and they come before my mind and my heart beats
> wildly and I begin to breathe heavily and sometimes I tremble
> with excitement – I feel *almost* sure that when once all the physical
> feelings have been indulged, this intense and almost painful
> excitement will subside, and whatever is pure and good and
> spiritual in them will survive.

The poor schmuck had blue balls, but it would have been a better
gag if he had been fooling only himself. Unfortunately, he was also
fooling her, and one feels for her even at this range. Dynastically,
the alliance of a British aristocratic scholar and a well-connected
American bluestocking looked good on deckle-edged paper. In fact,
it was hell, and the partner who suffered its most acute torments
was Alys, although Russell, typically, managed to convince himself
that *he* was the patsy. Having cajoled her ruthlessly into a cryogenic
marriage, he felt within his rights not only to fall for her sexier sister,
Mary, during a Continental holiday but to tell Alys all about it: 'I
am trying to fall in love with her and make these last days pass, and
I think I shall succeed enough to avoid too much impatience – she's
a fearful flatterer.'

Sharing a sitting room in a Paris hotel, Russell and Mary read
Nietzsche together by day and wallowed in Wagner by night. Probably
they weren't having full sex, because Russell would never have been
able to withhold the glad tidings from Alys, thee can bet thy life. He
certainly told her about his and Mary's tender goodnight kisses after
midnight discussions about the *Zeitgeist*. 'Why should I mind thee
kissing [Mary]?' Alys told him. 'Cried most of the morning,' she told
her diary. She cried most of the rest of her life. The immediate cause
of their estrangement, six years later, was Russell's unrequited but
spectacular passion for Alfred North Whitehead's wife, Evelyn – a
permanently convalescent beauty whose spiritual reluctance to put
out was matched by an earthy willingness to soak up Russell's money
in the form of gifts, trips and other freebies. Alys had a closeup of
the proceedings, because the Russells, fulfilling all the requirements

of Strindbergian claustrophobia, were sharing a house in Grantchester with the Whiteheads, where Evelyn faithfully reported to Alys every-thing Russell was saying – a possibility that failed to occur to Russell even while Evelyn was faithfully reporting to him everything Alys was saying. As Russell's last embers of feeling for Alys chilled to grey, he wrote her a letter that can be said to epitomize his ability to analyse his own emotions:

> Dearest, thee does give me more happiness than I can say – all the happiness I have, in fact. Thee is the only person I know well and yet really and thoroughly admire. I love the absolute certainty that all thy thoughts will be magnanimous and free from all pettiness. Since last winter I have known that life without thee would not be possible.

The writing was on the wall – though backwards, like Leonardo's. Life without her became possible two months later. His renowned account of how he got the idea in a flash, as enshrined in his ostensibly frank but deeply self-serving three-volume *Autobiography* (1967–69) – 'I went out bicycling one afternoon, and suddenly, as I was riding along a country road, I realized that I no longer loved Alys' – turns out to have more truth in it than you might think: there really was a bicycle. But there was no suddenly about it; he was merely bringing to a head what had been festering for years. As Alys went from being miscast to being cast off, she began a slow, limping exit to the wings of the drama, there to await in vain her cue for re-entry, with death a longed-for but elusive alternative. (She despaired when a lump in her breast turned out *not* to be cancer.) She always hoped that he would come back to her. He must have had something.

*

Mostly, he had a brain, and the ladies went for it, even when they didn't think much of his body. Lady Ottoline Morrell was grandly married but sported an impressive track record of adulterous bunk-ups with *prominenti* of all stamps. Anyone but the great philosopher would have spotted that this was a good reason not to try to get her all to himself. But Russell was so bowled over by an actual, consum-mated, thrashingly carnal love affair that he went ape. He counselled her to tell her husband, Philip, so as to avoid 'deceit and sordidness'. Typically, Russell had misread the object of his adoration completely.

Ottoline, who, unbeknownst to Russell, was still pursuing long-term affairs with Henry Lamb and Roger Fry, liked her life. She was loyal to her complacent husband. She was a realist. Russell, even though the warm impact of Ottoline's physicality had made him uncertain that he could now maintain contact with the cool world of mathematical logic, was, in emotional matters, still and forever an idealist. For once, the result was less Strindberg than Shaw, with the philosopher Russell spouting high-flown balderdash and the layperson Ottoline talking all the sense. His 'morality of passion', he explained to her, demanded the ability 'to behave as one might in a grand opera or in epic poetry', and he went on to vaporize about how 'rapturous it would be to die together like the people in Rosmersholm'. Sensibly planning to die in her comfortable bed like people in real life, Ottoline became more sparing with her favours. 'His intellect is supreme, but he lives up there so much that all the rest of him seems to have lost motion,' she told her journal. 'I feel it exhausting, as I have to keep in step with his intellect all the time, and also satisfy his heart.' Russell's intellect was at that time keeping in step with that of his dazzling new discovery, Wittgenstein, so he perhaps found it hard to slow down the pace. Satisfying his heart was not easy, either: satisfaction bred hunger.

When Russell was lecturing in America in his forty-third year, he fell for Helen Dudley, a Bryn Mawr graduate and would-be poet in her late twenties. She was glad to go to bed with him, and Russell responded to that gesture by offering her his hand in marriage, convincing himself that he was doing so principally because of his high esteem for her writing. He was not yet divorced from Alys. Nor was his love affair with Ottoline exactly over, though he filled her in on the news in the confident expectation that she would understand. 'My darling,' he wrote, 'please do not think that this means *any* lessening of my love to you, and I do not see why it should affect our relations.'

Ottoline understood, all right. When he got back to England, she refused to see him. When that stratagem failed to reignite his ardour, she saw him and threw him one. This time, she surprised him – and, presumably, herself – by manifesting an unprecedented physical desire. The delighted Russell immediately forgot all about his commitments to Helen. 'I am less fond of H.D. than I have tried to persuade myself that I was,' he told Ottoline. 'Her affection for me has made me do my utmost to respond. This has brought with it an overestimate of her writing.' Though Helen was about to set sail for England as had been arranged, she was clearly on her way to the wings. As war approached in Europe, Russell commendably sympathized with a generation's suffering, which he guessed to be forthcoming. But as Helen approached from America his sympathy for her evaporated.

Monk tellingly notes that Russell could think in terms of abstract populations but not of concrete individuals, unless the individual was himself. He knew he was a ghost, but he couldn't see how that fact might help explain why ordinary people were ciphers to him. In particular, he believed that females, as a sex, suffered from 'triviality of the soul': they didn't see the big picture, as he did. Helen, with her awkward insistence on arriving as requested, obviously had a bad case of it. 'I feel now an absolute blank indifference to her,' he told Ottoline, 'except as one little atom of the mass of humanity.' When Helen arrived in England with suitcases full of pretty clothes she fondly imagined to be her trousseau, he refused to see her.

Blind to the possible consequences, Russell contrived that the desperate Helen should take refuge in the household of none other than Ottoline Morrell. Helen told Ottoline everything and showed her Russell's letters, which the appalled Ottoline discovered to be full of the same exalted flapdoodle that had once been lavished on her. She found Helen's trousseau more tasteless than pathetic, but she had enough heart to be devastated by the revelations of Russell's pettiness and the capacity of his smarm to spread straight from the refrigerator, like margarine. Unimpressed by his reassurances that his 'sense of oneness' with her had only increased, Ottoline cooled to him. Soon Russell transferred his affections to Irene Cooper-Willis, with Ottoline playing the go-between. (This is *The School for Scandal* updated by Tom Stoppard. Don't try to figure it out now; just enjoy the flash and filigree as the principals rocket in and out of the parlour.) Irene, a celibate but bewitching young beauty, was ready to be Russell's research assistant but not his mistress. The affair aborted on the pad, but there was enough flame and smoke to bring Ottoline back at full speed. Into the cot with him she duly dived, for one last paradisiacal thrash, inspiring Russell to the whitest heat of his epistolary style:

My Heart, my Life, how can I ever tell you the amazing unspeakable glory of you tonight? You were utterly, absolutely of the stars
– & yet of the Eternal Earth too – so that you took me from
Earth & in a moment carried me to the highest heights ... it
blended in some unimaginable way with religion & the central
fires ... the mountains & the storm & the danger, & the wild
sudden beauty, & the free winds of heaven ... the depths &
wildness & vastness of my love to you ... a flood, a torrent, an
ocean ... what the greatest music yearns for, what made the
Sunflower be weary of time, what makes one's life a striving &
straining & struggling after Heaven.

Striving and straining and struggling for a single halfway original
phrase, he sent such letters day after day, like the artillery barrages
then lighting up the Western Front. Everyone writes badly to a lover,
but for specifying Russell's kind of badness – an interstellar bathos
ready to gush at the touch of a button – there are no words in
English, although there is possibly one in German: *Mumpitz*, meaning
the higher twaddle. But not even his prose was enough to turn
Ottoline off altogether. As people would later say in California, she
was always there for him: there to be informed of his latest depredations, incomprehensions, and marvels of self-deceit. On the basis
of extensive research, Monk is reluctant to lay the blame for the
madness of T. S. Eliot's wife Vivien on Russell's treatment of her
during their affair, but it could scarcely have helped. For this reader,
however, the prize episode of the book is Russell's deep, intimate
misunderstanding of the divinely beautiful twenty-one-year-old
actress Colette Malleson, who should have been one of the great loves
of his life. No doubt he believed she was, to judge from his prose. 'I
want to take you into the very centre of my being,' he wrote in 1916,
'and to reach myself into the centre of yours.' Russell said goodbye
to Ottoline all over again and invited Colette, who was already
married to the actor Miles Malleson, to the peaks of spiritual union:
'I love you, & my spirit calls out to you to come & seek the mountain
tops.' But the mountaintops, it transpired, held no place for her
aspirations to the stage: it wasn't a worthy ambition for any companion of his, and he did his eloquent best to talk her out of
it. Luckily, she had the strength to read him the news about the necessity of her staying true to her gift, but you can't help wondering

why he needed to hear it instead of figuring it out for himself. Why was the philosopher always the most blatant dunderhead on the scene?

The best that can be said for him in this instance is that he was concerned about the sexual temptation that Colette's vocation might put in her way. He was right to be: a handsome young director won her affections. That development threw Russell into such paroxysms of jealousy that her husband, a natural philosopher who was clearly better qualified in emotional matters than the professional, very generously worried about Russell's fate more than about Colette's. Russell resorted to composing a long, mordant analysis of Colette's allegedly deficient character, emphasizing her vanity and her inordinate need of sexual adventure. Whether or not this was projection, no term except damnable effrontery can cover the fact that he sent the character study to Colette. She stuck to her guns and went on seeing other men, thereby spurring Russell to a rare statement identifiable as normal human speech: 'You said the other day that you didn't know how to repulse people, but you always knew how to repulse me.'

Luckily for him, there was yet another young knockout on the scene – the twenty-five-year-old Dora Black, armed with a first-class degree in Modern Languages from Girton and an all-embracing hero-worship for Russell, whom she found 'enchantingly ugly'. She was the girl in the red dress. Truly desired, Russell responded as might be expected, cranking up his prose style into transgalactic overdrive even as she strove to hold him earthbound with her encircling arms. Colette did an Ottoline, returning to his bed to fill it when it was empty of Dora. Russell, who lied to each of them about the other and told Ottoline the truth about both, was at long last getting all the affection he could take. At this point, any male middle-aged non-philosopher who has become absorbed in Russell's emotional career to the point where the man's requirements have started to seem normal will find it hard to suppress an exhortation from the sideline: Hang in there, don't muck this up, you're doing better than Errol Flynn. But not even Russell could flourish forever in an atmosphere of total unreality. Along with the stars, the storm, the highest heights and the central fires, he wanted children. Dora was ready to give them to him. He ends the book married to her, and we close it with something like relief, as if after watching an unusually obtuse chimp navigate its way through a maze all the way to the bunch of bananas.

*

None of this, I believe, is a travesty either of Russell's love life or of Monk's account of it: Russell's love life *was* a travesty. The same is true for many men, and perhaps most: sooner or later, sex will make a fool out of any of us, and we are never more likely to talk balls than when they rule our brains. But most of us have not set ourselves up to instruct the world concerning what it should think and feel. Russell did. Fortunately for his memory, there is a parallel tale to be told, and Monk tells it well. All the generosity and forbearance that Russell so conspicuously did not bring to his emotional life he brought to his intellectual one, and there his true magnanimity is to be sought and found. When he learned that his work on the logical foundations of mathematics had been anticipated by the German scholar Gottlob Frege, he was generous to Frege instead of spiteful, and did everything he could to confirm the primacy of Frege's work over his own. Not even Wittgenstein, who shared Russell's proclivity for telling the brutal truth, was able to arouse his enmity. Russell, who arranged for the publication of the *Tractatus Logico-Philosophicus*, and promoted Wittgenstein's career in all respects, had every right to regard the astounding young Austrian as his protégé, but the protégé felt no obligation to protect his mentor's feelings; quite the reverse. Wittgenstein was worse than blunt in undermining Russell's confidence in his own achievement as a professional philosopher, and unrelenting in his contempt for everything Russell did as a popular one. When their friendship was broken off, however, it was at Wittgenstein's instigation, not Russell's. This showed true greatness of soul on Russell's part. It must have been a blow to discover that Wittgenstein did not share his conviction that a scientific philosophy was possible, but worse than a blow – a death threat – to be told that he was a bad writer.

Wittgenstein's qualifications for saying so were impeccable, because he himself was a very good writer indeed. He can be seen as one of the jewels in the glittering German aphoristic tradition that began with Goethe and Lichtenberg and included, in Wittgenstein's own time, Arthur Schnitzler, Karl Kraus and Alfred Polgar. Even in English translation, the habitually terse Wittgenstein inexorably emerged as the artist-philosopher that Russell, inspired originally by the poetic element in Spinoza, had vainly dreamed of being. But Wittgenstein, though a born master of language, was determined not to be seduced by it. Russell was seduced by it every day of his life. Wittgenstein set limitations on philosophy: 'What we cannot speak of we should pass over in silence.' Russell recognized no such limitations, and there was nothing he could pass over in silence. He gushed even when he turned off the faucet. Talking about ordinary life instead of the heady realm of love, he could leave out the stars, the mountaintops, and everything else in the instant-mysticism kit, but his plain language still took off under its own power, clear as crystal and no more yielding, as convinced of its elevated reasonableness as it was unconvincing about the stubbornly unreasonable texture of real life.

There are exceptions, and one of them is likely to remain a great book. *A History of Western Philosophy*, which was published in 1946 and is still the first general book for the lay man to read on the subject, shows what Russell's plain prose could do when the subject was safely in the past and some of his earlier exaltation of pure reason was in the past, too. However abstruse the topic, every sentence is as natural as a breath: for more than eight hundred closely printed pages, the exposition flows without a hitch. 'Whatever can be known,' he says in its concluding pages, 'can be known by means of science; but things which are legitimately matters of feeling lie outside its province.' Even this is open to question (there are very few important truths about politics, for example, that can be known by any means except a combination of science *and* feeling), yet at least it shows signs of the old man's having momentarily attained a measure of negative capability. Unfortunately, the bulk of his popular philosophizing was about current events, and was written, even into his old age, with all the overconfident flow of his initial, natural assumption, which was that political and social unreason was most easily to be explained by the mass of humanity's not being as bright as he was. A conviction of his superiority to mere mortals was part of his nature: we know that – know that now better than we ever did – because he was always inviting his latest love to join him on the heights above them.

*

There is a lot to be worried about in the current vogue for biographies of the great. To find out in advance that Picasso was a monster could be an invitation to underestimate his art, and to wolf down the details of Einstein's infidelity is certainly easier on the nerves and the ego than trying just once more to imagine those lights on the moving trains. Monk must have been aware of the dangers: after all, Russell behaved no worse than Einstein, better than Picasso, and a lot better than Matisse. But surely Monk has done the right thing in making Russell's personal life so prominent. Like the creatively fecund but personally unspeakable Brecht, Russell was a great man who used his prestige to back up his political opinions, and when someone does that we want to find out how he treated the people he knew, so as to assess the validity of his exhortations to the millions of people he didn't know. The unsung hero of this volume is D. H. Lawrence, who put his finger on what Monk bravely calls the central conflict of Russell's nature – or, rather, put his finger painfully *into* it, because it was a wound. Lawrence pointed out the irreconcilable discrepancy between Russell's ideal of universal love and his alienation from humanity. The devastated Russell generously declined to withdraw his lasting admiration of Lawrence, but one can't help feeling that this might have been partly because he didn't see all the implications of what Lawrence had said. As the autobiography reveals over and over, Russell could come to know things about himself after he was told often enough, but somehow he still couldn't take them in. He was in this respect the opposite of an artist, since the mark of the artist is to take in more than he can know.

It shouldn't have mattered, but in the long run it did. While Russell had no objections to colonialist wars against 'primitive' peoples (in his view, such wars spread enlightenment), he deplored wars between civilized nations. Unremarkable at first blush, this stand required courage in the war fever of 1914. Having consecrated his vows with a stretch in prison, Russell unwisely went on to pursue pacifism as part of his religion of reason. He erected peace into a principle instead of just espousing it as a desirable state of affairs: if enough people believed in peace, there would be no more war. The principle started looking shaky when Hitler came to power and set about incarnating the intractable truth that unless absolutely everyone believes in peace the few who don't will subjugate all the others. Einstein, a clear candidate for subjugation, gave up his pacifism straight away: he didn't have to be a physicist to figure it out. But Russell the philosopher was slow to get the point. And, even when he did, the principle was never given up. It was there waiting to lead him on to his biggest absurdity: unilateral nuclear disarmament.

To an issue that he might have helped clarify he added nothing but confusion. While there was a good case to be made for multi-lateral nuclear disarmament, there was none at all to be made for unilateral nuclear disarmament, since it depended on presenting a moral example to a regime that was, by its own insistence, not open to moral persuasion. Russell knew this: he had been one of the first visitors to the Soviet Union to warn against what was going on there, and when the Americans were still the only possessors of the atomic bomb he had recommended threatening the Soviets with it in order to change their ways. He knew it, but somehow he had not taken it in. I myself, as a multilateralist who did my share of marching from Aldermaston in the early sixties, well remember the hard-line-unilateralist Committee of 100 and its adherents: talking to them about modern history was like talking to a Seventh-Day Adventist about Elvis Presley. They were fatuous, but with the support lent them by Russell's immense prestige they could believe that they had been granted a vision of a higher truth, beyond the sordid realities of politics. The eventual effect, transmitted through the left wing of the Labour Party, helped to keep the Conservatives in power for a generation, because the public was unable to believe that Labour could be trusted with the deterrent – a distrust that proved well founded when Michael Foot, during his doomed general-election campaign, bizarrely promised to keep the deterrent for only as long as it took to bargain it away.

Russell spoke and thought as if the mass of humanity needed convincing that war was a bad thing. Somehow, he never quite took in the fact that most people already knew this but were genuinely divided as to what should be done about it, and something he never took in at all was that there is no such thing as the mass of humanity – there are only individuals. Failing to grasp that, he was, for all his real sympathy with the sufferings of mankind, paradoxically orating from the same rostrum as the century's worst tyrants. Trying to wake us all up, he could never believe that we were not asleep; that our nightmares were happening in daylight; and that his religion of reason could do little to dispel them. How could he not realize it? In this courageously frank first volume of what could well amount to a classic study of the personality of genius. Ray Monk shows us how – by showing us that no matter how brilliant a mind may be, its stupidity will still break through, if that is what it takes to assuage its solitude. With his eyes on the heights, Russell never noticed that his trousers were around his ankles: but now we know. They're ready for you on the set, Mr Wilder.

New Yorker, December 1996

KARL'S STRANGE ENGINE

Rebecca's Vest by Karl Miller

As compact and nutritious as a field ration, this deceptively slight autobiography is a classic from the day it appears. Whether its author appears is another question, which he is the first to ask. He takes off his helmet, and then the mask, but there is still the make-up. Fascinated by doubleness, the author of a highly original critical work on the subject, he calls himself a double man, but understates the case. There are more than two of him in there.

Just to start with, there are the child who is the father of the man, the man who is the author of the knotty style, and the knotty stylist who can straighten the prose of others. In a generation of outstanding literary editors, he stood out even from the rest: the back ends of the *Spectator* and the *New Statesman*, and both ends of the *Listener*, flourished under his tutelage. His recent departure from the *London Review of Books* was bad news not just for that paper but for the whole of letters. If he has indeed edited his last magazine, then an era is over. We should remember, however, the Stoppardian discovery that every exit is an entrance somewhere else. For Karl Miller to fall back for a better jump would suit the duplex nature of a limelit recluse who always relished the idea of leaving even as he arrived, seeing things through to the bitter end only on the understanding that he was sorry he ever started. Miller willingly appropriates D. H. Lawrence's observation about some dark-blooded miner, that his soul was a strange engine.

Miller's strange engine first turned its cogs in Scotland. A shilling version of his life would say that he was a fatherless boy from Edinburgh who did well at school, found out just how systematic the class system could be when he was drafted into National Service,

achieved upward mobility as a scholarship boy at Cambridge, and
went on to bulk large in the general transformation of the postwar
British arts world which now looks more like a functioning meritoc-
racy than any other aspect of the national life. Such would be a true
enough account, but it would imply that he had left Scotland behind.

He never has, and Britain is lucky that he is more of a Scots
patriot than a Scottish Nationalist, or he would make a formidable
champion for secession. Instead he favours a *Länder* solution, the
cherishing of regional identity. Much of his written work – he is
rightly sorry that there hasn't been more – is in critical but proud
appraisal of Scots writers and thinkers. Drummond of Hawthornden,
Burns, Sir Walter Scott – he knows where they are coming from and
belongs among their number. But he is not a bit provincial, for one
conspicuous reason: the province had schools that opened on the
world. In the Athens of the North he was taught Latin and Greek, a
background that gave him, eventually, the whole of Europe for
a garden. The inculcation of hard books – how enviable an upbringing
it now seems. It makes England, not Scotland, look like the province.

The vest of the title was worn by the Rebecca in *Ivanhoe*. Scott
clearly appreciated her abundance of cleavage. Miller appreciated it
in his turn. The boy bent over his books was also the boy who
watched some of the other boys having sexual intercourse with a
small hole dug in the earth. Sexual intercourse was tremendously in
evidence. Or, to put it Miller's way:

> 'The sexual intercourse of things' – pioneering epigram of James
> Hogg, in one of his parodies of the Lake School, for the world's
> blends and bonds and mucous mutualities – was tremendously
> in evidence.

He means that there was a lot of it about.

Unfortunately most of it was in the mind. The girls were hard to
get, yielding up their chaste treasures in the dark of the cinema
to stocking-top height only, whereupon the frail but firm hand
clamped down. Miller had obligatory recourse to secret diaries, basic
training in the ability to brood. The classicist chastened the romantic,
the romantic energized the classicist, and a personality was developed
which had the gift of attracting company by its air of solitude.
Fleetingly invoked, the name of Alain-Fournier fills the bill. Miller
often compares himself to young Werther but the hero of *Le Grand*

Meaulnes is a better fit. Karl Meaulnes must have wowed the girls even then.

Later on the girls became women and Karl Meaulnes pursued his sentimental education among them with what sounds like success, although the hints are so reticent as to achieve a better simulacrum of modesty than male memoirists commonly contrive. He doesn't claim it himself (and probably won't enjoy having it claimed for him), but his combination of certitude and vulnerability didn't hurt him at all with the female collaborators on his various publications. As with his eminent contemporaries Ian Hamilton and Terence Kilmartin, testosterone behind the editorial desk commanded an impressive loyalty amongst the surrounding oestrogen. Male contributors slaving for these hard taskmasters could easily fall prey to envy. We would have preferred to see our editors as the kind of limping squadron adjutant who looks after a chap's kit when he flies off to fight. But they were up there at the front of the formation, silk scarves fluttering in the slip-stream, the roar of their strange engines barely drowning the massed female sighs aimed adoringly from below.

The dandy in himself is one of the selves Miller explores. Without Cambridge he would never have broken out into his fastidious clothes. At Cambridge the double man became triple at least. Studying under F. R. Leavis, he deepened his seriousness, even to the point where he could see that the good Doctor, egged on by the implacable Queenie, had pushed seriousness to the verge of frivolity. But serious Miller was drawn to the frivolity of Mark Boxer, who incarnated the appealing notion that stylishness was a discipline too. All those of us who still keenly feel Boxer's absence will feel it more keenly for his presence here. His portrait is one of the many keepsake miniatures which would make this book a little wall of Hilliards if there were nothing else going on. But Miller being Miller, the other people, though he generously paints them as if they were there for themselves, are inevitably there for him. That people are dear to us according to how they help us grow is one of the book's many implicit teachings.

In later life Miller has been a professor (of English, at University College, London) and it is easy to imagine the Edinburgh schoolteacher that he might have been in his early life if academic brilliance had not led him away. Muriel Spark's Jean Brodie, haughty but susceptible, strikes a chord within his breast. The most valuable poise contains a passion. The clear intellect performs its intricacies of style only on the surface of the instinctual deep. One of Miller's favoured paintings is Raeburn's, of the skater on the loch, his arms folded with apparent insouciance, buoyed up by impending doom. The author of this book is on thin ice, and prefers it that way.

Self-pity, self-examination, self-renewal – they all saved him from self-satisfaction. He could easily have relaxed into the Establishment. Instead he has been one of the indispensable people who have helped the Establishment to shake itself up – an injection of responsibility which one would like to see institutionalized in its turn. But to keep a country's institutions alert takes a supply of functionaries who are bigger than the job, overqualified, containing multitudes. They are hard to come by. Placemen settle in.

At one stage there was a Miller who hobnobbed with aristocrats. Unlike Evelyn Waugh's aristocrats, some of whom tried to tell him that they were not the romantic paragons he painted them as, Miller's really were romantic paragons: the McEwen family, whose boy children came home from Eton on a private railway track to their country seat, Marchmont. A gifted and tragic bunch who embodied all of Miller's romantic longings – the death of his particular friend, Rory McEwen, is written short but with tears for ink – they could have pulled Karl Meaulnes in and made him *le grand* Miller, with Marchmont for his Coole Park. But another Miller, the footballer, drew him back towards the proletariat. Even at the time when I was seeing all of the best London literary editors at least once a week I was told that I would never get their true measure unless I saw them play football on the weekend.

I imagine he was Killer Miller. Certainly I wouldn't have wanted to try putting a ball past him, having felt his wrath at Langham Place when he was editor of the *Listener* and I wrote a radio column without having listened to the radio. As a result I had to listen to him. It was such a hell of a tongue-lashing that I left it to go on by itself and sprinted away down the corridor. His secretary, holding her high heels in her hands, just managed to catch me. It turned out that I wasn't fired at all. If the reason I never listened to radio was that I always watched television, I might try to redeem myself by reviewing that instead. Thus his generosity had an influence on my life.

There are scores of writers who would pay him the same tribute.

This book shows where that generosity came from – a mind whose outlook is fortified by the gaze within. If his prose does everything but fly, it is only because he lacks the fluent writer's actorish knack of completing himself on the page. Miller, already complete, can't allow himself the glib rush. But his considered pause, his capacity to dwell, gives us a unique book, whose only false note lies in its carelessly voiced double assumption that he will not edit again or write enough good books. Coming from a man well aware that at the same age Verdi was twenty years short of composing *Falstaff*, it sounds like petulance, as if the skater on the loch had decided to walk home in a huff.

Spectator, 25 September, 1993

GETTING LARKIN'S NUMBER

Philip Larkin: A Writer's Life by Andrew Motion

Somehow serene even in their consuming sadness, beautiful poems made Philip Larkin famous while he was alive. Since his death, ugly revelations threaten to make him more famous still. This unsparing biography furthers the work begun by the *Collected Poems* and the *Letters* of revealing how much more the poor tormented genius had to hide than we ever thought. The mood is catching. By now everybody with something on him is bursting into print. Glumly we learn that he wasn't just a racist, a wanker, a miser and a booze artist, he was also prey, in his declining years, to such nameless vices as forming a friendship with A. N. Wilson.

Larkin often said he wrote poetry out of an impulse to preserve. Unfortunately all who knew him seem to have contracted that same impulse: there is no souvenir they want to forget. The process began when Anthony Thwaite put together a posthumous *Collected Poems* which included all the poems Larkin had so carefully left out of his individual volumes. It was an impressive editorial feat, but the general effect was to blur the universal secret of Larkin's lyricism by putting his personal secrets on display.

The *Letters* continued the process, revealing how thoroughly Larkin could indulge in racism, sexism and all the other isms when he was trying to shock his unshockable friends. To anyone who knew him, or just knew of him, it was obvious that he was talking that way merely to vent his inner demons: in his public persona he was the soul of courtesy, and until his sad last phase, when his *timor mortis* got the better of him, it was impossible to imagine his being rude or unfair to anyone of any colour, sex or political persuasion.

But to know him is getting harder all the time. Too much information is piling up between the public and the essential man. Andrew Motion has done a meticulous job with this biography but its inevitable effect must be to make the selfless dedication of its hero's work seem self-seeking beyond redemption. Already it is almost too late to point out, for example, that if Larkin made racist remarks in order to be outrageous, then he was no racist. A racist makes racist remarks because he thinks they are true.

Having to argue like this means that the game is lost. No young reader will ever again read Larkin's great tribute to the black jazz musician Sidney Bechet ('On me your voice falls as they say love should/ Like an enormous yes') and respond to it with the pure admiration it deserves, since it so exactly registers the equally pure admiration Larkin felt for one of the great men in his life. The most that over-informed new young readers will be able to feel is that the old racist had his decent moments. The possibility will be gone to appreciate that Larkin was a fundamentally decent man; that in his poems he generously shaped and transcended his personal despair to celebrate life on our behalf; and that if he expressed himself unscrupulously in private it was his only respite from the hard labour of expressing himself scrupulously in public.

Still, it is always good to know more, as long as we don't end up knowing less. Here are the details to prove that the picture Larkin painted of himself as a perennial loser didn't necessarily match the way he seemed, even if it was a precise transcription of how he felt. He came up to Oxford as a shy boy with a stammer but to his fellow undergraduates he was an attractive figure, the kind of wit who makes his friends feel witty too. To the end of his life there were always people eager to crowd around him if he would only let them. Until almost the very end, Larkin was careful not to let them waste his time. He chose his loneliness. Like his diffidence, it was a wish fulfilment, at odds with the facts.

As a librarian he was a success from the start, rising with each move until, as the guiding light of the Brynmor Jones Library at the University of Hull, he was one of the chief adornments of his profession. Since tact, judgement and self-confidence were necessary at each step, his picture of himself as a ditherer isn't to be trusted. The rabid reactionary turns out to be an equally misleading exercise in self-advertisement. It was on Larkin's instructions that the Brynmor Jones Library built up its Labour Archive, with the Fabian Society

Library as chief treasure; now why should a rabid reactionary have done that? Well, one of the answers must surely be that if he felt that way, and even if he talked that way, he didn't actually *act* that way.

It would certainly help if this possibility could be kept in mind when it comes to the question of women – the only question that really matters to the lifestyle press, whose reporters are currently having a marvellous time patronizing Larkin as a lonely, furtive, perverted misogynist utterly unlike themselves. The old women who went as young girls to borrow books from his first library remember him well for his impeccable manners and helpfulness. His first mistress, Ruth Bowman, wrote: 'I'm very proud of you, dear Philip, and I love you very much. The fact that you like me and have made love to me is the greatest source of pride and happiness in my life.' Fifty years later she still remembered him as 'relaxed and cheerful, entertaining and considerate'. At a guess, it was his entertainment value that drew his women in, and his manifest stature as a great artist that kept them loyal through thick and thin.

Admittedly the thin could be very thin. There weren't *that* many mistresses, but he formed the habit of keeping several on a string at once, so that a few would have looked like a lot if he had wanted to present himself as the Warren Beatty of the literary world. Instead, through his poems and every other available means of communication, he complained endlessly about being rejected by the women he wanted, accepted only by those he didn't, and never getting enough love. This was damned ungallant of him and he was lucky to be forgiven.

It seems he almost always was. The woman to whom he did the most lying, Maeve Brennan, was annoyed enough after she found out to say that she was bitterly disappointed, but apparently still didn't believe that she had wasted her time. Even more convincingly, Monica Jones, to whom he told most of the truth, was there till the end, although the jealousies she suffered along the way must have been almost as great as her love.

Yet his misery was real, and they loved him in spite of it, not because of it. They all had to cope as well as they could with the certain knowledge that he was even more scared of marriage than he was of death. You don't need Freud's help to guess that the primary lesion might have had something to do with his parents. 'They fuck you up, your mum and dad' is clearly one Larkin line that can be taken as what he thought. Andrew Motion tells us more than we knew before about Dad, who admired the Nazis, although he could scarcely have admired them for helping Germany to achieve its economic recovery in the 1920s (Motion must mean the 1930s). When young Philip confessed his shyness, Dad's reply ('You don't know what shyness is') can't have helped with his son's stammer. He did help, however, with his son's reading: Dad was a well-read man.

On the evidence of this biography, a more likely source of horror at home seems to have been Mum. She could never let go of him or he of her, despite her inability to express herself in anything except platitudes. Mercifully only one fragment of one of her thousands of letters is quoted. It works like one of those revue sketches featuring Terry Jones in a headscarf talking falsetto: 'Here we seem to have a succession of gloomy evenings. It looks as though it will rain again, like it did last night. Have at last heard from Kenneth. He has written such a long and interesting letter thanking me for the handkerchiefs. I have written to thank him . . .'

Somewhere back there, we can safely assume, lay the source for a feeling of failure that could overcome any amount of success. But finding out more about how Philip Larkin was compelled to solitude can only leave us less impressed by how he embraced it – the most interesting thing about the man, because it was the key to the poet. It would be obscurantist to want the work of *post mortem* explication stopped. But Larkin's executors, in their commentaries, need to be much less humble on his behalf, or else they will just accelerate the growth of this already burgeoning fable about the patsy who has been overpraised for his – we have the authority of Mr Brian Appleyard on this point – minor poetry.

Andrew Motion has done something to show that Larkin chose the conditions in which to nourish his art, but not enough to insist that art of such intensity demands a dedication ordinary mortals don't know much about. To suggest, for example, that Larkin's last great poem *Aubade* broke a dry spell of three years is to ignore the possibility that a poem like *Aubade* takes three years to write, even for a genius. Those who revere Larkin's achievement should be less keen to put him in range of mediocrities who would like to better themselves by lowering him to their level, matching his feet of clay with their ears of cloth.

Independent Sunday Review, 4 April, 1993

UN-AMERICAN FILM DIRECTORS

PIER PAOLO PAIN IN THE NECK

Renaissance man is a description tossed around too lightly in modern times – actors get it if they can play the guitar – but for Pier Paolo Pasolini nothing less will do. From the moment he hit Rome after the Second World War until the moment his own car hit him in 1975, Pasolini single-handedly re-embodied about half the personnel of Burckhardt's *The Civilization of the Renaissance in Italy*. He was poet, novelist, scholar, intellectual, sexual adventurer, reforming zealot, creator of large-scale visual spectaculars – and all these things equally. To make a comparable impact, Raphael would have had to be elected Pope. To make a comparable exit, Michelangelo would have had to fall out of the Sistine Ceiling. Pasolini was a front-page event in every field he entered, including death. A boy he picked up in his Alfa Romeo sports car ran him over with it and left him helpless in the dust. Beat that, Renaissance! Not even Cola di Rienzo got trampled by his own horse.

Pasolini's sensational demise happened at Ostia, once the port where Julius Caesar took ship and Cleopatra came ashore. The ancient location widens Pasolini's frame of reference still further, to include the whole of Italian history. He was such a national figure that it becomes easy to lose sight of the individual. In a new biography (*Pasolini Requiem*, Pantheon) Barth David Schwartz mercifully doesn't, but his whopping book isn't helped by the bad practice of cramming in all the incidental research to prove that it has been done. European reviewers like to call this an American habit, but really it is a virus with no respect for borders. A more specific stricture to place on Mr Schwartz might be that a prose style so devoid of verve is no fit instrument to evoke a hero who crackled with energy even when he was being stupid. But Mr Schwartz, though a plodder, plods briskly enough to make his subject breathe, and some of the specialized knowledge was well worth going to get. In addition to his prodigious archival burrowings and the conducting of interviews on the scale of a door-to-door electoral canvass, Mr Schwartz seems to have acquainted himself personally with the sexually ambiguous (though unambiguously violent) Roman low life that was Pasolini's stamping ground, or prancing ground. The biographer is to be congratulated not least for coming out alive. The biographee, after all, got killed in there.

As for what he was doing in there, the first answer is obvious: he was cruising, although that word understates his predatory celerity. Better to say that he was pouncing. Quick off the mark and dressed to kill, he was a cheetah in dark glasses. In the *borgata*, the slumland of the Roman periphery, the population was mostly immigrants from the south who had come in search of prosperity and found misery. Petty theft and casual prostitution made up most of their economy. For a well-heeled and voraciously promiscuous homosexual like Pasolini, it was a dream come true. There were boys to be had for a pack of cigarettes or just a ride in his car.

He did his best to have them all. It remains astonishing, when you look at the shelf of books and rack of films signed with his name, that he found the energy to copulate even more prolifically than he created. People who knew him well were astonished, too. On location in North Africa for a film, his colleagues would retire exhausted to their tents after a long day and meet him coming out of his, all set to cruise the dunes.

But the spontaneous and seemingly everlasting abundance of sexual gratification was also the wellspring of his politics. The second and less obvious answer to the question of why he spent so much time in the lower depths was that he found them ethically preferable to the heights. He thought the truth was down there. Unlike other articulate, well-paid enemies of bourgeois society, Pasolini could actually point to an alternative. It wasn't a pretty alternative, but that was one of the things he hated about the bourgeoisie – its concern with mere appearances.

He hated everything else about the bourgeoisie as well, but in that respect he holds little interest except as an especially flagrant example of the modern middle-class intellectual blindly favouring, against common reason and all the historical evidence, a totalitarian substitute for the society that produced him. Valued by the PCI, the Communist Party of Italy, for the publicity he brought it,

Pasolini was allowed more latitude than any other mouthpiece. He often spoke against Party doctrines, and used the space given him by the Party's own newspapers to do so. But he was reliable, not to say predictable, in his denunciation of capitalism, neo-capitalism, consumerism, the bourgeoisie, bourgeois consumerism, bourgeois democracy, neo-capitalist democracy, consumerist democracy, and, for that matter, democracy itself, which he thought, or said he thought, could never achieve anything more than 'false tolerance' so long as it was infected by bourgeois consciousness.

It hardly needs saying that Pasolini had bourgeois origins himself: you don't get that kind of stridency except from someone in a false position. Raised under Fascism in a small town in Friuli – a province in the north-east of the country, where it bends towards Trieste – young Pier Paolo, a natural student, picked up the firm grounding in the etymology of the Friulian dialect which underpinned his lifetime achievement as a scholar and master of the Italian language. But he picked up no grounding at all in the life of the proletariat. He never did a day's manual labour then or later.

This is a standard pattern for revolutionary intellectuals and can't usefully be called hypocrisy, since if there is such a thing as a proletarian consciousness then it is hard to see how any proletarian could escape from it without the help of the revolutionary intellectual – although just how the revolutionary intellectual manages to escape from bourgeois consciousness is a problem that better minds than Pasolini have never been able to solve without sleight of hand. On this point Pasolini never pretended to be analytical, or even consistent. He was content to be merely rhetorical, in a well-established Italian tradition by which political argument is conducted like grand opera, with the tenor, encouraged by the applause or even by the mere absence of abuse, advancing to the footlights to sing his aria all over again, *da capo* and *con amore*.

Another aria Pasolini kept reprising was a bit harder to forgive. Mr Schwartz could have done more to disabuse the unwary reader of the notion that Pasolini might have had something when he not only awarded himself credentials in the wartime resistance but claimed the resistance as the *alma mater* of the postwar revolutionary struggle. Pasolini's resistance activities were confined mainly to writing obscure scholarly articles that the censors would have had to go out of their way even to find, let alone interpret. Again, there is no dishonour in this: people were shot for less. As in France, there was an understandable tendency in Italy after the war for people who had been helpless civilians during it to award themselves battle honours retroactively. Pasolini was just another schoolboy raised under the Fascist system who had the dubious luck to become a questioning adolescent at the precise moment when Fascism fell apart, and was thus able to convince himself that he had seen through it.

A more serious piece of mental legerdemain – and one that Mr Schwartz doesn't do half enough to point out – was Pasolini's lifelong pretence that the resistance was the prototype of the future Communist state, and for that very reason had been throttled by the ruthless forces of capitalism, bourgeois democracy, etc. Again as in France, most of the first and many of the bravest resistance fighters in Italy were indeed Communists. But the resistance movement soon became too broadly based to be called revolutionary; a better parallel is with Yugoslavia, Poland, or those other East European countries where not even opposition to the Nazis could unite the partisan movement, whose Communists regarded its bourgeois democrats as the real enemy, to be wiped out when the opportunity arose. This actually happened to Pasolini's brother, an active partisan who was liquidated by a Communist kangaroo court busily anticipating the postwar Socialist order. In most respects ready to concede that Pasolini was so cold a fish that even his passions were impersonal, Mr Schwartz seems not to have fully grasped that Pasolini was callous about his brother, too, claiming his death as a sacrifice in a historic struggle that, since it existed only in the minds of intellectuals, was never truly historic but always, and only, literary.

It could be that Mr Schwartz, for all he undoubtedly knows about Italy now, doesn't know quite enough about what it was like then. He is especially shaky in the crucial area of Italy's messy emergence from the war. A reference to German 'Junker 25 transports' might just be a misprint for what they ought to be, Junkers 52 transports, but his apparent belief that a German bomber could be called a Macchi – famously an Italian aircraft company – undermines confidence in his knowledge of the period, especially since he is making such a parade of specific references in order to evoke it: 'On April 6 [of 1944] Klaus Barbie's Gestapo in Lyons arrested fifty-one Jews ...' etc. If this is meant to be an ironic comment on the terrible bedfellows

Mussolini had acquired when he agreed to set up the Republic of Salò under German tutelage, it scarcely seems adequate. Why is there nothing about the Nazi assault on the Jews of Italy? It would not only have been more pertinent to the subject; it would have created a more realistic context against which Pasolini's later vapourings about the revolutionary resistance could have been judged. That the Nazi attempt to render Italy *judenrein* was a comparative failure was due at least partly to the historic reluctance of the Italian people to follow fanatics of any stamp further than the parade ground. There were plenty of bourgeois elements, including the rank and file of the Church, who risked their lives to save Jews. Mr Schwartz might have made more of this, especially since Pasolini himself made so little.

*

Pasolini's theatrical fantasies about a formative period of his own and his country's history were not casual. Like Sartre's quietly misleading suggestions that he had been a Resistance fighter in the thick of the action, they were fundamental to a political career of posturing histrionics. Pasolini never went as far as Sartre, although Mr Schwartz is kind to believe his claims of having escaped from the Germans in a hail of bullets. Pasolini's story was that when the regiment into which he had been drafted was ordered by the Germans to surrender its arms he and a friend threw their rifles into a ditch 'and then, in a burst of machine-gun fire, dove in after them'. The story continued, 'We waited for the regiment to march off, and then made our escape. It was completely an instinctive and involuntary beginning to my resistance.' Thus Pasolini, quoted by the English journalist Oswald Stack in 1970, and reprinted by Mr Schwartz without comment.

Well, it *might* have happened: German machine gunners missed, occasionally. A more plausible version is that Pasolini, like many others, managed to desert unnoticed in the confusion. Sartre let people believe that he had escaped from prison camp. In fact he had been allowed to go home. The heroism came later, in the telling of the tale. So it does for most of us. The best reason for not believing that there was any machine gunner, however, is that Pasolini said so little about the incident later on. If it had really happened there would have been essays, epic poems, movies, operas. A fabulist on Pasolini's scale could never leave unexploited a fact that had actually occurred.

Pasolini respected facts. He just didn't respect their context. You couldn't take his word about the meaning of things. But in his early days in Rome he was unbeatable at pointing out things that other people – bourgeois people – preferred to ignore. For a while, he had the only game in town. Propelled by the postwar economic recovery, Roman high life regained all its old extravagance. Out at its edge, in the *periferia*, Roman low life grew ever more malodorous, and for the same reason: the wealth that fuelled the party had drawn the poor people to the glowing window. Pasolini's mission was to remind the high life that the low life existed, to tell the *dolce vita* about the *malavita*.

He did it first as a novelist. His 1959 novel *Una Vita Violenta* has just been republished, by Pantheon, as *A Violent Life*, in the 1968 translation by William Weaver, of whom it should be said that the international reputation of modern Italian literature wouldn't be the same without him. Like Max Hayward with Russian, Weaver has been vital to the job of transmitting the cultural force of an off-trail language into the world's consciousness. (It remains a terrible pity that Weaver didn't find time to translate all of Primo Levi's books instead of only a couple of them.) But not even Weaver could translate the full impact of *Una Vita Violenta*, because the book depends on the shock effect of being written ugly in a beautiful language. Though Weaver's translation is rendered in the most faithfully squalid English, it is no more horrifying than *Last Exit to Brooklyn*, whereas it ought to turn the mind's stomach like the invective of the damned in Dante's Hell. Pasolini went searching for boys among the rubbish dumps and came back with a picture of how they lived. His Roman *borgata* was like a Rio *favela* without the flowers. In *Black Orpheus*, Marcel Camus's film about Rio, which was a worldwide art-house hit at about the same time, unquenchable poetry steams out of the garbage to meet the rising sun. In Pasolini's novel there is just the garbage, and human beings are part of it. When a flood comes, one of the characters finds it within himself to punctuate a career of theft by acting selflessly. But that is the only note of hope. The book was designed as a kick in the teeth for Pasolini's hated bourgeois enemy. It worked. His reputation as a teller of the awkward truth was rapidly established, and not only among the radical intelligentsia. After all, the awkward truth was true. You didn't have to be a Marxist to spot it.

Pasolini, however, did have to be a Marxist. Though never much concerned with elaborating a coherent social analysis, he never gave up on the class war. That became part of his tragedy, because the class he championed finally realized its only ambition, which was to be absorbed by the class he attacked. But at the time he was a recognized type of radical intellectual, valued even by the nonradical because of his dazzling verbal bravura, forgiven his excesses because he was such an adornment to the scene – a word hard to avoid, considering the theatricality of Italian political discussion. Again, Mr Schwartz might have made more of just how much forgiveness was required: 'He knew nothing about Stalin's purges' is a needless concession to Pasolini's wilful obtuseness. Italian Communist intellectuals knew all about Stalin. The best of them were trying to establish a brand of Communism that left him out – the hope that we later learned to call Euro-Communism, or Socialism with a Human Face. The best possible construction to put on Pasolini's polemical writings is that he was trying to do this, too. He had a promising model to follow – Gramsci, about whom Pasolini wrote the most sustained of his many remarkable poetic works, *The Ashes of Gramsci*.

Later on, in the flower-power phase of the nineteen sixties, Gramsci became a hero to thousands of young revolutionaries scattered all over the world; some of them even read a few selected pages, usually from the letters he had written in a Fascist prison. Pasolini got in early and read everything Gramsci wrote. Pasolini promised his hero's shade that the struggle would continue. What he couldn't promise was a solution to the problem posed by the fact that Communism in practice had turned out to need as much coercive apparatus as Fascism. At least part of Gramsci's undoubted charm was that he had died in jail without ever having to take part in the application of those theories he had elaborated with such humane subtlety. There was no guarantee that had he done so he would not have turned out like George Lukacs, Hungary's visionary turned cultural commissar – or, to go back to the beginning, Lunacharsky in the Soviet Union, who in 1929 was obliged to crack down on the same avant-garde artists he had previously encouraged.

Gramsci's seductive vision of justice could not have been brought about without unlimited state power. Neither could Pasolini's, and with him there was even less justification for believing it could. But plenty of Pasolini's admirers knew that. They knew him to be wrong but still they marvelled. *The Ashes of Gramsci* told them that they were dealing with a prodigy. Mr Schwartz forgets to mention one of the things that made the message clear: *Le Ceneri di Gramsci* is written in a version of *terza rima*, the same measure as the *Divine Comedy*. Pasolini cast his wild revolutionary document in the most hallowed of strict forms as a guarantee of national continuity. There is more truth than the author seems to realize in Mr Schwartz's solemn assurance: 'At poem's end, poet and Italy are one.' ('Poem's end' is an erstwhile *Time*-style construction that our author has unfortunately resurrected, employing it not quite often enough to reduce the reader to tether's end, just often enough to arouse the dreadful suspicion that a tin ear for English might be hearing Italian the same way.)

*

Pasolini the writer had established himself beyond question, if not beyond criticism. Bourgeois intellectuals who knew that his politics were nonsense still knew that he was a prodigy. He had ample evidence for his theories about a bourgeois conspiracy against spontaneity and social justice: busted on a morals charge, he was hounded for his perversity by Christian Democrat politicians and their attendant newspapers. Neo-Fascists joined in with delight. But the more awkward truth, for him, was that there was such a thing as an independent, middle-of-the-road intelligentsia, which was perfectly capable of recognizing that he was a classic case in the best sense as well as the worst. He himself was no faddist when it came to critical allegiances. When the name of Roland Barthes came up, Pasolini said that although he admired Barthes's work he would give it all up for a page of Gianfranco Contini or Roberto Longhi. As a student in Bologna, Pasolini had sat at Longhi's feet when the great teacher of art history made a case for the historical continuity of inspiration beyond the reach of any ideology. As for the philologist Contini, he was Pasolini's true conscience, as he was for a greater poet, Eugenio Montale, and for almost every other prominent artist in the postwar period. In the first marvellous years of his career, Pasolini reported to Contini by letter like a truant son to the father he had never had. Contini, the least radical of men, a true cultural conservative for whom learning was the world – and who mastered more of the world's learning than any other scholar – understood the tension in Pasolini between the irreconcilable forces of social rage and creative ambition. But so did many people less qualified. Pasolini was so obviously a star, and stars are on fire.

*

Pasolini loved stardom, which for a champion of the common man is always bound to present a contradiction. It can be reconciled, but it takes humour, and humour was not conspicuously among his gifts. If it had been, he might have been funnier about his need for an ever bigger stage. He preferred to believe that it was a political necessity. The movies reached people who couldn't read. While his literary reputation was still building up, Pasolini was already preparing to compromise it by contributing to the screenplays of the famous directors, which in Italy have traditionally been group efforts. In 1957, he wrote scenes for Fellini's *Le Notti di Cabiria*. Fellini gave him his first car, a Fiat 600, as part payment. The tiny *macchina* can be seen as the germ of a dangerous taste, but Pasolini didn't really need much encouragement beyond the thrill of being in on the most glamorous artistic activity available. The lowlife scenes of Fellini's *La Dolce Vita* were also written by Pasolini. In that so wonderfully, so *easily* symbolic moment when Mastroianni and Anouk are shown by the prostitute across the plank in her flooded basement room Pasolini's harsh knowledge of the periphery underlies Fellini's humanity.

Having so resonantly played back-seat driver, Pasolini was bound to grab the wheel. *Accattone*, his début movie as a director, in 1961, was the world of *Una Vita Violenta* made noisomely accessible to all, with no punches pulled, even in the casting: the bad teeth on display were the genuine article. The only star associated with the movie was Pasolini himself. The result was a triumph. Condemned out of hand by all the right people, it was a scandalous artistic success that was widely seen to spring from an even more scandalous reality. By a paradox whose consequences he would never cease trying to talk his way out of, Pasolini gained immediate and universal acceptance as the first fully authenticated multimedia genius ever to wear dark glasses indoors and a silk shirt undone to the third button. His subject matter was life beyond the margin; he himself was no more marginal than the Pope. How to reconcile this anomaly?

He couldn't, but he made a great try. If Mr Schwartz had gone lighter on inessential detail he might have found room for a few paragraphs pointing out what a continuous thrill it was to be in or near Italy when the film directors were all living in each other's pockets, poaching each other's personnel, and turning out movies that struck you even at the time as memories to be kept, partly because the people who made them so obviously had memories of their own. The glaring difference between the Italian cinema and the French New Wave was that the Italians hadn't sent boys to do a man's work. Quite apart from the international big guns like Fellini and Visconti and Antonioni, there was a whole row of domestic household names who could get the tragic recent history of their country even into their comedies. Anyone who wanted to know what really happened to young Italian deserters who ran away from German machine guns could have found out from Comencini's *Tutti a Casa*, a comic vehicle for Alberto Sordi which nevertheless brought out the full tragedy of the collapsing Fascist farce. Most of these directors were social democrats – moderates, if you like, or bourgeois liberals, if you insist – but they could produce a socially responsible cinema, and there was at least one Marxist, Gillo Pontecorvo, who left Pasolini's Marxism looking like the caprice it was. Pontecorvo's *The Battle of Algiers* was a political film in the way Pasolini's films never were.

But everyone at the time knew that Pasolini's role was to remain unpredictable by refusing to mature. He carried a licence to shoot his mouth off out of season, forever making statements because he could never make sense. Italian cinema had room for just one Godard-style head case, and Pasolini was it. The special exemption he held in the literary world also applied, on a larger scale, in the more spectacular world of the movies. Almost every film he made was indicted, sequestered, banned from the festival, reinstated, fought over, laughed at – above all, talked about. If he hadn't scandalized them, people would have been disappointed.

He was a spoiled child given a camera for his birthday, who made home movies about what had spoiled him. *Oedipus Rex* was an obvious love poem to his mother, played by Silvana Mangano at her most iconically beautiful, with Pasolini's alter ego Franco Citti in the title role. Starring in *Medea*, Maria Callas was his mother all over again: statuesque, mad about Jason, ready to kill anyone for him, including her own sons. In *Teorema*, Terence Stamp played Pasolini himself, the sexually omnipotent stranger who penetrated the bourgeois household and everyone in it, as if the plot of Jerome K. Jerome's play *The Passing of the Third-Floor Back* had been given a monkey-gland injection. Stamp, looking more beautiful than Mangano and Callas put together, was almost credible as the avatar before whom the whole household lined up seriatim to be ravished and transfigured. An earlier choice for the role, Lee van Cleef, might have made disbelief harder to suspend. The early choices for the role of Jesus Christ in *The Gospel According to St Matthew* were similarly unpromising. Jack Kerouac was one, Allen Ginsberg was another, and there was even a dizzy moment when Yevtushenko was considered. But Pasolini saw sense, cast a strikingly good-looking unknown, and made his best film, the one that shocked even the Marxists. It took the Gospel straight. Under the influence of Pope John XXIII, the Curia had decided that the occasional venture into the mass media need not be ruled out. The Franciscans put up the money for the movie on the sole condition that Pasolini's script stuck to the book. Pasolini might have done so anyway. Matthew's Christ comes with a sword. It was the way Pasolini saw himself: the man from nowhere, speaking authentic speech, potent beyond containment, loving the poor, transfiguring them by his touch. Authenticity was aided by the contractual and temporal impossibility of Christ's castigating the bourgeoisie, consumerism, American-style false tolerance, etc. All He was allowed to do was cleanse the temple, which will always need cleansing. As a Biblical film, *The Gospel According to St Matthew* has no peers and only one plausible emulator I can think of – Bruce Beresford's 1985 *King David*. That film, much derided even by Beresford himself, has something of the same startling, self-contained feeling of being there where it all began, away from here where it all ends. Recast and given the budget to finish the big scenes that were cut short when bad weather chewed up its shooting time, *King David* might have come even closer to the Pasolini film Beresford so admired when it came out, in 1964. But Hollywood was a bad place for Beresford to start from. To that extent Pasolini was right about American consumerism. He was just wrong about the Italian bourgeoisie, from which came the independent producers who backed his movies not just because they hoped to make money – always a gamble with a director out to get banned if he could – but because they respected his gift. The Franciscans respected it, too. Modern Italian society was more complex and fruitful than Pasolini ever allowed. He wasn't sufficiently impressed by how it had given rise to him. He was too busy being impressed with himself.

It did him in, in the end. History caught up with him in the late nineteen sixties, when the student rebellion outflanked him. His reaction to the student revolutionaries was the same as de Gaulle's. *Vi odio cari studenti*: I hate you, darling students. Pasolini cheered the police for hitting them. At least the police were poor, whereas the students were *figli di papà*, sons of daddy – in a word, bourgeois.

But by then it was becoming evident even to Pasolini that the class war was over and the bourgeoisie had won it. Belief in the socialist state was draining away in the West because it was already dead in the East. The only course left was to clean up democracy. Pasolini didn't take defeat gracefully. Using the regular front-page platform given him by the country's leading newspaper, the *Corriere della Sera*, he railed against every aspect of the new reforming spirit. He condemned abortion, divorce, even gay rights. He could have been preaching from the Reverend Criswell's pulpit in Dallas, except that he still considered himself the true Left. All this new stuff was just 'the American type of modernist tolerance'. The bourgeoisie was just boxing clever.

This was foolish, but there was worse to come. He condemned the poor, too. They had failed him, the way the Germans failed Hitler. Like many social commentators who love people by the class, Pasolini had never been much good at loving them one by one: apart from his sainted mother, he froze out everybody in the end – he was the authentic Brechtian iceman. But in the last phase he did the same thing even to his collective paragon, the poor people of the *borgata*. His undoubted passion for their way of life had always been riven by a contradiction. He thought they were authentic, speaking a tongue unspoiled by suave hypocrisy, honest in their animal lust. If all this had been true it would have been a good case for keeping them poor. But he also said that the slums they lived in were capitalism self-condemned, 'truly and really concentration camps'. (Pasolini also habitually trivialized the word 'genocide', thereby pioneering the unfortunate current practice of squandering the language appropriate to an absolute evil on a relative one.)

The tension between these two attitudes was fruitful for him as long as they could be held in balance. When it became evident, however, that the only wish of the poor was to join the consumers he despised, Pasolini could find no recourse except to enrol them among his enemies. In his three, increasingly dreadful last movies, his ideal pre-bourgeois world of freely available sex is successively discovered in Boccaccio, Chaucer and de Sade. The trilogy makes painful viewing. Escapism is too dignified a word. Pasolini was fleeing into a past that never existed from a present he couldn't face. In a notorious front-page piece for the *Corriere* he dismissed his once-beloved Roman sub-proletariat as having succumbed to 'a degeneration of bodies and sex organs'. Pasolini even had the gall to suggest that education was ruining them. For the admirer of Gramsci it was a sad betrayal. Gramsci had always been delighted by any evidence of his proletarians' improving themselves. Pasolini wanted them to stay the way they were. When they showed signs of independent life, he lost interest in them.

Perhaps too kindly, Mr Schwartz doesn't make much of the possibility that they were losing interest in Pasolini. One of the most famous men in the country, recognizable at a glance, he still drove by night into the territory of the Violent Life. But time was ticking by. Once, the car and the clothes would have been enough. Now he needed his fame. What next? Charlus with his rouged cheeks? Aschenbach with his rinse? Rage, rage against the dyeing of the hair. Luckily, Pasolini never had to face the sad, slow twilight of the predator gone weak in the hams. He died the way he had lived, dramatically.

He had always thought that life was like that: drama. It was the belief that made him the kind of Communist who sounds like a Fascist. His politics were an insult to his intelligence. But there was a saving grace. The Italians are cursed with a language so seductive it can gloss over anything; Pasolini could always make it reveal more than it concealed, even when he talked tripe. He cut through the mellifluous uproar to speak the unspeakable. Pasolini's matchless ability to be irritating in every way meant that he was also irritating in the ways that count. Beneath Pasolini's politics lay his perceptions, and some of those remain permanently true. Free societies feel free to waste human lives, pushing them to the edge and calling them part of the landscape. The better we are at telling ourselves that this is inevitable, the more we still need telling that it won't do.

New Yorker, 28 December, 1992 and 4 January, 1993

MONDO FELLINI

Asanisimasa is a seeming nonsense word that crops up early in Fellini's *8½*. Later on you find out that it isn't nonsense at all, but a real word expressed in a children's code, like one of the language games Mozart played with his sister. Simpler even than pig Latin, the code works by inserting an 's' after each vowel and then repeating the vowel before moving on to the next consonant. Take out the padding and *asanisimasa* contracts to *anima*, the Italian for 'soul'. At the heart of Fellini's greatest film, one of the greatest works of art of the century, is a single word.

To get to it, though, you have to do more than crack a childishly simple code. You have to follow the director down a long corridor in an old-fashioned luxury hotel. It is late at night. Along the corridor comes Marcello Mastroianni in the role of Guido Anselmi, a renowned Italian director buckling under the strain of starting work on his latest, make-or-break film before the script is really finished. Guido is wearing a black hat with its sides curled up, he has hangdog bags under his eyes, and his overcoat is draped over his forearm. Surely this is the studied sartorial insouciance of Fellini himself – a clear confession that the director is his own hero. We know who this is. We know what must be going on in his head: anguish, remorse, panic. But without breaking step in his forlorn march he suddenly twists and flicks one foot sidewise while it is in midair, as if he were momentarily attacked by the memory of a dance. Why does he do that?

I first asked myself this question in Florence, in 1963, when *8½* came out. Even in the delighted shock of that first viewing, it was clear that *8½* had dozens of such apparently self-contained moments, enigmatic yet instantly memorable: the squeaky crackle of Guido lying back with languorous angst on a bed heaped with the eight-by-ten glossies of actresses from whom he has to choose the supporting cast; the sheeting that shrouds the scaffolding of the uncompleted rocket ship flapping in the sea wind at night; Guido's father going down into his hole in the ground; the ancient cardinal's face inhaling the steam in the sauna at the spa; Sandra Milo, Guido's airhead mistress, trying to walk in two different directions at once when she spots Anouk Aimée, the terrifyingly poised wife; Guido slumped in the preview theatre in front of the intellectualizing screenwriter who has nagged him beyond endurance and who, in the beleaguered director's imagination, has just allowed himself to be hanged. If you could have stopped the film from moment to moment, it might have looked like any film in which a visually gifted director lights fireworks that will illuminate the darkness of an unilluminating script. But the film established its coherence in the first few minutes and unfolded inevitably. It was a film about an unfinished film – about a film that never even started – and yet it looked and sounded more finished than any film you had ever seen. About a director who didn't know what to do next, it always knew exactly what to do next. It was a cosmic joke.

That much I got, though I couldn't understand all the dialogue. At the time, I knew barely enough Italian to follow the story. My future wife, who spoke Italian fluently, was sitting beside me: she disliked having her concentration broken but provided whispered explanations when asked, filling in the details about the lying, cheating husband, who is insufficiently consumed by guilt for having granted himself romantic privileges on the strength of his creative gift, while his classy wife faces yet another crisis in the endless process of deciding whether to put up with him or walk away. The film should have functioned as a pre-emptive counselling session – an advertisement for the advisability of filling out the divorce papers before signing the marriage register. But the aesthetic thrill over-whelmed everything. Long before the lights went up on the stunned audience, everyone in it knew that this was a work to grow old with – one that, as T. S. Eliot once said about Dante's poetry, you could hope to appreciate fully only at the end of your life. You couldn't expect, then, to tease out the meaning of the film's single moments. First, you had to absorb the impact of its initial impression, as authoritative and disabling as that created by the two great wide-screen Botticellis in the Uffizi – only a few hundred yards away from the cinema where *8½* was playing *in prima visione* – which slowed

your step and kept you at a distance while you strove to refocus your
brain along with your eyes.

In the subsequent three decades, growing older if not wiser, I
have seen *8½* every time it was re-released. Now there is a video of
it: not a perfect way for a newcomer to see the film but, for anyone
who knows it well, a handy *aide-mémoire* to the order of its events
– an order that, though precisely calculated, is inherently bewildering,
because the chronology of the immediate narrative sometimes
includes scene-long figments of Guido's self-serving imagination
and is continually intersected by divergent ripples spun out from
his underlying memory. On the whole, 'personal' films are to be
distrusted, if by personal it is meant that they are personal to their
authors. (After the *auteur* theory took hold, no director could make
a film bad enough to be dismissed: a kludge on the scale of John
Ford's *Seven Women* was discovered to be personal instead of lousy.)
But *8½* is the kind of film that becomes personal to its viewer.
Whether *8½* is really about Fellini is a question raised by the film
itself – a question answered, in part, by the uncomfortable certitude
of any married man who watches it that it is really about *him*. Men,
we're all in this together. Fellini had us figured out.

Until almost the eve of the start of production on *8½* the Guido
Anselmi character wasn't a film director. We know this because Deena
Boyer, a journalist born in America but raised in France, was trusted
enough by Fellini to be given unprecedented access to the preparation
of this film about the preparation of a film. Even the best movie
books are usually more entertaining than indispensable; hers breaks
the rule. It was first published in French, as *Les 200 Jours de 8½*, but
I have never seen it except in German, as a tatty secondhand Rowohlt
paperback called *Die 200 Tage von 8½*. There is no point in trying
to be omniscient about a work of art whose stature depends upon
its knowing more about life than you do, but Boyer's supply of first-
hand information is handy for dispelling illusions, and the illusion
that Fellini set out to make a film about a film director is a crucial
one to have dispelled. Woody Allen's *Stardust Memories*, in part a
copycat of *8½*, could hardly work if it were not about an artist in
a crisis. But Fellini's ur-hero was *l'homme moyen sensuel* in a crisis.
At first, he was 'just anyone', or, as Fellini told Boyer, 'a man who
goes to a watering place and starts thinking about his life'.

Guido graduated from being just anybody after Fellini decided to give him a career, so that the audience could get a handle on what his immediate crisis was about. Guido graduated from being just anybody to being a writer, Boyer records. If *8½* had actually been made on that basis, it would have provided an interesting parallel to Antonioni's masterpiece of two years earlier, *La Notte*: same leading man, same professional anguish, same lustrous camerawork by Gianni Di Venanzo. But, as the start of production drew near, Fellini, with Mastroianni already cast, opted for the calling whose nuts and bolts he and his star could most easily show. Thus, very late in the game, *8½* acquired the solid-seeming foreground that snares your initial attention while the psychological background sends out tendrils through its interstices to gather you in. All the fascination, all the *fun* of the Italian film world, the *mondo del cinema*, is right up front working its charm: the randy production manager getting off with bimbo bit players, the producer carrying on like a prima donna, the prima donna melting down like a maniac, the deals, the double deals, the chaos, the creativity.

*

Above all, the creativity. It's getting hard for younger generations to grasp, as time goes by, but in the nineteen fifties and sixties Italy was the true centre of the film world. Before the *auteur* theories promoted by *Cahiers du Cinéma* in France, by the magazine *Movie* in Britain, and by critics such as Andrew Sarris in America forced the movie-mad intelligentsia all over the globe to reassess the Hollywood heritage instead of just enjoying it – a vital preparatory step in the development of the Planet Hollywood we all so uneasily inhabit now – the lesser nations produced the films that seemed to matter most, and of the lesser nations Italy led the pack, ahead of France, Sweden, Poland, India and Japan. It was as if Italy had risen reinvigorated out of the ashes of the war, a phoenix with a body by Farina and the Klaxon voice of Giuseppe Di Stefano: sexy, strident, attention-getting, bung-full of tradition yet terrifically up-to-date. Italian movies were a worldwide art-house attraction even before *La Dolce Vita* came out, in 1960. After that, they were a sensation. Fellini, with his big hat and loosely slung coat, was in all the photo magazines. Apparently, he lived at a table in the Via Veneto, looking tolerant but reserved while being mobbed by students and paparazzi. (Actually, he never went there or anywhere else in public except to be photographed, and he put up with it only so that his face could pull in money with which to make movies – but we couldn't tell that from looking.) He wasn't alone. Film artists of impeccable intellectual credentials lived in coronas of personal publicity. Everybody had just worked with everybody else or was about to. The general effect was to make Italy look like an updated opera, with props and costumes shipped in from the future: *Cavalleria Rusticana* with a Ferrari onstage instead of a horse, *Tosca* on a Vespa. The effect, in short, was magnetic.

Australians of my generation on their way to Britain stopped off in Italy to absorb an atmosphere they had correctly divined to be a magic compound of culture and hedonism. Those of us who stuck around long enough to pick up the language found that the film world was even more effervescent than we had guessed. In Florence there was an unending supply of American Fulbright scholars who were supposed to be studying Mannerist painting but still found time to keep up with all the gossip of the Rome-based industry, as if Pasolini were as important as Pontormo, Bolognini as Bronzino. They didn't have to haunt the library to get the facts. It was all in the papers. Producers, directors, cameramen and actors were getting married, divorced, sued, betrayed, killed, buried and born again in a pattern constant only in its unrelenting turbulence. Everyone was a star.

Essentially, each Italian film was a collaboration, usually involving three or more writers, two or more of whom would be directors next week and one or more of whom was a producer last week, but the money ran out. All those egos, however, were born to clash: hence the fizz, and hence the air of dedication, detectable in comedies and serious films alike. It is unfair to Antonioni to read his career backward – from the disaster of *Zabriskie Point*, through the awful, wilful obfuscations of *Blow-Up* to the brain-curdling deterministic lethargy of *Red Desert* and *The Eclipse* – and to decide that the spaced-out pacing of his high-impact central movies *La Notte* and *L'Avventura* was a bogus claim to seriousness. You didn't have to be mad about Monica Vitti (and we all were, even the women) to decide that those films were definitive treatises on the loss of love, all the more convincing for moving no faster than a snail's funeral. They retain their integrity when seen now, if we can suppress our awareness of how the director himself fell to pieces. Seen at the time, they looked monumental, but they didn't stand alone: bustling at their feet was a metropolis of the imagination.

On the subject of the mature Italian male's sexual dilemma, the comedies of Pietro Germi looked at least as thoughtful as any dirge by Antonioni, and packed in a lot more incident. (In Germi's *L'Immorale*, Ugo Tognazzi runs around frantically to keep three fully fleshed female characters happily out of touch with one another until he finally conks out – not from guilt but from an overtaxed heart.) Watching the comedies of Germi, Salce, Comencini, Monicelli and a half-dozen others as they appeared, we got an education in just how comprehensive and satisfying a popular art form could be without ceasing to be either popular or artistic. The entire national life was up there on the screen, with an interval for drinks.

Over and above the comedies, there was the straight stuff. Postwar neo-realism had evolved into something even better: realism, with a fact-based imaginative scope that could take in anything, even the deep-seated, dangerously retaliatory corruption of the country that had given rise to it. In 1963, Francesco Rosi's *Le Mani Sulla Città* (*Hands Over the City*) helped to light a fuse under the Italian political system which finally burned its way to the dynamite more than two decades later. In 1966, Gillo Pontecorvo made *The Battle of Algiers*. A radical film of such power that it remains compulsory viewing even for conservatives, it put the dazzling first features of Bertolucci and Bellocchio into sober perspective, making them look childishly hipped on their own anger. In short, the Italian cinema of those years was a lush field for someone to stand out from. Fellini did, head and shoulders.

*

Even more than *La Dolce Vita*, *8½* is a clear demonstration of how Fellini became Italy's national director and its ambassador to the world – the ambassador who never left home. The totality of his films is more than the sum of its parts, but all his films are contained, at some degree of compression, in *8½*: they all lead up to it or lead on from it. Rich even by his standards, his supreme masterpiece first conveys its wealth through its sumptuous visual texture. Since *Nights of Cabiria*, for which the designer Piero Gherardi joined his entourage, Fellini had already put more of his country's visual excitement into his movies than any other director except perhaps Kurosawa. In

8½, with Di Venanzo lighting Gherardi's sets, Fellini excelled even his own previous efforts at pulling his tumultuous homeland into shape.

The lustre isn't just the look of Italy; it's the look of Fellini. Compared with him, the world's other great national directors hardly cared about what the camera could do. Buñuel never moved the camera unless he had to. Renoir called for a bravura setup only if there was no other way to make a narrative point: that much-studied, Ophuls-like long exterior tracking shot in *Le Crime de Monsieur Lange* is there just so you can see exactly how far the hero has to run along corridors and down flights of stairs. And you can't imagine Bergman actually enjoying what in his case you feel inclined to call the physical side of it. But Fellini, even in his maturity, is like Orson Welles playing with the toy train set for the first time. In *8½*, through sets built by Gherardi to look real and real locations lit by Di Venanzo to look like sets, the camera sails and swoops weightlessly yet without a flutter, as if following grooves in space. As Boyer's book reveals, there was no question of Fellini's standing aside and letting Di Venanzo make all this happen. Fellini was with him behind the camera: the instructions given to the operator, Pasquale de Santis, were their joint work, with Fellini always in the ascendant, specifying every aspect of a black-and-white *mise en scène* gorgeous enough to make colour look famished. Fellini was so sure of getting what he wanted that it didn't bother him if he was unable to check his work. He almost never looked at rushes, although for much of the shooting of *8½* he couldn't have even if he had wanted to: the laboratories were on strike.

Not only were there hardly any dailies, there were practically no scripts. Only two complete copies of the script existed anywhere near the production. Fellini had the picture in his head. To a large extent, it happened the way you feel it happened: like a marvellous, fluent improvisation, with a freedom of expression which extended to the actors – even to those who were amateurs and needed dozens of takes to get a tricky scene right. According to Fellini's usual practice, the players, whether professional or amateur, were cast for their faces. For Fellini, *la faccia* was everything. In a little book of 1980, *Fare un Film*, Fellini said that he would have preferred not to decide on his cast until he had seen every face in the world. Fellini had always taken delight in casting untrained faces and getting precise performances out of them, but until *La Dolce Vita* he mainly confined them to the lower ranks of the cast. In *8½* they are up among the leading figures. The role of Guido's increasingly apoplectic producer (clearly modelled on Fellini's real-life bagman, Angelo Rizzoli) is played by an industrialist, Guido Alberti. Physically ideal in his pampered rotundity, he uncorks a performance that a trained actor would be proud of. (Alberti went semi-pro afterwards: he'd got the bug.) Similarly, the screenwriter is played by a real screenwriter, Jean Rougeul. Possessing a face that begs to be slapped, he, too, is physically ideal, but it is remarkable how good he is at the lines, or how good Fellini makes him. Contrary to legend, in Italy it does matter if an actor can't say the lines properly: though Italian films are post-synched, the lips have to match the words in anything except a long shot. Rougeul, a Frenchman, had to work hard. He does an amazing job of being repellent. When he gets strung up, the audience laughs.

In a TV interview given by the late Alexander Mackendrick to Stephen Frears, Mackendrick said he had always found mixing untrained actors with trained ones doubly fruitful, because the untrained caught discipline and the trained caught naturalness. This effect can be seen working at a high pitch in *8½*. The prinicipal players have no star mannerisms: they are just people. Mastroianni and Anouk Aimée, playing Guido's wife, Luisa, aren't on-screen together for much more than fifteen minutes, but the way they connect across distance burns at the centre of the film: these are the embers of a long love, too spent to keep either party warm yet still too hot to handle. As his mistress Carla, Sandra Milo pulls off the impossible trick of being a nitwit angel that a smart man might like to know almost as much as he would like to lay. To fatten her up for the role, Fellini made her eat until she groaned. In *Fare un Film* he calls the character a *culone*, which more or less means that her brain is in her behind. Milo convinces you that it's a good brain anyway. Purely physical, ecstatically devoted to her exciting lover – he is the White Sheik from one of Fellini's early films, but in a black hat – she is not to be blamed that he is bored with her almost as soon as she steps off the train. It isn't her fault: it's his. This is about something deeper than adultery. If it was just the story of a man caught between wife and mistress and satisfied with neither, it would be *La Dolce Vita*. But *8½* isn't about the melodrama in the life of its protagonist, it's about the psychodrama in his mind.

'Didn't you know the devil is Saraghina?' The question that rings through *8½* rang through Fellini's life. In *8½* the young Guido, making an appearance in the mature Guido's memory, hears that question from the priests and doesn't know how to answer. Saraghina is an enormous, blowsy, barefoot madwoman who lives on the beach and dances and exposes herself for Guido and his fellow inmates of a church school. After a flagrant exhibition by Saraghina, the young Guido gets caught, led off by the ear, and made to kneel on dried peas while the priests put him to the question. In real life, Fellini never made a secret of Saraghina. Fellini commonly told interviewers anything that would get rid of them, but on the subject of Saraghina he either always told the same lie or else it was a fact. In *Fare un Film* – cobbled together from a baker's dozen interviews and articles by other people, but reprocessed by Fellini and bearing his signature – the Saraghina story is given neat. He says that while he was at the church school in Fano, the only period in his childhood when he spent much time away from his native town of Rimini, he visited Saraghina often and paid the price for inciting her to her revelatory routine. (She was cheap: her name meant 'sardines' and she would do her number for a few of them as payment.) Refusing to believe that Saraghina was the devil was obviously the essential early decision of Fellini's emotional life. He preferred to believe that she was an angel.

Whether of not the Saraghina episode ever happened to Fellini, or merely something like it – or, still more merely, numerous and diverse episodes scarcely at all like it but he synthesized them later in the way that artists do – for *8½* Saraghina is one of the elements that help to dramatize Guido's memory as a convincing determinant of his imagination. The memory of Saraghina is the gross, unfrocked and irrepressible guarantee that Guido's imagination can't be a thing of refinement: the most he can hope for is to make refined things from it, but his imagination itself must remain primitive, shaped incorrigibly by the initial impact of her uncorseted oomph. Guido is unsettled by the knowledge that his memory should dominate his imagination in such a way. He still half regrets that he can never give the priests a satisfactory answer, still hopes that the cardinal in the steam can show him the true path. But Fellini himself, judging from the sum of his films, seems to have been glad enough, if not exactly grateful, to have a story in his mind that would help him to script and shoot the male sexual imagination as a divine comedy.

The mind is the house of the Lord, and in the house of the Lord there are many mansions, and one of them is a honky-tonk. Fellini's central boldness is to embrace that fact and body it forth without shame, but without any knowing pride either – just the embarrassment necessarily involved in being consciously human. Self-revealing without being self-exculpatory, he is not offering *carte blanche* for adultery, a concrete act that needs excusing at the very least and is often a crime. Besides, there are married men who have never committed adultery, and one or two of them have even reached the White House. But there is no married man who has not, like President Carter, committed adultery in his heart – meaning, of course, in his imagination, which grows out of his memory, and has been with him always.

This interior imbroglio is *8½*'s real subject. In real life Guido is merely entangled. In his mental life he is tied to time: the rope that threatens to drag him by the leg from the sky back down to the beach is a doubly exact metaphor, because the beach is where Fellini's imagination began its life. Saraghina was as meaty, beaty, big and bouncy as all the world's women rolled into one and that's what Guido has wanted ever since – all the women in the world. Not every woman he wants is an uncomplicated *culone* like the one played by Sandra Milo. There is also the young, vital ideal of fructive beauty, played in *8½* by Claudia Cardinale, whose looks and personality made a unique contribution to Italian movies in the early sixties before she went international later in the decade and rather dissipated the effect. Silvana Mangano, Sophia Loren and Monica Vitti could all act better. Even Virna Lisi could act better, although few ever appreciated her as an actress because she was so beautiful. But Cardinale wan't just beautiful, she had the knack of incarnating a dream type, the aristocratic peasant. Visconti used her for that quality, twice and at length, in *Vaghe stelle dell'Orsa* (hardly seen outside Italy, it had a title from Leopardi – *Beautiful Stars of the Bear* – and a plot from hell, but she looked unputdownably scrumptious) and his much-mangled international blockbuster *The Leopard* (she was the gorgeous up-market earth girl that Burt Lancaster and Alain Delon both cherished as the personification of authenticity, a judgement which received ironic reinforcement from the film as a whole, camped as it was somewhere between Sicily and the abstract outworld we have since come to recognize as Planet Hollywood). In *8½* Fellini got the same charge out of her as a glorified walk-on, a bit-part with billing. Practically all she does is turn up. But she triggers Guido's mixed vision of carnal purity and we believe it. Dante's Beatrice on the cover of *Vogue*. Petrarch's Laura with an agent, an unblemished spirit in perfect flesh, she is infinitely desirable: we know he'll be longing for her on the day he dies, if only because he has never touched her. As a token of her power to stir his imagination, even her appearance in the actual now has a tinge of the altered, heightened pseudo-reality of the hero's wish world, whose bridal candour, we come to realize, doubles as white mourning. When she and Guido are for a little while alone together, in the empty piazza in Filacciano, the authentic architecture around them, built long ago by other hands than Gherardi's, is the only setting in the film that looks artificial, and the breeze that stirs Cardinale's black feather boa blows only for her, rather in the way that the envoys from the beyond in Cocteau's *Orphée* are contained in their own micro-climate. Cardinale is Guido's dream walking, but when she realizes that he is idealizing her she laughs, and he realizes that she is right.

Another version of breathtaking unavailability is played by Caterina Boratto, as the guest at the spa who does nothing but descend the staircase of the grand hotel and cross the lobby. Statuesque in a personal cloud of white chiffon, she is a poised blast from the past of the Italian cinema. Boratto was a diva of those escapist movies, made at Cinecittà in Fascism's heyday, in which the protagonists indicated their luxurious lives (*Vivere!* was the title of her big hit of 1936: *To Live!*) by talking into white telephones. To present a white telephone star as a womanly ideal is Fellini's indication that in Guido's sexual imagination even the ideals of subtlety and refinement have something cartoon-like about them. The women in his brain are all caricatures. He knows they are, but he's stuck with it. His mind is in poor taste.

All the caricatures get together in one of the film's most elaborate sequences. When he hears the word *Asanisimasa* pronounced by his old friend the vaudeville mindreader, Guido is propelled back in his memory to a favourite place of his childhood, the barn fitted out as a small wine-factory – a *fattoria* – where he was teased, tucked up, looked after and generally spoiled by older women. Guido goes back to the same *fattoria* in his imagination, to stage a wish-fulfilment scene in which all the women in his life, along with all the women whom he would like to be in his life, live together in harmony: united, instead of divided, by their common desire for him. They all take their tune from the old peasant women who teased him and tucked him up. Their only role is to spoil him. They compete in nothing except subservience. His wife is there, smiling in acquiescence: she understands his needs. Every woman he has even fleetingly noticed in the course of the film's real-time story turns up as a worshipper. Women we have never seen before are there too: this place has been in business for a long time. A black girl dances through, flashing an open-mouthed white smile before snapping it shut. (I can still remember, from the first time I saw the movie, how a single American male groan outsoared the collective Italian male whimper in an audience whose females has already audibly made it obvious that they found the whole scene a *sciocchezza* – a foolishness.)

But this isn't just the place where Guido's dreams come true. It is also where they go sour. An early love, an exuberant soubrette, has outlived her desirability. Desperately she tries to interest him again but she stands revealed as just a not very good singer and dancer. Guido is ruthless with her: she has to go upstairs, where he consigns the women he no longer wants. (In real life, Fellini might have been ruthless with the actress who plays her: Boyer reports that the actress sang and danced too well, so he made her repeat the number until she was exhausted and in tears. However it happened, pathos certainly got into the scene.) Guido is suddenly recast as a monster. His dream women rebel, having realized that the same thing might happen to them. He has to get his whip out and drive them like animals. It is a clear confession, on Guido's part, that his sexual imagination is an unrealizable, incurably adolescent fantasy of banal variety and impotent control.

Just as clearly, it is Fellini's confession too. This is really why he made Guido a film director: not just to give him a believable role, but to show him cracking his whip over his tumultuous desires – to show him marshalling fantasies. Fellini is assuming that in this respect a film director is just everyman writ large, or at any rate writ more obvious. It is a big assumption, which will provide ammunition to condemn him if it is rejected as an excuse. Fellini's real-life wife, the distinguished actress Giulietta Masina, was on the set to witness the filming of 8½'s key scene. It was her dubious privilege to watch her husband's surrogate setting about his harem with a whip to bring them back into line. Masina had no doubt long before been made aware of Fellini's belief that what goes on in a man's mind he can't help, so he had better be judged on his conduct. What she thought of that belief is one of the many secrets of their long marriage. What Fellini thought of his wife is brought out explicitly in *Fare un Film*, where he ascribes their marriage to a decision of fate and would obviously, had he been a believer, have ascribed it to a decision of God. But you don't need to read his book to know what she meant to him. All you have to do is look at the films, which from *La Strada* onwards are about their marriage even when she is not in them. Sometimes, indeed, they are at their strongest on that subject when she isn't there. In *8½* Anouk's face, *la faccia*, is enough to establish that this wife is no willing victim but a strong, independent woman with as much class and style as her famous husband, if not more.

Anouk's incandescent performance shows why a director needs his prestige. Able to persuade her that she was participating in a serious project, Fellini talked her into acting against her charm and in line with her magnificent bone structure. Fully exposed by a boyish hairstyle, those knife-edged facial planes that kept her beautiful for decades could take on overtones of a hatchet when she was angry, and Fellini made sure that anger was almost the only emotion she was allowed to register. We are obliged to conclude that if this is a long-suffering wife, it isn't because she's a patsy. The film's moral edifice pivots on this point, because if it isn't accepted then the whole thing looks self-serving. The plot provides Luisa with a young, handsome, adoring admirer. She can't get interested in him. Is Fellini saying that she forgoes mere devotion because her faithless husband is more fascinating? Most feminists would say yes. They would have half a point, but only by hindsight. Fellini was a feminist *avant la lettre*: he had already proved that much with his early films, all of which feature, and some of which focus on, men's manipulation of women.

God knows he had enough to go on. In the early sixties Italy was still in the grip of a chest-beating male supremacy stretching back to the Borgias, among whom Lucrezia probably took up poisoning just to get some attention at the dinner table. The first week I was in Rome, the papers were running editorials about a young Italian male whose Dutch girlfriend had told him she wanted to break off their affair because her real boyfriend was about to arrive from Holland. The Italian boy stabbed her sixteen times with a carving knife. The editorials daringly suggested that this sort of thing was giving Italy a bad image abroad. It was still a bold innovation to suggest that the crime of honour was unforgivable. From Sicily as far north as Naples, if a girl refused a man's hand in marriage he could still get her by raping her, because then no other man would want her. (Scandal arose only when *he* didn't want her either, on account of her being no longer a virgin.) As for men pestering young women in the streets, there was no north and south: Milan was as bad as Messina. Foreign women suffered most. They were assumed to be whores just for being there. In Florence I used to get so angry at what I saw that it would spoil the visit. After the Florence flood in 1966 there was a startling change, which hit the other big cities not long after. Suddenly the women's magazines, which had previously been almost exclusively preoccupied with the mysteries of the trousseau, started carrying articles about how to divorce a sadistic husband without getting killed. Women's rights got a look in at last.

But anyone interpreting Italy then from the vantage point of now should realize that feminism was starting from a long way behind. Looking at Fellini's wide screens full of big breasts and accommodating thighs, it is easy to decide that he was part of the problem. The truth is that he was part of the solution. He was saying that men should be held responsible for what they did, not for how they felt. It was an especially important message for a country in which what men did could beggar belief. Trying to change the way a man felt who had just stabbed his girlfriend sixteen times, you might possibly persuade him to stab his next girlfriend only fifteen times. The trick was to call his outburst of passion by its proper name, murder. And to do that, you had to argue that passion was every man's property, and the management of it his responsibility.

Feminism was one of Fellini's touchstones of liberty. The anger he aroused in feminists later on was because of his other touchstones, one of them being the liberty to express the full squalor of the male mind. He did it with such bravura that it struck the censorious eye as a boast. It wasn't, though: it was an abasement, and Anouk's tight-lipped fury is there to prove it. '*Vacca!*' is the word she spits at the *culone*, Carla. It means 'cow' and in Italy it is a harsh word for one woman to use about another – the last word, the fighting word. Luisa is insulted by the banality of her rival. For Guido to take a mistress might have been forgivable. But if this is what he dreams of, what sort of man has she been living with?

If Fellini had not driven a wedge between how Guido thinks and how he acts, Guido would stand condemned, and Fellini along with him. But the wedge is there, in the beautiful form of Luisa. Guido once dreamed of her, too, and he is still involved with her even though she has become real – the best evidence that she must have been the most powerful dream of all. Luisa is what the German socialists used to call a *Lebensgefährtin*, a lifetime companion. Strong in her anguish, graceful even in despair, she is the true Felliniesque womanly icon. Anouk looked the part. Masina's misfortune was that she didn't. When it came to the crunch, she didn't have the right face to play herself.

In *La Strada* and *Nights of Cabiria*, Masina played the waif. She could be funny, resilient and even tough, but with a face like a doll she just couldn't transmit flint-like fury. You always wanted to pity her, and the point of Luisa is that she finds her husband pitiful, and hates him for it. Fellini followed *8½* with *Juliet of the Spirits*, the all-colour extravaganza which is nowadays the most neglected of his major films. This time Giulietta Masina plays the wife. With the inexorable proviso that her face is borrowed from a Cinderella who will never get to try on the shoe, the film is an opulent, radiant, unmanningly reverent tribute to her stature in Fellini's life. This was the last film Fellini made with Gherardi and Di Venanzo. They both excelled themselves. The sets are a cumulative marvel from an unsung opera and the photography makes colour film look as if it were being invented all over again. Giulietta's imagination and memory are explored like Guido's in *8½*. In addition, there are layers of Jungian analysis, parapsychology, voodoo and drug-induced hallucinations. Fellini subsequently told *Cahiers du Cinéma* that he didn't need LSD to have visions, but there can be no doubt that he was willing to try anything in order to give his votive offering to his wife the depth, weight and splendour he felt she deserved. The inescapable problem was that it was all within his gift. The idea was to show her liberating herself from her psychological burden. But it was his idea, not hers. In *Fare un Film*, Fellini movingly looked forward to the day when women would give us their view of the world. There could be no question of his generosity. But that day hadn't yet come, and for the meantime he was stuck with his own stuff.

*

He still had plenty more, but first he had a crisis to get through. *Juliet of the Spirits* tanked in a big way, he broke with Gherardi, lost Di Venanzo, swapped Rizzoli for Dino de Laurentiis, sailed straight into a real-life *8½* situation with a film he couldn't start, and wound up suffering from what seemed like terminal depression. Most directors would have quit at that point and gone off to give lectures, but Fellini was on the verge of a string of films that are, at the very least, all interesting sidelights on *8½*, and some of which, in one aspect or another, actually supersede it. Peter Bogdanovich once pointed out that Fellini's first few movies, the ones we rarely see, would have been enough to establish him as an important director. It should also be said, but rarely is, that the films after *Juliet of the Spirits* would have been sufficient to work the same trick. A few weeks ago, on a plane between London and Bangkok, I watched videos of *Fellini Satyricon* and *Fellini's Roma*. I still didn't enjoy *Satyricon* very much: except for the scene where the patrician married couple commit suicide to get away from the moral squalor – a clear echo of Steiner's unexpected yet inevitable exit from *La Dolce Vita* – it just doesn't offer enough relief from its own all-consuming animality. The people in it behave like pigs, but not even pigs behave like pigs all the time; sometimes they just lie there. (Fellini was too decent to be any good at decadence, and even if he had been, decadence dates: this is the reason some parts of *La Dolce Vita* now look *passé*.) *Roma*, however, came up fresh as paint. The traffic-jam scene is a far more effective comment on modern barbarism and insanity than anything in *Satyricon*, which was supposed to reflect our own age but made it look good by comparison. In *Roma*, the threat of industrial society's inhumanity is made real by the intensity of the humanity. The *trattoria* on the street, with the tram clanging past, looks like the way of life we all want but suspect that only the Italians have ever had. It was probably never quite that folksy in Rome: Fellini is remembering Rimini.

When I got back to London, *Amarcord*, the film that actually does remember Rimini, was showing on television as part of a memorial season. I had always recalled it as a delight, but now it looks like a masterpiece. It hasn't changed; perhaps I have. *Amarcord* (in the dialect of Rimini, the word means 'I remember') is like all the child-hood flashbacks in *8½* condensed into one. Saraghina is there again: a nameless tobacco vendor this time, but with breasts bigger than ever. Our young hero, appropriately called Titta, gets his head caught between them, and this counts as a big adventure. Everything here is small-time: the cinema, the bar, the square. The cars of the 'Mille Miglia' automobile race howl through town, but they are going somewhere else. The big, lit-up liner sails away. The citizens remain, eating, drinking, having families, and occasionally dressing up as Fascists. It takes a while for the viewer to realize that this is a film about Fascism, and longer still to realize that this is *the* film about Fascism. Especially in the late sixties, Fellini was accused of having said nothing about politics. He defended himself by saying that he saw politics purely in terms of personal liberty, and in *Fare un Film* he explains that the life led in *Amarcord* was the soil from which Fascism grew and can always grow: a life of arrested adolescence, narrow horizons, mean dreams, easy solutions and – saturating every-thing – ignorance. The film bears out his analysis in every respect. He shows the disease with a clarity that defines the cure: Fascism is undisciplined nostalgia, a giving in to childish wishes, the cuddle continued, the tantrum in perpetuity.

 Fellini's Casanova is the film he should never have made. Artisti-cally, it has some interest; strategically, it was a disaster. Some critics decided, on the strength of its weakness, that he had been an eroto-maniac all along. But *Casanova* is a dud precisely because Fellini was no pornographer. If he had been, his films would be running continuously on Eighth Avenue and making a lot of money. Casanova the seducer is the wrong hero for a man who wanted to submit to his women, not dominate them; Fellini craved their individuality, not their similarity. (So did Casanova, incidentally, but the statistics made it look otherwise.) Fellini had nothing but contempt for Casanova and wanted to prove it – a bad plan for an artist whose forte was his range of sympathy. The film was such an unequivocal stiff that you wept for Donald Sutherland, who must have felt honoured to be in it and devastated when it didn't work out. (Sutherland had previously starred in Larry Tucker and Paul Mazursky's *Alex in Wonderland*, a now forgotten but considerable homage to *8½*, in which a young American director has trouble starting a movie.)

Casanova is in Fellini's next big film and last masterpiece, *La Città delle Donne* (*The City of Women*, 1980) – only this time he is called Dottore Santo Katzone. (Since *cazzo* is the Italian word for 'cock' and -*one* is the enlarging suffix, the name means that he has a big one.) Katzone, like Casanova, is really just another version of Don Juan, and must suffer the same fate: to find his own endlessly repeated excitement an endless disappointment, to suffer the built-in letdown of the permanent hard-on. Katzone, though not on-screen long, is probably the best stab at Don Juan's pitiable doom since Mozart's. Bergman, in *The Devil's Eye*, gave his Don Juan too much finesse: his punishment is to have the woman disappear at the moment he embraces her, whereat he gently recoils with a polite sigh. Katzone gets what he wants, and it eats him up. He can feel himself coarsening even as he thickens, turning into one of the phallic sculptures that decorate his room, a petrified forest of dildos in which he is the only flexible component, and only just. Snaporaz, the film's hero, has no desire to be Katzone. Played by none other than Marcello Mastroianni in full panic mode, Snaporaz (the name seems to be one of Fellini's many code names for a liar) is, like Guido in *8½*, a married man battling his sexual imagination, but this time it's in colour, and the women of his desires come on in choruses, in kick lines, in cabarets with Las Vegas lighting effects: they slide down poles and go up in balloons. At the beginning, he gets off a train, and he spends the rest of the film trying to get back on. (It sounds like the same train scene that was cut from the end of *8½* when Fellini realized that the circus finale was the only possible wrap-up.) He is trying to hide out in his own fantasies, but the militant feminists are in there, too, and they want his guts for garters and his scrotum for a handbag.

Mastroianni's brilliantly conveyed helplessness didn't save the film's reputation. An unflinching portrayal of a man at bay was widely condemned as a conscienceless parade of unreconstructed male chauvinism. By this time, Fellini was routinely being called sentimental, even by critics who conceded the historical importance of his central films. Sentimentality was supposed to be his weakness. His case wasn't helped by *E la Nave Va* (*And the Ship Sails On*, 1983). The ship-of-fools format is a certain loser unless the ship makes landfall: we are given no tangible social life for comparison, so the artificial one on the ship has to refer to itself, with cramped results. But faces, as always with Fellini, stick in the memory: Pina Bausch playing a blind woman, staring straight out of the screen with eyes like those of the dead sunfish on the beach at the end of *La Dolce Vita*, when Mastroianni sees the girl who incarnates his lost innocence . . . Even at the end of Fellini's career, there was something in each new movie to remind you of all the others – something to remind you that there was a man behind the film, and that he had a woman beside him to whom he felt bound to explain himself. The explanation was always about the difficulty of marriage and the emptiness of the alternatives. It was always about Fellini and Masina. *Ginger and Fred* was charming, but unworthy of them: the story of a couple of old hoofers who couldn't really dance that well, it gave Masina and Mastroianni all too many opportunities to be cute. But Fellini and Masina *could* dance that well: they were people of majesty, not puppets of fate. Pathos was inappropriate.

*

I called some friends in the Czech Republic recently, who said they were looking forward to seeing *8½* the next evening on a satellite movie channel. Fellini distrusted television. In the later part of his life, when big movies were harder to finance, he made films for television, but he always disliked the restrictions: the TV screen didn't have enough information in it; the shot could never go deep; the lighting had to be too even. Above all, he disliked the atomization of the audience – one, two, or, at most, a few people in front of the set, eating, drinking and talking. He thought that the movie house as he had known it for most of his life was the last church. He valued its sacred aspect. Well, TV screens will get bigger, and the resolution will get better. It doesn't take a clairvoyant to envisage the day when all you can see in the cinema you will be able to see at home, without some lout behind you laughing through his popcorn at all the wrong moments. Every movie of any consequence that has ever been made will be there in front of you at the touch of a button. But *l'aspetto sacrale* probably won't be coming back. On the information highway, each of us is going to be alone in the middle of a hundred lanes of traffic. It will be a lot like trying to walk out of Los Angeles on the freeway system.

In any case, most of the entertainment that people all over the world touch their telephones to get will be manufactured somewhere in the San Fernando Valley. And I suppose a more horrible fate for the world can be imagined: American films at their most mindless have seldom been as toxic as any totalitarian country's films at their most sophisticated. On the whole, back in the sixties, we were right to restate our enjoyment of the old Hollywood as admiration, to turn fandom into scholarship.

But this development had one lasting deleterious consequence. The attention that had been focused on the great national directors of other countries began to lapse. Renoir, Bergman, Ray, Wajda, Kurosawa, Ozu, Fellini: we had been preoccupied with them for a long time; we had grown bored with endorsing their obvious eminence; and, anyway, they could look after themselves. So we sort of let them go. Yet they had something that their successors didn't always have – we could see that Truffaut might be another Renoir, but Godard obviously wasn't anything of the kind – and that the American directors didn't have at all. To begin with, the earlier masters were mainly true filmmakers, not just directors who were nothing without the right producer to bring them the right script. They developed a project from the beginning and got the whole of their country's life into it, and they went on doing this until they were old and grey. In America, Orson Welles might have done that if his personality had been different. Peter Bogdanovich might have done it if his life had been different. But it has always been hard to avoid the conclusion that what really needed to be different was America itself.

Not that Hollywood lacked a sense of history. Contrary to what foreign intellectuals usually thought and had such fun expressing, Hollywood always expended huge energy on getting the historical details right, right down to the buttons on the costumes. Where history went missing was in the people. Even today, when some of the cleverest people in the world are writing and directing Hollywood films, the characters on the screen are usually present only in the present. They haven't got a past, except as a series of plot points. They might say wise things, but not from experience. They are happily married until they love someone else, and then they leave the person they were with and go off to be happy with the other, as if love were some kind of moral imperative. And if one of the miracles of modern Hollywood is the energy that is lavished on these sleepwalking ciphers, another is how the people doing the creating often end up behaving like their creations.

Too many of the people busy with their careers in Planet Hollywood are just boys and girls, whereas a man like Federico Fellini was a man. Called 'sentimental' by those for whom his emotions were too big and too pure, he was really the enemy of sentimentality, which he had correctly diagnosed as being only a step away from cynicism. The typical aria of sentimentality is from an operetta: it breathes the perfumed atmosphere of *Leichtsinn*, that dreadful Viennese word which makes the heart heavy the moment it is sung. In *8½*, Mastroianni at first glance looks like a refugee from an updated production of *Die Fledermaus*. But there is no *Leichtsinn* here, no glibly wry tolerance of other people's suffering, no easily borne betrayals. Instead, there is melancholy. It comes from the self-examination without which life is not worth living. Fellini's is the tragic view of life, the gift of the old countries to the new ones where people think their life is over if they are not happy. It is the view of life formed in that aspect of the mind which, even when all the religions are dead, dying or preaching holy war, we still feel bound to call the soul. *Anima*: the word denotes a thing.

Fellini was by no means a perfect man. He was not an ideal man. He was a real one. His individuality resided in his being able to see what was universal about himself; he had a scope, within and without, that made him in postwar Italy what Verdi had been for the Risorgimento: the great cultural figure of Italy's recuperation, and, beyond his own country, one of the great men of the modern world.

Fellini was even beyond the cinema as a specific art. Though he was the master of all its techniques, he pursued it not as one art form among others but as if it were art itself. The last scene of *Les Enfants du Paradis* is magnificent, but it is just cinema. Its director, Marcel Carné, would have been lost without Jacques Prévert's screenplay, and Baptiste and Garance were only symbolically separated by the crowd flowing past the Théâtre des Funambules – they could have met again around the corner. The last scene of *8½* is often compared with Carné's flag-waving finale, but the difference is the difference between substance and stylishness, between a revelation and mere flair. Fellini's outburst of exuberance has a grief in it that leaves the children of paradise looking like the children they are –

patronized by their parents, the makers of the film. Fellini patronizes no one. He knows himself too well. When Guido joins the circle with his wife and all the people he lives and works with, the spectacle is no pretty ring out of an Arcadia by Poussin. It is an acknowledgment of a truth that the most prodigious artists realize with their souls, even if they sometimes deny it with their mouths: that, despite their uniqueness, they are not alone, that they live and work for the people, of whom each of them is only one.

The evidence suggests that Fellini, for all his mighty ego, was a man with no vanity (except about his thinning hair), and that he experienced his talent as a responsibility to be lived up to as long as his life lasted, even when his best collaborators were gone, the money had run out, the young directors who had hoped to emulate him had given up or gone abroad, and Italy's *mondo del cinema*, stripped of its atmosphere by the voracious gravity of Planet Hollywood, was reduced to a lifeless satellite. As long as the art prince Fellini was alive, the Italian film industry had a face.

But though *la faccia* is gone, *l'anima* yet lives. Fellini's films are already popping up everywhere, even out of the armrests of airline seats, and at least one of them will be watched in awe when human beings live in spaceships and have at last grasped that the longest voyage is inside the mind. *8½* will transmit the distillation of a national culture to an international, homogenized future that might well be condemned to have no other source of such qualities except the past. It is the work of a man who could realize his gift because he realized what a gift is. A gift comes from Heaven, as an elation of the spirit. For its recipient not to enjoy it would be ungracious, despite the grief it might bring – which is why Fellini told Marcello, before he began his long, weary walk down the corridor, to flick that foot.

New Yorker, 21 May, 1994

WHO *WAS* THAT MASKED MAN?

Peter Bogdanovich doesn't need a career, because he has a destiny. The same once applied to his hero Orson Welles, and it is a tribute to Bogdanovich's mind, soul and stature – all increasingly rare attributes in modern Hollywood – that the comparative powerlessness of his mature years should remind us so much of how Welles's exultant precocity came unstuck. In at least one dimension, the comparison works to Bogdanovich's advantage: his opening moves, though uncannily assured, might not quite have ranked with Welles's for their lasting impact, but his endgame, despite a private life undeniably baroque in some of its salient aspects, is showing a lot more class. Welles wound up narrating commercials for social-climbing brands of mid-price wine, and one of the reasons for his inability to get a film financed was that he was a spendthrift: prodigal even with peanuts, he was the enemy of his own best gift. Bogdanovich, though he might never be allowed to direct another movie, looks admirably determined to keep at least one side of his best gift well tended and fruitful.

Right from the jump, he could write about the movies with a cogency that placed him in the top flight of critics, and as an interviewer he has always been without peer. His latest book, *Who the Devil Made It* (Knopf), is just further confirmation of a quality he seems to have had since the cradle. When it comes to movies, the master of the medium is often a buff but rarely a scholar – he hasn't the time, even when he has the inclination – yet Bogdanovich somehow always managed to service his debt to the creativity of his past masters while he was busy with his own: articles and interviews, slim monographs and fat books were all done with manifest love, despite his being in a tearing hurry. Here, from the new book, is Bogdanovich on the Lubitsch Touch. First he defines it as 'a miraculous ability to mock and celebrate both at once'. Then he gives an example.

> In 'Monte Carlo,' alone in her train compartment, Jeanette Mac-Donald sings 'Beyond the Blue Horizon' in that pseudo-operatic, sometimes not far from ludicrous way of hers, and you can feel right from the start that Lubitsch loves her not despite the fragility of her talent but *because* of it: her way of singing was something irrevocably linked to an era that would soon be gone and whose gentle beauties Lubitsch longed to preserve and to praise, though he would also transcend them.

When a critic can quote so creatively, his criticism becomes a creation in itself. Among Bogdanovich's previous volumes, *Pieces of Time* remains a model of how a miscellany of pieces can add up to a lodestone, and *This Is Orson Welles* rivals Truffaut's mega-colloquy with Hitchcock as an example of how a sufficiently instructed disciple can get his master to talk revealingly about the nuts and bolts in the mechanism of his miracles. Bogdanovich was, and remains, the kind of star student who goes on studying after he graduates.

Being a star student was how he got into movies in the first place. He started off as an enthusiastic young archivist, putting retrospective screenings together for the Museum of Modern Art in New York. Catalogues for the retrospectives would include interviews with veteran directors, conducted *in extenso* by Bogdanovich himself. His licence to pester gained him entrée to the Hollywood studios, where in time he was allowed to try his hand as a director, perhaps because it was less trouble than showing him the door. After proving his competence with a low-budget effort called *Targets*, he was off and running like Craig Breedlove. But when his run of hits – *The Last Picture Show* (1971), *What's Up, Doc?* (1972), *Paper Moon* (1973) – was wrecked by the failure of the musical *At Long Last Love* (1975), his wunderkind's privilege of creative freedom was brutally withdrawn. (The memory of that deprivation must surely have been rekindled by the recent success of Woody Allen's *Everyone Says I Love You*, another musical full of people who can't sing, but this time with the sour notes meeting critical approbation.)

Bogdanovich, his career as a director already in irretrievable trouble, was then stricken by tragedy on a Greek scale. In 1980, his muse and mistress, a twenty-year-old *Playboy* centrefold named

Dorothy Stratten, was murdered by her low-life husband: *The Killing of the Unicorn* was what Bogdanovich titled his subsequent book about the event. On any objective scale, the Unicorn was not greatly talented as an actress, but Bogdanovich can be forgiven for thinking otherwise, because she was greatly beautiful. Unable to get over his loss, Bogdanovich began looking after her thirteen-year-old sister, whom he married seven years later; the dream lived on. But his fame faded, to the point where his name is now starting to sound foreign. Perhaps he never was a typical American in the first place. The tradition behind his work was American, but the way he *thought* of it as a tradition was European. Now that the work has dried up, the thoughtfulness remains, and might well be his lasting contribution.

Extraordinarily concerned in his films with the integrity of his technique and the burden of what he was saying with it, he has shown in his publications where he got that concern from: his predecessors. He was Hollywood's Mr Memory even while he was its golden boy. Now that he has become the Man in the Iron Mask, he is free to cultivate the archives at his leisure. Executives who played a part in condemning him to strangle in his own beard might be in for an unpleasant surprise. What makes them pygmies is that there once were giants: it's a cliché, but on the strength of the documentation assembled in *Who the Devil Made It*, Bogdanovich looks as if he might raise it to the status of an axiom.

The book comprises interviews with veteran filmmakers – Allan Dwan, Howard Hawks, Alfred Hitchcock, Fritz Lang, Sidney Lumet, Leo McCarey, Otto Preminger, Don Siegel, Josef von Sternberg, Raoul Walsh and others less famous though sometimes even more ready with illuminating war stories of their craft. These were (and sometimes are: a few yet breathe) men rooted in history as much as in Hollywood. Their collected memories make the past look fearfully rich beside a present that is poverty-stricken in everything except money. 'Whoever invented spending millions of dollars has absolutely ruined the picture business,' Allan Dwan told Bogdanovich in the late sixties. It might have sounded like an old man's bitterness then. Said today, it would simply sound accurate – except, of course, for the amount of money. For 'millions' read 'hundreds of millions'. A mere million buys you one pout from Val Kilmer in *The Saint* and maybe two drops of sweat from Tom Cruise in *Mission: Impossible* as he hangs there reprising the heist scene from *Topkapi* at a hundred times the outlay for a tenth of the impact. Today's blockbusters, despite the technical bravura of their components, rarely strike us as being very well put together: the tornado twists, the mountain blows up, the dinosaurs eat the scenery, and you are supposed to be lost in wonder, but instead you are left wondering why you are meant to care, because the characters risking death have never been alive and there would be no story without the scenes that interrupt it. The special effects leave NASA looking underfunded, yet the general effect, despite oodles of expertise, is one of a hyperactive ineptitude – of the point missed at full volume, as in the unstoppable monologue of a clever, spoiled child. Mountains of money in labour give birth to ridiculous mice. There's a reason, and this book's radiant bullion of reminiscence illuminates what it is.

To put it bluntly, the old guys had to tell a story because they couldn't blow up the world. There were limitations you couldn't spend your way out of, and in overcoming them lay the essence of the craft, its economy and brio. Don Siegel says it for all the others when he unveils the secret of shooting on the back lot: 'For instance, if there's an area which looks weak, I decide that I'll pan down to the feet of the guys walking and then come up where the area's good ... At the moment where it's weak, I'm closest to the feet. This is no hard and fast rule, just an example.' When you remember that one of the main reasons that *Heaven's Gate* nearly bankrupted United Artists was that Michael Cimino couldn't live with the idea of a background that looked weak for even a single square yard, you realize that there is a whole aesthetic, and hence a morality, embodied in Siegel's attitude. To accept and transcend limitation can be a source of creative vibrancy, whereas to eliminate it with money almost always leads to inertia. On his seventeenth, and last, day of shooting *Baby Face Nelson*, Siegel did fifty-five separate camera setups, and they're all in the picture. ('It cost $175,000 to make,' Siegel told Bogdanovich, 'and it took a lot of bookkeeping to make it *up* to $175,000.') Warren Beatty, given the choice, would have gone on editing *Reds* forever, but no amount of editing could lend tension to the footage, in which only Jack Nicholson behaved as if he owned a watch. *Reds*, a pioneering effort in the annals of modern wastage, was made in order to indulge the creative whims of its maker. *Baby Face Nelson* was a cynical, cost-conscious piece of exploitation. Which was the work of art? All right, which would you rather see again tonight?

Reality is a useful brake on megalomania. Besides this key point (continually and hearteningly endorsed by almost everyone in the book), there is plenty of other stuff that merits thoughtful attention from the current generation of moviemakers, who so often not only can't do anything small but don't even want to, except as a career move on the way towards doing something big. Leo McCarey took credit for very few of the hundred or so Laurel and Hardy films that he was effectively responsible for, but his vision shaped that of his actors. 'At that time,' he says, 'comics had a tendency to do too much.' (There has never been a time when they had any other tendency, but let that pass.) In *From Soup to Nuts*, Hardy as the *maître d'* came in to serve a cake. He tripped, fell, and buried his head in the cake. It was McCarey who shouted (in 1928 the audience couldn't hear him), 'Don't move! Just don't move! Stay like that!' Seeing it now, all you get to look at is Hardy's back, stock-still as you rock back and forth with the best kind of laughter – the kind you bring to the joke, participating in it with your imagination.

*

The movies are a collaborative art, then – or, rather, they were a collaborative art *then*, back at a time when the audience didn't feel left out. But this is to talk like a curmudgeon. Actually, there are more good, solid, humane, well-plotted, and well-acted movies being made now than ever before. Compare a densely textured political thriller like *City Hall* with the average FBI gangbusting melo of the forties – one of those movies in which the agents sneak up on the spies while a yelping commentator on the soundtrack tells you what they are doing (sneaking up on the spies). But there is no comparison. The movie business now is immeasurably more sophisticated than it used to be. Sophistication, however, is a two-edged sword. It abrades the innocent delight necessary for the making of, say, a screwball comedy. (Bogdanovich's triumphant latter-day contribution to the genre – *What's Up, Doc?* – is the surest testimony that we should put the best possible construction on everything that has happened to him since the death of Dorothy Stratten: only a man capable of deep love could celebrate a wild girl's pilgrim soul with so much joy.) And, above all, it erodes the concept of a modest sufficiency. It ought not to – in almost any other field, the sophisticated rein themselves in – but in the movies it somehow does. People who have made small, intelligent movies dream of making big, dumb ones, persuading themselves that if all values except production values are left out some kind of artistic purity will accrue.

So the creators get carried away. And they want to carry us away with them, but without giving us anything to hold on to except a train being chased by a helicopter through a tunnel. To adapt the famous words of Gertrude Stein, it is amazing how we are not interested. The hero *couldn't* be doing that, even if it looks as if he were, so the only point of interest is how they worked the trick. Whereas in the old days, even if he didn't especially look as if he were doing that, he *could* have been doing that. So we were with him, and we didn't care how they worked the trick. We let them care. That was their job. They didn't expect to have articles written about it, or to be interviewed – least of all in advance, before the movie was even finished. They worked from pride, but the pride was private. Somewhere in there is the difference between then and now. Then we participated in the movie without participating in its making. Now it's the other way around, and now will pretty soon become intolerable if we don't remember then. This book will help, like all of Bogdanovich's other books.

It might even help us remember his movies, which were marked from the beginning by a rare compassion for those blasted by fate. The great scene in his first great success, *The Last Picture Show*, was when Ben Johnson told the normal boys off for their 'trashy behaviour' in humiliating a halfwit. In one of his later movies, *Mask*, the director's challenge, met with subtlety and grace, is to transmit the awful self-consciousness of a superior mind as its grotesque containing skull closes in on it. Bogdanovich's understanding of fate's unbiddably cruel workings is rare among filmmakers anywhere in the world and almost unheard-of in America. He seems to have been blessed with it from birth. But the blessing brought a curse with it. Fate came for him, too. The killing of the Unicorn left him inconsolable. Since then, he has been living a story so sadly strange that not even he could plausibly make a movie of it. One would like to believe that he doesn't want to, since without a deep, literate conviction that the movies can't do everything, he would have less of a gift for celebrating everything they have done.

New Yorker, 7 July, 1997

FRONT-PAGE MONARCHY

PLAIN-CLOTHES POLICE STATE

A hidden camera is far enough. Intercepted telephone calls were already far enough, but we were too fascinated with the results to be sufficiently disgusted by how they were obtained. The results obtained by the hidden camera are nothing remarkable, if you discount the good looks of the subject, which we knew about anyway. The manner by which those good looks were on this occasion recorded, however, was so repellent that even the tabloid editors – including, apparently, the editor of the *Sunday Mirror*, after his fellow editors rounded on him – finally realized that a line had been crossed, although none of them seemed to grasp that they had all crossed the same line years before. Thugs who had been making a good living beating up helpless victims suddenly discovered that one of their number had supplemented his bare hands with brass knuckles. 'You fool,' they cried, 'don't you realize it's supposed to be *fists*?'

One of the characteristics of the totalitarian mentality is to erect opportunism to the status of a principle. To describe the behaviour of a pack of not very bright journalists in totalitarian terms might sound extreme. But it is another kind of wishful thinking, and a dangerously misleading one, to suppose that totalitarian impulses don't exist in a democracy. They are repressed, but they are there. One totalitarian impulse is to create a subhuman class which may be persecuted without compunction because it is beneath compassion. The moral squalor of French journalism under Nazi occupation was no sudden putrefaction. The rot set in with the Dreyfus case. Anti-Semitism polluted French journalism – even the higher, literary journalism – in a long process which had established the Jews as a special case well before the Nazis arrived to round them up.

Mass murder was only the sudden physical translation of a long spiritual contempt which had been propagated in French journals. Some of the journalists were not without talent. But they were without pity, and what had given their callousness free play was the principle of free speech. It was a cruel paradox.

In Britain the same paradox now ensnares the famous. It takes a less cruel form, and is scarcely likely to have such a vile outcome; but while being careful not to diminish a great tragedy by equating it with something inherently more trivial, one can still suggest that there is an instructive comparison to be drawn. In recent years there has been a steadily growing tendency to treat the famous as if they were without the right to a private life – always an important step in depriving a group of human dignity, even if, as in this case, there is no further wish to deprive it of life itself. (Quite the opposite: to ensure a supply equal to the demand, the press is ready to help almost anyone become famous, if only to provide fodder for the style-file supplements that we all deplore even as we fight over the first look.)

It can be said that with politicians and other public officials the private life and the public role are intertwined, so that everything they want concealed, even if it breaks no laws, should be open for inspection. (It *was* said, often, by Richard Ingrams of *Private Eye*, although when his turn came he was quick enough to decide that he had been a private citizen all along.) But the thin argument grows thinner still when it comes to those public figures who are famous for their achievements. Some of them seek publicity for all they do, and so should be ready to take the flak with the kudos; but clearly most do not, or, if they once did, learned better, holding, surely correctly, that the appreciation they attract is for their public performance, and that their private lives are their own business. Since most journalists obviously feel the same way about themselves, they know they are wrong to contend otherwise, but increasingly they have done so anyway, the contention growing more hysterical as its self-serving basis stands revealed. It has been years now since anyone prominent in any field could offer himself to be the subject of a profile without taking his life in his hands. By the time open season was declared on the Prince and Princess of Wales, bad faith among journalists had already whipped itself up into a righteous passion. It is often said in print, in the more august journals, that the royal family made a mistake in letting publicity into the Palace; but this is just a pious way of saying that they asked for it. The idea that they brought it on themselves is basic to the cast of mind which invents a subhuman class as a preparation for giving it the treatment. From the Peloponnesian war onwards, for the guards watching the prisoners starving in the rock quarry there has always been that consoling thought: *It's all their fault for letting us do this to them.*

The more august journals have had good sport in recent days pointing out that the less august ones are steeped in confusion, what with the *Sun* high-hatting the *Mirror* over tactics scarcely less questionable than its own. Posh editors ought to shed their delusions. To anyone on the receiving end of this stuff – which includes the public, who feel far closer to the Princess than to any editor – the press looks like one thing, and that thing is a juggernaut: oppressive, relentless and overwhelmingly nasty, a sort of plain-clothes police state. The cheap press stirs up the muck and the expensive press sifts through it, spreading it about so that everyone gets a whiff.

This unfortunate vertical integration of grunge and informed comment is naturally best exemplified by the Murdoch papers, whose upper-echelon editors have long been obliged to pretend that their colleagues down in the yellow depths have nothing to do with them. *Wehrmacht* commanders who claimed to have got all the way from Berlin to Moscow and back again without noticing what the SS was up to were not believed. Those who did notice but said it wasn't their responsibility deserved a hearing, but couldn't complain if they were heard sceptically. Not that I hold, as some do, that Rupert Murdoch is an evil tyrant. My energetic compatriot is not to be dismissed so easily. He is a man of principle. But the principle is commercial. He has well-reasoned intellectual objections to any institution that can't be quoted on the stock exchange. His broadsheet editors, however strong their illusion of independence, are perforce caught up in his heroic voyage to a future where no tradition, however hallowed, will restrain enterprise.

But other broadsheet editors should be slow to assume that they aren't at least partly in the same boat, even if they are kicking in the opposite direction to its drift. By discussing the mess that the tabloids have created, they can't help but reinforce the impression that the press has turned into a remorseless machine for chewing up the private lives of eminent people and spitting out the pieces.

Editors of responsible broadsheets and magazines, suitably horrified by this latest excess, nevertheless announce that a privacy law would be a cure more virulent than the disease. They are probably right, but could be surprised by the dearth of public outrage if such a law is brought in. Nobody outside the system really believes that voluntary curbs will work for long. Like Mr Murdoch's sudden conversion to a decent reticence, they will be seen as a stratagem, a lull declared by the storm. The best answer would be for the posh papers to leave the pop papers strictly alone in their strange world of soft-core pornography and freeze-frame soap opera. The pops would be less noxious if they were isolated. For that to happen, however, the political parties, and especially the Conservative Party, would have to stop cooperating with them. Hillary Clinton has never written a column for the *National Enquirer*. It is not pleasant for admirers of Virginia Bottomley's sunny face to see it smiling above her byline in some festering rag featuring transsexual mud-wrestlers on the opposite page, and it was always a poser, when Lady Thatcher was in power, to see her keeping company with Woodrow Wyatt, considering the company *he* was keeping in the *News of the World*.

Both in money and in votes it pays to slum, but the poisonous side-effect is to lend the junk papers legitimacy, and so foster the illusion that journalism is a profession, instead of what it is, a trade. Plumbing is a trade because the man who fixes your tap and the man who wrecks your sink are both called plumbers. Medicine is a profession because the man who takes out your diseased kidney is called a doctor and the man who takes out your healthy one and sells it is called a criminal. The solidarity between good and bad journalists is illusory. It would help if they were not all so keen to sit down together at such functions as the annual *What the Papers Say* luncheon, which I myself lost the urge to attend when I realized that I might inadvertently clink glasses with the editor who helped to kill Russell Harty.

Splitting the quality press from the trash press would not be easy, especially within the Murdoch empire as at present constituted, but if it could be done it would at least have the benefit of resolving the permanent identity crisis of Peter McKay, who fills half his column in one kind of paper lamenting the fatigue induced by reading about the Princess of Wales in the other kind of paper, to which he himself regularly contributes on the subject of the Princess of Wales. Ben Jonson would have made him the hero of a play. Kinder spirits would put him out of his misery.

Meanwhile the Princess of Wales is in hers, and the Prince along with her, if I know him. I do know him to speak to, and her too, but in both cases the speaking acquaintance will undoubtedly evaporate when this piece comes out, because both of them must have long ago grown sick of having their relationship talked about in the press, and the press definitely includes *this* part of the press talking about *that* part of the press. But with the damage done, I might as well throw in my two cents' worth, to go with the million dollars' worth of unsolicited advice that the sundered twain are inundated with every day. I think that the Prince and Princess of Wales, much as they both loathe what press intrusiveness has done to them since their separation, have rather underestimated its role in driving them apart in the first place, and that if they could put some of the blame where it belongs, instead of all of it on each other, they might be persuaded to get back together behind the barricades, if only to put up a fight against this monster before it consumes the rest of us.

The monster is not republicanism, but press intrusion into private life. As it happens, I am for the monarchy, but only as a preference. In my own homeland, Australia, the alleged tide of republicanism is already flowing the other way, largely because the people have begun to remember that Prime Minister Keating, who is so certain about Australia's future as a self-assertive nation state, was once equally certain, when he was Treasurer, about its future as an economic miracle. The benefits of retaining an off-shore, cost-free head of state who is out of politics and sets a limit to ambition have begun to sink in, helped by the stridency of the abolitionists, whose personal aspirations are all too apparent.

Even if Australia were to go republican, however, the monarchy here, though it would be badly damaged, would probably survive. It will probably survive even if the Prince and Princess of Wales divorce, although if the explosion propels young William early to a tottering throne he won't thank his parents for giving him a broken home as a prelude. What might or might not happen to the monarchy, however, is not the main reason why these two should renew their alliance. The main reason – and this comes from conviction, not from mere preference – is that they have let the press define for them what a marriage is, and in so doing have made a mistake with potentially ruinous consequences for everybody.

The press is not qualified to keep the conscience of the married.

At almost every level, with the occasional exception of a proprietor miraculously immune, its practitioners have done everything except stay married. They know more about divorce and remarriage than they know about marriage. For the Prince and Princess of Wales the journalists promoted an ideal marriage, and then detected a bad marriage, and finally condemned a sham marriage, but in all three cases it was a fantasy, because all they had ever been talking about was a difficult marriage, and all marriages are difficult. Every marriage has something wrong with it. Marriage has something wrong with it. What it has wrong with it is people. The more individual they are, the less they are designed to live together. If two people were meant to live together easily they would have half a personality each. Mr and Mrs Rupert Murdoch might be an ideal couple – he bringing out the *News of the World*, she running the beautiful house in which it is never read – but scarcely any other couple is. A lasting marriage isn't dreamland: it is reality.

As things are now, the Princess, though brave as a lioness, is being dragged down. The Prince should overrule any advice from his camp which suggests that he can survive her fall uninjured. He will be dragged down next. They have already had sufficient experience of living apart. The time has come for them to live apart together, drawing what profit they can from everything they have so harshly found out. With their private life restored, they might each love other people. It would be no great innovation. Most people who love once love again, and have even been known to fall for the person they once married, after realizing that the person they let go was in a trap, and the trap was in themselves. We might delude ourselves that what happens to the beleaguered couple in private will still be our concern, but really it will be unknowable, as marriage, in its essence, always is. But there will be an important practical result.

They will be back in business, and for that they both have excellent qualifications, both mutually and as a complement. We have been encouraged to forget, in the hubbub, that the Prince of Wales is a man out of the common run, a fact he would have had less trouble proving had he been born a commoner. (Indeed if you think that the chief role of the royal family is to exemplify an ordinary life, his excess of ability has always threatened to unbalance the whole institution.) What has been less noticed about the Princess, largely because of her startling glamour, is that she has a good mind too. It is not an academic mind (journalists who read three books a year have always been swift to point that out) but it is an original one, and she has learned to speak it with increasing precision, even as the hyenas close in.

On the subject of the children they are more in agreement than they might suppose. One of the first things I heard him say was how determined he was, when some potentate gave him a miniature electric-powered sports car for the boys to ride in, that the boys would never get to see it. When the Princess flies economy class with the boys now, she is pursuing the same idea. They might have different opinions about how to realize it, but the aim is the same. They both want the children to know what reality is, and there she can help him. Neither of his parents was born as heir to the throne: he has had to find too much out for himself. She knows all there is to know about being a child from an unreal background.

In that last dubious advantage lies the key to those qualities she has more of than he does. The reaction she gets in the hospitals and the hospices is no mere contrivance. The wounded and the lonely spot her immediately as one of them. And even if there were an element of the actress, how bad would that be? Female journalists whose every sentence is an imposture are fond of belittling her as histrionic, but where do they suppose the histrionics come from? If she plays a part, she plays it from a deep impulse, and from the same impulse comes an authentic gift for making the weak feel that they have a representative. No wonder the Queen seems desperate at the thought of losing her.

For all I know, the Princess is a hell of a handful close to. But she is a man's woman if I ever saw one. Falling for her is a lot easier than falling off a log. The problem is what to do about her next. Having married her, the Prince was obliged to watch her grow and change, while she had to cope with all the ways in which he was determined not to alter. I imagine his life-lines entangled her like a net. Their life together would have been difficult anyway. But publicity made it impossible. It was just too good a story.

The only way out of the story is to get back to reality. With private life regained, their public life might be managed better. It will still be to some extent a PR operation, but at least the publicity will be for something that can thrive in the limelight, as no marriage ever has, or ever can. They will have a battle on their hands, but even if they are living apart, if they are living apart together they are well equipped to fight. All he needs to accept is that he is the Hurricane and she is the Spitfire. In the Battle of Britain, the Hurricane was the worthy gun-platform that could take the punishment and the Spitfire was the bobby-dazzler that could turn inside the German fighters and demoralize their pilots with its sheer speed. The Spitfire broke them up and the Hurricane knocked them down. In the flypast afterwards, the Spitfire flew first and got most of the publicity. But it took both of them to win. There is a hint there about protocol. The Prince might consider letting her walk in front to mop up the photo flash, while he takes the credit for his wisdom. A change in procedure is all it will be.

But the institution will have been preserved. And let us be in no doubt about what institution that is. It isn't just the monarchy, which might very well be coming to the end of its time, although I hope not at the hands of those who see a role for themselves in its replacement. It is private life, the touchstone of civilization, our only guarantee against the mob – which is us too, but at our worst.

Spectator, 20 November, 1993

REQUIEM

No. It was the first word of that cataclysmic Sunday morning: 'no' pronounced through an ascending sob, the consonant left behind in the chest voice as the vowel climbed into the head voice, the pure wail of lament whereby anyone, no matter how tone deaf, for one terrible moment becomes a singer. But there was not one terrible moment. There were, still are, hundreds of them, joining up in a long aria of anguish interrupted only by exhaustion. Hundreds of millions of people who loved her but never met her must be crying like this. Those who did meet her, and knew her faults, should have some detachment. But somehow it works in reverse. The physics of this unprecedented metaphysical explosion, this starburst of regret, are counterintuitive, like relativity. The more you know she was never perfect, the less you, who are not perfect either, are able to detach the loss of her from the loss of yourself, and so you have gone with her, down that Acherontic tunnel by the Pont de l'Alma and into the Halls of Dis, the inane regions, where loneliness is the only thing there is, and the lost are together but can never find each other, because it is like looking for a shadow in the dark.

No, there was not much I knew about her. But I knew it well. At one period, starting either just before or just after her official separation (I can't remember, and although a glance at the dates of her letters to me would tell me, I can't bear to look at them) and ending well before her death, I lunched with her often enough to goad the lurking press into some arch speculation about whether I was helping to mastermind her PR campaign, especially on television, my area of expertise. Rather to my secret disappointment, it was taken for granted that there was no romance. (My wife, well aware that she is married to a romantic egomaniac, found that aspect particularly amusing.) When the mid-market tabloids ran a page of photographs featuring the men supposedly in Diana's life, my photograph was always among the venerable, sometimes senescent, advisers, never among the young, handsome and virile suitors. The assumption was that although she might listen to what her privy counsellors said, she would never look at any of them twice. In my case, that assumption, unlike the one about my role as the *éminence grise* behind her television adventures, was dead right.

No, there was nothing between me and her beyond a fleeting friendship. Many other men knew her better. Some men knew her intimately, and now, at last, I do not envy them, because what they have in their memories must make loss feel like death. (I never thought I could be sorry for James Hewitt, the dim former cavalry officer who repaid her for her favours by selling his story, but think of where he is now, deprived even of the reason for his ruin, his empty head already rotting on Traitors' Gate.) As for the man who knew her most intimately of all, Prince Charles, he is a man as good and honest as any I have ever met, and I know him well enough to be sure that today he is on the Cross, and wondering whether he will ever be able to come down. My own knowledge of her is minute compared with his and theirs, but now, for the first time, I wish I had never met her at all. Then I might not have loved her, and would not feel like this, or at any rate would feel it less. But I did meet her, and I did love her.

No, it was not a blind love: quite the opposite. Even before I met her, I had already guessed that she was a handful. After I met her, there was no doubt about it. Clearly on a hair trigger, she was unstable at best, and when the squeeze was on she was a fruitcake on the rampage. But even while reaching this conclusion I was already smitten, and from then on everything I found out about her at first hand, even – especially – her failings and her follies, only made me love her more, because there were none of her deficiencies that had not once been mine, and some of them still were. In her vivid interior drama I saw my own. I didn't find out much, but what I did find out I found out from close up, from a few feet away across a little table; and I knew it certainly, and it made me love her more truly. I was even convinced (this was not for certain, but it was a deep and ineradicable suspicion) that she would get herself killed, and that conviction made me love her to distraction, as if I had become a small part of some majestic tragic poem: an obscure, besotted walk-on mesmerized by the trajectory of a burning angel. I feared for her as I loved her, and the fear intensified the love. It was too much love for so tenuous a liaison, and one of the reasons I never spoke of it in public was a cheaper fear – the simple, adolescent fear of appearing ridiculous.

No, you don't have to tell me. I am appearing ridiculous now, but it is part of the ceremony, is it not? And what flowers have I to send her except my memories? They are less than a wreath, not much more than a nosegay: just a *deuil blanc* table napkin wrapping a few blooms of frangipani, the blossom of broken bread. London has gone quiet; the loudest human sound is the murmur of self-communion; and we are told that half the world has done the same. In the old times, when the plague came, people would cast off their sense of self, say what was on their minds, find what had always been in their minds but had remained unsaid even to themselves, and make love to strangers. There will be no *Totentanz*, this time, no orgies, no mass kicking over of the traces. But there will be something of the same liberation from the very British drive to protect the self, and I will be surprised if some of the new openness does not remain. The lake of flowers submerging Kensington Palace has released a perfume that has changed the air. And although those who did not participate in the vigil might sit in judgement on us for our mass delusion, we will judge them, in our turn, for their inhuman detachment.

No, nobody can escape her image in these days after her death – it is as if the planet were being colonized with her replicated smile – and each time I see it, it brings back a reality that was even lovelier. I first saw Diana – the living human being, not the image – at the Cannes Film Festival. Sir Alec Guinness was getting a lifetime-achievement award, I was to be the master of ceremonies at the dinner, and Charles and Diana had come down from London just for the evening. There was a reception beforehand. The whole British film world stood around nursing drinks. It was like watching a movie composed of nothing except cameo appearances. A bit of some TV crew's lighting rig fell on a PR girl's head and she regained consciousness in the arms of Roger Moore: she thought she was in a James Bond movie. Then Charles and Diana came in and started working the room. With astonishment, I suddenly found myself on the roster of familiar faces Diana wanted to meet. There she was, right in front of me, and I instantly realized that no kind of film, whether still or moving, had done her justice. She wasn't just beautiful. She was like the sun coming up: coming up giggling. She was giggling as if she had just remembered something funny. 'I think it's terrible what you do to those Japanese people. You are *terrible*.' She was referring to the clips from Japanese game shows which I screened on the TV programme that I hosted each week. I started to protest that they were doing that crazy stuff to each other; it wasn't me doing it to them. But she quickly made it clear that she was only pretending to be shocked. She said she never missed my show and always had it taped if she was out. While I was still feeling as if, all at once, I had been awarded the Booker Prize for fiction, the Nobel Prize in Physics, and the Academy Award for Best Actor, she switched the topic. 'Ooh. There's that odious man Maxwell over there. Don't want to meet *him* again. Yuck.'

No, she really meant it. She made a face as if she had just sucked a lemon. And that did it. I was enslaved. Looming hugely at the far side of the stellar throng, the publishing tycoon Robert Maxwell was doing his usual simultaneous impersonation of Victor Mature and King Farouk: a ton and a half of half-cured ham wrapped in a white tuxedo, his pan-scrubber eyebrows dripping condescension like spoiled lard. At the time, the old crook hadn't yet been rumbled. Some of the cleverest men in Britain were still working for him and helping to vilify anyone who questioned his credentials. But this young lady, with a head allegedly composed almost exclusively of air, had the bastard's number. On the other hand, after knowing me not much more than a minute she had just handed me a story that would have embarrassed the bejesus out of the Royal Family if I had passed it on: it would take only one phone call, and next morning the front page of every British tabloid except Maxwell's *Mirror* would consist almost entirely of the word 'Yuck'. Either she was brave to the point of insanity or else I radiated trustworthiness. I decided it must be the latter. For the air of complicity she had generated between us in so brief a time, the best word I can think of is 'cahoots'. We were in cahoots.

No, it couldn't last. With the two-minute mark coming up, she started regretfully signalling that our lifelong friendship would have to be temporarily put on hold. Her pursed lips indicated that although she would rather stay talking to me until Hell froze over, unfortunately her duties called her away to schmooze with far less illustrious people than me. Her mouth saying that she was looking forward to my speech, her eyes saying, 'Plant you now and dig you later,' she fluttered a few fingertips and swanned off in the direction of Sir Alec. What would she say to him? *Help me, Obi-Wan Kenobi. You're my only hope.* I wish I hadn't just thought of that.

*

No, I didn't see her again for a long time. But I thought of her often, and especially when I saw Charles. In those days, I was one of the outer ring of his advisers. The system worked – probably still works – like this. The inner ring of advisers are on call full time for anything. In the outer ring, you get called to the centre when the upcoming job touches on your areas of competence: in my case, television, Australia and occasionally the arts. Flattered to get the nod, I gladly made trips to see him. Born to a life in which people magically appeared when needed, he sometimes had trouble remembering that his fifteen minutes with you at Highgrove or Sandringham would cost you a whole working day, but apart from that he was impeccably sensitive, courteous, and just plain thoughtful – a quality of his which is continually underestimated, and one which will make him a great king when his turn comes, as come it must. (Diana's declaration, in her *Panorama* interview, that Charles might never reign was the single biggest mistake she ever made, but haven't *you* said foolish things about the person you loved after it all went wrong?) Our meetings, though invariably friendly and increasingly funny, were always strictly business, so it was no surprise that Diana wasn't around. But when my wife and I asked him to dinner he came alone, his wife was never mentioned, and sadly I began to realize that that was no surprise either. The word was out that they were sticking together for the sake of the monarchy and the children but were otherwise going their separate ways.

No, it couldn't go on like that. I still think it should have, and right up to the divorce I published articles in the *Spectator* saying that they owed it to all of us to stick together somehow, or else the press would be confirmed in its hideous new role as a sort of latter-day Church of England with witch-finders for priests. But I was making the fundamental mistake of being more royalist than the King. The two people at the centre of events were pursuing happiness, American style, and it was becoming more obvious all the time that they had known enough unhappiness to justify the pursuit. During

Charles's fortieth-birthday party, at Buckingham Palace, I met her again. There were no cahoots this time. She said that she had enjoyed my latest documentary and that she was glad to see me, but she didn't seem to be glad about anything else: the lights in her face were dimmed down to about three-quarter strength, so she looked merely lovely, at a time when her full incandescence should have been outshining the chandeliers. Charles did his formidable best to jolly everyone along. The Duchess of York chortled around in her usual irrepressible manner, a bumper car in taffeta. It was fun to go for a piss, stand in a reverse lineup of hunched dinner jackets, and gradually discover that I was the only man staring at the porcelain who was not a crowned head of Europe. But generally there was something missing, and nobody could be in any doubt what it was. She was still there physically, but her soul had gone AWOL; and without that soul the party had no life.

No life, and no future. Soon the press were piling it on, and steadily the intrusiveness got worse. It became known that she was trying to lessen the effects by getting a few media figures on her side. It was manipulation, but what else does a marionette dream of except pulling strings? So I thought I knew what it was about when she sent me an invitation to lunch at Kensington Palace. I thought there would be at least half a dozen of us there to receive the gentle suggestion that a few supportive words would not come amiss. (Even for my generation, words like 'supportive' are losing their inverted commas by now: her unashamed use of me-speak has influenced the language.) But after I was shown up the staircase to the sitting room I found myself alone. When she came into the room, it was as if that first conversation in Cannes had been frozen by the pause button and now the button had been touched again to re-start the tape. 'Sorry there aren't any film stars,' she said. 'There's just me. Hope you don't get bored.' The cahoots were back. We sat down at a small table in the next room and immediately established the protocol that would become standard, and which I will always cherish as one of the best running gags I was ever involved in. She ate like a bird while encouraging me to eat like a wolf, as if I weren't being fed properly at home. There was a catch under the joke: that I *had* a home, she made it clear, was enviable. She envied me my long marriage. When I told her that I had been a neglectful husband and father, and that my guilt had begun to erode my peace of mind, she said that I must have done *something* right, if we were all still together, so I should take comfort from that. Her own marriage, she said, was coming apart. She told me why and how. I could hardly credit my ears. Armed with nothing else except what she told me then, I could have gone to a telephone and blown the whole thing sky high. But the cahoots ruled that out. The tacit bargain was: You tell me what you can't tell anyone else and I'll tell you what I can't tell anyone else, and then neither of us can tell anyone else about what we said.

No, it wasn't mutual therapy. But I suppose it was a mind game. There must have been dozens of other people that she played it with, but she infallibly picked those who would never break the deal. (If she had chosen her lovers on the same principle, she would have given a lot fewer hostages to fortune, but desire doesn't work like that.) She would make each of her platonic cavaliers believe, or at any rate want to believe, that he was the only one. The joker in her real life doubled as the ace of diamonds in the game: it was her childhood. Everything in her tormented psyche turned on what had happened to her at the age of six, when her parents separated and left her to a loneliness that nothing could cure. Then, while I was clearing her plate after I had cleared mine, she popped the question: 'Something like that happened to you, didn't it?' It was the Princess of Wales who was asking me, so I gave her the answer. Yes, it did. When I was six, my mother got the news that my father had been killed on the way home from the war.

No, my mother cried. No, no, oh no. I was the witness of her distress, I couldn't help her, and I had been helpless ever since. I sometimes thought, I said, that everything I had ever written, built or achieved had been in order to offset that corrosive guilt, and that I loved the world of women because I feared the world of men. Diana touched my wrist, and that was it: we were both six years old.

No, it was no trick. It might have been a mind game, but her mind was her most vivid reality, the battlefield on which she looked for peace. It was a good mind, incidentally. Of all the poisonous dreck ever written about Diana in the newspapers, the most despicable was based on the assumption that she was stupid. Journalists who read three books a year and had scarcely two ideas to rub together about anything called her an ignoramus. The truth was the opposite. Schopenhauer ('Chopin who?' I can hear her say), who was a great reader himself, pointed out the danger of letting books get between us and experience. What Diana knew was based on experience, and she knew a lot, especially about the mind. Well aware that her own was damaged, she sought comfort from those who would admit to the same condition. She spent too much time with gurus, spiritualists and exotic healers, but that wasn't frivolity: it was desperation. For the rest of the time, which was most of it, she had a remarkable capacity to do exactly the opposite of what she was notorious for: far from being obsessed with her own injuries, she would forget herself in the injuries of others. It was the secret of her appeal to the sick and the wounded. When she walked into a hospital ward, everyone in it recognized her as one of them, because she treated them as if they could have been her. They *were* her. She was just their souls, free for a day, in a beautiful body that walked so straight and breathed so easily. The sick, she would often say, were more real to her than the well: their guard was down, they were themselves.

*

No, I didn't figure all that out straight away, but as time went on it became more apparent to me that I was her patient. I missed her after that first lunch, with a mild version of the forlorn longing I have seen among friends of mine when their shrinks go on holiday. So I did something so presumptuous I still don't believe I had the brass neck to go through with it. *I* asked *her* to lunch. The separation was practically official by now, she was kind of up for grabs, so why not, you know, *ask her to lunch*? I made the phone call to her secretary and hung up feeling like someone who was going to get a flea in his ear the size of a hummingbird. But ten minutes later the secretary was back on the line. The Princess of Wales would be delighted. How about the Caprice?

No, I didn't get there half an hour early – only twenty minutes. I took up my elaborately casual position at the corner table, double-cleaned my fingernails with my door key, and watched the forecourt through the window. As always, she was on time to the minute. When she stepped from the chauffeur-driven car, it wasn't just the way she looked that stymied me. *No escort.* She had been threatening for a while to start going out without an escort, and now she was actually doing it, the crazy little twit. The chill of fear I felt was probably useful in making me appear cool as I rose for an air kiss that stopped every knife and fork in the room, as if time had been switched off. The rattle of cutlery started again after she sat down, and there we were, tête-à-tête. It wasn't cahoots yet, though. By this time, two camps had formed, Charles's and Diana's. Diana's people were busy calling Charles a stuffed shirt, and Charles's people were just as busy calling Diana a dingbat. I wanted to make it clear to her that I was for both of them, and against anything that would make them irreconcilable. I couldn't, either in public or in private, say a word against the Prince. Putting it in jokey form – always her preferred way of hearing a lecturette – I told her that if we were caught talking high treason she would be given the privilege of dying by the sword, whereas I, a commoner and a colonial, would be lucky if they even bothered to sharpen the axe. She laughed, said she understood completely, and made it evident that she admired Charles's qualities as much as I did. Things bubbled along nicely. Cahoots again. I got both our meals to eat as usual, and from the next table the director-general of the BBC was looking at me as if I were a combination of Errol Flynn and Neil Armstrong. He was stuck with the Home Secretary. Christ, what fun she was. But the chill of fear came back when she started to talk about the possibility of going on television with a personal interview. I knew it wouldn't be with me, but that wasn't the reason I counselled her against it. I said if that happened the two-camps thing would go nuclear, and continue until there was nothing left. She would be on the run forever, and there would be nowhere to go. Nowhere would be far enough away. She seemed convinced, but of course she was pretending. She had already decided.

No, she wasn't always the straight goods. She often pretended. She would listen to advice and warnings that – as you'd later discover – had been rendered obsolete by what she had already done, and pretend to consider them. Then, when the news came out, you found that she had been watching you lead yourself up the garden path. It could hurt.

No, I don't think she was being malicious, or even mischievous. There was just a lot of stuff she couldn't share. At least once, however, she lied to me outright. 'I really had nothing to do with that Andrew Morton book,' she said. 'But after my friends talked to him I had to stand by them.' She looked me straight in the eye when she said this, so I could see how plausible she could be when she was telling a whopper. I would have been terminally pissed off if I hadn't suspected that she knew I knew, and just didn't want to be remembered as admitting it. In the *Panorama* interview, she did admit it, so I had two reasons for feeling that historic programme as a personal wound, quite apart from my premonition that it would wound her. It multiplied her popularity, but it propelled her in the direction I had spent a lot of time telling her she should never think of going: over the wall, out of the country, away from her protection.

No, there was no chance she would listen. She *hated* the protection. She saw the protectors as assailants. She believed, against all the evidence of her own beautiful eyes, that there was some kind of enchanted place called Abroad, where she would be understood and where she could lead a more normal life. This place called Abroad became a recurring theme in future conversations at other restaurants. Kensington Place, in Kensington Church Street near Notting Hill Gate, was one of her favourite hangouts, and she thought it funny that I always booked a table against the back wall, instead of up front, near the window. There was an acre of unshielded glass and she – *she* – wanted to sit near it. It scared me rigid. Sometimes I could barely eat my own lunch, let alone hers. But it seemed she would rather have gone down in a hail of broken glass than live in fear. She could live in her own fear – the fear of never finding happiness, of never making the pieces fit, of Mummy and Daddy never being together again – but she could never live in mine, the fear for her life.

No, she never took my advice even once. Well, just once. Before she went to Japan on her big solo diplomatic trip, she asked me what would be the best thing she could do there, apart from all the hospitals and stuff. She knew that I was a student of the Japanese language and Japanese literature, and she thought I might have some nifty scheme up my sleeve. I told her I did, but it wouldn't be easy. I told her that if she learned even a few words of the language – just the standard phrases about how pleased she was to be there – she would knock them out. I could lend her my teacher, a gentle but determined little woman called Shinko. Diana, after her standard protestations about being too thick, said she was up for it. Shinko, quietly experiencing the same emotions as I would have done if I had been asked to teach the Emperor of Japan croquet, marched up to Kensington Palace and did the job. Diana flew to Japan, addressed a hundred and twenty-five million people in their own language, and made the most stunning impact there since Hirohito told them that the war was over.

No, she didn't forget. When she got back, she called me to lunch at Bibendum. We did all our standard numbers, culminating in the hallowed dessert routine, by which I ordered one crème brûlée with two spoons and finished the rest of it before she had swallowed her single mouthful. As usual, she had finessed that deadly third glass of wine into me without my even noticing. But there was an extra *petit four* with the coffee. It was a little red box that opened to reveal a pair of cufflinks: gold ovals enamelled in pink with the chrysanthemum of the Japanese imperial family. '*Domo arigato gozaimash'ta,*' she said. Thank you very much for what you did. 'Did I get that right?' Yes, I told her: you got that right.

No, there is not much more. Our last lunch was at Kensington Palace and Harry was present with one of his friends, so there were no cahoots. She was putting distance between us. Later on, quietly and nicely, I was dropped from her list. I understood completely. I had wanted her to be Queen. I had wanted, when I grew old, to see her in the gradually, properly altering beauty of her middle age. I had wanted to see her beside Charles, on the day when he took his proper place as the most intelligent and concerned monarch this country has ever had. I had wanted to have lunch with her once a year and do the dessert routine again. But she wanted life. She was going on to those other, faraway adventures which she knew I didn't believe in. I hoped I would hear about them someday.

No, I never saw her again. Neither will anyone now. Not even once. Never even once again.

No, I can still see her. She's leaving the Caprice, heading for the back door, because a Range Rover full of photographers has just pulled up in the street outside. She's turning her head. She's smiling. Has she forgotten something? Is she coming back?

No.

New Yorker, 15 September, 1997

POSTSCRIPT TO A REQUIEM

Complete with all its stylistic arabesques, the preceding obituary is reproduced in the form it took when it was first published in the special edition of the *New Yorker* which appeared in the week of the accident. The following weekend, a slightly shorter version appeared in Britain, in the *Sunday Telegraph*, and that was the version which was subsequently reprinted, sometimes in further abridged form, in newspapers and magazines in other languages, and was reproduced in its entirety in the book *Requiem* which came out to mark the anniversary. Not at my initiative, but with my agreement, the second version was shorn of the first version's opening paragraph. Some London journalists, usually professing more sorrow than anger, had taken particular exception to this, quoting it dutifully as evidence of how at least one of Diana's admirers had lost his head. Even the second version, as I have subsequently discovered, provides ample opportunity for critics deploring the state of modern journalism (or anyway deploring the modern state of *my* journalism) to demonstrate how a once-keen critical brain can be softened to sponge cake by the moist air of celebrity. When the *Requiem* volume came out, one of its reviewers – somehow contriving to forget that it was he, and not I, who was a member of the sweating team of Stakhanovite shock-workers currently pouring forth yet another load of loosely mixed sand and gravel on the topic of Diana – kindly said of my piece that I must have regretted ever having written it.

When I read what he and some of his colleagues said, I *did* regret having written it, but only for the moment. Self-justification is a bad reason for writing a postscript to anything, but I would be conspiring at my own hanging if I failed to record that on this topic my fellow scribblers were the only people I heard from who said that I had done the wrong thing. Other people said that I had spoken for them. From all over the world I received letters by the hundred. The harshest

admonishment any of them proffered was that if I had let grief
unhinge my equipoise, that was only appropriate, because they too
had felt bereavement with such force that all their normal stability
had trembled on its base. To be fair to my colleagues in the media,
those I knew personally were ready – unusually ready, but those were
unusual times – to concede that my cry from the heart had struck a
note whose authenticity they recognized, even if it had come from
a heart that had spent too much of its existence worn on a sleeve.
One famously unfoolable TV critic had been telling me for years that
the Royal Family was a swindle perpetrated on honest labourers such
as herself. She phoned me in such a fit of tears that she could hardly
choke out her message, which was that her anguish was made worse
because she had not expected it could ever happen – that she too
had been slammed into a wall, and all her best hopes for herself had
been stopped with no appeal. Since she had previously, in private if
not in print, been vocal in her opinion that Diana was a genetically
engineered hybrid of a minx, a prize poodle and a sacrificial goat,
this was a dramatic reversal of her past feelings. She said she knew
it and that made it worse.

She was no isolated case. Stuff like that was going on all over
London. I saw strong, respected men looking as if one of their
children had died in their arms. It made me feel a bit better about
snivelling at my desk, and it made me feel a lot better about having
written my poem, because I had got out some of the strangely
personal grief that I now knew a lot of people had been feeling, and
feeling all the more intensely because it was against their expectations
and convictions – against their will. It was not so much the amount of
the emotion, as its contrary nature, that made the episode historically
remarkable, and might well, eventually, make it recalcitrant to historical assessment, because a lot of intelligent people later on decided
that they had been wrong to shed tears, and the less honest among
them are already saying that they never did. The whole convulsive
purgation of pity and terror is coming to be remembered as a weak
moment. That it might have been a strong moment is not an idea
anyone very much wants to pursue. I don't either: empiricism, not
mysticism, is what I value in British culture. But there is nothing
empirical about pretending that something didn't happen.

If you believe, as I do, that a poem is any piece of writing that
can't be quoted from *except* out of context, then a poem is what my

lament for the Princess is, at least in the eyes of its author. In the eyes of some of my critics it was a suicide note, and they might well be proved right in the long run: perhaps what was left of my reputation as a writer of critical prose was wrecked for keeps. But the point was that it didn't seem to matter at the time, because what we self-appointed public mourners said was for her, even if – especially if – we seemed to be grieving for ourselves. A few detractors alleged in print that my tribute was nothing but an opportunistic effort to boost my importance by claiming a friendship that had had small basis in fact. (My own assurances that the friendship had had small basis in fact were taken to be Machiavellian deceptions aimed at furthering this end.) A suitably attentive textual analysis could easily support that view, and *folie de grandeur* might well have been my subconscious impulse. But as far as I can remember my feelings, they were precisely the opposite. Though writing about myself has always been my stock in trade, on that occasion I was as close as a pathologically solipsistic man can ever be to self-denial. All I could see, even in a mirror, was her face.

Who was she? She was us. That was her secret and her nemesis. All of us must spend our lives fighting the internal battle between what we are and what people want us to be, and many of us are handicapped in the struggle by a deficient or fluctuating sense of what we are. But Diana was unusual, even among the stricken, for a sense of self that within a single hour could wink out to nothing or expand to embrace the world. As I said in my obituary – from the viewpoint of *de mortuis nil nisi bonum,* it was the only real boldness in the piece – I suspected quite early on in my fleeting acquaintance with Diana that she was mentally unstable. It has sometimes been put to me since then that if I knew that about her I should have had nothing to do with her. I can think of two answers, the first more obvious than the second. The first answer is that her living presence had the same effect as some of Botticelli's models obviously had on Botticellli, who might well have been at his most serious when he conceded that Savonarola was right to want his pictures burned, but was at his most human when he behaved as if the beauty before his eyes was a heavenly mandate to get painting immediately. In my trade I meet a lot of women who are renowned for looking perfect. Diana didn't look that, but she did look alive. She looked like life itself. To the argument that no man of sense would have thought twice about her if she had been a check-out girl in Tesco, the only possible reply is that she would have been the classiest thing to hit Tesco since bottled water.

But as the late Sir Kingsley Amis might have put it, she *wasn't* a check-out girl, was she? No, she was the Princess of Wales. So I bathed in her starlight the same as any other man who got the nod. And once admitted to her acquaintance, there could not have been many men who wanted to be rid of her before she wanted to be rid of them. She was too fascinating, and was made even more so by one's awareness that she knew how to be fascinating, and was working the trick as a baseball pitcher might keep his arm in shape by throwing rocks at a tin can. If Ortega was right to say that a man flirts so as to make the public woman momentarily reveal her private personality, then Diana knew how to reward flirtation, and the reward became only the more precious as you realized that a different private personality was being revealed every time. The lights were on, and everybody was at home. She was an all-star cast of knockout troublemakers: Bathsheba, Salome, Helen of Troy, Circe, Medea, Dido, Messalina, Francesca da Rimini, Lucrezia Borgia, Mary Stuart, Catherine the Great, Lola Montez, Thérèse Raquin, Anna Karenina, Marie du Plessis, Mata Hari, Isadora Duncan, Aimée Semple Mc-Pherson, Mildred Pierce, Eva Peron, Betty Blue, Betty Boop, Jessica Rabbit. You were looking at the inspiration of literature from the beginning of history, and she had never read a book. Try not being fascinated by that.

The second answer, the less obvious one, is the one worth expounding, because an awful lot of pious rhetoric has been lavished on the pretence that it had no substance. As many protean personalities do, but to a degree made irresistible by her beauty and position, she had the gift of reflecting a man's best self back to him. At one level it was part of her gift for deception, and what *that* gift was like when it was working against you I hate to think. (It certainly worked against her: when she realized what her charm could do to disarm an editor, she made the supreme mistake of believing that she could manage the press, as if a fire could be put out with selective squirts of petrol.) But at another level it was enchanting, because she couldn't have made it work with so many people unless she was genuinely receptive to the possibilities of life, having so many of its creative impulses within her own soul. There was always an easy thousand words to be written – some of the name columnists on the Diana beat were paid for the words at a pound each – about the remarkable extent to which she was uneducated. Few ever wrote about the remarkable extent to which she was educable. She must have had a natural feeling for words, for example, because by the time I knew her she had taught herself to speak with verve and to the point. She had read, and continued to read, nothing except hocus-pocus, but apart from the occasional malapropism she was a pleasure to hear.

At her funeral service, the melody that best reflected her later tastes was the work of Verdi, not Elton John. She came a long way in her appreciation of music, and the best inference was that this was because she was a born listener, just as she was a born dancer. It was often pointed out that she had no idea of how dedicated a real ballet dancer's life has to be. I suspect that she had a very good idea, and regretted that she had found out too late, or anyway had begun in the wrong place. (The old Irish joke whose punchline is 'I wouldn't start from here' applies exactly.) Deborah Bull's marvellous writings are now with us to make clear what the life a real dancer has to lead is like, and incidentally they tell us about the sort of background from which she has to emerge. It is rarely an aristocratic one. Diana's upbringing could scarcely have been more inimical to any kind of concentrated effort. All the more remarkable, then, that she became so appreciative of concentrated effort in the short years of her adult-hood. It was one of the forces that combined to pull her apart. She couldn't see a doctor in action without wanting to be his nurse. She envied anyone with a vocation. You could call it bubble-headed dilettantism if you liked, but to assume that it was part of some sophisticated pose was a failure of the imagination. For those bent on her destruction in print, it would have been more accurate and thus more useful to call her naïve. Though she had the con artist's deadly knack of assessing a stranger's character from how he spoke and stood, she would take his role in life at his own estimation, and captivate him by being in awe of it. No doubt there is something crazy about a woman who can't meet a ditch-digger without letting him think that she harbours a frustrated dream of digging ditches. But ask the ditch-digger what *he* thinks. He thinks that she has flattered the life into him.

Of the harm she could do there is still no full telling, and I rather hope that we will never be told. But of the good that was in her there is not enough said. Writers shame themselves who devote their valuable skills to calling her charitable impulse a grandstand play. It is true – this can never be said too often either – that the kind of charity work Prince Charles does is a hundred times more demanding of time and discipline than anything his dizzy wife ever attempted. But with this talent as with any other, the Gods are erratic in how they dish it out, and they gave Diana the talent to visit the helpless with an injection of the Holy Spirit. How much she did with that talent is open to question. I suppose her compassion for landmine victims would have carried more conviction if she had cared less for the genius of Gianni Versace. But there should be no doubt that her damaged psyche carried unusual powers of sympathy. They couldn't do much to help her – turned inwards, pity was one of her most lethal enemies – but they could do wonders for other people, a category which surely included, at least in the early stages of a liaison, those men who were granted the dubious blessing of her intimacy. In retrospect, redeeming features in Dodi Fayed are hard to find, but it is a safe bet that when he was near her he was at his best. She probably saw something in him, and got him to agree. It was the key to her way with the men in her life, most of whom, we should remember, have honoured her memory by keeping their counsel. The poor, damned James Hewitt was the exception, not the rule. (Even Will Carling *tried* to shut up, but found that the press pack was rather heavier, and faster on its feet, than any other pack he had ever faced: he must have thought that Jonah Lomu had been cloned into a regiment.) She overestimated Hewitt as she overestimated every-one, a tropism typical in those who lack self-esteem. Part of her downfall was that all her geese were swans. But Hewitt was unique in taking revenge on her for her credulity. From the men she cared most about we have heard nothing, a silence whose full fortitude is hard to estimate from outside. Only Prince Charles, subject to overwhelming pressure, has said so much as a word, and all who wish him well can only hope that he never feels bound to say another. The men who know most have said least, and the man who knows everything has said almost nothing, and that's how it should be.

I never knew anything except the pleasure of her company, but perhaps I should say here why I was reluctant to talk even about that. I was and remain a part of the press, so there is no point in my trying to high-hat the whole institution. I would like to think that writing thoughtful articles in my own house is a higher activity than sticking my foot through the door of someone else's, but in the long run investigative journalism is the foundation of a free press, and a free press is something I am for, out of political conviction. I just don't believe that a free press should be free to investigate the private lives of people who are in the limelight for any other reason except, through election or official appointment, their consent to public accountability. The argument that if you have nothing to hide you have nothing to fear was heard in Salem, and is always repudiated by its proponents at the moment when attention shifts to them. By force of circumstances I had that much worked out long before I met the Princess of Wales. In the 1980s I wrote and presented a TV series called *Fame in the Twentieth Century*, and it necessitated a lot of reading that didn't show up in the final script. I was reading about the phenomenon of modern celebrity, and how it affected lives. It emerged, progressively and inexorably throughout the century, that there was a paradox in the very nature of a free press. It was a free press that shielded the democratic societies from the murderous tyranny of the totalitarian ones, but it steadily came to exercise a tyranny of its own, just as pervasive if much less violent. People became trapped by what was written about them, and they were never more trapped than when they thought they were guiding the process of publicity by cooperating with it. The best they could do, by doing so, was to become riders on the storm.

So when I first lunched with Diana in a public restaurant, my first thought was for my own welfare. Already enjoying the questionable privilege of a small measure of celebrity of my own, I knew the phone would start to ring that same afternoon, and I knew that anything I said would go straight into the database, to be quoted from in any context from then on, especially if the context was unfavourable. From the minute I sat down I was already cast in the role of Eats With Princesses. For the sort of commentator for whom 'antipodean' is a long, hard, funny word, anything I said on the subject would be grist to the mill. So for my own sake I resolved to keep my trap shut. But there was an additional element, and a much more important one. I was already appalled by the sheer amount of what was being written about her, whatever its nature. Not all of it was nonsense, but even the sensible stuff was part of an avalanche. Silence might have been a small gesture, but sometimes a small gesture is the only meaningful one you can make, especially when you are afraid. And I wasn't just afraid of having my own small name attached to her big name, in the way that superannuated Mafia button-men, their achievements forgotten, find themselves remembered for their connections with Frank Sinatra. I was afraid of the storm. I didn't want to be part of it. I was afraid of what it had already done to her, and of what it would do next.

The only significant thing I left out of the obituary was that I counselled her against going to America. When she raised the subject of how Jackie Kennedy had managed her later life, it wasn't hard to guess what was going on in the Royal head. I told her that Jackie Kennedy had, to a certain extent, been able to choose privacy; that the same choice would never be available for a runaway Princess; and that she would need a private army, because the sidewalks of New York were very wide, and it was a long walk between the front door and the limousine. I all but told her what was really on my mind, which was that if she went to the United States she would almost certainly be assassinated. To say so at the time would have sounded like paranoia. Alas, it sounds less like that now. All I was wrong about was where the storm was taking her. It wasn't to America, it was to Paris and the tunnel.

Anyway, the phone rang most days until her death. I suppose it would have rung less often since if I had kept to my rule and gone on saying nothing even when she died. The only excuse I can plead is shock. My answering machine filled up with messages from every publication and television channel: some of the names I knew all too well. People whose attentions had helped drive her to the wall were begging my help in decorating her coffin with their cheap wreaths. There were calls from Australia, from America, from Hong Kong. What it must have been like for those whose acquaintance with her amounted to more than a few short hours, Christ only knows. Not to respond was easy. It has been just as easy since. But on that awful day after the night Diana died, a great natural psychologist made it hard. Tina Brown called from Long Island and told me what she hoped I would do. When I said that I couldn't possibly, she read my voice and asked what else I was going to do for the next few days.

It was the right question. Like so many others, I had been surprised by my own wretchedness and needed distraction from it with a job of work. Much has been made since of how the country and the world went mad in a self-regarding ecstasy, a populist frenzy that threatened the rule of reason. There is truth in that argument. The devastated Royal Family had a right to their seclusion. So-called popular opinion had no business hauling them out of it, although it was my impression that it was the press, and not the people it presumed to speak for, who stormed the gates. There is even something in the admonition that bigger tragedies happen every day. There is something, but not, I think, all that much. It is all too true that less illustrious victims are taken by the hour in circumstances inconceivably more cruel, and that there have been times when much younger ones have been taken by the million. But anti-populist oracles seldom consider the possibility that the people might already have known all that. Nor, if they knew all that, were they necessarily weeping at such a brutal reminder that sudden death, if it could come for her, could come for anyone, and thus for them. To believe they were weeping solely for themselves, you have to believe they were all selfish. My own bet, based on my own experience, is that the much-derided masses felt the pain of losing someone they loved.

No doubt they got above themselves, but I would be the last person to say they had no right to. Not that I favour populism as a political creed. I ceased to believe in the credentials of New Labour when Tony Blair read the lesson at Diana's funeral. I wish John Prescott had read it instead: we might have heard the tones of sincerity, whereas populism comes down to a calculation of what will play, and there is no calculation colder than well-rehearsed sentimentality. Diana as the icon of demagogues is a frightening prospect. Julie Burchill is probably an extreme case, but it was very disturbing to find that someone who had gone on record as positively *liking* the idea that Stalin had killed millions of innocent people should also go potty for the Princess. Pundits who think of the people as an instrument to be played upon – and of course those who fear such a possibility think the same way – have been hailing Diana as a voodoo talisman. There will probably be more of that to come: not so rabid, perhaps, but more insidious for seeming reasonable. I wish I could say that I foresaw such things might happen, and wrote my piece as part of a pre-emptive antidote. But I didn't need prescience to see the radiance of the icon. What I wanted to celebrate and lament was the radiance of the human being. She might have been less radiant had she possessed more integrity – she would have been less concerned to project her inner fires – but a human being she was.

Thankfully lost in my work, I spent four days writing about her, and have said nothing else about her until now. What I have offered here is not a defence of what I wrote, but a description of its circumstances, for anyone who might feel bound to make a serious study of what went on at an extraordinary time. I can't tell whether I was right to predict that the impact of her death would change the emotional climate of the country, but I can't tell if I was wrong either. The good news is that people in real life, as opposed to professional gossips, seem less inclined to suppose that celebrity status is a bed of roses, and are more likely to give away some of their precious time. I detect her example in that first effect, and her legacy in the second: if it is true that she was self-obsessed, by just so much she dramatized her selfless acts, and to copy those is no less useful for being fashionable. The bad news is that the press scarcely let up for a year. The *Daily Mail*, for instance, carried a Diana story almost every day, and often her picture on the front page. Though the pressure eased off a bit after the anniversary, it is not as if the flood has dried to a trickle: there is still a steady stream. The expenditure of energy that has gone into all this is daunting to think about. Most of it adds up to less than nothing, but for a generation of journalists to spend the best part of a career hunting the Snark, and then go on hunting it after it is dead and buried – well, it can hardly come to good. But there is money in it, because people want to read the stuff; and to believe that the stories would vanish if the people really ruled is wishful thinking.

Winding down, I should perhaps say at this point, to block a possible line of reproof, that of the several thousands of pounds the piece earned all over the world, every penny was given directly to charity. The same will be true, in perpetuity, of the proportion of royalties for this book that is generated by the total pages devoted to the same subject, with an additional percentage to cover the possibility – slimmer now, thank Heaven, than would have earlier been true – of its sales being artificially increased by the allusion to her name. If a lawyer working for the Diana Memorial Fund feels justified in taking a salary, there are no doubt business ethics to justify it. But for a writer, on the level of elementary morality, there can be no quibbling: money made out of Diana's death is blood money, and that's final.

Let me conclude this postscript by saying that I am under no illusions. For better or for worse (almost certainly for worse, as far as my reputation goes) my valediction for the Princess will be identified as the *experimentum crucis* of my career as a journalist, always supposing that anyone cares. I had always wanted – why hide the obvious? – to earn a place, however small, in the abstract and brief chronicles of the time. Out of the blue, in one sad week, I did. To that extent I too, like so many others, have been touched by her fate, but I have better reasons than that for wishing her fate had been otherwise. If she were still here, if she had never gone into the tunnel, history would have passed me by. It didn't, but it is not just for my sake that I wish it had.

1999

DIFFERENT OCCASIONS

INCIDENT AT ST DENIS

For Ian Hamilton's 60th birthday

Out near the left corner post, Miller, with characteristic hauteur, beat Ungaretti and launched the cross without even looking inward. Hamilton, moving in at top speed from right of centre, instantly calculated where he would have to be to intercept it. There were two Italians he would need to outrun, Montale and Quasimodo. Both were fast, but they were facing the wrong way. With his unrivalled footballing brain, Hamilton knew already that he would get there. The problem would be to strike the ball into a space that the Italian goalkeeper, Pasolini, was already moving fast to close down. With only thirty seconds left before the whistle, and the score level at five all, this last, slim, desperate chance could decide the World Cup in England's favour. It was all down to Hamilton. He had scored all five of England's goals, three of them from his famous upside-down overhead backward somersault bicycle kick, but if he missed this one he would not be forgiven. Experience would help. He and Miller had been in the front line of the England squad since Moore, Charlton and the rest had helped them to that first World Cup success – the prelude to so many others – at Wembley in 1966. On that occasion, too, a typically sly pass by Miller to Hamilton's unerring right foot had clinched the issue. That had been a while ago, of course: Hamilton would be the first to admit it. Miller never admitted anything, but even he, if threatened with a cocked automatic, would concede between clenched teeth that he might no longer be quite capable of the ninety-yard diagonal run that had left Beckenbauer floundering before the back-flick to Hamilton had yielded the decider. Still, that was the great thing about this game. You might lose the odd tiny fraction of a mile per hour for each decade at the top, but you made up for it in wisdom, guile, grit and craft.

As Hamilton, after feinting to Montale's left, hurdled over the Italian's hacking right leg, his mind played its familiar trick of expanding, for a crucial split second, into another time, another place, another life. For strangely enough, this man, who ranked amongst the nonpareils of football ('There is another Pele called Maradonna,' Brian Glanville had once written, 'and there is another George Best called Paul Gascoigne, but there is no other Hamilton') was cursed, or blessed, with an imagination that furnished him with a whole separate existence. In his dreams, which came upon him most intensely when he was awake, and were at their most luxuriant in moments of professional footballing crisis, he was a poet, critic, editor, biographer and all-round man of letters. Unlike most imagined lives, his was full of vivid detail. He did not just vaguely dream of being a poet. There were actual poems, composed instantaneously in his head even as it was still ringing with the impact of the opposing goalkeeper's drop-kick clearance sent back past that stunned individual into the top corner of the net at seventy miles an hour. It was happening now.

> In the corner of my eye
> You move to the kitchen.
> Why do I not tell you
> That I ate the last bran flakes
> During the night?

It was the first stanza of a new poem which he knew would complete itself in the next few seconds of furious physical action. Such compositions – terse, acerbic, pregnant with *angst*, armoured to the core against any probe for sentimentality – lay at the heart of his early and still recurring conjured persona as the hard young literary guru of Soho. The same scenario would replay itself endlessly in his mind at moments like this. In his imagination, he entered once again the decrepit pub in Greek Street. The grand name he had invented for this sticky-carpeted dive, the Pillars of Hercules, was designed to create an ironic distance from its squalor. The place fell silent as he strode slowly in, dressed in black like Doc Holliday breasting the swinging saloon doors of Tombstone. Gripped in his lethal right hand were the galleys of his little magazine, the *Review*, the rarely appearing periodical in which established poetic repu-tations were riddled and left for dead. Propped against the bar, his worshipping acolytes tried unsuccessfuly to look casual as they sensed his entrance. Which of them would be next for the bullet? Which of them would next discover that no amount of loudly professed loyalty was proof against the unswerving integrity of their chosen editor? Once again he bathed in the furtive glance of fear, even as now, in real life, he saw apprehension in the eyes of the Argentine fullback, Borges, the only man he had left to beat before he faced their legendary goalkeeper Sabato, who was already on his way out to narrow the angle. Borges was practically sideways in mid-air, launching a tackle designed to cut Hamilton's lithely muscled legs from under him. He could let it happen, get the penalty, and finish the match that way. The second stanza flashed into his head.

> Perhaps because
> I need your disappointment
> To equal mine. The hallway
> Is full to waist level
> With buff envelopes.

The poem was already half done. Soon it would finish itself, just as he would finish this goal. A goal it would have to be: a penalty was the coward's way. It wasn't his style. His style was integrity, and that meant what he must do now: beat the tackle with all the skills he had first developed as a youth in those endless hours of kicking a crushed tin can through his letterbox while being attacked by the family dog, and had gone on honing through hundreds of First Division and international matches in which the opposing backs had dedicated themselves to marking him out of the game. With a delicacy and precision made doubly incredible by the speed at which he was travelling, he nudged the ball through the space left under the hori-zontal body of the Brazilian fullback, de Moraes, and launched himself over it as the crowd's continuous roar rose to an orgiastic frenzy. Hamil-TON! Hamil-TON! It got boring sometimes, all that adoration.

He was still in mid-air when he began to calculate the options available to the rapidly advancing goalkeeper, Cabral. Here once again, if it were needed, was startling evidence of Hamilton's greatest single gift: the ability to compute possible trajectories even while his finely tuned physical capacity was fully committed to the action of the present instant. ('If the photon-stream of the Hamiltonesque footballing mode can best be resolved through a lens which owes more to Heidegger than to Heisenberg,' George Steiner had once written, 'perhaps the crux of our appreciation lies in the very synchronicity of *spurlos* intellection and breath-bereaving *Affekt* which we, simultaneously deceived and undeceived, are delightedly aware unites us in belief even at the moment when we are unable to believe our eyes.') De Moraes was already behind, flailing helpless on the turf, automatically signalling innocence to the referee for a foul which he had not managed to commit. Hamilton descended to rejoin the ball as Cabral checked his own headlong rush and distributed his weight evenly to both feet, ready to launch himself in whichever direction the hurtling Hamilton might choose to strike. It was the supreme moment of decision.

> As I forge through them
> To the front door,
> It sounds like cereal being eaten
> Without milk.

Hamilton had nobody left to beat except the Norwegian goalkeeper, Ibsen. It would not be easy. Ibsen stood ready to go either way. But Hamilton the footballer could read an opponent's intentions in the same way that, in his imagined role as Hamilton the literary biographer, he could read the complex creative psychology of his chosen subject. Just as, in his reveries, he had penetrated to the central motivation of Robert Lowell's paranoia and J. D. Salinger's strange reluctance to offer himself up for questioning, so now, in reality, he infallibly analysed the Scandinavian's notorious coiledspring poise. The bacchantic tumult of the crowd was not enough to muffle the crack of a heavy-calibre rifle shot as Hamilton struck the ball with all his force to his opponent's right while imparting to it, with a long-practised flexing of the foot, the special spin that would curl it to the left. Even as he did so, Hamilton was looking into the grandstand out of the corner of his eye. Kate was there, taking a day off from filming *Titanic II*. Jennifer and Courteney were on either side of her: production of *Friends* had been suspended for a day at their insistence. Julia was only just arriving, typically: later on she would probably babble that the private jet from Los Angeles had run short of fuel. He was getting sick of Julia's excuses. If she kept that up, her suite in the women's wing at his chateau on the Loire (*Hello!* had done a special supplement, back in the days when Sigourney and Michelle were still in residence) might just have to be reassigned to young Gwyneth, who God knows had put in enough requests. Even now, with all the women on their feet cheering, Gwyneth looked the most ecstatic. Good girl. Hamilton was resolving to reward her with a new Porsche even as Ibsen read the trick, reversed direction in mid-air, and got a hand to the ball.

> Now you have the milk
> But without cereal.
> Tough break.
> Let's call it a draw.

The poem was completed but the goal was not. The German goalkeeper, Festschrift, had got a hand to the ball but of course he couldn't hold it. Hamilton's shot, moving at only just below the speed of sound, had been too powerful. Hamilton knew what must happen next. He had planned it all along. The only chance with Festschrift was to get him with the second bite of the cherry, not the first. The ball rebounded in a high arc. From behind, the fullbacks Enzensburger and Grass had recovered fast and were moving in. Hamilton was upside down in mid-air when he glanced into the stands and saw Julia, Jennifer, Kate, Courteney and Gwyneth all clutching their distorted faces in horror at the prospect of his missing this most vital of all goals. But he was not going to miss. He never missed with the upside-down overhead backward somersault bicycle kick with the special spin. '*Ach, du Schweinhund Hamilton mit deine magische Talent!* screamed Festschrift as the ball streaked past him into the net.

Slack-jawed with awe, the referee finally remembered himself and blew the whistle. A hundred thousand people were shouting too loudly to hear it. Nor could the object of their adulation. But he didn't need to. He knew the job was done. On his hands and knees, suddenly weary, Hamilton glanced towards the grandstand and realized at last why Julia had arrived late. He had forgotten but the girls had not. Julia had brought the cake. They were all lighting the candles.

Damned pity it took such a long time, but there was a lot more football in him yet.

From *Another Round at the Pillars*, a *Festschrift* for Ian Hamilton, edited by David Harsent, Congo Press, 1999

THE YEAR IT DIDN'T HAPPEN

It was the only year I ever thought of at the time as being a special year by itself, so it's the only one I can look back on with any sure recollection as to its events. Other years interchange their events in memory. When I was writing the first draft of the television series *Fame in the Twentieth Century*, I worked from memory, and found out only while checking for the next draft that I had continually got things out of order. Memory rearranges even the biggest, world-scale happenings into a more manageable sequence. Memory edits. Memory would have edited 1982 if, before the year began, I hadn't persuaded Karl Miller of the *London Review of Books* to serialize an *ottava rima* verse chronicle which would treat the year's news as it came, with no benefit of hindsight. It was typically generous of Miller to be attracted by this prospect, because there was no guarantee that much of interest would actually happen.

And at first, indeed, everything seemed drearily normal. General Jaruzelski, ruling Poland, rounded up all the Solidarity activists and penned them in the open air while the snow fell. As things went in the East, nothing could be more humdrum than that. Roy Jenkins stood for the Glasgow seat of Hillhead with every chance of losing it for the SDP, whereat, it was predicted, the new party would disintegrate. Here again, the predictions couldn't have been more predictable, especially from Tony Benn, who had branded the SDP a media party, with no policies. My own view was that for the SDP not to have the Labour Party's policies was policy enough, but a win for Jenkins still looked like a lot to hope for. Mark Thatcher got lost in Africa, which had to happen. The railway union ASLEF went on strike, which also had to happen. Freddie Laker's airline went broke, which seemed as if it had to happen too, since few people realized at the time that an independent entrepreneur who complained about being sabotaged by BA might just have a case. In Northern Ireland,

John de Lorean's factory for building gull-winged sports cars had proved to be the most efficient way of combusting the British tax payer's money since the ground-nut scheme.

Mrs Thatcher gained fewer points for denying funds to these crashed buccaneers than she lost for having presided over the new spirit of free enterprise in which they had somehow contrived to fail. Her principles were working against her. Michel Foot hailed the Peace of Bishop's Stortford, a new deal by which the Labour Party would somehow bind up the differences within itself, thus rendering the SDP superfluous. Abetting this process with unsurprisingly miraculous timing, a plot was uncovered: Labour's Militant Tendency had not only been conspiring to remove all non-Marxist MPs after the next election victory, they had written their plan down. Happening to meet Neil Kinnock and his charming family taking a half-term tour of St Paul's, I found him delighted by this development and was thus able to get some personal colour into my poem, but things were looking pretty staid. At just this point my chosen year started behaving as if the power had been switched on.

Jenkins won in Hillhead. Overnight, like Eurydice glanced at by Orpheus on their way out of Hades, the Labour Party went backwards into history. There would be a new party of opposition. Mrs Thatcher would be hard pressed to defeat it. She was the most unpopular Prime Minister since, since ... But just when we were absorbing the shock of these wonders, wonders were succeeded by epiphanies. Argentina occupied the Falklands. Lord Carrington – observing the quaint, not yet quite extinct custom by which Ministers who presided over catastrophes resigned in contrition – presented his embarrassed Prime Minister with his head, which for a while looked like the only thing she had to throw at General Galtieri. In the House of Commons nobody shouted louder for war than Michael Foot, but by left-wing intellectuals it was taken for granted that for Britain to fight would be a preposterous exercise in post-Imperial nostalgia, jingoism after the fact. One of my most brilliant friends published an article instructing the fleet to turn back.

The sinking of the *Belgrano* confirmed thinkers on the Labour Party's left-wing in all their suspicions about Mrs Thatcher. Actually, we can now see, those same thinkers were helping to sink the Labour Party, because nothing weakened the opposition to Mrs Thatcher like reluctance to admit that in the matter of the Falklands war she was a realist. The *Belgrano* had been a victim, not of her ruthlessness, but of the Royal Navy's long memory for the day when they let the *Bismarck* out of their sight, thereby almost losing a whole convoy and World War II along with it. The Falklands war, small-scale in historic terms, was still a momentous event, and Mrs Thatcher managed it well. The best way to counter her afterwards would have been to say, truthfully, that while to show determination in war is admirable, it is not as taxing as to show creative imagination in peace, when there is no single object in view. But nobody – at least nobody in the House of Commons – said so, and she came out of the war doubled in stature, with the Labour Party nowhere in sight, although as yet it would have taken a clairvoyant to spot that no other party or group of parties would have a chance against her either. With a glittering future seemingly assured, the SDP's choice of Dr Owen as its leader seemed merely stage-struck, not disastrous.

At Buckingham Palace, the Queen played host to an undistin-guished visitor, one Fagan, who appeared beside her bed at dead of night to bum a cigarette. Suspicions that the Palace might not be quite so suavely in charge of its affairs as had been thought were soon quelled. The IRA bombed a military band in London: things were getting back to normal. In Cambridge an undergraduate poetess called Sue had a devastating effect on previously imperturbable dons, allegedly because of her fluent gift for the sonnet form, and not because of her beauty: things were very normal. History had left Britain and was happening out there in the world, as was only proper. Squeezed by Begin's invading armies, Yasser Arafat and the PLO pulled out of Beirut, whose ruins filled the world's television screens, except for the sad hiatus in which Princess Grace died – by accident, scarcely history at all, just terribly regrettable, a containable tragedy. Then it was the Lebanon again, where Begin and Sharon were res-ponsible for an uncontainable tragedy – the massacre in the camps. All of us who believed in the state of Israel's right to exist had suddenly to face the fact that it was run by men too stupid to appreciate why getting stuck with a label like *massacre in the camps* was contra-indicated, PR-wise.

At the time, that was my pick for the incident that would have the most fatal resonance in the future. As things turned out, it just blended into a dreadful, see-sawing sequence of atrocities which can probably never be ended; only, at best, brought to some kind of

balance. A better choice for an event with a long shadow would have
been the Royal decision to deny Koo Stark her manifest destiny as
the bride of Prince Andrew. Discreet, strong-willed, keen for the job,
as bright as any woman willing to share her life with the future Duke
of York was ever going to be, Koo, though she had admittedly been
photographed with her clothes off, at least looked good that way.
Though we didn't yet know it, to shut her out left the way open for
Sarah Ferguson, whose impact on Buckingham Palace would be
roughly the same as that of alcohol on the Eskimos.

But to spot that would have taken a crystal ball. There were bigger
issues where all the trends were already running but you just couldn't
believe they would go on that way. My brilliant friend who had
instructed the fleet to turn back gave up writing about British politics.
Another brilliant friend still wrote about British politics but now did
it from America. With Reagan and Thatcher triumphant, everything
was blamed on their unscrupulous populism. No other reason than
public gullibility could be adduced for their success. It had not yet
become fully clear that the real reason for the success of the Right
was the collapse of the Left. Throughout the West, the dream of the
socialist state was already well embarked on its long day's dying, but
you had to be a cynic to believe it.

In the East you had to be a fanatic to believe anything else, and
the really big news of the year was precisely that – they were running
out of fanatics. The most tremendous event of the year was the one
that didn't happen. Lech Walesa was allowed to live. Jaruzelski locked
him up but didn't kill him. Brezhnev checked out, Andropov checked
in, and still the Russians let the Poles get away with it. In December,
Walesa walked free. The Soviet tanks didn't come. The will to rule
by terror was gone. With that gone, the whole thing was doomed.
Looking back from now, it is easy to see how everything followed
from that one non-event. Looking forward from then, we didn't dare
even guess. Full of happenings, it would have been a big year anyway.
But what made it the biggest year of the late twentieth century was
something that didn't happen at all.

From Picador's *21st Birthday Anthology*, 1993

DESTINATION EUROPE

To introduce a special issue on the subject, the New Yorker *asked me to sum up the history of Europe in a thousand words. For my next trick, I will run a mile in four seconds.*

Suppose the world were an animal curled up into a ball, like a threatened armadillo, and you wanted to blow its brains out: the best way to do so would be to put the barrel of your gun against Europe and pull the trigger. The United States might be nettled by this dubious favouritism; in the century now waning, it has been called upon to save Europe from itself twice – three times if you count Stalin's opportunistic incursion. But even the United States would have to admit, if pressed, that it is itself a largely European creation, a giant offshoot of the most productive piece of geography in the planet's history. Behind that admission would be a tacit acknowledgment that, although America may have the power, the energy, and most of the money, Europe has the pedigree. As David Copperfield (the Broadway illusionist, not the Dickens character) is reported to have said to Claudia Schiffer while they were touring the Louvre and reading the dates on the paintings, 'Talk about your *old!*'

As a word, Europe goes back a long way: Assyrian inscriptions speak of the difference between *asu* (where the sun rises; i.e. Asia) and *ereb* (where it sets). As a place, Europe is old even by the standards of dynastic China and Pharaonic Egypt. As an idea, though, Europe is comparatively new: the word European didn't turn up in the language of diplomacy until the nineteenth century, and to *think* of Europe as one place had always taken some kind of supervening vision. Whatever unity existed within it came not through a unifying idea but through the exercise of power, and did not last.

The Pax Romana prevailed for more than two centuries: it left us the Latin language and all its rich derivatives, and it left us the law – and slavery, and militarism. Dante spent the best years of his life in exile: a member of a political faction, he was exiled from his beloved Florence not by another faction but by another faction of the *same* faction. The university system pioneered the notion of intellectual unity, but intellectual was all that it was. Erasmus the wandering scholar was at home everywhere he went in Europe, but his wanderings were forced on him, and his humanism would have died young if he had been caught napping where the knives were out. The Church united Europe in the one faith – Christendom is a peaceful-sounding word – but finally the faith itself split. Nothing could stop the rise of the nation-states, or stop them from fighting once they had arisen. And those states whose destiny it was to fight one another had been forged from fiefdoms and principalities that had warred upon one another, from walled cities that had laid siege to one another, and from fortified hill towns that had laid siege to one another for the valleys in between. The colossal efforts of Charlemagne, Louis XIV and Napoleon – though they gave us, respectively, the restoration of learning, the apex of the comfortable arts, and the crucial new reality of the career open to the talents – all depended on military might. Kaiser Wilhelm II's similar dreams seem more explicitly violent only in having left behind little that was constructive; and Hitler's demented venture, though it united an unprecedentedly large proportion of Europe, left nothing in its wake – nothing except destruction, and this: the idea of European unity stopped being an intoxicating vision and started being a mundane necessity.

The centrifugal effect of the Nazi regime in Germany scattered the best brains of Europe all over the planet. Exiled to faraway New Zealand, the philosopher Karl Popper developed his argument that there could be no such thing as universal fixes – that the most that society could or should hope to do was to correct specific abuses. This perception surely applies to a united Europe: speculation about what utopian goals it might achieve counts for little beside a firm grasp of what it sets out to avoid – any recurrence of the internecine conflict that was already ancient when Athens fought Sparta and that reached its hideous apotheosis in the Second World War. In the middle of the twentieth century, it had become plain for all to see that Europe's glories – justly renowned even when they had to be rebuilt stone by stone – were merely its structure. Beneath them was the infrastructure – a network of burial mounds linked by battle-fields – and it stank of blood. Hegel said that history was the story of liberty becoming conscious of itself. European history has culmi-nated – at last, and in our time – with Europe becoming frightened of itself.

As happens so frequently in human affairs, fear has accomplished what neither reason nor culture ever could. Cultural unity was no illusion – had it been one, Hitler would not have been so eager to dispel it – but cultural unity had not been enough. When the musicians played for Mengele in Auschwitz, it did not mean that art and civilization added up to nothing, but it did mean that they did not add up to everything. Beside the broken bodies of the tortured innocent, the life of the mind was felt to be irrelevant – as, indeed, in any forced comparison it is.

To make sure that no such forced comparison happens again is the task in hand. It is not an easy one. In place of the conquerors' fevered dream of a Europe united by the sword, the peaceful com-mercial republics of the New Europe make do with such cultural manifestations as the Eurovision Song Contest – a kitschy classic that every year draws a huge television audience, whose more sophisti-cated members amuse each other with jokes about how dumb it is. The jokes keep changing. For years, Norway's songs reliably lost ('*Norvège . . . nul points*'); then they started winning. More recently, much derisive hilarity has attended the earnest efforts of Turkey. Between laughs, though, the less sophisticated but more thoughtful viewers should take heart: there was a time when the Turks stood at the gates of Vienna and bristled with the armed intention of getting into Europe by less tuneful means.

What the snobs are really afraid of is a United States of Europe that mirrors what they imagine the United States of America to be: an agglomerate dissolved into homogeneity, a consumer society consumed by mediocrity, or, at best, a mindless mimicry of Euro-savvy in which a dauntingly exact copy of Michelangelo's David presides over Forest Lawn's departed Angelenos and an actual-size Parthenon wows visitors to Nashville. But they are wrong about America, which is more than that; and they are wrong about the

New Europe, which, as the millennium looms, bids fair to attain a last, unprecedented, and very welcome greatness, through a just peace. Talk about your *new*!

New Yorker, 28 April and 5 May, 1997

A VOICE IS BORN

If you love music, you can't be tone-deaf: the only reason you can't hold a tune is that you haven't got the notes. More than a year ago, this was one of the first things my singing teacher Ian Adam said to me when I edged through his door like a dental patient. Ian Adam is famous within the showbiz world for his ability to turn actors into singers so that they can star in musicals and thus do what actors like to do best – stunningly reveal a hitherto unsuspected talent. Ian's lack of fame outside the showbiz world is due not just to his innate modesty, but to the touching reluctance of the stars in question to concede that the hitherto unsuspected talent was ever less than fully formed. Yet almost invariably the talent was scarcely there to be suspected before Ian Adam helped them reveal it, or – in the majority of cases, but let's keep that a secret – supplied it in its entirety.

The latter is certainly what he is doing for me. I was never an actor, but still less was I ever a singer. In the forty-five years between the demoralizing month in which my once pure alto voice broke and the blessed day I slunk up to his door in South Kensington, there was hardly a tune I could carry, with the possible exceptions of the first phrase of 'Che gelida manina' (all on the one note) and selected fragments of Cole Porter's 'True Love' (written specifically for Grace Kelly after it was discovered that she had the vocal range of a mouse trapped under a cushion). I couldn't even sing 'Happy Birthday' successfully. With the arrogant humility of the wounded animal, this was the first thing I confessed to my new mentor, and he began the necessary soothing process by saying he was not surprised: 'Happy Birthday' is actually quite hard – something about the interval leading up to 'birthday' in the third line being impossible to manage if you haven't got the notes in between. 'But that's why you're here, dear boy. Now let's breathe.' And he started showing me how to breathe.

Learning how to breathe was the nominal reason for my attendance. I had been told by several musical people that some singing
training might help stave off a problem with my speaking voice which
was starting to show up with advancing age. When I go to market
in television, my speaking voice is the only thing I've got to sell.
Nobody stays tuned for the bewitching symmetry of my features: if
I can't address the audience in my trademark effortless drone, I'm a
dead duck, and I had begun to notice that after a two-day studio
rehearsal for a big show, when I got to the taping session on the
second evening I was a bit short of puff, and hoarseness threatened.
A hoarse effortless drone could be a switch-off.

Having been assured that the antidote lay in diaphragm breathing,
and that this was something only a singing teacher could teach, I
fronted up for the cure, and in no time started feeling the benefits
of breathing deeply for the first time in my life. The secret is to get
all the air out by pulling your diaphragm in, and then, by letting
your diaphragm out, filling your lungs entirely with brand-new air.
If you breathe with only your chest, the way most of us do all the
time, you're running on just the top half of a fuel tank, and the bottom
half might as well contain marsh gas. The technique is soon learned,
although it takes years, starting young, to master it completely. (Any
of those three tenors can take on a full load with a single twitch and
you won't even see it happen unless you're ogling his abdomen
instead of the soprano's cleavage.) But you don't have to be that
good. After your first week of proper breathing, your teacher has
already established the basis on which he can start cleaning up the
mess you made of your singing voice after it broke. Women don't
have the same problem, but they, too, have to learn to breathe
properly if they want to add a few soaring notes above the squeak
they always thought they were stuck with, and the main reason they
squeak is that there isn't any air coming out, because they haven't
taken any in.

You will have guessed already that behind the nominal reason
there was a real reason. Wanting to be Jussi Björling or Giuseppe di
Stefano and sing all those wonderful arias into the adoring face of
Victoria de los Angeles or Maria Callas – that was a dream. But just
wanting to sing a pretty popular song – that seemed a real, legitimate
possibility, except that it was impossible, seductively near yet cruelly
out of reach. After four bars of my 'Strangers In The Night' strangers

were talking about noise pollution. And now here was this kind gentleman telling me it didn't have to be like that. Yes, I *would* be able to sing those golden standards and even a few carefully selected arias too. But first I had to realize the crucial importance of the magic word 'support'. He pointed to my nether regions. The focus of the whole business, he explained, is not up there in the head and throat, but down there behind the scrotum. With singing, the standard military exhortation in times of danger applies in all cases: you have to keep a tight arsehole. The only tension should be in your tripes, not in your gullet. Try to sing exclusively from the throat and you'll bust a gut.

Clenching the fundament as you expel your full tank of clean air upwards over the vocal chords, you support the voice. That way, the few notes you've already got won't crack or slide about, and you are creating the opportunity to add new ones on top of them. The initial work of augmentation is done through vocal exercises. Ian has perfected a set of these which are niftily designed to circumvent your perennial expectations of failure by springing on you by surprise the missing note he has decided you are just about ready to hit. When you first hit it, it sounds lousy, but this is the precise point where he reveals himself as a master psychologist. Well aware that a honking klutz like me dreams of unfurling shimmering skeins of melisma in the upper register like Tito Schipa, he knows that the main psychological inhibition is the fear of sounding less than perfect. He convinces you that when you hit the note in any form, however horrendous, the job is already done.

The rest is just the mechanical work of lifting the roof of the mouth, keeping the lower jaw back, hoiking it up at the sides, flattening the back of the tongue, maintaining the support, and so on *ad* seemingly *infinitum*. Just all that, but lesson by lesson you can hear the new note sounding more natural. Flatteringly – and, wonder of wonders, believably – he assures you that it sounds far less forced than any notes you've already got. Meanwhile he is already helping you build the next note up the scale. Again it starts off sounding like an alley cat in a trouser-press, but week by week that dreadful noise is climbing higher and higher, the new notes underneath it are becoming usefully available, and the repertoire of melodies that remain recognizable, even while you murder them, is steadily increasing.

Of Ian's psychological strokes, the masterstroke is to slake your clandestine ambitions by giving you a few of your so-long-dreamed-of *chansons* and arias right from the jump, so you can take something home to sing in the bathroom. (If the bathroom door starts caving in under protest, you can always test your new stuff out in a deserted park on a rainy day.) Knowing by heart every decent melody that has ever been written in any genre, he knows exactly which ones to pick that will fit your burgeoning range without straining it too much at the top. (It doesn't hurt to strain it a little, just to go on reminding yourself that there's a note up there you can soon have, as long as you remember that it can't be had by wishing, only by work.)

After the first few weeks I was making something better than a cry for help out of Donaudy's pretty lament, 'O del mio amato ben', and in less than three months I could hit all the notes of Fauré's gorgeous 'En Prière', even if most of them were *sans* overtone and the desired legato line showed a few rough welds at the joints. Best of all, inside four months I had my first aria, 'Prendi l'anel ti dono', a surefire showstopper from *Sonnambula*. Sounding challenging enough to chill the blood, but in fact far more easily negotiated than 'Dancing in the Dark', it was cunningly designed by Bellini so that the tenor, with minimum effort and maximum parade of daring, could bring the house down. All I brought down with it was the bathroom, but I was singing an aria!

But, as Ian kept on patiently explaining, it's seldom the *tessitura* that makes things tricky: more often it's the intervals. A lot of good stuff is written entirely within the stave, but a song can demand only a narrow range and still flummox you by the jumps you can't make from one note to the next without grinding to a halt, consulting your mental tuning fork, and starting again. While never precisely forbidding the project, he pointed out that my self-assigned task of getting on top of the 'Flower Song' from *Carmen* was asking for trouble. After one unsolicited hearing he pinpointed where the trouble was, but didn't tell me until I figured it out for myself. My own candidate for the most ravishing of all tenor arias, a love-letter to enslave Circe, the 'Flower Song' is a relative doddle throughout except for a vicious booby-trap in the seventh line: in 'De cette odeur je m'enivrais', the interval between the two last syllables is a killer. I went on killing myself with it in private for about six months before he told me the cruel truth. I was trying to sing the consonants 'vr' instead of the vowel 'ais'. When he got me to sing the syllable without the consonants I could hit it with ease. 'Practise that for a while, dear boy, and you can fudge the consonants in later. It's *admirable* how much you care for the words – you really are *amazingly* sensitive to language, it's a privilege to hear you speak on the television, *so* articulate – but if you try to pronounce the consonants too accurately when you're *singing* you'll have trouble jacking your gob open to do the vowel. We have to be a bit *ruthless*.'

Going light on the consonants is a very good general trick for joining up those scary little black dots at the top of the stave. All trained singers, no matter how illustrious, use it as a crutch. It's the reason why their consonants, during the bravura bits, tend to sound like Henry Kissinger's. Even Björling, probably the greatest tenor after Caruso, sang in French as if it was his native Swedish, and sang in Swedish as if he was half drunk. (A lot of the time he was, but that's another story.) Joan Sutherland got through her entire career without uttering very many consonants at all. Often she turned a whole aria into a cadenza, and if you're still looking for an argument-winning reason to prefer Callas for the title of top diva of the modern era, you could suggest with some justification that Callas sang the words, whereas Sutherland sang only the music. And we singers don't sing just to make a nice noise, we sing to give back to the language the wings it lost when the angels fell.

After such knowledge, what forgiveness? Knowing a little bit more about the technicalities now, in the opera house I have become, if no less easy to please, at least a bit harder to fool. For a tired tenor to transpose a high note downward isn't as heinous as Mike Tyson biting the other guy's ear off to get out of the fight early, but it isn't honest either. From here on, I'll know when to sit on my hands. Let us, however, not kid ourselves, dear boy: those singers up there can really sing. They're doing it for a living, and all I'm doing is dreaming aloud. But at least the dream is no longer confined to the interior of my head. My current practice number is 'Fenesta che lucide', a funeral song in dialect variously attributed to Bellini and to that prolific Italian composer Ignoto. Grittily catchy as a dirge from *The Godfather*, plangently lovely beyond all measure, it laments, in phrases that pulse like pent-up weeping, the death of the singer's sister. Whether or not I have truly mastered its haunting melody, people certainly look haunted when I sing it. I sing it in the street, like Mario Lanza yodelling as he toddled in *The Great Caruso*. Heads turn.

And even the most deeply buried dream of all has come true. *I have sung the duet in the restaurant with the pretty girl.* When Frank Johnson and Petronella Wyatt took me to lunch at Simpson's in the Strand for the purpose of inveigling me into writing this suicidally inadvisable piece, the subject came up of which show songs were harder than operatic arias. I suggested Cole Porter's 'So in Love', which bristles with lethally placed examples of the most awkward sound to sustain beyond a quaver, the long 'i' diphthong. In that blackberry-stained *mezzo* voice of hers which is so much more enchanting than her politics, *la* Wyatt began to sing it, and after the first stanza I joined in, *pianissimo* but *con amore*. As our last notes faded away, the whole restaurant burst into applause. It might have been because I had stopped singing, but I like to think it was a tribute to our joint impact – just as I like to think that Mr Johnson's twitching smile throughout the performance was a sign of envy rather than embarrassment, and that he pulled his jacket over his head only because the beauty of what he heard was too much for him to bear.

Spectator, 19 December, 1997

PETER COOK

In the restaurant on top of Ajax mountain at Aspen, Colorado, my wife and I had just started eating lunch when Barry Humphries suddenly appeared beside us and said that Peter Cook had died the day before. I hadn't known, and hated not having known, guilty that I had enjoyed the previous evening's dinner. I ate my lunch but didn't taste it. Later on I was glad that it was a fellow comic writer, one of my masters, from whom I had found out that another of my masters was no longer with us. It fitted the way that Peter's influence worked. He got used early to the adulation of a wide public and eventually decided that he could do without it: long before the end, fame had to chase him far harder than he chased it. But among his fellow practitioners his lustre was undimmed, unequalled and unchallenged, a large part of the binding force that joined them even as their individual ambitions forced them apart. Just as the astronauts riding up on their rockets all worshipped Chuck Yeager, the jet pilot who never joined them in space because he flew too well with wings, so the media millionaires all knew that Cook was the unsurpassable precursor who had done it all before they did, and done it better. Indeed his superiority was easier to take after he ceased to exercise it. In his last years, when he sat at home reading newspapers while defying alcohol to dull his brilliant mind, he was a cinch to love. Early on, when we were all struggling to get started and he was effortlessly up there dominating the whole picture, to feel affection for him took self-discipline. Admiration was too total. You couldn't write a line without imagining him looking over your shoulder, not very impressed.

To imagine him doing that was particularly easy if you were coming up to Pembroke College, Cambridge, which I did in 1964. His legend haunted the place with an intensity unrivalled even by that of Ted Hughes. The poet, after all, had only begun to practise his art there. But the comedian was already the leading man in his field before he went down. I thought, perhaps incorrectly, that I could write poetry of my own without worrying too much about Hughes. But there was no question of doing comedy without worrying about Cook. When Eric Idle drafted me to assist him in producing the Pembroke Smoker in the Old Library, he made it clear to me that the tradition begun by Cook had to be kept up, even if it was unlikely that our concert would emulate Cook's in forming the basis of a West End hit revue. Cook created *Pieces of Eight* while still *in statu pupillari*. He had two revues running in the West End before he sat the Tripos. At the porter's lodge, so the story went, his accountant was told to wait because a Hollywood producer had not yet left. Stories about Cook grew with the telling, but only because of the magnitude of the initial impetus. It would be our task, Idle informed me, to be worthy of his example, at least to the extent of not perpetrating a disaster. Together we built a stage out of beer crates.

In subsequent years, when I had installed myself as perennial sole producer of the Pembroke Smoker, I always had Cook's damnably precocious originality in mind to keep me humble. When Germaine Greer did her famous Striptease Nun routine, or her sensational rendition of 'Land of Hope and Glory' in which her mouth moved out of synchronization with the words while the audience fell thrashing out of their chairs, I would stand proudly in the wings, confident that he would have approved. I only wished that I could have been as confident about my own efforts. Most of them were comic monologues, and none of us ever delivered one of those without remembering who had been on before us. That tiny beer-crate stage could feel as big and lonely as a Roman arena.

We had all felt his influence long before that, of course. With mingled envy and awe I had memorized the whole of the *Beyond the Fringe* LP, including the liner notes, the year I arrived in London. But in Pembroke those four indecently gifted young people started to become real, simply because I could hear the exemplary echo of Cook's footsteps on the flagstones. He was practically a physical presence, although strangely enough he was the last of the quartet that I actually met in real life, and it was more than twenty years later before I experienced the delights of his conversation. When I finally did, it immediately became apparent why he was producing less for the public. It was because he was lavishing it on his life. He gave it away to his friends. In an hour of casual talk he spilled out enough wit and perception – in him the two things were uncommonly near allied – to keep anybody else going for a whole television season. That was the cruel fact which so few of his obituarists, even at their most laudatory, could bring themselves to face: he wasn't just a genius, he had the genius's impatience with the whole idea of doing something *again*. He reinvented an art form, exhausted its possibilities, and just left it. There is always something frightening about that degree of inventiveness. Leonardo used to scare people the same way, by carving in ice, painting on a wet wall, or just never getting around to creating any more of the masterpieces that everyone – wise after the event – knew that he was capable of. But he knew that better than they did. Cook, *mutatis mutandis* (he couldn't paint, but then Leonardo couldn't imitate Harold Macmillan), was in the same case. He didn't lose his powers. He just lost interest in proving that he possessed them.

In a television special called *Postcard from London* I filmed a conversation with Cook and we did a good deal of incidental chatting while the magazines were being changed. More recently, in his last years, I had the pleasure of his company when he sweetly agreed to descend from his mountain fastness and become the most adventurous guest in every season of my weekly talk show. On screen he was invariably magisterial, but off screen he was even better than that. Most good speakers husband their resources, especially when it is getting late. Few of them will play to an audience of one. He would give his whole wealth without hesitation. I wish we had spent more time talking about the Dear Old College but it didn't work out that way. In my experience, he wasn't much of a one for reminiscence, and he wasn't kidding about his profound indifference to Establishments of all types. It would be sentimental to suggest that Pembroke, or even Cambridge, formed him. It would be truer to say that he formed them – to the extent, at any rate, of providing one of those periodic injections of concentrated intelligence which our venerated institutions depend on for their continued vitality. He did the same for the whole country. A supreme master of the language that unites this nation, he was the laughter in its voice: sceptical, critical, yet always joyful, revelling in the verbal heritage which for him was the tradition that really mattered. (It was a pity that he never read from

The Anatomy of Melancholy, because there are whole stretches of it which you would swear he wrote.) If his college ever puts up a statue to him, it should be rigged to speak, as a reminder that the illustrious roster of Pembroke poets which began with Spenser surely included Peter Cook.

Pembroke Magazine, 1995

MY LIFE IN POP

The music business being what it is, it's practically impossible to quote a song lyric without paying through the nose. But I can quote this one for free because, about thirty years ago, I wrote it. 'Perfect moments have a clean design,' sang Pete Atkin last week, launching the first stanza of his opening number at the Everyman Theatre during the Cheltenham Literary Festival. 'Scoring edges that arrest the flow/ Skis cut diamonds in the plump of snow/ Times my life feels like a friend of mine.' Pete was centre stage, accompanying himself on guitar, and the pretty melody already held his audience breathless: not an empty seat in the place, and not a sound except from him.

Feigning casualness in my chair at stage left, I arranged my weary eyelids to yield an appropriate aperture for conveying serious humility while simultaneously counting the house. Terraces of angelic people went up into the sky like the final scene of Dante's *Paradiso*, and not one of them was eating popcorn. Would they all still be there after an hour and a half of this stuff? Worry about that later: so far, so good. It was a perfect moment.

Much of the perfection lay in its unexpectedness. Until very recently, I had thought that the hundred or so songs James and Atkin wrote between the late Sixties and late Seventies had been consigned irretrievably to the same warehouse as the Sinclair C5, the Sony Watchman, Albert Finney's record album and Naomi Campbell's novel. For the forgotten fad, there is always a place in nostalgia. For the bright idea that never catches on in the first place, there is nothing that lingers except the disappointed sigh of its creator. At the time when Atkin and I were active as songwriters, young men wore side-burns, flared trousers and round-tip Paisley-pattern shirts with a high content of polyester. If any of that hideous kit ever comes back, it will be because there was too much of it for the embarrassed folk

memory to burn. Some young pretender to John Galliano's crown
will find a heap of his father's quondam glad-rags in the back of the
broom cupboard and get the idea that what was popular once might
be popular again.

But our songs were never popular in that sense. Hundreds, and
then thousands of people liked them, but not millions. The Atkin
albums – there were six of them all told – achieved respectful reviews
and even respectable sales: if I had published collections of poetry
that sold in those figures I would have been a happy man. People
who bought the albums rarely got rid of them. As the years went
by, their resale price went up and up: they are notoriously hard to
find second hand. The trouble was that in the years when they were
coming out they were hard to find first hand. Record company
executives didn't know how to classify what we were doing, and the
shops didn't know where to put it in the racks. Pop? Rock? Jazz?
Folk? All too often we were filed under Easy Listening, which was
the last thing we were. Whichever way you sliced it, by music business
standards we were a minority interest. And in a mass medium, the
penalty for being a minority interest is the kiss-off, usually without
hope of resurrection.

When Lazarus emerged from the tomb, none of his friends wanted
to hear about what it felt like to come back to life. They wanted to
hear about what it felt like to be dead. Did it hurt? Well, yes it did.
We put ten years of effort into trying to break through, and it all
ended with a funeral bell. After that, there was a Clive James compul-
sively active in several fields of various repute and there was a Pete
Atkin with an increasingly important career in BBC radio, culminating with his magisterial production of *This Sceptred Isle*, a hit series
whose collected earnings on audio tape – none of which go to him
– will contribute a large chunk to Sir John Birt's retirement package.
There was a James and there was an Atkin, but there was no more
James and Atkin. There was a him and a me, but there was no
more us.

Over the last twenty years I have spent as little time as possible
wondering what became of us, because the sense of loss was too
piercing. 'I Wonder What Became of Me', a miniature masterpiece by
Johnny Mercer and Harold Arlen, was one of the Broadway show
tunes that Atkin and I found we shared an admiration for when we
first started to write together. It was a downbeat, near-suicidal song,

and so, it would turn out, were a lot of ours. We were always careful to crank out the occasional jollified show-stopper to avoid the possibility of our listeners hanging themselves, but on the whole we, and especially I, inclined towards melancholy. My favoured thematic area at the time was the absurdity of love in a world dedicated to destruction, and quite often I wasn't even as funny as that. Pete would make even a death threat sound like a murmur of desire, but there must have been times when he looked at one of my sketches for a lyric and wondered whether it might not have been better tackled by Captain Nemo sitting at his pipe organ near the bottom of the Atlantic.

Yet even our most doom-laden efforts were written on a tide of optimism. We had a terrific time, and I think some of that afflatus got into what we turned out, giving a joyous lilt to even the bleakest dirge. We used to meet late at night in the Footlights club-room, which in that era was a first-floor walk-up in Petty Cury, a decrepit lane which has since been replaced by the kind of blond-brick shopping mall where people in training shoes buy fluorescent haversacks. Snugly installed with a pint each from the bar, we put our songs together at the old upright piano, Pete changing the melodies to fit my words, me changing the words to fit the melodies, both of us working towards each other like tunnellers from different sides of the world. Upstairs, the massed hearties of the University Yacht Club were either dancing a reel or else attacking the floor with sledgehammers. Downstairs, the loosely stored merchandise of Macfisheries sent up the odour of the ocean after a thermonuclear blast. But nothing could break our concentration or poison the atmosphere of shared endeavour. We knew what we were after. Total expression, and popular success.

Pete loved rock and roll. He had a fierce, though not undiscriminating, interest in everything rock was turning into, from Fairport Convention at the soft end all the way across to Randy Newman at the ragged edge. But he also loved the traditions of Broadway and Tin Pan Alley. He wanted to get everything into his melodies. I felt the same about lyrics. I wanted to get every form of writing into them: poetry, drama, reportage, aphorisms, gags. But I also wanted to get every *form* into them. I liked the grab-bag lyrics of Bob Dylan but would have preferred them tightly rhymed; vowel rhymes were too loose. I wanted those clinching syllables to match up, as they always had from the courtly love lyrics of the troubadours all the way through to those stomping numbers Leiber and Stoller wrote for Elvis Presley. Word play, slang, literary allusions: let's have it all. Why not?

There was nothing Pete couldn't set. I could write a long, complicated verse full of tricky internal rhymes and he could make it soar and swoop like an aria. Even better, I could follow the flashy verse with a childishly simple chorus and he could fill every black-and-white phrase of it with emotional colour. Remembering Sydney Harbour on a Saturday afternoon, I wrote: 'Between the headlands to the sea/ The fleeing yachts of summer go.' He set the two syllables of 'fleeing' to the same note-length as the single syllable of 'sea' and the yachts sped up in front of your mind's eye, as if their spinnakers had been snapped open by the wind. Here were melodies you could touch, and my words were there inside them like amber-breathing butterflies, transfigured and vivified into a sumptuous compound that would never come apart. Talk about a lucky break!

I loved what we were doing. Better yet, when Pete sang our numbers in the Footlights revues on the Edinburgh fringe the audience loved what we were doing. Better even than that, when the albums came out – *Beware of the Beautiful Stranger, Driving Through Mythical America, The Road of Silk, A King at Nightfall, Secret Drinker* – the people who bought them loved what we were doing. They wrote letters to tell us. Strange, wild-eyed young men would come up to me in the street, quote a phrase and give me their blessing. I didn't see how we could lose. What could go wrong?

Everything. The rocket sat on the pad for year after year, spilling impressive plumes of boiling liquid oxygen but resolutely refusing to lift off. I blamed the record companies, the BBC playlist committee, the journalists, the weather. I even blamed poor Kenny Everett for managing to get himself fired in the very week that he was playing one of our songs every time he went on the air. It was a long time after we packed it in that I started blaming the real culprit. Myself. You could have total expression, or you could have popular success, but not both. What I had created was an insuperable marketing problem. Guilt-ridden at having led my gifted colleague down a blind alley, I put it all behind me.

What I never guessed was that the market would change, and that the old, rigid recording industry would melt down like the Soviet

Union. There was a new form of distribution on the way: the Internet. Early this year, when some bright young spark in my office taught me how to switch the thing on, there it was: the rocket finally lifting off.

On the Pete Atkin website (www.peteatkin.com) anyone who wants to can find out everything, including how to buy the first two albums, reissued on a single CD. (Seeformiles C5 HCD 664). There are photographs, music sheets, chord sequences, learned analyses. What really floored me, however, was to see all the lyrics I had ever written come popping up one after the other. Many of them I had utterly forgotten, but somebody had remembered. There really is a life after death: a nice thing to find out while you're still alive. It was a perfect moment, like the one at Cheltenham. The audience was still there at the end, by the way, and their applause made the trousers of two ageing men flare as in days of old. If we still had sideburns, they would have been on fire with pride.

Independent, 21 October, 1999

EMPHASIS ON OZ

LES MURRAY AND HIS MASTER SPIRITS

Over the hundreds of years it has taken for the colonies of the old European empires to become nations, there have been cases – most notably, of course, the United States – where a creole literature has made an important addition to the literature of the homeland, but there has been no case quite comparable to that of Australian poetry in this century. The Spanish poetry of the Americas comes close – a history of poetry in the Spanish language that did not give Ruben Dario a crucial place would be no history at all – but even that has little to compare with the burgeoning of Australian poetry in the last hundred years. Trainee midwives on tenterhooks, Australian nationalists eager for every sign of a successful parturition from the homeland have a lot to go on. Though it remains necessary to call them unwise, it would be unwise to call them fools. What they really want is for Australia to become the new USA: the ex-colony that made it all the way to the status of world power. The more likely realization of so gullible a wish would be Australia as an extra American state – a new Alaska with a better climate, or at most a new California with a better social security system. But since it undoubtedly would also have a better literature, there is something to be said, from the cultural viewpoint, for these dreams of autarky. Sir Les Patterson, Minister for the Yartz, has never been entirely wrong on that point: it is only by missing the larger point that his view becomes ridiculous. A culture can never flourish as a hedge against the world. It isn't a bastion for nationalism, it is an international passport.

The best known internationally among his generation of Australian poets, Les Murray would count as a nationalist if there were such a thing as a purely political view. Up to and including the prospect of severing all monarchist ties with Britain he believes politically in the Australia he gave a name to: the Vernacular Republic. But as his collections of densely wrought essays prove, when it comes to culture he also believes that such a thing as purely political belief can't be had. The secret of his pre-eminence as a writer of critical prose in Australia today is his capacity not to simplify what he would like to change. Blessed with a sense of history and the gifts to articulate it, he would be an important man of letters even if he never wrote a poem, and he would be a vital shaping influence of Australia's emergent poetic tradition if only by dint of his anthologies. Murray favours what Ezra Pound used to call the active anthology: one whose poems are chosen because they are all inventions, and not just representative of their authors' reputations. Wide-ranging and generous in his choices, adept – sometimes too adept – at leaving himself out of the picture, he chooses from the creole heritage to bring out the full complexity of the relationship between the Australian poets of previous generations and the old Empire that was always on their minds even when they tried to repudiate it.

Murray's anthologies could easily have been more tendentiously selective. In his *New Oxford Book of Australian Verse* he includes a striking proportion of aboriginal poetry: any Mexican anthology that included so much Indian poetry would be accused of pushing the *mestizo* ideal to the point of nationalist fervour. But not even his Oxford book tries to pretend that the imperial past was a state of false consciousness from which Australia had to awake before it could breathe free air. Because he has played so straight with the complexities of history, Murray has established impeccable credentials for himself as an interpreter of his country's present. As a consequence, everything he does as a man of letters takes on a growing burden of responsiblity. His poetry can look after itself: none better. But he finds his merest book review being scrutinized for political resonance, and an anthology like his new, quirkily named *Fivefathers* acquires a significance beyond the literary. Speaking as a devout cultural reactionary, my own first reaction to Murray's latest survey of his literary forefathers (Fivefathers equals forefathers plus one: I just got it) is that if all the other nationalists were as judicious as he, the prospect of a republic would be a lot less daunting. To borrow Thomas Mann's classic formulation about Goethe, Murray is radical enough to understand the good.

Murray's five fathers were all active in what he tellingly calls the pre-Academic era, when Australian poets had to make their way without any support from the as yet undeveloped academic industry, and were not necessarily the worse off for it. First-time readers of Australian poetry in Britain, at whom this Carcanet publication must principally be aimed, should be warned that another criterion for inclusion is death. None of these five fathers is among the living or even the recently departed, which means that there are some comparable contemporary figures who are not present and should be sought elsewhere. There are fathers like A. D. Hope, mothers like Judith Wright and Gwen Harwood, and sisters, cousins and aunts who should ideally be here too. But Murray's anthologizing activities always lead you in that direction: each of them feels like the beginning of the ideal inclusive book, the one that, nothing but art, contains *all* the art. What we need to remember is that such a book can no longer be compiled: Australian poetry has become too big a subject – has become a *field*, to which we need a *guide*, and eventually quite a few more of those academic help-words of which Murray is so rightly suspicious, believing as he does that they threaten the death of personality. Like all true humanist critics an implacable enemy of literary theory, he wants us to experience his five fathers as living men, and it is permissible to suspect that he wants this with particular urgency in the case of the first father in the queue, Kenneth Slessor, from whose work Murray's selection is particularly lavish and – dare one say it? – loving. Of this father, Murray speaks as a true son.

At Sydney University in the late 1950s, most of the young poets were men but would haunt the cafeteria of the women's Union, Manning House. The reason was simple: in Manning House you could linger over a single coffee cup for hours without getting thrown out, whereas from the men's Union ejection followed precipitately upon the first gurgling of the dregs. With the conspicuous exception of Murray – even in those days, he stood out like Sydney Greenstreet miscast as Ginger Meggs – few of the Manning House poets had the heritage of Australian poetry much on their minds. My own *Stammtisch* would be decorated with slim Faber volumes in their original glamorous wrappers, all purchased from Tyrrel's second-hand bookshop at the Quay end of George Street: Auden, MacNeice, T. S. Eliot and the occasional impressively fat black-bound fascicle of Pound's *Cantos*, which inchoate effusion I held at the time to be omniscience distilled into a crucible of obsidian. Robert Hughes wouldn't even be reading in English: if he hadn't already memorized it, he would be carrying *Mon coeur mis à nu*, muttering lines from it while he drew caricatures in the margin. Home-grown literary magazines like *Meanjin* and *Westerly* were for old lecturers in gowns who cared about Vance Palmer and were sincerely, absurdly, bent on setting up a Department of Australian Literature. For them, and for Murray.

For the rest of *les jeunes*, the very concept of an Australian literature seemed far away, yet even those of us already committed in advance to a breakaway existence knew about Slessor. Everyone owned a copy of *One Hundred Poems*. In those days books of poetry published in Australia looked and smelled like books published in the Soviet Union throughout its benighted career: i.e. they looked like tat and smelled like glue. Cherishably well-presented volumes like the Edwards and Shaw edition of A. D. Hope's *The Wandering Islands* were the very rare exceptions. Slessor's *One Hundred Poems* was an Angus and Robertson booklet bound in an uneasy combination of paper and stiff cardboard. It was pitiably unimpressive to look at. But we all knew that the stuff inside it was the best Australian poetry anybody had yet seen. Shamefully, at least one Manning House *habitué* for too long employed this awareness as an excuse to dismiss everyone else, and even in Slessor's case I had been away from Australia for twenty years before I took his full measure as an artist, memorized everything, and began the long job, which his example necessitated, of getting the national literature into perspective within my own mind.

The main point to make about Murray's relationship with Slessor is that Murray saw Slessor's pivotal importance straight away, and with a thoroughness that helped determine his own attitude to his privileges and duties as a poet in Australia, as opposed to the poets *from* Australia that most of the rest of us vaguely dreamed of ourselves as being, if not yet then some day soon. At his own table in Manning House, Murray always looked as if he was dug in to stay. A boy from the country for whom Sydney was exotic enough, he approached Slessor personally, made his admiration clear, presented his own work for criticism, and was eventually rewarded with Slessor's acknowledgment that he, Murray, had been determined by fate to pick up and carry on the torch that Slessor had dropped. In private life, when the company is suitable, Murray has been known to recount the details of this apostolic succession. His pride is justifiable, and a nice example of the anecdotal human scale that still vestigially applies to the Australian literary life even in this later age of arts-section hype, globe-girdling travel, and the isolation that forms unbidden around famous names. I got that story out of him over a glass of white wine at Australia House the last time he read in London, and it was only a few weeks ago, in Bloomsbury, at a publisher's jamboree for booksellers, that David Malouf easily secured my agreement to the proposition that Murray's critical prose was by far the best thing of its kind being written in Australia now. The idea of an Australian international literary mafia is not a very good one (principally because it is not a very good metaphor) but if there is something to the notion of an extended family of those devoted to literature, then in a large part it goes back to Slessor, a godfather in the best, most benign sense, even when – perhaps especially when – he was no longer creative.

Just why Slessor has to be thought of as dropping the torch, rather than merely setting it into an iron ring against a stone wall to burn by itself once his arm was tired, is a subject Murray is ideally equipped to treat one day, in an essay that should be a pleasure to read, even if tragic. The foundations have been laid by Geoffrey Dutton's excellent biography, but we need an analysis that traces the line of destruction from the personality into the poetry. Alcohol had something to do with it; and alcoholism in turn had something to do with Slessor's disappointment in the culture that had grown up, or failed to grow up, around him: a disappointment which had somehow been prepared for, within his estimation of himself, by his comparative failure as a war correspondent *vis-à-vis* such stars as Alan Moorehead; and so on. But there can be no doubt about the intensity with which the torch burned while he could still run with it. In his 'Five Visions of Captain Cook', when he wanted to evoke the confidence that the junior officers of the *Endeavour* had in their captain's powers of navigation, he did it like this.

> Men who ride broomsticks with a mesmerist
> Mock the typhoon.

Just try forgetting that. Slessor favoured the extended, multi-part poem, but he was always epigrammatic even at his most thematically expansive. After returning to it many times over thirty or more years, I can now see his twelve-part poem 'The Old Play' as a masterly set of varied tones and dictions, but his sheer power of compressed evocation is still at the heart of it.

> In the old play-house, in the watery flare
> Of gilt and candlesticks, in a dim pit
> Furred with a powder of corroded plush,
> Paint fallen from angels floating in mid-air,
> The gods in languor sit.

Otherwise an admirer of Sickert, I have always found his theatre paintings disappointingly dark: his muddy palette is meant to call up faded glory, but only the fading shows. In Slessor's lines you can see the glory. *Furred with a powder of corroded plush* is something better than an image: it is an attitude, regret distilled into an elixir. In his most famous multi-part poem, 'Five Bells', such stellar moments gravitate together and join up: the whole effort is alive with sayability, assembled from a kit whose parts are quotations.

> The naphtha-flash of lightning slit the sky,
> Knifing the dark with deathly photographs . . .
>
> You have no suburb, like those easier dead
> In private berths of dissolution laid—
> The tide goes over you, the waves ride over you
> And let their shadows down like shining hair . . .

I have never written or even spoken about Slessor without quoting those last two lines. Precisely registering what the surfer sees on the sand beneath him when he ducks under an incoming dumper, they were with me when I left Sydney; they were my way back to him when I later sat down to read everything he ever wrote; and perhaps, eventually, they were my way home. But Murray's extensive selection proves that such clean, clear, shapely, and striking simplicity – the speakable directness that many of us would like to feel is, or should be, the defining characteristic of Australian poetry – was hard won from a deep complexity of mind and spirit, and from an inherently tortuous connection with the whole heritage of European culture. Slessor was a learned man who knew just where and when to place his epigraphs from Heine. Natural utterance did not come naturally: it was a quiet triumph of sustained artifice. Finally our realization of the full impact of his poetry depends on *his* realization that the search for a personal voice would have to be self-conscious, if only because the demand for a national voice had taken on a political dimension. In this regard it is a pity that Murray did not have room to include more of Slessor's light verse (the term was never more of a misnomer: the merest lyric drips with melancholy) from the two collections *Darlinghurst Nights* and *Backless Betty from Bondi*, because it was those two books that most clearly pointed up the source of the dicipline that sharpened his sense of form and loaded his line without blurring it – Tin Pan Alley. The impact of the American forces during World War II, both as comrades in arms and as what amounted to an occupying power, decisively shifted Australia's position in the old Empire, and Slessor not only presaged the whole event during the Depression years, he set the lingusitic limits for it, outlining the tonal range in which an Australian poet, as an agent instead of a patient, could write about a wider world.

The other four of the Fivefathers wrote about the world before it widened. As a result they seem further back in time than Slessor does, even when their period of flowering was more recent. Murray puts a high value on Roland Robinson, who spent a lifetime trying to incorporate the totemic properties of traditional Aboriginal poetry into his own. The same urge, less subtly realized, inspired the Jindyworobak movement. Robinson had a wider range of tones than the Jindyworobaks, but he was still, and thus still is, limited by the assumption that a proper name from an Aboriginal language has automatic resonance. Nobody would expect to get away with this when quoting from any other foreign language: it is always a plea by a would-be anthropologist with a political programme, and it always stops a poem dead in its tracks.

> Now that the fig lets fall her single stars
> of flowers on these green waters I would be
> withdrawn as Gul-ar-dar-ark the peaceful dove . . .

Later on in the same poem, Geek-keek the honeyeater shows up, demanding the same good faith that his name is not a misprint, or a harassed blacktracker's short way of saying 'Take a hike, honky' to an importunate enquirer. As was bound to happen, the subsequent recovery of actual Aboriginal poetry by specialists in the original languages – a process amply drawn upon in Murray's Oxford anthology, and which continues – pointed up the essential wilfulness of this whole premature attempt to lend native art dignity by misappropriating its detachable tokens. Even at the time, the general impression was of petty larceny masquerading as ethnology, like André Malraux swiping statuettes from pagodas. Later on, in retrospect, the sad spectacle of wasted time spread like a dry lake through a generation. Robinson was an especially poignant example because he had the talent to compose thoroughly in English without having to doll up flat language in borrowed trinkets: the Australian love poem has a sumptuous heritage, and Robinson's 'The Creek' is one of the loveliest poems in it.

> I make my camp beside you, a dove-grey
> deep pool fretting its fronds and tangled
> flowers. Waratahs burn above you. You
> give me billyfuls of rainwater wine, a
> bright wing-case, a boronia petal, a white
> rose tinted tea-tree star.

All of this bush detail is easily recognizable and appreciated by any Australian and none of it would be made more poetic if it were to be substituted for by an aboriginal word: indeed the opposite effect would be achieved, to the detriment not only of English but of the aboriginal language as well, which would be made to sound as the Jindyworobaks invariably made it sound – like a formula for boredom. But there was nothing shameful about their doomed fight. It was part of an impulse to make a new nation conscious of the awkward fact that it had existed as a country long before its colonial history began: a fact which it was in the interests of its bourgeoisie to overlook, and of its powerful squattocracy to deny.

For all practical purposes, 'squatter' was the Australian word for the creole or the sabra in his most self-confident form: the squatters inherited the earth and it would have been no surprise if whole generations of the landed families had grown up thinking of nothing except their own interests. Australia has yet another reason to bless its luck that so many of its landed gentry cultivated the arts and sciences as well as the soil. However close their connection with 'home', meaning England, they did a disproportionate amount to form the character of the country they were born in – endowing its art galleries, enriching its universities, setting a humane course for its cultural institutions. David Campbell, Murray's third Fivefather, was a glistening example of a type that filled the Australian social pages only a generation ago: the MacArthur-Onslows, the Bonythons. They are still there, but nowadays keep a lower profile. Campbell's profile filled the sky. While at Cambridge before the war he played rugby for England. In the RAAF he won two DFCs. He would have made such a perfect husband for Princess Margaret that the joy his poetry takes in his colonial background – seemingly exultant that his background is in the foreground – acquires overtones of heroism.

> Here's to Sydney by the summer!
> Body-surfing down a comber
> Where the girls are three a gallon
> To a beach of yellow pollen . . .

For daring young men like Campbell, the arts they practised with such confident grace seemed just another part of *noblesse oblige,* and all the more daunting for their seeming ease. Like the black bullock's horns mounted on the grille of the returned Mosquito pilot Kym Bonython's white Bristol sports saloon, Campbell's poems were the bagatelles of a dandy. But the successful throwaway gesture is fated to live, and Campbell's perfect little poem 'Mothers and Daughters' is remembered today by men who, when they were young, got no closer to the incandescent women it describes than the social pages of *Pix* and *Women's Weekly,* leafed through at the barber's in sullen envy.

> The cruel girls we loved
> Are over forty,
> Their subtle daughters
> Have stolen their beauty;
>
> And with a blue stare
> Of cruel surprise
> They mock their anxious mothers
> With their mother's eyes.

For the sons of the squatters, at home anywhere in the world where there were country houses, turning up breezily at Buckingham Palace to collect their gongs, Australian cultural isolation was a non-problem. To James McAuley, Fivefather number four, it was a burning issue, and he eventually reached the conclusion that there was no salvation outside the church. For McAuley in the late – some might say the sclerotic – phase of his conservatism, the Catholic church was not just the symbol but the living presence of the international order he thought his country needed to be part of, or it would have no standards except its own. There was a paradox in his position, because the church stood behind and above the heritage of Irish immigration that gave the Labor party its electoral strength and provincialism its abiding force. Luckily he thrived on paradoxes. They appealed to his sense of symmetry. He had a formal gift that comes singing out of this anthology with the chamfered and inlaid neatness of a Van Eyck angel's spinet. In stanzas lusciously sonorous he evoked austerity as if thirsting for a vinegar-soaked sponge.

> Where once was a sea is now a salty sunken desert,
> A futile heart within a fair periphery;
> The people are hard-eyed, kindly, with nothing inside them,
> The men are independent but you could not call them free.

Since free was exactly what the independent men *did* call themselves, McAuley could not expect to be popular for taking this position, but he didn't care. A local Ortega relishing his role as a fastidious rebel against the mass-market future, he was fated to embrace austerity all too successfully – the later epic poetry was thought tedious even by lifelong admirers – but he never lost his unmatched capacity to conduct a prose argument through a poetic form: 'Because', a lament for his parents and the love he never got from them or could give back, is one of the great modern Australian poems and would be worth acquiring this book for just on its own.

The same might be said for several of the poems in the selection from the last of the Fivefathers, Francis Webb, whose fitting task is not to fit into this book or any other except those entirely his. Even at the time, Webb was a one-off, an El Greco-style stylistic maverick: making an entirely unexpected appearance in a tradition, he could be seen to have emerged from it, but he distorted the whole thing. Webb was a clinical case, a schizophrenic who spent a lot of time in hospital and eventually disintegrated, but Murray, with typical penetration, has never fallen for the easy notion that Webb's poetry is psycho in itself. The answer to the biologist's trick question of whether there was something wrong with El Greco's eyes is no, because if there had been he would have compensated for it. Similarly

Webb's poetry is the way it is because of his inner vision, not because of scrambled perceptions. If his cognitive apparatus had been muddled he would have attempted simplicities. As things were and are, his synaesthetic effects have to be compared with Baudelaire, Rimbaud and the hallucinatory extravaganzas that the British Apocalyptic poets of the forties aimed for without achieving. The guarantee of Webb's urge to transcendental integration was the purity of his fragments. Wherever two or three of his admirers are gathered together, you will hear these particles flying. (My own favourite hemistitch, from a poem omitted here, is 'Sunset hails a rising': one day I'm going to call a book that and lay the beautiful ghost of an idea that must have come to him in one of his fevers, like a cooling drop of sweat.) In the enforced retreats of his hospitals and the injected lucidities of his drugs, there might well have been something prophetic about Webb. Certainly he guessed that the Australian poets would become a success story, and feared the consequences.

> Now yours is the grand power, great for good or evil:
> The schoolboy (poor devil!) will be told off to study you . . .

Webb was Murray's predecessor in guessing that an efflorescent culture would set the challenge of studying it without ceasing to love it. With music and painting, both of which flourish in Australia as if the molecules of the air had been redesigned specifically to nourish them, it is easy to keep passion pure: when the orchestra strikes up, the commentary must cease, and in the art gallery you can always neglect to hire the earphones. But when the academic age dawned it became chasteningly clear that poetry would be hard to separate from its parasitic buzz. One of the penalties for success was a proliferation of middle-men, and eventually, as feminism institutionalized itself, middle-women. The new *Oxford Book of Australian Women's Verse*, however, is a welcome sign that the essentials are being remembered. Unlike the notorious *Penguin Book of Australian Women Poets* of 1987, Susan Lever's anthology is unburdened by didactic jargon and makes commendably little fuss about the necessarily agonizing problem of getting everybody in without leaving too many good poems out. Fledgling feminists will receive an encouraging message about self-realization growing with time. Those of us who have always taken the importance of women poets in Australia for granted (in the fifties we were male chauvinist pigs almost to a man, but none of us was going to argue with Gwen Harwood or Judith Wright) will be left free to detect a more edifying progression. Presumably it must apply to the men as well, although perhaps the women – careful now – were always more likely to register its effects: anyway, in this verse chronicle, as the century wears on, the poets become more, instead of less, precise about domestic detail, until nowadays, against all expectation, the housewife tradition looks unbreakably strong.

One of the great strengths of the generation that included Judith Wright and Gwen Harwood lay in the harsh fact that they had no time to be careerists: they wrote from necessity, in the exiguous spare time left over from looking after their men. You would think that the new freedoms would have led to a plunge back into time, a local re-run of the *rentier* aesthetic leisure once enjoyed by the bluestockings of Britain and America, an inexorable push towards the free bohemian status of Edna St Vincent Millay: that the ethereal would beckon. But not on this showing. It was once uniquely Gwen Harwood's way to write about music and philosophy as if they were the bread of life she had brought home from the shops. But here is the proof that it has since become standard practice, thus helping to create, for the Australian reader, perhaps the least alienated and divisive literary culture on earth. Try this, from Susan Hampton's 'Ode to a Car Radio'.

> My right eye leaking blood coming home
> from Casualty, patched, pirate view, & changing gears
> past Rooms to Let $12 p.w. beside Surry Hills Smash Repairs
> & a beer gut emerging from a pub door at ten, well,
> you can picture the general scene
> & click! clear as glass, the flute opening
> to Prokofiev's *Romeo and Juliet*, cool & sweet
> as a parkful of wet trees.

Ms Hampton was one of the hectoring editors of the aforementioned Penguin anthology but I forgive her, as long as she goes on writing like that. Prokofiev gets into the poem unquestioned, which is exactly the way things ought to be, because Australia is a place where classical music is in the air. It didn't happen by accident. Australia became a clever country because clever people, many of them refugees from harsh political experience in Europe, were wise enough not to accept unquestioned the prevalent intellectual assumptions about the necessary divorce between democracy and art. For the poets of the pre-academic generation, art was in their lives as sustenance and salvation. Their successors have caught the habit, in the only tradition worth taking the trouble to define, the handing on of a copious view. One of my favourite poems in this book is by Vicki Raymond, whose work I will seek out from now on. Talking about static electricity in the office, she brings off a quietly tremendous coup worthy of the poet whose name she invokes.

> You can even feel it through your clothes,
> which crackle lightly like tinfoil.
> It's as though you were turning into
> something not right, but strange; your hair
> floats out like Coleridge's
> after he'd swallowed honeydew.

According to the notes, Vicki Raymond is an an expatriate who has lived in Lodon since 1981. Well, it's an Australian poem wherever it was written. The expatriates are part of all this too, but if put to the question they would have to admit that the vitality grown at home in their absence has come to form the core of the total astonishment, generating the power behind what makes a small country recognizable to the world in the only way that matters – its voice, the sound of freedom.

TLS, 5 July, 1996

GEORGE RUSSELL: A REMINISCENCE

George Russell is a great teacher and I was the worst student he ever had. It could be argued that the opinion of a bad student ought not to be allowed to count for much in the assessment of a teacher's quality. But George Russell's eminence as a teacher is not in doubt. Too many star students would willingly give testimony about his influence on their lives. What might perhaps add an extra, unexpected dimension to the eulogistic chorus is the testimony of a student whose biological resistance to being taught was a phenomenon of immunology. If George Russell could influence even me, there must have been something uncanny about him.

Having, to nobody's surprise greater than my own, conned my way into the English Honours school after two undistinguished years of the ordinary pass course, I joined George's high-powered class in Anglo-Saxon, opened my newly purchased textbook for the first time, and sat there as if staring at a cobra. Until that moment I had had no idea that Anglo-Saxon was a foreign language. My petrified gaze must somehow have aroused George's sympathy, not normally a commodity that he made freely available to dolts. George could be pretty cutting with anybody whose unpreparedness or plaintive outcry disturbed the rhythm of the class. 'Thank you very much,' he once publicly told a girl who had nowhere near finished protesting about the difficulty of a term exam, 'I think we've heard enough of your piping treble.'

But at least she, like all her classmates except one, had attempted to decode the set text. George knew exactly which one of the students sitting at the desks in front of him was trying to bluff his way through the whole course by memorizing the translations. That he took me under his wing instead of booting me back to the pass class can possibly be explained with reference to his religion. No doubt it imposed on him some form of spiritual mortification. I was his hair shirt.

The woman to whom I am now married was at that time a fellow student – the sort of student that every teacher dreams of teaching. Her presence by my side must have made up for the fact that I was the sort of student every teacher dreams of getting rid of, because together we were invited by George and his wife Isabel to dinner at their house in Pennant Hills. George picked us up in his car at Pennant Hills station. The visit became a regular thing; which says a lot for Isabel's tolerance, because for someone who drank George's wine as if it was water I got a great deal of talking done. My companion, needless to say, was the soul of moderation, possessing the judicious self-assessment appropriate to an academic record unblemished by any grade lower than A or honour other than first. She delighted the Russells.

But I think it fair to say that it was I who fascinated them. Wide-eyed behind his glasses, George watched enthralled while the contents of his cellar vanished inside me. I think he took a scientific interest in seeing if one of the finer things of life could work its civilizing influence even on someone who was throwing it in a high curve over the taste buds so that it didn't touch flesh until it hit the back of the throat. When my powers of monologue flagged, he would put one of the pearls of his impressive collection of classical records on the radiogram. Here again I proved a hard nut to crack, and here again he proved strangely forbearing. I can remember his laughing appreciatively, instead of in derision, when I compared Brahms to oxtail soup. When it became clear that a classical recital was to be a regular after-dinner feature, I started to retaliate by bringing along some Thelonious Monk and Charlie Parker LPs. George generously tapped his feet to ''Round Midnight' and 'Salt Peanuts' while I made faces at Monteverdi. If he construed my grimaces as a sign that the great music was striking deep into my unwilling soul, he was prescient, because there was to be little manifest evidence until many years later. Without giving too much of the game away, however, I might confide at this point that I am today no longer disposed to compare Brahms with oxtail soup, and that I could bore you pretty thoroughly with my opinions about what Emil Gilels gets out of the two piano concertos that Rubinstein doesn't, and about how Karajan drags the tempo in the Fourth symphony. Then, though, I was apparently impermeable, partly because paralytic. At the end of the evening, George drove us all the way back to town, to obviate the possibility of my boarding the electric train and falling out of the opposite door on to the track. Though I am assured that he invariably drove us all the way to Town Hall, today I can't remember us having even once crossed the Harbour Bridge. It must mean that I was unconscious every time.

In class I stayed awake but it didn't make much difference. For the Union Revue I adapted an Anglo-Saxon text about the Battle of Maldon into a sketch in which two warriors from each team faced off across a very small river and pronounced incomprehensible war-cries. The sketch was a big hit with those members of the audience who were familiar with Old English texts. This was as close as I came to any kind of rapport with our ancestral tongue. Less forgivable was how I remained impervious even to George's special seminars in which he touched upon a wider field, the Middle Ages in Europe. Unfortunately I had no Latin and it didn't occur to me at that time to acquire any, busy as I was with such important matters as editing the literary page of the student newspaper *Honi Soit*. But I can remember now being impressed even at the time by George's grave humility as he introduced a discussion of *European Literature and the Latin Middle Ages*, by Ernst Robert Curtius. 'This,' said George, his hands poised above the volume as if he were about to break bread, 'is a great book.' Then he opened it. It hardly needs saying that I had neither the preparation nor the spare time to corroborate his opinion, but the moment stayed with me.

Only the rare teacher is as fond of his promising young writers as he is of his promising young scholars. Christian Gauss of Princeton knew that Edmund Wilson was an outstanding student, but he was equally proud of his class dunce, Scott Fitzgerald. Gauss realized that Fitzgerald's divine gift for the rhythmic sentence was the cause of his immaturity: facility outran understanding, and would do so until experience provided a measure of resistance, something solid to be carved. In a teacher it takes more than brains, it takes clairvoyance, to realize that a callow chump might be carrying the seeds of literary life. I don't suggest that I had it in me to write *This Side of Paradise*, but I certainly had a startling capacity to talk fluent tosh. George listened tolerantly as I informed him of my plans to spend five years in Europe doing odd jobs while looting the area for its cultural wealth and composing poetic masterpieces by night, before returning to take my rightful place as an Australian man of letters, position and political influence. He heard me out with a patience aided by cold beer. Somewhere between the University and Redfern station there was a pub where we sometimes met at the end of the working day when George was on his way home by train and I, after two hours in Fisher Library sleeping off the effects of a long lunchtime in the Forest Lodge, was preparing for a hard evening's dissipation in the Royal George, the headquarters of the Downtown Push. Sipping reflectively, George ventured the suggestion that in the unlikely event of my scheme's failing to reach immediate fruition I might drop him a line, because if the necessity ever arose for me to take refuge once again in a university, he had a certain amount of pull at his old Cambridge college. Grandly I let him know that the possibility would never arise: the place of the artist was not in the cloisters, but in the world.

The place of this artist turned out to be in the soup. As I write this note, the second volume of my unreliable memoirs is about to be published, whereupon the full story of how I failed to ignite the Thames will be edifyingly available for any reader still harbouring the delusion that all the Australians who sailed for England in the early Sixties achieved instant success. I, for one, achieved a depth of oblivion from which I could see to climb out only by the light of my lucky stars. George, as ever conscientious beyond the call of duty, or perhaps once again impelled by the self-mortifying requirements of his lay religious order, wrote me fulsome references by air-letter so that I might apply for jobs which a glance must have told him had a dead end. Finally, when I had at last concurred with the otherwise universal opinion that I was unemployable, he wrote the letter which secured me a place at Cambridge.

Safe inside the oak doors of his old college, Pembroke, I immediately set about betraying his trust by giving my principal attention to Footlights. What reading I found time for was off the course. On one of George's visits to London I met him for a drink and gave him an account of my progress that was probably the real reason for the sour look which at the time I put down to the unspeakable English beer. My degree was obtained more by turn of phrase that by proof of diligence and I must have been the only graduate in memory who got himself registered as a Ph.D. candidate merely so that he might

become president of a dramatic society. Mine was scarcely an academic record. It was almost a police record. Always I read any book
except the one specified. But I never stopped reading. Nor did I ever
stop listening to music or looking at paintings. In George's house I
had somehow got the idea, more by osmosis than observation, that
an education was something you went on acquiring all your life.
Perhaps I got the idea too well, and too often postponed what I
should have tackled early. But I got the idea.

The moment when George said mass over his holy book has
stayed with me ever since, and now, when I look up from the
typewriter at the bookshelves in my office, I can see my own copy
of *European Literature and the Latin Middle Ages*. Beside it is another
book by Curtius, his *Essays on European Literature*, which includes the
two important long pieces about T. S. Eliot. Next comes *Gesammelte
Aufsätze zur Romanische Philologie*, which contains Curtius's definitive
review of Gianfranco Contini's edition of Dante's *Rime*. I bought that
one in Cambridge in 1968, before I could read any German. Then
there comes Curtius's pioneering little study of Proust, and then an
authentic rare bird, the first edition of his *Balzac*, Verlag von Friedrich
Cohen, Bonn, 1923. Where did I buy that? My inscription on the
flyleaf reminds me: Staten Island, two years ago, in a house full of
books bought from the descendants of European refugees from
Hitler. The thousands of abandoned books stacked two deep in the
shelves were a whispering testimony to the cultural disintegration
that Curtius first feared, then experienced, and which gave *European
Literature and the Latin Middle Ages* its pessimistic tone. I could write
an essay on the subject. It might not be an outstanding essay, but it
would touch on the main points. It has taken a long time, but I am
some kind of student at last.

Still not a good student, however. A writer can never be that: not
this writer, anyway. Borges, book mad if anybody was, divided the
two things neatly in *Historia universal de la infamia*, when he said
that writing comes before reading and is less considered. The same
dichotomy is fundamental to Croce's aesthetics, and I suppose Schil-
ler's celebrated distinction between the naïve and the sentimental
amounts to the same thing. But these are weighty names of learned
men, and merely to adduce them is to concede that you can't be a
writer without at least wanting to be a reader as well. A writer
who took literally Schopenhauer's imprecations against book-learning

would not be concentrating his energies, he would be inhibiting their renewal.

We would all like to set our minds in order, and that applies most to those of us who are obliged to lead disorderly lives. As I consume, in the TV studio, hundreds of hours that I might have spent making yet another attempt to get somewhere with Greek, my great teachers are with me as an ideal. (Probably *their* great teachers were with *them* as an ideal, when they were wasting their time reading my emptily fluent essays, and certainly when they became, later on, Professors with departments to run.) I remember George Russell standing at a lectern, silently reading a photostat of a medieval manuscript, the hurrying world shut out. I remember H. J. Oliver, when I was in his office for the first time and transfixed by his collection of those first-issue Everyman volumes with the gilt spines, pointing out gently, so as not to daunt, that the real collection was at home. Nowadays I have my collection too: books bought during assignments in Munich, Vienna and Salzburg, in Tokyo, Peking and Hong Kong, in San Francisco, Los Angeles and Tel Aviv. Some of the books I buy I will have to wait to read until I can read the languages they are written in. But at least I know what should be desired. I think it was while George was holding a seminar about the austere dedication of the Brethren of the Common Life that he first mentioned Rachel. She wasn't a real woman, she was a spirit – the spirit of contemplation. For the monk, to be denied her company was to be left desolate. To forsake Rachel was madness.

Expounding this concept, George spoke as both a man of religion and a humanist. At the time I had little idea of what he meant. A quarter of a century later I am still proof against religion of any stamp, and will no doubt remain so until my pagan grave. But humanism, the thirst for concentrated meaning that turns a classic text into a fountain of refreshment, has by now become as vivid for me as the river of light became for Dante. I wish I had good enough Latin to read the *Annals* of Tacitus as I can read his *Histories*, or to read his *Histories* as I can read his *Agricola*. Yet after my first hour with the *Annals*, an hour spent sweating to unpick even a few of its compressed sentences – whose elliptical density, like that of Shostako-vitch's string quartets, is the guarantee of their truth and of the truth's private defiance of state terror – I could at last see our horrifying twentieth century for what it has been, a time like any other: a time like *all* the others. When I closed the book I held my hands above it as if to touch it might burn them, and only later realized that the gesture had been an echo. *Benedictus benedicat.* So George Russell has had his influence, beginning with a few words and coming to fulfilment far away, as an important part of his pupil's attitude to life. There are other, better pupils with less erratic tales to tell. But I was the test case, the one sent to try him; and he came through.

From a *Festschrift* for George Russell, 1984

PREFACE TO AN AUSTRALIAN CLASSIC

By the time I at last met Robin Eakin personally, on the *sable d'or* of Biarritz in the early eighties, she was called Robin Dalton and had been one of the most influential literary agents in London for half her career. We were introduced by our mutual friend, Michael Blakemore, whose talents as a director extend to real life: wherever he is, the stage teems with creative people, and in those years, in Biarritz every summer, there was always enough prominent human material spilling out of his house and down to the beach for everyone present to have begun a *roman-à-clef* except the novelists, who were already writing about what happened the *previous* summer. John Cleese and Michael Frayn came to the house to work on films and scripts; Tim Pigott-Smith came there to be obscure for a while after starring as Merrick in *The Jewel in the Crown*; and that trim form under the big straw hat, watching the children play in the shallows of the advancing tide, belonged to the exquisite Nicola Pagett.

But there was never any doubt who was the *grande dame* of the scene. It was Robin. She had a cut-glass accent that you would have sworn had been first turned and chiselled in the nurseries of Belgravia. I was relishing her company long before I realized that she was Australian, that she was Robin Eakin, and that she had once written a classic book. I had never even heard of *Aunts Up the Cross*, which sounded to me like a feminist tract about capital punishment in ancient Rome. When I read it, I realized that it was a prize example of a genre I had been looking for: the small Australian book that was better written than the big ones, the actual fragment of *echt* literature with a small 'l' that would make me feel less unpatriotic about all those behemoths of Literature with a capital 'L' which had been failing to convince me for so long. My party-piece recitative based on the opening page of *The Aunt's Story* had been making me feel guilty for years. (I used to get a big laugh on the one-line paragraph

'And stood breathing' but I always felt ashamed: perhaps it only *sounded* ludicrous.) After I read *Aunts Up the Cross* the guilt vanished. Here at last was the living proof that a civilized, unpretentious, fully evocative prose style had been available in Australia ever since the young Robin Eakin handed in her first school essay. All we had ever needed to do was look in the wrong place. As so often happens, the true art was filed under entertainment.

To say that *Aunts Up the Cross* is beautifully written risks making the book sound like a filigree. It is anything but. Social information, moral judgement, comic action and tragic incident are all packed into sentences which have the density of uranium and would also have its weight, if they were not so proportionately constructed that they take off from the page like gliders picked up off a hill by a thermal from its face. Soon you, the lucky first-time reader of this marvellous little creation, will be in the light yet firm grip of its opening paragraph. Before that happens, let us analyse its first two sentences, because there will be no chance to do so once the third sentence reaches back to draw you on. Study this, you upcoming, unreliable memoirists: study this and weep.

> My Great-aunt Juliet was knocked over and killed by a bus when she was eighty-five. The bus was travelling very slowly in the right direction and could hardly have been missed by anyone except Aunt Juliet, who must have been travelling fairly fast in the wrong direction.

It's the gift that money can't buy and no amount of literary ambition can ever find a substitute for: the prose that sounds as if it is being spoken by the ideal speaker. Yet the spontaneity is all designed: 'very slowly' is exactly balanced against 'fairly fast', 'right direction' against 'wrong direction', and the impetus would be ruined if an editor – as almost any magazine editor nowadays would, especially if asked not to – were to insert an otiose comma after 'right direction'. The whole book is as precisely calculated as that, with the result that calculation scarcely seems to enter into it. When you get to the end, however, you find that Aunt Juliet and the bus make contact again, and you realize that you have been led a dance – a dance in a circle that might have been choreographed by Poussin, if Poussin had ever lived in the Kings Cross area of Sydney.

Robin Eakin did live there, in that unlikely Arcadia. When I was growing up after the war, Kings Cross was featured in the newspapers and magazines – not yet subsumed under the collective name of The Media – as Sydney's Montmartre, Schwabing, Soho and Greenwich Village, a reputation which seemed mainly to be based on the occasional appearance in the streets of Rosaleen Norton weighed down by mascara, sometimes as late as 11.30 in the evening. When Robin Eakin was growing up there before the war, Kings Cross, for her family at any rate, spelt something more interesting than any Bohemia – gentility in reduced circumstances. She grew up in a house full of life; a house full of lives. In that nest of gentlefolk – Turgenev is one of the many names with whom she can be mentioned in the same breath – there was drama on every floor. *The Madwoman of Chaillot* was being staged on the mezzanine. *Les monstres sacrés* inhabited the verandah. No wonder she has spent so much of her time in and around theatres: she was born in one. She revelled in it. For her, Heaven was other people. She shames me in that regard. When I look back at my own book of memoirs, I see that its first critics were right: there is only one character in it, and everyone else is a walk-on. *Aunts Up the Cross* is just the opposite: its only half-realized character is the author herself.

If the book has a fault, that's it. When she casually lets slip that she had read all the major novels of Meredith before she was twelve years old, you want to know everything else about her education, and there is nothing like enough about the young love life of a woman so striking in her maturity. Though her evocation of Sydney in the war years ranks with the on-leave passages of T. A. G. Hungerford's *The Ridge and the River,* you can't help feeling that her American service personnel are miraculously well behaved. But the book was written in what was still an age of reticence, and the upside of that is better than the downside: where tact rules, frankness really startles, and no text of such brevity ever had so many flashpoints of shock. Aunt Juliet making contact with the bus is the very least of them. I mention no more because nothing should be allowed to dissipate the economy with which every telling vignette and intermezzo is prepared and resolved. I only say that the moment when the author's mother causes the death of the plumber is one of the great throwaway paragraphs in modern Australian letters. Read it, and then imagine how Xavier Herbert would have thrown it away.

He would have thrown it away like an old refrigerator full of house-bricks: it would have taken him a hundred pages plus.

Aunts Up the Cross is all over in two hundred pages minus. A fan's foreword should show the same regard for brevity, so I will back out with one last unreliable memory before her reliable ones begin. I think it was while we were walking along the esplanade of the Côte des Basques (by which I mean we could equally have been in the drawing-room of her holiday-home maisonette, but I would rather you heard waves in the background) that I upbraided her for having written no more than this one perfect book. She fobbed me off with another drink – all right, it *was* the drawing-room – and politely neglected to state the obvious, which was that she had written something so sensitive to its own past, and so responsive to its own present, that it contained its own future. All the books she might have written later were already in it. What she was too modest even to think was that all the books the rest of us wrote later are in it too.

From an introduction to the reissue of *Aunts up the Cross*, 1997

RUNNING BESIDE RON CLARKE

One tries not to fall for the lure of the freebie, but when an Australian national hero offers membership of his gymnasium in return for a preface to its prospectus, it would be a churl who turned him down.

Having run 5,000 metres against Ron Clarke on several occasions and matched him shoulder to shoulder in the home stretch, I can give other distance runners of our calibre the following tip for defeating him tactically: start ten minutes earlier. If you and he are both running on adjacent treadmills at Cannons gym, it can be done. A lot of things can be done for the human body at Cannons. Things have been done even for my body, which was probably the nearest to a total wreck that ever stumbled out of the locker room in baggy shorts and a too-tight T-shirt. I didn't get back my youth. I didn't get back the full splendour of that original V-shaped figure that stunned the beach so long ago. But I got my weight reasonably under control, regained the habit of exercise, and above all rediscovered the pleasure of a healthy sweat.

*

When I was young in Australia I swung upside down from trees, half-killed myself clown-diving at the baths, and rode my three-speed bike for twenty miles at a time through the storm-water channels of the Sydney suburbs. I burned energy as fast as I generated it. Then about thirty years went by when I burned no energy at all, with results that most of you can guess at and some of you know all too well. It is this latter group that I address now: we of a Certain Age, victims of Time's depredations, the invasion of the body-snatcher. The greatest danger we face, when we try to get our bodies back, is of overdoing it. The great virtue of a properly run gymnasium like

Cannons is that we aren't allowed to. The staff are on the alert, making sure that no new member with one foot in the grave will try to pull it out so fast he sprains a thigh. The watchful dedication of these young guardians is eloquent testimony to how the health movement has calmed down from its initial wild enthusiasm and become part of the landscape instead of just a craze like the hula-hoop or Rubik's cube.

*

A craze was what it used to be. It all started with jogging. The so-called health editors of the Sunday newspapers filled pages with copy advising out-of-condition executives about where, when and how often to jog. One health editor was so impressed at his own easy breathing after a six-mile jog that he went off to do the same course again. Before he was halfway around he wasn't breathing at all. The following week there was a new health editor. Like his predecessor he was really an out-of-condition executive himself. Jogging shattered many a calcified Achilles tendon before the general realization dawned that it had to be done under controlled conditions.

By the time that was grasped, the more trend-conscious out-of-condition executives had given up jogging and moved on to lifting weights. Men barely capable of lifting a double brandy were pounding themselves into the carpet lifting weights at home. They were the wrong weight. There was nothing wrong with the principle. There was just a lot wrong with the practice. People who had spent thirty years getting out of shape weren't going to get back into it in thirty minutes. Luckily the gymnasium movement arrived before they all ended up in traction.

The great majority of Cannons members, of course, are young executive types who have never been very far out of condition in the first place and consequently have little trouble either getting back into it or else simply maintaining an impeccable physique. I try not to hate them. Some of the women look very cute in leotards and I try not to ogle them, an activity reprehensible at my age, and no longer tolerated even amongst the young. But I can't help sneaking a sideways look at the aerobics classes. It must be fun to bounce around like that. Certainly it seems to induce an intense camaraderie. In the snack bar afterwards you can see the aerobics experts describing their moments of glory to each other like fighter pilots after a dogfight. The après-sweat social facilities at Cannons improve after each rebuild of the premises. If I had my life over again I would spend most of it in the gym, staying in my magnificent original trim as I strode manfully between the Nautilus machines and the punching bags, writing my books at a cafeteria table with nothing to drink except a can of Dexter's, buffing up my immortality.

*

Life didn't work out that way. An old buffer has nothing left to buff up. But he can put the brakes on his decline, and feel hale again if not hearty. Like the other older senatorial figures who come to the gym I enjoy my solitude, the only hour in the day when nobody wants anything from me. You can see us in the sauna, each alone with his head in his hands, getting back in touch with the physical life, re-establishing the almost but not quite lost connection between the sound mind and sound body. There's something Roman about it. A thousand years from now, when they dig up the railway station, find a gymnasium underneath it, and decide that ours must have been an advanced civilization after all, they won't be far wrong. I can recommend without reservation that anyone worried about the deceptive comfort of his or her swivel chair should follow my lead and rekindle that old flame immediately: don't let even a single decade go by.

An introduction to *Total Living* by Ron Clarke and others, 1995

ON THE LIST

Grizzled Aussie expatriates who thought they were safely holed up in this country have been shaken to their foundation garments by the explosion of interest in the subject of Australian republicanism. There was no dodging the issue. Some said it was the first eruption of a long-simmering volcano. Others thought a squib had gone off. The initial evidence supported the latter theory. Meeting the Queen during her tour of Australia the Australian Prime Minister's wife had several times failed to curtsy, while the Prime Minister himself, on at least one occasion, had physically touched the Monarch.

For a while it was not established whether these were deliberate acts of *lèse-majesté* or examples of disarming Australian casualness. But the prominent British art critic, Brian Sewell, was already certain. The *Evening Standard* ran a full-page article from him recommending that all Australian expatriates in Britain should be deported back to their inherently treasonable country.

My own name was high on the list, with a full description. I reacted with some alarm. Though Auberon Waugh once made the same suggestion, he had been talking about voluntary repatriation, like Enoch Powell. Brian Sewell's tone was less kindly. I had always thought he sounded like a decorative attack dog, a sort of pit bull poodle, but this time he was really barking. Those British cultural journalists of the second rank who enjoy baiting Australians as a form of licensed racism had previously worn muzzles. Brian Sewell gave you a taste of what it must have been like to be Jewish in occupied Paris when Brasillach was writing for *Je suis partout*. First the denunciation, then they wake you up during the night.

Sleeping that night with my passport in my pyjamas pocket, I was woken early by a telephone call from the *Evening Standard*. Quelling the urge to answer in a disguised voice and exit backwards through the bedroom window, I bravely asked them what they wanted. It turned out that Prime Minister Keating, responding in Parliament to a taunt about his behaviour *vis-à-vis* the Monarch, had condemned Britain's shameless indifference to Australia's fate during the Second World War. Would I care to comment? I told them to ask Brian Sewell.

There was no getting out of it that easily. Over the next few days, *Newsnight*, *The World At One* and most of the newspapers were all on the trail. Everyone wanted my expert opinion on the Australian constitutional issue. Did I *look* like an expert on the Australian constitutional issue? I tried on a false beard, but it made me look like Tom Keneally, who *is* an expert on the Australian constitutional issue. He is in favour of an Australian republic. I'm not, but I'm not sure why. To get out of having to dodge any more questions, however, let me give the few answers in my possession.

Paul Keating is a man of conspicuous virtues. He has a nice line of invective which could have made him a successful debt collector in another life. When the moment came to pull the lever which dropped Mr Hawke through the trapdoor to the waiting crocodiles, Mr Keating did not pretend to share their tears. His boldness is proved by the unblushing confidence with which he now proposes to rebuild a national economy that all Australians, including possibly himself, are well aware he destroyed in the first place. He will probably make a good, long-serving Prime Minister in the not impossible event that the opposition remains so short of credible leadership that it can't beat even him.

But he knows nothing about the modern history of Australia or anywhere else. He left school early and has too readily excused himself from making up his educational deficiencies late at night. Instead of reading English books, he collects French clocks, which can tell him nothing except the time. Compared to most of his predecessors as leader of the Labor Party, he is an ignoramus. Dr H. V. Evatt might be said to have been privileged, because he went to Sydney University and had a dazzling academic record; and Bob Hawke was even more privileged, because he went to Oxford University and drank beer; but Ben Chifley, though his school was the footplate of a locomotive, found out about the world by asking. Paul Keating doesn't ask. He can't be instructed because he is always instructing. Tempted out of his field, which is bare-knuckle politics, he finds himself compelled to relay, as a substitute for what he has found out from experience,

stuff he has got out of the air. What is of interest is not his belligerence
but how the stuff got into the air.

As Alistair Horne made clear, when the posh papers wheeled him
into the argument, the idea that Britain deliberately did less than it
could to save Malaya, Singapore and finally Australia, has no basis in
fact. It shouldn't have needed Mr Horne to point this out. Repub-
lican-minded Australian revisionist historians have been able to float
the notion only by blinding themselves to the obvious. The Malaya
campaign was a bungle which cost Britain dear, and if there were
any plans by Britain to abandon Australia, they were scarcely more
sweeping than Australian plans to do the same. Planning against the
worst is a military necessity. When the Australians counted up their
resources they had to face the possibility that if the Japanese got
ashore the only defensible perimeter would be the eastern seaboard:
'the Brisbane line'. This proposal, which was drawn up in some detail,
is no reason for the inhabitants of Adelaide and Perth to now demand
a separate country of their own. Luckily the American navy fought a
crucial draw with the Japanese navy at the Battle of the Coral Sea
and the Australian army stymied the Japanese army in New Guinea,
so the prospect of abandoning Australia ceased to loom. But it might
have happened, because it might have had to.

The Australians showed more resentment for the Americans who
came to their rescue than for the British who had been so ineffective
in defending the Empire. The idea that Australians *should* have borne
ill-will towards Britain was hatched subsequently by revisionist historians with an interest in republicanism. It is a legitimate interest,
especially in view of Britain's undoubted indifference to the sensi-
tivities of Australia and New Zealand at the time of its belated entry
into the Common Market. But to play fast and loose with the truth
in order to further a political interest is not legitimate, and nothing
is more likely to make Australia go on seeming provincial than this
propensity on the part of its artists and intellectuals to tinker with
ideology. You can understand it from the Murdoch press. Its proprietor favours Australia's cutting itself off from Britain because he
has cut himself off from both countries, in pursuit of some dreary
post-capitalist Utopia in which the hunger to acquire is exalted as a
spiritual value, and the amount of debt magically testifies to financial
acumen. But there is no good reason why some of Australia's most
creative people should share his bleak vision.

And yet they do. In Australia the conspiracy theory of history wins in a walk and the cock-up theory comes nowhere. At the Dardanelles, three times as many British troops were uselessly thrown into the same boiler as the Australians, but the fact doesn't get a mention in the Australian-made film *Gallipoli* because its writer, David Williamson, favours a republic. Williamson is a gifted man who must know the truth. But he has an end in view. The conspiracy theory that Britain cynically exploited Antipodean cannon-fodder in both wars is seen to further this end.

I wonder if it will. Ordinary Australian people, less bound by the requirements to write a neat article or a clear-cut screenplay, are more likely to favour the cock-up theory, especially if they are old enough actually to remember what the war in the Pacific was like. Indeed, some of them might be inclined to extend that theory to a full-blown view of the world's contingencies, one of them being that if the British had done everything right in Malaya, they might still have lost.

It is racism of a particularly insidious kind to imagine that the Japanese were able to advance only because we retreated. General Percival, commanding for Britain, was certainly no genius, but even if he had been Montgomery and Slim rolled into one he would have had trouble with General Yamashita, a strategic prodigy in command of an army which comported itself brilliantly all the way down to platoon level. After the fall of Singapore, a jealous Tojo banished Yamashita to Mongolia, but with the war almost lost he was brought back to stop the rot on Luzon, where the Americans, by then wielding limitless resources, found to their horror that his troops had to be cooked out of their holes, and came out shooting even when they were burning.

Mr Keating's assumption that a modernized, Asia-minded Australia needs to be a republic might be greeted with some puzzlement by present-day Japan, whose economic clout dominates the region and whose Emperor, at his coronation, spent a night in the embrace of the Sun Goddess. Mr Keating's real problem, however, is with my mother. Though fiercely proud to be Australian, she has made a point of seeing with her own eyes all the officially visiting members of the Royal Family since the present Queen Mother, then the Duchess of York. When the present Queen first visited Sydney in 1954, my mother came in by train to wave. She was there again for the Queen's visit this year. The two women are very like each other, sharing the same past, if not the same income. My mother did not, and does not now, regard my father's death as a pointless sacrifice on behalf of British interests. She believes that he was defending civilization. Though Mr Menzies took care to keep her war widow's pension small so as to encourage thrift, she voted for the Liberal Party as often as for Labor, and always according to her assessment of which party had the firmer grip on reality. She has personally elected every Australian prime minister for the last sixty years and if Mr Keating thinks he can do without her vote, it might be his turn on the trapdoor.

Nor should he put too much faith in the argument – much touted by the Murdoch press and slyly put forward as fact by the Australian broadcaster Mike Carlton in his entertaining article in the *Sunday Times* – that as Australia's demography alters to put people of Anglo background in the minority, the majority are bound to prefer going it alone. Whether from Europe two generations ago or from Asia in the last generation, many of Australia's migrants were refugees from political instability, and won't necessarily favour any proposal that encourages more of it in their chosen home. Their progeny might be persuaded, but let it be by reasonable argument, on a basis of truth. Meanwhile for Australians like myself, resident in Britain but still holding on loyally to their Australian passports, caught between Mr Sewell and Mr Keating, queuing in the 'Other Passports' channel while ex-SS tank commanders are given the quick welcome reserved for the EEC, there is nothing to do but wait, and screen all incoming calls.

Spectator, 7 March, 1992

UP HERE FROM DOWN THERE

When London Calls by Stephen Alomes, Cambridge

Billed as a senior lecturer in Australian Studies at Deakin University, Stephen Alomes, with his latest book *When London Calls* – subtitled 'The Expatriation of Australian Creative Artists to Britain' – has made a timely intervention in the perennially simmering local discussion about why the Australian expatriates went away and what should be thought about them by the cognoscenti who stayed put. As its provenance and panoply suggest, this is most definitely an academic work, but the reader need not fear to be dehydrated by the post-modernist jargon that threatened, until recently, to turn humanist studies in Australia into a cemetery on the moon. Instead, the reader should fear a different kind of threat altogether.

There was a time when Australian academics could be counted on for a donnish *hauteur* when it came to treating journalistic opinions relating to their subject. Alomes goes all the other way. Without knowing much about it, he loves the world of the media. If there is ever a Chair of Cultural Journalism at Deakin University, he could fill it the way he fills his reporter's notebook. He gets out there on the interview trail himself. Most of the big names he wants to talk to, if not already dead, don't want to waste any more of their lives giving soundbite answers to the kind of questions that their work exists to answer in full, but he has the professional pest's remedy for that. He either gives them short shrift or plugs the lacunae from his clippings file, in which, it seems, any British journalist's merest mention of an Australian expatriate's activities – especially if the opinion is adverse – is preserved like holy writ, and in which anything that even the most uninspired Australian journalist makes of the British journalist's opinion is carefully appended, the whole dog-eared assemblage being regarded by its assiduous compiler as a pristine *Forschungsquelle* out of which he may construct his own opinions by an elaborate system of cross-reference. This method seems particularly Swiftian in a book which nominally devotes itself to the proposition that Australia need no longer be in thrall to how its creative efforts are perceived in the mother country. Australia is a land mass of three million square miles and geographers have long debated whether it should be called a continent or an island. The bizarre spectacle of Alomes's self-cancelling thought processes should be enough to settle the discussion. It's an island all right, and it's flying like Laputa.

No doubt seeking to legitimize his gift for inaccurate précis, Andre Malraux recommended telling the kind of lies that would become true later. In Australia it is by now widely proclaimed among the intelligentsia that the era of provincialism is over. Would that it were true, but on the evidence provided by the mere existence of a book like this it isn't yet, and later might mean never if the facts aren't faced. One of the facts is that in Australia any discussion of the arts is likely to be bedevilled with politics. Another is that the politics are likely to be infantile. As opposed to the quality of the discussion, the quality of the arts is not the problem. With a size of population which only recently overtook that of the Ivory Coast, Australia has for some time been among the most creatively productive countries on earth. In the mortal words of Sir Les Patterson, we've got the arts coming out of our arseholes. Painters, poets, novelists, actors, actresses, singers, directors: our artists are all over the world like a rash, and the days are long gone when the stars who stayed away were the only ones we had.

Nobody now would be surprised to hear that the only reason Cate Blanchett left home was to get away from her more gifted sister. In Sydney a new Baz Luhrman lurks on every block, and Brisbane bristles with *prêt-à-porter* Peter Porters. Alomes has predicated his book on the up-to-date assumption that if Australia should happen to go on producing cultural expatriates, it won't be provincialism that they flee from, because there no longer is any. The way he says so, however, would be enough in itself to make any current expatriate think twice before coming home for anything longer than a brief incognito visit, and might well recruit new expatriates by the plane-load.

On a world scale, the average cultural expatriate in the twentieth century took flight because if he had stayed where he was he would have faced death by violence. His average Australian equivalent has faced nothing except death from boredom. It might sound like a privileged choice until you find out how lethal the boredom can be. Try a sample sentence.

> In this period groups and institutions were either offshore repli-cations of Australian support organisations or precursors of official and unofficial Australian organisations.

To be fair, Alomes doesn't always succeed in being as unreadable as that. There are lingering signs that the once-excellent Australian school system has not yet fully given up on its initial aim of teaching pupils to write coherent prose. Apart from the use of 'manifest' as an intransitive verb ('Sayle's happy knack of being on the spot where things were happening manifested early') and a failure to realize that the adjectives 'new' and 'innovative' are too similar in meaning to be used as if they were different ('The film was innovative and new') he writes a plain enough English for someone whose ear for rhythm either never developed or was injured in an accident. There are whole paragraphs that don't need to be read twice to yield their sense. The question remains, however, of whether they sufficiently reward being read once, except as an unintended demonstration of the very provin-cialism whose obsolescence their author would like taken for granted.

The answer to the question is yes: just. Leaving his overall inter-pretation of them aside, the raw data are of such high interest that they inspire even the author to the occasional passage of pertinent reflection, some of it his own. He names the names of those Austra-lians who came to London when that was still the thing to do. After World War II the tendency for the painters who went away to stay away became ingrained. Arthur Boyd, Sidney Nolan and Charles Blackman all made a life in England, even when their imaginative subject matter was drawn either from their memories of Australia or from the visits home they could make more frequently as they pros-pered. Alomes gives details of which painters resettled in Australia later in their careers, or else merely appeared to while maintaining their British base, and of whether their work was regarded as Austra-lian-based or international. He occupies himself with the questions of domicile and national loyalty as if his subjects thought about these things then as hard as he does now. What seldom strikes him is the possibility that to *stop* thinking about such matters might have been one of the reasons they took off in the first place.

If Alomes had widened the scope of his book to include other destinations besides London, he would have had to deal, among the painters, with the problem posed by Jeffrey Smart, who, at the height of his long career, not only remains a resident of Tuscany but rarely paints an Australian subject even from memory. Smart had a clear and simple reason, freely admitted in his autobiography, for leaving Australia half a century ago. As an active homosexual, he had a good chance of being locked up. But his other reasons are of more lasting interest, and one of them was that he had no personal commitment to a national school of painting that depended on Australian subject matter. He knew everything about what the national painters had achieved, but he saw them in an international context. In short, he wasn't interested in nationalism.

The same can be applied to the musical luminaries here listed: Richard Bonynge, June Bronhill, Charles Mackerras, Malcolm Williamson, Yvonne Minton, Joan Sutherland and so, gloriously, on. Alomes flirts with the idea that the performing artists – the instrumentalists especially – might have hindered the development of Australian music by leaving, but he doesn't follow up on the possibility that by raising the prestige of Australian music throughout the world they might have helped more than they hindered, simply by making a musical career seem that much more exciting to a new entrant. Postwar, the arrival of Sir Eugene Goossens raised the level of Australian orchestral music, but the departure of Joan Sutherland made Australia a planetary force in grand opera – like the extra shrimp that Paul Hogan later threw on the barbie. Our Joan's impact on Covent Garden resonated throughout the world.

The resonance reached Australia itself: when the winner of the *Sun* Aria Contest set out for England, she sailed on a ship that launched a thousand sopranos. The effect that the international prestige of our expatriates had on aspiring artists in their homeland is a big subject for our author to pay so little attention to. But he pays no attention at all to an even bigger subject. He notes that the *prima donna assoluta* got a rapturous reception on her 1965 homecoming tour but neglects to mention that her every record album was received with the same enthusiasm – quietly, in thousands of middle-class households. Throughout the book, he takes it for granted that the expatriate artists ran the risk of being out of touch with an Australian audience: not even once does he consider that they might have been *in* touch with an Australian audience in the most intimate possible way – through their art. He is keener to treat the whole phenomenon of expatriation as if it had a *terminus a quo* in the old colonial feelings of inferiority and a *terminus ad quem* in the now-imminent attainment of independent nationhood: because the stage at home was too small, gifted people needed to leave, and now that it isn't, they needn't. But the Sydney Opera House was already built when Joan Sutherland repatriated herself as a resident star, and although she was congratulated by music lovers for choosing to spend the last part of her career at home, she also had to cope with the patronizing opinion that her career must have been over, or she wouldn't have come back. She also faced persistent questioning – of whose impertinence Alomes seems not to be aware – about why she was not in favour of an Australian Republic. Nostalgia for Switzerland must have been hard to quell.

On the continuing problem of how a successful expatriate can make a return without being thought to have failed, Alomes could have been more searching, but at least he mentions it. The theatrical expatriates have always suffered from it most. They are all here, starting with Robert Helpmann before the war, and going on through Peter Finch, Bill Kerr, Leo McKern, Diane Cilento, Michael Blakemore, John Bluthal, Barry Humphries and Keith Michell. Michell is usefully quoted as telling a journalist 'the trouble is, when you go home, everybody says you're on the skids.' This is a handily short version of a Barry Humphries off-stage routine that he has been known to deliver to anyone *except* a journalist. Humphries relates that when he stepped off the plane on one of his early trips home, a representative of the local media asked him how long he planned to stay. When Humphries explained that he was back only for a few days, he was asked 'Why? Aren't we good enough for you?' For his next trip, he armed himself with a more diplomatic answer to the same question. When he said that this time he might be back for quite a while, he was asked 'Why? Couldn't you make it over there?'

Perhaps Alomes might like to use this parable in a later edition, although he is unlikely to get it confirmed by Humphries himself, who has already committed suicide often enough without handing the

Australian press any more ammunition. Meanwhile Alomes reports a usefully rueful comment from the distinguished theatrical producer and film director Michael Blakemore, who apparently wondered whether his film *Country Life* – a retelling of *Uncle Vanya* in an Australian setting – might not have been better received in Australia if he had launched it in America and Europe first. Blakemore was really saying that the home-based Australian journalists did him in. Alomes might have made more of that, but true to his title he is more interested in the Australian journalists who went abroad.

The list starts with Alan Moorehead, who in Europe built a justified legend as a war correspondent before moving on to write his best-selling books about the Nile. Robert Hughes has several times paid tribute to Moorehead's influence as exemplar and mentor. Moorehead was a true heavyweight, but the pick of his many successors who took the road to glory in the Street of Shame form a by no means trivial list: Paul Brickhill, Sam White, Philip Knightley, Barbara Toner, Bruce Page, John Pilger and the explosively charismatic swagman Murray Sayle, he whose happy knack of being on the spot when things were happening manifested early. They all had that happy knack, and they all shared the conviction that wherever the spot was, it wasn't in the land where they were born. You would think that at least a few of the survivors might have gone home by now, if provincialism was really over, but among the big-name byliners no instance of a permanent return is here recorded. There are less illustrious figures whose sojourns in Fleet Street and subsequent repatriation are solemnly celebrated. No doubt they brought something home with them, but what they took away with them in the first place seems, on this reckoning, no great shakes, and one would have thought that their inclusion stretched the term Creative Artist pretty far. Two women who turned out yellow drivel for the British tabloids ('You can tell a man by his underpants') have their itineraries traced in detail, in keeping with Alomes's tendency, throughout the book, to count heads without caring about the size of hat.

A conspicuous example of that same tendency is Jill Neville, enrolled among the expatriate writers. By a rough calculation she gets three times as much space as Patrick White. No doubt she had a magnetic personal attractiveness. Unduly given to the bad journalistic practice of name-checking his way through networks as if that did something to illuminate the individuals caught up in them, Alomes makes much of Jill Neville's role in Peter Porter's life and in the circle that formed around Charles Blackman and Al Alvarez in Hampstead. Alvarez wasn't Australian but he liked Australians. His recent book *Where Did it All Go Right?* shows how much he liked Jill Neville. If not precisely a *femme fatale*, she certainly had the knack of making grown male intellectuals fight like schoolboys. By the time I met her, she had been brought low by illness and the familiar cumulative effects of a career in which literary ambitions do not fulfil themselves, to an extent that makes the income from ordinary journalism matter significantly less. To be trapped in Grub Street and sick too is a hard fate. But even in the early grip of the cancer that took her away, Jill Neville still had charm. The question was whether she had any talent. My own assessment would be that she more or less did – her fiction, without being incandescent, retains something better than documentary value – but Alomes doesn't say whether she did or she didn't. He just parades her along with all the other expatriates as if she had the same rank, and pays her more attention than almost any of them because she happened to know so many of them personally.

The matter of talent becomes an embarrassment when Alomes gets to what he calls the Megastars, because if he can't talk about what they have to offer, then he can have no reason for being interested in them apart from their celebrity. The usual four suspects are rounded up. Robert Hughes gets fleeting treatment because he settled in New York instead of London. Germaine Greer, Barry Humphries and myself are worked over at length. I wish I could say I felt flattered to be included, but flattened would be more like it. Ian Britain started this Gang of Four caper with his book *Once an Australian*, which at least had the merit of crediting his individual subjects with a vestigial inner life that might yet survive somewhere inside the airless perimeter of their fame, in the same way that the presence of water on Mars cannot yet be ruled out. Britain was able to contemplate that his chosen specimens might have become famous *for* something – if only their way of putting things – rather than just through wanting to be famous. But Alomes has gone beyond that. With his innovative and new filing system, he has no need to form a personal estimation of anything that his Megastars might have actually done. He can just trawl through the press coverage.

Let me start by getting myself out of the road as quickly as possible. I only wish our author had done the same, but it all goes on for pages. A detailed case study is built up of what Alomes calls a 'professional Australian', smarming his way upwards in the capital city of imperialism by shamelessly peddling his colonial identity to con the Poms. For all I know, and in spite of its plethora of factual errors, this dossier fits the culprit: it takes a saint to be sure of his own motives. All I can say in rebuttal, if not refutation, is that I can't remember the Poms being as easy to con as all that. Even for Rolf Harris, the didgeridoo and the wobble-board weren't enough by themselves: he had to sing. And as far as I can recall after almost forty years, I had to compose a few ordinary, unaccented English sentences before I could get anybody's attention. My freckles were already fading fast, and putting zinc cream on my nose would have looked like frost-bite.

If it was conceited of me to expect some attempt at assessing the way I write – if only to demonstrate how I worked the scam – such an attempt was the least to expect when it came to the case of Germaine Greer. If you leave out her way of putting things, all you are left with is the things she puts. Her various attitudes have been shared at one time or another by many, and there might even be some who share them all. Perhaps somewhere, gathered around some dusty well, there is a group of women farsighted enough to perceive that clitoridectomy is a breakthrough for feminism. But it would be even more amazing if they could write. Germaine Greer can write, often amazingly. Her distinctiveness is in her style, where all she feels, observes and believes adds up to a passion. It might be better if it added up to a position, but it would take a fool to deny its power, and a dunce to ignore it. Alomes ignores it. Instead, he applies his method. What she said to the media, or what the media said she said, is sedulously quoted. The contradictions and anomalies that emerge are marvelled over, as if consistency had ever been among her virtues. Deep thoughts that various mediocrities have thought about what she thinks are duly shuffled into a heap, which you would have to set fire to if you hoped for any illumination. But at least obfuscation is not the aim. In the case of Barry Humphries I'm afraid it is. The stuff about him is a scandal.

A serious fellow even while he was alive, the avant-garde novelist B. S. Johnson once informed a table and the people sitting around it – I was one of them, so I can vouch for this – that he did not admire Shakespeare, because real people don't talk in verse. Showing similar powers of insight, Alomes is able to detect that Dame Edna Everage, Sir Les Patterson and others among Barry Humphries' range of stage zanies do not correspond to any actual people in our country's now advanced state of development. He further concludes that Humphries' international theatrical success is therefore damaging to Australia's image abroad. When Ian Britain favourably reviewed this book for the Melbourne *Age*, the strictures placed on Humphries were too much even for him, and he tried to point out the obvious: that Humphries' fantastic characters were found just as entertaining by an Australian audience as a foreign one. More could be said on those lines, but I doubt it would be enough to convince Alomes, who is too hipped on his idea of the 'cultural cringe' (a term he employs interminably) to let go of the possibility that large sections of the Australian audience look up to Humphries precisely because he looks down on them. Alomes wouldn't put anything past the middle class. Like many Australian soft-option academics who fancy themselves as radical political thinkers, he resolutely refuses to grasp that a middle class is the first article a liberal democracy manufactures, and the last it can do without.

Of all the people in the book, Humphries is the one to whom the term Australian Expatriate Creative Artist applies most, and of whom its author knows least. You would never guess from what is written here that Humphries, throughout his career, and in addition to commanding a mandarin prose that integrates the wild inventiveness of the Australian idiom at a level beyond the reach of even his brightest critics, has devoted tireless energy to the study, rediscovery, preservation and furtherance of Australian music, literature, painting and architecture. Humphries is learned on a world scale, but his learning began at home, and always goes back there. An expatriate he might be, but a patriot he has always been. Everyone knows that, except Alomes and the dunderheads in his filing system, prominent among whom is Dan O'Neill, described as (and this is Alomes talking, not Sir Les) 'literature scholar and radical academic at the University of Queensland'. In 1983 Radical Dan apparently asked 'How much longer can this curious ritual last, a Londoner with quick uptake, retentive memory and verbal flair coming over here on a regular basis, to tear the living fang out of us for being "Australian"?' I love that 'verbal flair': obviously a very compromising thing to be caught in possession of, like a bottle of anabolic steroids.

Not all of the names brought in to help lynch Humphries are ciphers. One of them belongs to the gifted playwright David Williamson, whose towering presence in this shambling rank of irascible homunculi is enough to prove that Alomes's book is a more serious matter than it might appear, although never in a way that its author might like to think. Williamson is quoted as calling Humphries 'a satirist who loathes Australia and everything about it'. As it happens, Humphries is a difficult customer in real life and there are things about his stage act that some of us find difficult too. I wouldn't like to be in the first three or four rows when Sir Les is propagating rancid zabaglione from the dilapidated cloaca of his mouth, and I have always sympathized with the country wife in the fifth row when Dame Edna asks her what she had to do to get the pearls. Without question there is an implacable animus boiling somewhere behind the personae. But to discern in Humphries 'almost a total hatred of Australia' (Williamson again, apparently) takes something more than a lack of humour. It takes nationalism, which is where we get down to the nitty-gritty.

For any free nation, an upsurge of nationalism is something it needs like a hole in the head. The holes are usually provided by whatever force emerges victorious from the resulting turmoil, and the heads by its innocent citizens. If the history of the previous century taught us anything, it taught us that. But one of the charms of the Australian intelligentsia is that the generality of its members aren't bound by an historical context. Unfortunately they aren't informed by one either, a deficiency which makes innocence less cute when it comes to politics. When the Australian Republican Movement gave itself a name, it was merely naïve in supposing that the concept of an historically predetermined *Bewegung* would fail to arouse bad memories. But there was nothing naïve, and much that was nasty, in the ARM's collective fondness for wondering whether Australians who questioned its visionary mission were quite Australian enough.

Beginning with the discovery by Paul Keating that Australia's destiny was to Stand Tall, it was suggested, with progressively increased intensity all the way to the eve of the recent referendum, that anyone who believed otherwise was guilty of standing short. Nationalist rhetoric was off and running like one of those bush fires that burn down whole states. It was too late for anyone to say, without risk of being fried to a crisp in the media, that Australia already *was* a nation: that it had thrown off the shackles of British imperialism even before the federation of its constituent states; and that it was much envied in a world which had seen many other nations with older names smashed to pieces and forced to start again – or, like Argentina (a country directly comparable to Australia up until the end of World War II), remaining intact only at the cost of being consumed with grief as their natural blessings, social cohesion, public benefits and civil rights were irrevocably frittered away in one constitutional crisis after another.

It was too late for anyone except the Australian public, who declined to vote for the republican proposal as it was put to them, and might well do the same again even if the proposal is different. It should be evident, indeed, that unless all the proposals are the same – i.e. unless there is an agreed republican model – then the republic will remain merely a nice idea, like a popcorn mine or the Big Rock Candy Mountain. Personally I hope that the republicans *can* agree on a model: firstly because we might need it – the Royal Family might decide to give up – and secondly because, during the necessary discussion, the intelligentsia will be obliged to examine what it did wrong last time, and might reach the salutary conclusion that its propensity for questioning the loyalty of its ideological enemies came home to roost.

Whether a wise expatriate should come home to roost is another question, especially if he has been tagged as a conservative. But it probably wouldn't matter much if he stayed away. I called Alomes's book 'timely' because in the débâcle of the lost referendum it should teach his fellow savants, simply by its grotesque example, that the nationalist line of thought, especially when applied to culture, is a busted flush. But I fear it could still take many other books to teach them that the ideal of cultural autarky has always been a pipe-dream, in whatever country the pipe is smoked. Heine, without whom German poetry would be cut in half, spent two thirds of his life in Paris. He was sheltering from repression and prejudice, but Thomas Mann, even after Hitler's death, never came home to Germany, because he doubted whether Germany was ready to come home to him. Stravinsky operated on the principle that Russia went with him wherever he went, which was everywhere except the Soviet Union. Picasso was Spain in spite of Spain, and for James Joyce the

condition for returning eternally to Ireland in the circulating river of
his work was never to set foot there again.

An artist is the incarnation of his country, wherever he might
happen to hang his hat. And as for those countries that have never
had direct experience of what tyranny, repression or officially imposed
obscurantism are, they have always exported cultural figures as copi-
ously as they have taken them in. Why William James stayed in the
United States and his brother Henry never came home is a question
open to a hundred answers, but sensibly the Americans long ago gave
up on wondering which of them did their country the bigger favour,
because it became evident that they both belonged to their country
only in the sense that their country belonged to the world.

A nation's culture either joins it to the world or it is not a culture.
Although Australians should try to be less impressed with the size of
their country on the map, and remember that it contains far fewer
people than Mexico City, they are right to be proud of how large
their little nation looms in the world's consciousness. The expatriates
have played a part in that. It might not be the biggest part, or even
a necessary one – Les Murray got the whole of the modern world
into his marvellous verse novel *Fredy Neptune* without ever leaving
home for long – but they have certainly played a part. Which is not
to say that a nation's expatriate Creative Artists need always be
thought of as ambassadors, or think of themselves that way. The
place they came from, even if it is the first thing in their hearts,
might be the last thing on their minds, and they might remain
convinced that they came away only to commit what Françoise Sagan
once called the crime of solitude. But if they commit it with sufficient
grace, their homeland will claim them anyway, in the course of
time.

TLS, 26 January, 2000

Postscript

I could write a book about Australian nationalism, and have recently
been plagued by a nightmare in which I actually have to. In the

nightmare I occupy a cell in the old Long Bay gaol, an institution now happily disestablished, but which in my youth was still playing host to the most hard-to-hold recidivists in New South Wales, including, off and on, the notoriously elusive Darcy Dugan. A small man who could make himself smaller to wriggle between iron bars, Dugan got himself into the language by getting himself out of any form of incarceration the screws could devise. There was a prison tram, a windowless steel box on wheels, which used to take criminals back and forth from Long Bay to the court in Paddington. It once left Long Bay with Dugan inside it and arrived in Paddington without him. He was next seen in Queensland. From the top of the hill near my house I could look across Botany Bay to Long Bay gaol and wonder whether Dugan was still there. He made me feel better about school, but I was well aware even then that I lacked his talent. In my nightmare, there is no getting out of the cell. (Scratched into the wall about five feet from the floor is the rubric 'D. Dugan was hear breefly.') The screws want to see a fresh thousand words at the end of each day or they won't feed me. No outside exercise is permitted.

On the other hand, any visitor is allowed in. Gough Whitlam shows up. He demands to see my references to him. I show him the one about his habit of quoting verbatim from the *Almanach de Gotha* being somewhat anomalous for a professed Republican. He replies with a long exposition of the Bowes-Lyon family tree. Representatives of the Australian intelligentsia arrive. They tell me how shameful it was that our diplomats once had difficulty explaining to President Suharto of Indonesia why our Head of State did not live in Australia. They do not tell me if the Indonesians had any difficulty explaining why every occupant of their administrative structure above the level of receptionist was called Suharto and half the economy was in Switzerland. Paul Keating arrives to read the bits about him. He calls me a maggot for suggesting that he lowered the tone of parliamentary discourse by calling anyone who questioned his Republican policies a maggot. My cell is full. So is the corridor. I will never get my book finished, but I am not allowed to stop writing it. Stephen Alomes arrives, wanting to know why I tried to nuke *his* book before it could get out of the silo. I tell him *this* is why: because I didn't want to spend the rest of my life here, compelled to make sense of a subject with the same ontological status as the man who shagged O'Reilley's daughter.

Darcy Dugan arrives, weighed down with chains. An Australian journalist recognized him in Vancouver.

2000

LET'S TALK ABOUT US

In the 1950s, John Douglas Pringle caused a sensation in Australian intellectual life with the publication of his book *Australian Accent*. A real, live, distinguished British journalist and editor had written about us! He had found Australia interesting! Half a century later, it is a measure of how interesting Australia has become that another real, live, distinguished British journalist and editor, Michael Davie, is unlikely to cause an equal sensation with his book *Anglo-Australian Attitudes*. Davie's book is at least as good as Pringle's, but times have changed, and where there was once a famine of commentary there has in recent years been a feast, a feast which in the year of the Sydney Olympics threatens to escalate into a saturnalia. The delicious suspicion that the whole world might be watching lends an extra, international cachet to this wonderful new national sport of self-examination at which Australians have so quickly become so good. It's the biggest thing since synchronized swimming, and it's all ours. Hands up anyone who hasn't written a book.

With so much activity on the part of the home team, it is harder for the visiting pundit to get a look-in, no matter how impressive his paper qualifications. In the post-Whitlam period Davie had a two-nations connection with Australia, rather like Pringle's in the late Menzies era. Where Pringle was the Pommy ring-in editor of the *Sydney Morning Herald*, Davie was the Pommy ring-in editor of the Melbourne *Age*. Davie was even better than Pringle at cracking the whip over the unruly prose of his young Australian journalists while simultaneously laying himself open to the burgeoning cultural life around him – and by his time, of course, there was a lot more burgeoning to deal with. Beyond those capacities, however, Davie was the carrier of an extra propensity which could help this book make its voice heard even in the current hubbub. He had an acute ear for bluster. He liked the confidence of Australians, but when they were all shouting the same thing at once he showed a subversive tendency to wonder why. *Anglo-Australian Attitudes* is the fruit of that tendency. Davie gives his endorsement to the rise of national self-awareness. But the rise of self-assertive nationalism earns his disapproval, all the more damning for being so quietly expressed.

Davie has always had the kind of whisper that can shout you down. One of his most piercing whispers in this book is addressed to the orthodox nationalist precept that Australian troops at the Dardanelles were used as cannon fodder by a cynical British high command. Not after Gallipoli but after *Gallipoli* (i.e. after the movie, not the event – a sign of the times) the idea became very popular among the Australian intelligentsia, probably because it so neatly encapsulated the Manning Clark train of thought about the permanent colonial status underlying Australia's parade of independence, a necessary subservience dictated by the machinations of capitalist imperialism. In recent years the idea has buckled under academic scrutiny: in the fourth volume of the *Oxford History of Australia*, Stuart Macintyre quotes the statistic that matters. The film, of course, didn't mention any British dead at all, and it's quite likely that hardly anybody who saw the film is aware that the British were even present. But they were, and suffered a total of fatalities more than double that of the Anzacs, and just about three times that of the Australians taken alone. The notion that the Australians were sent in by the British to die in their stead at Gallipoli should therefore have been a non-starter. But the film *Gallipoli* ensured that there was no stopping it. Davie's whisper might help to slow it down. He quotes the figures, having always been in favour of the kind of journalism in which the hard facts appear in an early paragraph, and aren't left to the end, where they might be cut.

Davie has the patient humility to pick up on the results of dull-looking academic archive sifting and transfer them to the world of the media: a task that the higher journalism should always tackle, but seldom does. Better than that, he is ready to do some hard graft in the archives on his own account. A latterday wandering scholar, he has somehow found time to journey from state to state, request access to the papers of previous state governors, and actually read them. The results should be equally fascinating to those who smile on the old imperial connection with Britain and to those who would like to be rid of its last vestiges. Particularly before Federation, some of the governors were formidable men. In the twentieth century the standard of originality went down as place-men settled in, but there was still the occasional star figure. Starriest of all was Alexander Hore-Ruthven, the first Lord Gowrie, who practised for being Governor-General of Australia with a preliminary period as Governor of South Australia from 1928 to 1934. Davie has read Hore-Ruthven's papers and found much to admire on top of their impeccable style.

Hore-Ruthven began his turn of duty under the impression that a governor might have a role in politics. When he attempted to mediate between the wharfies and the shipowners he was told by the state government not to do it again. Governors were doomed to spend much of their time being masters of ceremonies and incarnating, along with their hard-working wives, the apex of social life. Especially since they were likely to bring large resources of cultivation to the latter role – along with plenty of their own money, the post being designed for gentlemen who would not complain about ending up out of pocket – Davie rather admires them for their dedication to a non-job, while he fashionably allows that the whole arrangement has always been superfluous to requirements. But on that point he might have drawn a more edifying conclusion from the story he recounts of how Hore-Ruthven helped the Governor of NSW, Sir Philip Game, to dismiss Jack Lang. Unusually for one so pertinacious, Davie glosses over the significance of that incident.

Like Gough Whitlam forty years later, Jack Lang really proposed to govern without a parliament, the very thing that reserve powers are designed to stop. In Lang's case they stopped it efficiently. One might conclude that the governor system thus proved itself to be the very opposite of powerless, even if its one and only power was to supersede all other powers at a moment of crisis. But Davie feels safer calling the state governor system antiquated and cumbersome, while simultaneously conceding its quiet charm. He doesn't seem keen to dwell on the awkward fact that at the vital moment it worked, perhaps because that would lead him into the uncomfortable side of the perennial debate about the Whitlam dismissal, which turns on the question of the reserve powers. There have to be some. So who gets them? The answer you give dictates not just whether you are for or against a republic, but, if you are a republican, what kind of republican you are. Judging from internal evidence, most of this book was written before the referendum, but there would have been time to add a few pages of protest if Davie thought that its outcome had been a debacle. Instead he takes the calm attitude that the republic will arrive anyway. But he is probably glad that it didn't arrive at a time when Australia's past was still a subject of caricature. The strength of his position depends on his capacity to see the inevitability of the unravelling of the Anglo-Australian ties while simultaneously wanting to tell the complicated truth about what they were like when they were still ravelled.

In 1985 Davie's contribution to *The Daedelus Symposium* was called 'The Fraying of the Rope'. He welcomed the decline of the old deference but made a telling citation from his hero Sir Keith Hancock, who had quoted an Indian professor to the effect that Australia, if it repudiated its European inheritance, would be no use to India. Davie has elaborated his position since then but his sense of historical responsibility is still at the core of it. For Robert Gordon Menzies the ties with Britain were so important that he held back his country's Asian future with an almost treasonable zeal – or so we were encouraged to think, until Macintyre established that Menzies, at the opening of the war, did a better job than his legend allows in resisting pressure from Churchill to neglect Australia's specific interests in favour of Britain's. Davie is not inclined to follow Macintyre's lead on that particular point: while questioning the validity of the classic David Day thesis that Britain deliberately left Australia at Japan's mercy, Davie still believes that Menzies in 1941 should have been thinking and acting closer to home, instead of hoping to share with Churchill the task of running the Empire's war. But whether or not Davie is right about Menzies' behaviour, he is surely right about Menzies' motivation: Menzies was acting from quite the opposite of a colonial inferiority complex.

To arrive at this conclusion, once again Davie has gone unerringly to the document that matters: in this case the diary that the young Menzies kept when he visited Britain in the mid-thirties. Davie shows convincingly that for Menzies the tradition that mattered in British politics was Whig. What really counted for him about Britain was its parliamentary freedom, not its royal panoply. He was a Cromwellian, not a Cavalier. If the absurd ecstasies of pomp and circumstance that marked his twilight years – the plumes and velvet of his honours royally conferred, the vow of eternal love to the Queen – were compensation for any feelings of being an eternal outsider, it was because he was a Scot, not because he was an Australian. In the post-war period, his pride in Australia and faith in its future made untenable any suggestion that he thought of his own country as a backwater. The suggestion was made anyway, and still is: but Davie's opinion of Menzies is a useful contribution to a necessary process by which Menzies is slowly emerging in his true stature as a creative political leader who did at least as much looking forward as harking back. It was the harking back that made him a joke, but had he been just a joke, so would have been the large proportion of the electorate that voted for him – and for any country's intelligentsia there is no more dangerous moment that when it unites in finding the common people politically inadequate.

On the general question of whether Britain abandoned Australia at the beginning of the Pacific war, Davie has nothing original to offer except common sense. Not long ago, during the full ascendancy of the Other People's Wars thesis, there was not much common sense to be heard on the subject. Lately there has been more, but you could scarcely call it a glut, so a fresh contribution is always welcome. Although he never looked it when I knew him, Davie is old enough to have seen service in the Royal Navy (on the cruiser HMS *London*) at a time when a Japanese torpedo might easily have provided explosive evidence that Britain was doing its best in our part of the world. The question turns on how good that best was. Davie faces the full, sad facts about the inadequacy of Britain's preparations and our foolishness in thinking that everything was going to be all right. But he also shows that with the Singapore catastrophe, as at the Dardanelles, Britain did too much damage to its own interests to allow any validity whatsoever to the idea that it was intent on betraying Australia. The Donald Day theory simply doesn't wash. The disaster in Malaya wasn't a conspiracy, it was a cock-up. Plenty of people have said this by now, but it is always useful to have someone say it well, with such a clear head, and in such a clear style.

Not even Davie, however, is clear-headed enough to get beyond the assumption that it took incompetent generalship on our side to give the victory to the Japanese. There will be no fully mature opinions on the subject until it is accepted that the Japanese army would have taken Singapore anyway, even if our forces had been deployed to their optimum effectiveness. The disaster would have just taken longer. Writers who glibly suppose that only a failure on our part could have permitted a Japanese success are succumbing to racist assumptions without knowing it. At the beginning of the war the Japanese were superior in almost every department and their command of the air alone would have been enough to make them hard to stop. Failure to realize this opens the way, paradoxically enough, to underestimating the magnitude of Australia's achievement when they *were* stopped, in New Guinea. In the story of how the Japanese onslaught in Asia and the Pacific was turned back, Kokoda was a crucial moment, and it was ours: it happened because the Australian soldiers were valiant. Revisionist history, by displacing attention towards the moment when Britain supposedly machinated to leave us in the lurch, has had the effect of diminishing our country's real status – an unfortunate but not unfamiliar consequence of rewriting history along nationalist lines.

To trace the rise of the Republican movement in modern times, Davie characteristically sets about investigating the background to Geoffrey Dutton's trendsetting *Nation* article of 1963. Somewhere in the middle eighties (Davie is sometimes a bit vague about when *he* did things: British reticence) he called on Dutton in Melbourne and got the full story that Dutton himself never wrote down for publication. It turns out that Malcolm Muggeridge, down under on a visit, provided the spark. It was not long after the Queen Mother's Royal Visit of 1958, enjoyed by Dutton as a comedy. (In his journal – from which Davie, again characteristically, is able to quote – Dutton poured scorn on those intellectuals who boycotted the ceremonies and thus cut themselves off from the entertainment.) Muggeridge's own, non-Royal visit took place during the aftermath of the ruckus he had kicked up in Britain by disparaging the Royal Family. At dinner in Adelaide, Muggeridge put the question of what was being done about an Australian republic. Two of his interlocutors were Rohan Rivett, editor of the Adelaide *News*, and its young proprietor, Rupert Murdoch. They said something had to be done but it was too early. In other words, before they got behind the idea it would have to be a ball already rolling. Dutton's article rolled the ball.

An obscure, smoky restaurant on the Anzac Highway, a group of influential men deciding their country's destiny – here is a play by David Williamson in the making. But what to call it? My own title would be *The Silvertail Conference*, thus to emphasize an aspect that Davie could have made more of. The opening section of his book is a penetrating analysis of the class structure that Australia is not supposed to have – an evocation from which the squattocracy emerges in all its easy splendour, complete with its hallowed ties to 'home'. Davie notes that the grand families have traditionally not taken an overt part in Australia's political life, preferring to exert their influence behind the scenes rather than run for office. (Malcolm Fraser might have been cited as a conspicuous exception to this rule, but it will still serve as a rule of thumb.) He also notes that of the participants at this historic dinner, Murdoch (Oxford) and Dutton (Cambridge) were both from grand families. But he neglects to note a possible connection between the rise of a republican movement and a moneyed elite exerting its influence in an extra-parliamentary manner. Such a connection can be denied, but its possibility has to be considered, because when it came to a referendum there were plenty of Australians who suspected that their libertarian sympathies were being manipulated by an elite. When Malcolm Turnbull, another glittering son of a grand family, found himself too prominently placed for the good of his cause, it was an illustration of the real reason for that political shyness on the part of the gentry that Davie seems so puzzled by, and even to regret. The Australian electorate is very unlikely to accept any constitutional system that overtly transfers power in the direction of an oligarchy, and wise oligarchs know it.

Davie might well object at this point that during the forty years since I left Australia he has spent almost as much time in my homeland as I have in his, so he has a better right to speak about recent developments. I would gladly concede that, but with one proviso: nothing quite beats being born and brought up in the country you want to pontificate about. It isn't just that I know for a fact, without having to look it up, that the Australian Prime Minister whom Davie calls Joe Chifley was really called Ben. It's that I sat there on the carpet in front of a radio set taller than I was and listened to Ben Chifley's grating voice while my mother told me she respected him as a true man of the people. She always voted for Ming anyway, but that was politics: Australian politics. It was made clear to me from an early date – bred in my bones, in fact – that patriotism didn't just mean pride in the Fair Go, it meant pride in my country's innate distrust of any form of dogma that treats people as a mass. In this book Davie gives me several elegant strokes of the cane for a crime he can't quite bring himself to specify, but it sounds like a lack of patriotism. Let me caution him in turn that he should beware of what Orwell once called transferred nationalism. One of the tragedies of the transferred nationalist is to miss the point about the new country he adopts, and the point about Australia is that its citizens never cease to be patriotic until patriotism becomes compulsory, whereupon their individuality takes over.

Caught in the middle between two national loyalties, Davie's book gives the sense that it has been squeezed out of him: for all its freshness of perception, it is short of breath. Bill Bryson's *Down Under* is big and brash: HMS *London*, make way for USS *Nimitz*. Bryson is an outgoing American personality on a generous mission to find out whether there is any kind of country joining up the Australian cities where he has previously been on book tours. On the flight in, he still doesn't know the name of the current Prime Minister. I once landed in Mexico without knowing the name of the current President, but that was because the President whose name I *had* looked up had been deposed during my flight after his sister was caught in Switzerland trying to put half of Mexico's GNP into a private bank account. The Australian Prime Minister's name is John Howard, for Christ's sake: it isn't hard to remember. He might be, but his name isn't. To make such breezy condescension even less appealing, there is Bryson's comic style, which depends on exaggeration without benefit of metaphor. When I say, for example, that to read Bryson on the subject of crossing the Nullarbor by train is like crossing the Nullarbor on foot, I am exaggerating, but also speaking metaphorically. If I were to say that reading his book took me a hundred years, I would merely be exaggerating.

I would also be lying. Once the reader gives up on the idea that any of the author's heftily visible preparations for a wisecrack will ever yield results – page two is a good spot to call it quits – the book turns out to be not without value. Bryson has the genuine curiosity that comes down through the American tradition of travel-talk reportage from Mark Twain, who rode on stagecoaches and paid attention to the other passengers when they conversed, argued or shot each other. Bryson talks to everyone he meets, visits museums no matter how unpromising, and is generally not afraid to do the corny thing – a very important attribute, because there is nothing like sophistication for cutting you off from experience. A big smile in a rented car, Bryson gets a long way on bonhomie. He can even, despite his relentlessly facetious style, be amusing: perhaps because death and tragedy are involved, his account of the monumental incompetence of Burke and Wills is sufficiently deadpan to elicit an appropriately hilarious response. Burke and Wills's qualifications for exploring the dead heart of Australia were exactly those of Laurel and Hardy for painting a house, and Bryson, for once, proves that he knows enough about vaudeville not to spoil the comedy with too much whizz-bang punctuation from the band in the pit.

One might say that Bryson has never been in Australia long enough to find much to dislike, but there is a killing description of a bad meal in Darwin to show that he is capable of invective. The bottom line is that he likes Australia, and being so famous he will probably sell millions of books saying so, many of them within Australia itself. But it is becoming a nice question whether there is much room left for visitors from civilization to come flying in and marvel that we have hotels more than two storeys high. Back in the 1950s, there was a story in it when the black musician Winifred Atwell crossed the Pacific to play the piano and liked Sydney so much she wanted to stay. There was another story in it when she wasn't allowed to. In the razzmatazz of Australia's current jamboree, it is sometimes forgotten just how narrow-minded Australian society seemed only forty years ago. Sometimes I forget it myself. From the perspective of social-democratic politics I nowadays find the Ming dynasty under-rated, but if I had been condemned to live through its protracted decline, would I have wanted to face a future in which I wasn't allowed to read *Portnoy's Complaint*? We were barely allowed to *have* Portnoy's complaint. There was a fantastic amount not happening.

Peter Conrad hasn't forgotten any of it. His icily scintillating article about his life-long alienation from Tasmania heads up a very keepable special issue of *Granta* devoted to Australia. Patiently edited by Ian Jack, who must have needed a cattle-prod to corral some of the more elusive among his illustrious contributors, the booklet is clear proof that writers born and raised in Australia are nowadays quite capable of discussing their country's drawbacks without feeling that they are lending ammunition to foreign philistines. Among the bleak views, Conrad's is the bleakest. 'Australian troops were always available to die in Britain's wars,' he intones. 'At Gallipoli, they were used by the imperial generals as cannon fodder . . .' The riff is familiar, but less usual is the way in which Conrad detects a more comprehensive imperialism, as an envious world closes in on its last theme park.

Conrad might be on to something here. Those of us who think that Barry Humphries was not just joking when he identified Australia as the newest top dog among nations should remember that this is the age of celebrity, in which to be loved by the whole world is to be in some danger. On the whole, though, Conrad's article is less a disquisition on geopolitics than a cry from the heart. It was because of his personal circumstances that he thrived as a literary pundit in England. For the same reason, the Englishman Howard Jacobson – whose contribution is as sensuously funny as you might expect – thrived as a literary pundit in Australia. Each man wields a brilliantly inclusive style, but neither has a chance of summing up what has really been going on in Australia since they first passed each other in mid-ocean. For all we know, the key event of the whole period since World War II was something Menzies didn't do – he didn't, for example, put Arthur Calwell's immigration policy into reverse. If Ming had really been so committed to Australia's future as a British nation, he might have tried to do that. But he didn't, and the way was left open for his beloved, sleepy, conformist and wowser-ridden country to change in ways he could not predict.

Australia's literary intellectuals might have to face the possibility that their effectiveness as political commentators is coming to an end, and that this might be a good thing. The journalists are taking over, just as they did in the United States, where the advent of expert political commentators such as Elizabeth Drew left the inspired but tendentious pastiche of the Mencken heritage where it belonged – in the past. As that excellent volume *The Best Australian Essays 1999* revealed, no poet or novelist is going to write political commentary as pertinent as Mungo MacCallum's, because he is right there on the campaign plane with his raw material. Michael Davie remembers when the political journalists always mistook the country's mood because they never left Canberra. But now the politicians travel and the journalists travel with them. With insularity no longer the keynote, the ivory tower is no longer the vantage point: leg-work, contact and close observation are everything. It's still Australia, but it's a different country, and its writers and artists had better accept that they can no longer get an overall grasp of it just by intuition:

they're going to have to read about it in the newspapers and the magazines, just like everybody else.

In the newspapers, the magazines and the books – and most of the books are nowadays by journalists, and thank God for it. Since the middle 1970s, we have gradually become accustomed to such books being on hand when we need them: Paul Kelly's fine trilogy is only the most conspicuous example. In the Pringle period they scarcely existed. When Donald Horne's *The Lucky Country* came out in 1964, it was so singular that its underlying thesis was taken as holy writ, an *ex cathedra* endorsement of the exciting idea that our country could be saved from its long failure only by political realism, which would entail a preliminary admission that the country's international position up to that point had been essentially servile. From that time forward, most of the informed voices spoke on Horne's side, but there were signs even before the referendum that a true discussion was developing. The mere presence of Paul Sheehan's *Among the Barbarians* on the bestseller lists was an indication that those who looked with disfavour on the wholesale denigration of Australia's anglicized past didn't necessarily consider themselves romantic – they thought *they* were realists, too.

Since these were the very people that the less judicious republican activists had grown fond of calling unpatriotic, the result of the referendum can be seen as a blessing for everyone, and especially for the republicans. Had they won, they would have faced the impossible task of presenting, to an audience they had only just finished insulting, a model of the state on which they themselves had not yet managed to agree. Now they have time to clarify matters both for themselves and others, although the latter part of the task, especially, will require listening as well as talking. We can look forward to a battle of the books, in which books written by journalists are bound to play a key role. As this article goes to press, the justly lauded Australian expatriate journalist Philip Knightley is about to publish his *magnum opus* called *Australia: A Biography.* I have seen the unbound proofs, which teem with pertinent facts and original judgements. Reviewing the finished work will take an article not much shorter than the book, but perhaps I can jump the gun legitimately by citing a real-life conversation Knightley had with Ryszard Kapuscinski.

Knightley records how Kapuscinski assured him that there was an answer for despairing citizens of the quondam Soviet satellite countries who now found it impossible to live the way Americans would like. There *was* such a thing as a just society that was also free: it was called Australia. Knightley believes it, and the belief makes his book a labour of love even at its most caustic. As I write these last lines here in London, Knightley has just said in the *Sunday Times* that Australia seems so attractive to live in now that he wonders if he was right to leave. I know what he means, but the fact remains that we all remain: nobody leaves, and nobody forgets. As Knightley recalled in his contribution to *The Best Australian Essays 1999*, he once, so very long ago, pestered Menzies for a quote outside Kingsford-Smith airport in Sydney. 'Young man, I don't know you,' said Ming. 'I have not been introduced to you, and I have no wish so to be.' Travel as far and as long as you like, you can from your mind a moment like that banish never.

Australian Review of Books, September 2000

WRITTEN TO BE SPOKEN

In the years of my apprenticeship I devoted a lot of effort to making writing sound like speech. Ideally, I think, any kind of sentence, at any level of ambition, should obey the rule of never needing to be read again to get the sense. If it can obey that rule – which is the rule of speech – then it is more likely to invite being read again to get more of its meaning. But there is still a difference between prose written to be read and prose written to be read out. Prose designed in the first instance to be spoken will tend to be much more linear in construction, and thus susceptible to – because more tolerant of – rhetorical tricks. For the pieces reproduced in this section, I don't claim the title of oratory, but I do hope to avoid the accusation of rhetoric. One of them is a television script, on the subject of *Hamlet*, whose hero warned about the negative effects of sawing the air with one's hand. It is a piece I might have reproduced earlier, but thought to leave aside because at the time I still believed there were no exceptions to the rule that words written to pictures could not survive being melted out of the amalgam. But on second thoughts, the pictures for this *Hamlet* script were pretty skimpy – I wandered around castles of the type that Shakespeare 'must have' known about even if he never actually entered them, etc. – and a lot of people kindly wrote to say that they would like to possess the script in a less unwieldy form. Eventually, of course, one hopes that the audience feels the same way about anything one writes to be spoken. Indeed I can't think of any other way to be impressive, as a would-be latter-day Pericles, *except* to say something that sounds more carefully composed than it needs to be – which is practically the definition of good writing anyway. Whether these pieces pass that test I leave the reader to judge, but the reader can be sure that I was trying hard. The Anzac Day address, for example, is the kind of thing nobody should ever take on unless he has a fair idea of what he wants to say, and a better than fair idea of how to get it said. People remember. Admittedly it is said that the people who actually heard Lincoln's address at Gettysburg forgot every word of it, but that just proves the favour he did us by allowing it to be reprinted. (Sir Kingsley: 'Yes, but *you* aren't Abraham Lincoln, *are* you?')

HAMLET IN PERSPECTIVE

Fifteen years ago I was an undergraduate at Cambridge and then later on I stuck around for a while as a postgraduate. I hope I was too weatherbeaten to fall for the mystique that these old dens of privilege supposedly generate, but I can't deny that I've got the sort of affection for Cambridge that anybody feels for a place where he read a lot and thought a lot and wasted a lot of time. Hamlet feels the same way about his university – Wittenberg.

Hamlet has to act out his destiny on the sleet-spattered battlements of Elsinore, while Horatio makes regular trips back to Wittenberg for the port and walnuts and the relative safety of academic intrigue. Many a time in Fleet Street, as I've sat there sucking my typewriter and waiting desperately for inspiration, I've envied those of my contemporaries who stayed on to become academics – the Horatios. In other words, I identify with Hamlet. In my mind's eye, he even looks a bit like me. Perhaps a couple of stone lighter, with blond hair and more of it: one of those rare Aussies who happen to fence quite well and stand first in line of succession to the throne of Denmark.

I don't think this is mad conceit because I think all men and most women who've ever read or seen the play feel that its hero is a reflection of themselves. What's more, I think Shakespeare felt the same way. All his characters in all his plays – men or women, heroes or villains – are aspects of himself because his was a universal self and he knew it inside out. Shakespeare was everybody. But Hamlet is probably the character who comes closest to reflecting Shakespeare's whole self. When I think of what Shakespeare was like, I think of Hamlet. Shakespeare probably didn't behave like that, and he almost certainly didn't talk like that. Hamlet talks a great deal and Shakespeare probably spent most of his time listening. At the end of the night's revelry in the tavern, he was probably the only one sober and the only one silent. Nor was Shakespeare famous for being indecisive. From what little we know of him, he was a practical man of affairs. But he was a practical man of affairs in the theatre, which gave unlimited scope to his imagination. He was an art prince, like Michelangelo. If he'd been the other kind of prince, his imagination would have become his enemy, the enemy of action.

In Shakespeare's time, the biggest question of the day was how the Prince should rule. When *Hamlet* was being written, as the sixteenth century turned into the seventeenth, the stable reign of Queen Elizabeth, amid universal trepidation, was drawing to its end. The Earl of Essex, 'the glass of fashion, and the mould of form, the observed of all observers', had dished himself through not knowing how to do what when. Essex died on the block somewhere about the time that Hamlet was being born on the page. Shakespeare was a keen student of these weighty matters. He was a keen student of everything. Not that *he* ever went to university. His university was the theatre. The same has held true for a lot of our best playwrights, right down to the present day. Osborne, Pinter, Stoppard – they were all educated in the university of life. Shakespeare was a gigantic natural intellect who had no more need of a university than Einstein had, who didn't go to one either. But Shakespeare did have a contemplative mentality. We know that much for certain because we've heard so little about him. Only in the theatre did Shakespeare create experience; in the outside world he was content to reflect upon it.

Shakespeare knew that he was a man of outstanding gifts. Talent of that magnitude is never modest, although it is almost always humble. He knew that he could dream up a whole kingdom and breathe so much life into it that it would live in men's minds, perhaps for ever. But he also knew that he didn't have what it took to rule a real kingdom for a week. He lacked the limitations. He wasn't simple enough, and it was out of that realization that he created Hamlet, who is really a changeling. Hamlet is what would happen if a great poet grew up to be a prince. He might speak great speeches, but the native hue of resolution would be 'sicklied o'er with the pale cast of thought'.

'To be, or not to be' – I wish I'd said that. By now that speech has been translated into every major language on earth and most of the minor ones, and it is remarkable how the first line always seems to come out sounding the same. '*Sein, oder nicht sein,*' runs the German version, '*das ist die Frage,*' which perhaps lacks the fresh charm of the English subtitle in the recent Hindi film version – 'Shall I live, or do myself in? I do not know.' Today, Hamlet belongs to the world. He's come a long way from Elsinore. And there's no reason why not. After all, Shakespeare not only didn't go to university, he didn't go to Denmark, either.

The plot he inherited. A Scandinavian scholar called Saxo Grammaticus wrote an early version. Hamlet was called Amleth and his wicked uncle Claudius was called Feng, who sounds like the leading heavy in *Flash Gordon Conquers Denmark*. Saxo's story was the basis for a later English stage version by Kyd, of *Spanish Tragedy* fame. Shakespeare took over the property and transformed it out of all comparison, although not out of recognition; that old warhorse of a plot is still there inside it. Shakespeare civilized it. He moved it inside the mind and inside the house. He updated *Hamlet* into the Elizabethan age.

One of the things that makes Shakespeare a great man of the theatre is that he knew the real thing when he saw it. He knew that power couldn't be wished out of the world. If power were used wisely and firmly, then everyone might thrive. If it were mismanaged, corruption ensued as surely as rats brought plague, and the whole State went rotten. Shakespeare believed in order and degree. He believed in justice, too, but he didn't think there was any hope of getting it unless the civil fabric was maintained. The idea of social breakdown was abhorrent to him. He knew that he was a kind of prince himself, but he had no illusions about how long his own kingdom would last if the real one fell into disarray. To Shakespeare, Hamlet's tragedy was not just personal but political. Like Prince Hal in an earlier play and like Mark Antony in a later one, or even King Lear, Hamlet has responsibilities. And because Hamlet can't meet those responsibilities he gets a lot of good people killed for nothing and loses his kingdom to the simple but determined Fortinbras.

Nowadays we tend to see Hamlet's blond head surrounded by the flattering nimbus of nineteenth-century Romanticism, which held that Hamlet was a sensitive plant with a soul too fine for the concerns of this world. But Shakespeare was too realistic to be merely romantic. And, of course, he was too poetic to be merely realistic. He knew that there was more in this world than the mere exercise of power. He could feel it within himself – imagination, the supreme power. But even that had its place. In the wrong place it could have tragic consequences. The first reason Hamlet hesitates is dramatic. If Fortinbras were the play's hero, it would be all over in five minutes instead of five acts, with Fortinbras heading for the throne by the direct route – over Claudius's twitching corpse. But the second reason Hamlet hesitates is that he has puzzled his own will by thinking too precisely on the event.

Throughout history, the thoughtful onlooker has been astonished at the man of action's empty head. Napoleon and Hitler, to take extreme examples, did the unthinkable because they lacked the imagination to realize that it couldn't be done. With Hamlet, it's the opposite. More than 300 years before Freud, Montaigne, a great student of the human soul, whose essays Shakespeare knew intimately, identified the imagination as the cause of impotence. Because Hamlet can't stop thinking, he can't start moving. Hence his melancholy. Happiness has been defined as a very small, very cheap cigar named after him, but really Hamlet is as sad as a man can be. He's doubly sad because of his capacity for merriment. Clowns don't want to play Hamlet half as much as Hamlet wants to play the clown, but always the laughter trails off. He loses his mirth and the whole world with it. He does this with such marvellous words that he stuns us into admiration. No actor can resist turning Hamlet's defeat into a victory.

From the moment the part was there to be played, every important actor has looked on his own interpretation of Hamlet as defining him not just as a talent but as a human being. And every Hamlet has studied the Hamlet before him in an almost unbroken succession from that day to this. Burbage, the original Hamlet, gave way to Joseph Taylor; Taylor gave way to Betterton. Pepys saw Betterton play Hamlet in Lincoln's Inn Fields, in 1661, and said that Betterton played the Prince's part beyond imagination, 'the best part, I believe, that ever man played'. Pepys spent a whole afternoon learning 'To be, or not to be' by heart. And as the seventeenth century became the eighteenth, Betterton was still playing Hamlet in his seventieth year, when Steele saw him and said that, for action, he was perfection. Hamlet was at centre stage all over the world. In London he was at Covent Garden, he was in the Haymarket, but, above all, he was at Drury Lane, where great actor after great actor strove to convince the audience that to play Hamlet stood as far above ordinary acting as Hamlet in the play stands above the Players.

In the early eighteenth century, the great tragedian Wilks played Hamlet at Drury Lane. According to contemporary accounts, when the Ghost came on, Wilks climbed the scenery. When he climbed back down again, some time later, he used his sword not to fend off his companions who were trying to keep him from the Ghost but to attack the Ghost. And he did this while wearing a complete tragedian's outfit – full-bottomed wig, plumes and a cape. The outfit was the only complete thing about his performance because, like most of his successors, he cut the text drastically. When Garrick came on, he came on in elevator shoes and stole one of the Ghost's best lines. 'O, horrible! O, horrible! most horrible!' Dr Johnson thought Garrick was over the top, but most of the playgoing public concurred in the opinion that Garrick was unbeatable in the role.

As the eighteenth century gave way to the nineteenth, Kemble arrived and the romantic interpretation of Hamlet began to arrive with him. Hazlitt didn't think much of Kemble in the role. He thought he played it with a fixed and sullen gloom, but I think we recognize that gloom as the beginning of the romantic interpretation of Hamlet which has persisted almost down to our own day. Hazlitt didn't think much of Kean, either. He thought his performance was a succession of grand moments, but had no real human shape. Everybody else thought Kean was marvellously natural, especially in his appearance, and he *looked* like the Hamlet we know today – short hair, black clothes, white lace collar. And on they came – Macready, Barry Sullivan, Edwin Booth, whom some people thought was the ideal Hamlet but who had his thunder stolen by Irving – and the total effect of the nineteenth-century actor-managers was to establish Hamlet as the romantic, alienated outcast, the poet who perhaps couldn't write poetry but could certainly speak it, the man who was just too good for this world.

As the nineteenth century gave way to the twentieth, a truly revolutionary actor-manager arrived on the scene – Johnston Forbes-Robertson – revolutionary because he widened the focus of attention from the central character to the whole play, and never again was it possible to argue plausibly that the play was anything less than the miraculous sum of its parts. Nowadays we never think of any interpretation of the central character, no matter how brilliant – Gielgud's vividly mental, Olivier's vividly physical – as anything more than a contribution to the total character, just as we never think of any cut version, no matter how consistent within itself, as anything more than a contribution to the total play.

The world could go on changing unimaginably and Hamlet would still have everything to say to us. Whenever we hear of some new atrocity and wonder impotently what life is for, we always find that he got there ahead of us. Hamlet poses the eternal question of whether life is worth living. The answer that he appears to arrive at is that it isn't, but the way he says so makes us realize that it is. Hamlet has been given the creative vitality of Shakespeare himself. Even though robbed of will, he's still the embodiment of individuality. Hamlet is what it means to be alive. So all those actors were right, after all. Hamlet's tragedy really is a triumph. A prince of the imagination, he inherits his kingdom in eternity, even if Fortinbras inherits it on earth.

Boris Pasternak, who translated *Hamlet* into Russian, also wrote a famous poem in which Hamlet faces something even worse than his own doubts – a world in which his doubts are not permitted.

> Yet the order of the acts is planned,
> And there is no way back from the end.
> I am alone.

Pasternak wasn't the first, and probably won't be the last, to see Hamlet as the supreme symbol of liberty. As the doomed Prince of Denmark, Hamlet must act out his tragic fate, but as a mind he remains free. He fails in the outer world only because his inner world is so rich. Scorning necessity, he reflects upon his own existence – 'In my mind's eye, Horatio'. Hamlet is the human intelligence made universal, so he belongs to all of us. 'For which of us,' wrote Anatole France, addressing Hamlet, 'does not resemble you in some way?' We're all like him because we all think, and it's because, on top of all its other qualities, its hero incarnates the dignity of human consciousness, that *Hamlet* is the greatest play by the greatest writer who ever lived.

BRING BACK THE OVERQUALIFIED

A speech to the Royal Television Society

It's a bit more than forty years now since I was first in this hall, which has always struck me as a holy place: not just because of its ecclesiastical appearance, but because of the spirit that pervades it. I was first here as a guest, the year before I came up to Cambridge myself as an undergraduate in another college. My host was a fellow-Australian who was proud of being here at King's but had already learned the educated Englishman's trick, still a distinguishing mark in those days, of underplaying any emotion that might redound to his credit. We were sitting there at one of the benches to take lunch. A few aged dons were shuffling in to have lunch served to them up here at the high table. When you're that young anyone old looks very old, but none of the older men looked as old as one man. He couldn't even be said to be shuffling. It took him about ten minutes to get from one end of the hall to the other. I had plenty of time to study his appearance. He looked a bit like a photograph I had once seen of E. M. Forster. 'Who's that?' I asked my friend, who finished chewing and swallowing before he answered with calculated casualness: 'It's E. M. Forster.'

So I went back to my London bedsit and watched television for a whole year. I liked what I saw. It was entertaining and informative, and often both at the same time, this latter trick being worked by the presence on screen of people who knew what they were talking about and had the knack of putting the explanation in as they went along. While the young John Birt was still stacking his cross-referenced copies of *Eagle* in chronological order, television was already one big Mission to Explain. Twenty-five years later, Rupert Murdoch, the all-time most bizarre McTaggart lecturer despite stiff competition,

would make his famous accusation about an irresponsible élite giving
the public what they thought it needed instead of what it wanted.
If the same accusation had been made in those days, its fatuousness
would have been self-evident. Whoever the élite were, they weren't
irresponsible. They vied with each other in service to the nation. The
BBC hierarchs were outdone only by their ITV opposite numbers
in the vocation to enlighten the people. Lord Bernstein, Sir Denis
Forman – they were grandees of the Great and Good. Sir Lew, later
Lord, Grade, far from being a cost-calculating cynic, was already well
embarked on the philanthropic course which would eventually lead
him to spend more on the production values of Franco Zeffirelli's
New Testament than on raising the *Titanic*; Noele Gordon in *Cross-
roads* had a smaller costume budget than Robert Powell on the
cross, and the biblical cast list teemed with knights of the realm
playing bit parts. Below their tea towels, their faces blazed with the
light of dedication.

But that was then, and this is now, and what worries me about
television now is that gradually but inexorably the screen is emptying
itself of the contribution that once came from the kind of people
I can only call the overqualified. Their contribution was especially
conspicuous in documentary features, the field of television in which
I myself have been most active, so I suppose I've had personal reasons
for concern, and you must allow for my bias if I emphasize the point
too much. But I can remember vividly that when I first came to this
country I would switch on the black and white TV set to enjoy
features written and presented by people like René Cutforth: people
who could talk well about the present because they had some background in the past, and about the past because they were marinated
in history; who could write to pictures in a compressed yet clear
manner without traducing the complexity of events; and who could
make a programme snap along like a good essay. You would switch
on the set not just because of the subject, but because it was them
treating it. Features like that were more common than not.

Thirty years later, they are less common than not. The typical
feature now is written by a producer or an attendant pundit and
narrated in voice-over by an actor. Whole channels sound like what
an Equity AGM would sound like if actors ever went to one. As a
member of Equity myself I am glad to see the actors get the work,
but the results tend to lack personality in the strict sense of the

word. The actors try hard – they try all too hard – but what they intone sounds as if a committee wrote it, and the general effect is of a long commercial. One of the consequences is that the viewer is helpless to attribute not only praise, but blame. Earlier this year I saw a BBC 2 programme about the Holocaust in which the actor delivering the voice-over mispronounced the word Auschwitz more than forty times. If he had been a presenter in vision we could have blamed him. As it was, there was nowhere to place the blame except on the production team, and, by extension, on the controller and the whole of the BBC. Nor did the producer have the excuse that Jeremy Isaacs had when Lord Olivier misread every second line in the script of *The World at War*. The actor voicing the BBC 2 feature was not very eminent and could have been easily set right. The feeling that the overqualified are giving way to the barely competent is hard to avoid. On the whole the BBC did reasonably well over the VE and VJ Day period, but it was notable how the programme about the Burma campaign, presented by Charles Wheeler, stood out. It was because of Charles Wheeler. His presence gave the programme authority. He had the qualifications because he was overqualified. Having seen the places and read the books, he not only knew what was involved, he knew how to say it, in clear language tactfully contrived to sound simple; and how to deliver it in a way that drew no attention to himself except admiration for his dedicated artistry. It isn't his fault that he looked like a member of a dying breed.

So whose fault is it? It isn't really anybody's. It's an historical tendency. There used to be dozens of these people on the screen and now there are hardly any. They haven't been bumped off. One or two of them have been edged off, but most of them seem to have just died off, with the passing of time. What alarms me is that they haven't been replaced: not, at any rate, with people of their type. There are superficial reasons that can be adduced for this. One of them I would call the Ford Cortina fallacy: the idea that if a subject is sufficiently fascinating it can present itself, with no single narrator. But few subjects are that fascinating in themselves: as the original proponents of the presenterless, multiple-interview, flashily edited documentary feature have no doubt been painfully discovering since they became channel controllers, even for a killer whale people are more likely to switch on when it looks as if it wants to eat Sir David Attenborough. There has to be a human face there. Bob Peck's sepulchral voice is not enough, except if the subject is the evolution of the funeral parlour through the ages.

Another superficial reason is the Mission to Explain: a good and necessary idea, it got diverted into the news department, where there is less room for it, and away from documentary features, its proper province. Thus the impeccably overqualified John Simpson gets a few minutes to report from the battlefield and has to fufil his mission to explain in the *Spectator*. On screen he seems mainly to have a mission to get shot at.

But the deep reason, I believe, is a lingering nervousness about whether an élite is justified in delivering enlightenment to the public. It's hard to believe, at this distance, how persistently the left wing, when it existed, used to attack the broadcasting élite for its paternalism. An élite was held to be a very bad thing for a society to suffer from, and the more paternalistic it was, the more manipulative it was felt to be. What else was the Establishment but a tool of Late Capitalism? This line of thought attained the status of religious belief in the 1960s, when the youth movement turned the universities into broadcasting stations of their own. Right here in King's, on the other side of that door at the end of the hall, in a room which is now the student bar, a Free University was set up in permanent revolutionary session. Though it had all the appearance and noise level of a Trotskyite crèche, it was taken seriously by those present. I myself attended several of its soirées and made a stirring speech against the evils of *in loco parentis*. But as one of the older dons remarked at the time, the parents were't as loco as they looked. Several of the more radical undergraduates – the ones who had reduced their daily intake of food to a single bowl of rice in order to proclaim their solidarity with Chairman Mao's struggle for world freedom – condemned the Machiavellian cynicism of King's in having provided the Free University with a room and tea-making facilities. They called this an act of repressive tolerance.

It was. On the whole, and in all its institutions, repressive tolerance was the way the Establishment neutralized attacks from the left. The unspoken assumption was that there was a solidarity between the ruling élite and its critics, the more promising of whom, it was correctly anticipated, would one day join its ranks. There was a large measure of tacit agreement that the ruling élites were as permeable as they needed to be and that there was enough social mobility to

ensure that talent would rise. That it would *want* to rise was supposed
to be guaranteed by an educational system that imparted knowlege
not for utilitarian ends but as an absolute good. The broadcasting
system was meant to play a large part in this process and largely
did. Attacks mounted from the left thus found themselves short of
ammunition, and had to make up for it by shouting slogans. Although
the broadcasters exhausted themselves keeping a cool head in the
hubbub, accusations that they were too much in thrall to the market
answered themselves. What nobody expected, until Mrs Thatcher
came to power, was the accusation that the broadcasters were too
little in thrall to the market.

I don't think that the camel's back was broken, but perhaps
its heart was. Vilified from two directions, the older generation of
mandarins lost some of their confidence, and the younger generation
started off without it. There was a loss of belief, and especially in the
area I am talking about tonight. The left wing's simplistic loathing
of paternalism, and the right wing's disingenuous advocacy of the
sovereign people, combined to produce a lasting, toxic residue: a fear
of putting anyone on the screen for long who might look or sound
as if he or she (especially she, sadly enough) has been blessed –
whether by background, education or the hand of God – with an air
of authority not shared by the viewers at home. One result was this
fading away of the old soldiers. Another was their partial replacement by these disembodied voices. And perhaps the most disturbing
result of all, visible in all too many fields of television now, has
been the gradual but seemingly unstoppable emergence of fresh faces
with nothing to say for themselves. I'm not here to mock them: not
just because I don't want them to mock me back for my own faults,
but because I'm sure most of them are nice, honest people. I don't
belong to the school of thought that says Terry Christian was invented
by the *X-Files* special effects department. He looks to me like a brave
young man struggling deperately against odds. What I question is
the notion that television personalities chosen to be unthreatening
present no threat.

If so seductive but wrong-headed a notion is to be countered, the
first thing to say is that this isn't the way the viewers at home feel.
It's the way the broadcasters feel on their behalf. We already know
that whichever party can make education educational again will
probably win the next election. We should also already know, but have

been slow to catch on, that a television screen populated exlusively by specialized media creatures who have studied nothing seriously in their lives except how to read an autocue is going to leave the whole system looking poverty-stricken, however lavish the graphics. The viewers give their loyalty to people who impress them, not to ciphers. The evidence is already in. In the case of game shows, an area which is as close to a pure market as television offers, the viewers won't switch on just for the game. They want to see the person who runs it, and it has to be a person who looks and sounds like something more than just an automaton invented for the screen. At the moment the person most people switch on is Michael Barrymore. Better than the format he fronts, he's a naturally bright, gifted and elegant man, with a real personality rather than a manufactured one, and with a life beyond the screen – rather more life beyond the screen, it turns out, than we at first thought, although I doubt if revelations of his personal complexity will make him less popular. In America, where the daily press is not so virulent as ours but the television executives are more timid, he might have been destroyed: but that's America's problem, like their network television system as a whole.

American network TV is a very dangerous analogy to draw upon when discussing the British equivalent. It was on the American analogy, I suspect, that the BBC began making its ill-advised prophecies about the necessary shrinkage of the audience share for the four main channels *vis-à-vis* cable and satellite. But the reason why the US network audience was ripe to shrivel was that nobody with an IQ in three figures could bear to watch. The commercials were so close together that any alternative arrangement was bound to find favour. For British television executives to make a prophecy on the basis of the American experience merely risked the prophecy's fulfilling itself without ever having validated the analogy. The only part of the analogy that really *might* come true concerns the American network anchor men. As the audience for each network shrank, the anchor men's salaries expanded, because the difference they made became more decisive. The remaining audience for CBS news switched on because Dan Rather was anchoring it, with the result that a man with a tenth the qualifications of Jon Snow ended up earning a hundred times the money. It got to the point where Rather's salary increased at double the rate of the audience's decline, just as long as he kept the share. Earlier this year, no doubt more by luck than judgement, I myself was fronting a prime-time show that kept an audience share of never less that 40 per cent for the entire run. If somebody told me that I could have a bigger pay cheque every time the audience grew smaller, just as long as I kept the share, my first response would be 'Where do I sign?' But I would like to think that my second response would be desperation. We're in this for more than the money, aren't we?

Well, aren't we? Of course we are. Even the faceless moguls who won the franchises turn out to have faces after all, and they want to be able to shave in the morning with their eyes open. We want to go on having a broacasting system worth working a long day for, and we want to restore it where it has lapsed. In this one area I have picked on – the supply, or lack of it, of overqualifed screen personnel – I believe the lapse now amounts to a real crisis. Other areas will repair themselves, in the light of experience. Some lapses came from a good impulse. The justifiable idea that regional accents were insufficiently represented on the air waves led to the unjustifiable and damaging conclusion that there was no such thing as standard English. But there is, and the clearest proof lies in how well it is spoken by members of precisely those minorites who might legitimately complain of discrimination if they chose. When all the women on television speak like Zeinab Badawi, and all the men like Trevor McDonald, we'll be all right again: and there's an end to *that* discussion. But this more fundamental matter, about the failure in recruitment of authoritative figures to the screen, can only be tackled when we realize that the class war is over, and put it behind us. The public already has. The public knows that it is better to be Richard Branson than the Marquess of Blandford. The public doesn't need our pitiable tabloid newspapers to tell them that. So why can't *we* grasp it? Is it because we are still haunted by this guilty embarrassment about belonging to an élite? But the people who run television are *necessarily* an élite, and that is a bad thing only to the extent that the élite perpetuates itself as an oligarchy.

Left-wing ideology died in the West because it was already dead in the East, and right-wing ideology, after its brief period of respectability under Mrs Thatcher, is already a rump. Social engineering of either kind has reacquired the status it should never have lost, that of a fantasy. If the fantasy lingers, it is because liberty so inconsiderately refuses to produce perfectly fair results. But a society, and a free society least of all, can't be homogenized in pursuit of absolute justice. Such a course must always lead to greater inequalities than ever, when the last, self-seeking élite retreats to an enclave, there to rule by decree or cower within its walls. Society can't be regimented in any lasting way, not even by Hitler or Josef Stalin. Nor can it be atomized in any profitable way, not even for Bill Gates. Society can only be bound together, in its common humanity. In that continuing task, the broadcasting system, and especially television, has a responsibility. There is no escaping from it: not into personal wealth, desirable though that might be; not into management systems, scientific though they might sound; and never into the idle supposition that the majority audience consists entirely of minorities each of which can be appealed to if its needs are identified. The final minority is the individual, and he or she is a person like us. If *we* sometimes don't know what we want or need until we are shown it, how can the audience? What individuals want and what they need are two terms neither of which can be entirely resolved in terms of the other. So the broadcasting élite is stuck with its dilemma, and the dilemma is the job. We can never be certain, and yet we must act with certitude. Finally we have to do what we feel like and hope they like it. The charge of irresponsibility will always be hard to dodge. That's the responsibility, and we might as well call it a privilege. After all, even if we're leading a life of sacrifice, it doesn't look that way tonight.

King's College, Cambridge, 15 September, 1995

PRESENTING THE RICHARD DIMBLEBY AWARD

It's my honour to present this award to a man who writes so well that his art criticism and cultural comment would have made great television even if they had never left the printed page. Everything he writes has pictures in it. To write so vividly you have to see vividly in the first place. Blessed with the incomparable advantage of having been born and raised in Australia, he got clear blue sky into his eyes when young and has been seeing the world through it ever since.

Above all he could see how the art of painting reflected the world. Setting up a powerful base in New York, he wrote art criticism which brought in the whole society that produced the art. Though his intellectual resources threatened to burst the bounds of any medium to which they were confined, it never occurred to him that television, even American television, was beneath him: it was *there*, to be entered at its weak point – its growing dearth of the authoritative voice. Through that weak point could be made the strongest effect, and his effect was instantaneous. Just when we thought that the great tradition of the comprehensive television arts essay established by Kenneth Clark was fading, suddenly there was *The Shock of the New* to prove that it could be not just recapitulated but even transcended. About the notorious pile of bricks in the Tate Gallery our award-winner said everything necessary in a single sentence: 'Anyone *except* a child can make such things.' This was better than wisdom. It was wit: wisdom with wings.

His most recent BBC series, *American Visions*, was a gift to America for which not only Americans should be grateful. Anyone who watches television anywhere in the hope that it can still make life better instead of just more bearable should be glad that there is still someone who incarnates what cultural comment ought to be:

overqualified yet uncondescending, serious without solemnity, packed tight yet with unimpeded flow, providing us, as if it were our birthright, with the priceless bonus of television's simplest yet most precious blessing – the talking head who brings words alive. I have known this man since we were students together and have never ceased to wonder at his gifts, yet the millions of people throughout the world who have watched and listened to him in delight know the best thing about him as well as I do. Tonight I am proud to represent them in paying tribute to a prince of the English language. The Richard Dimbleby Award for Outstanding Contribution to Factual Television goes very deservedly to – Robert Hughes.

From a presentation speech at the BAFTA Awards, 1997

ANZAC DAY DAWN SERVICE ADDRESS

It's said that whenever Winston Churchill fell prey to the fits of intense depression he called Black Dog, he would dream about Gallipoli and the Dardanelles, of the dead soldiers in the water and on the cliffs. The Dardanelles campaign had been his idea, and it was a brilliant idea: if it had been successful it would have altered the course of the war, breaking the murderous stalemate of trench warfare on the Western Front. It would have stemmed the slaughter. But it wasn't successful, the enemy was waiting, and all that was altered was the course of many young lives – and of those, too many belonged to us, to Australia and New Zealand, little dominions with not much population, and certainly none of it to spare.

There was a harvest of our tallest poppies. A bitter harvest. Recently – by commentators with their own, no doubt heartfelt and even admirable purposes – the notion has been encouraged that the Anzacs were fed into the battle to save British lives, as Imperial cannon-fodder. The cruel fact was that three times as many British troops as Anzacs went into that cauldron and never came out. But the British were counting their troops in millions anyway, and soon they would be counting their dead by the same measure. For us, young men dead by the thousand was a lot, an awful lot, and the same was still true in the second war, and always will be true if it happens again.

But nothing quite like those wars, not even Vietnam, ever has happened again, or is likely to, and that consideration, perhaps, is nearer the heart of this ceremony than we might easily realize. The memory is fading, even as the myth grows, and it is fading precisely *because* we have got the world our parents dreamed of. In our generation and probably for all the generations to come, the privileged nations no longer fight each other, or will fight each other. It is, and will be, the sad fate of the underprivileged nations to do all

that. In the meanwhile the way is open for our children to misinterpret history, and believe that a ceremony like this honours
militarism. Except by our participation in this moment of solemnity
– the solemnity that always courts pomposity, unless we can forget
ourselves and remember those who never lived to stand on ceremony
– how can we convince our children that the opposite is true?

Militarism, in both the great wars, *was* the enemy. It was why the
enemy had to be fought. Almost all our dead were civilians in
peacetime, and the aching gaps they left were not in the barracks but
on the farms and in the factories, in the suburbs and the little towns
with one pub. The thousands of Australian aircrew who died over
Europe, and are commemorated here by this stone, would, had they
lived, have made an important contribution to Australia's burgeoning
creative energy after World War Two. We might have found our full
confidence much sooner. But without their valour and generosity we
might never have found it at all. Had Hitler prevailed, and Britain
gone under, nowhere in the world, not even America, would have
remained free of his virulent influence. Those of us who are very
properly concerned with what the Aborigines suffered at the hands
of Anglo-Saxon culture should at least consider what they might have
suffered at the hands of a Nazi culture, as it would undoubtedly
have been transmitted by the occupying army of Hitler's admiring
ally. They would have been regarded as a problem with only one
solution – a final solution.

When we say that the lives of any of our young men and women
under arms were wasted we should be very careful what we mean.
We who are lucky enough to live in the world they helped to make
safe from institutionalized evil can't expect any prizes for pro-
nouncing that war is not glorious. They knew that. They fought the
wars anyway, and that *was* their glory. It's obviously true that
the world would have been a better place if the wars had never
happened, but it's profoundly true that it would have been an infinitely worse place if they had not been fought and won.

All our dead would rather have lived in peace. But there was no
peace. Now there is, and perhaps, in our protected, cushioned and
lulling circumstances, one of the best ways to realize what life is really
worth is to try to imagine the intensity with which they must have
felt its value just before they lost it. Sacrifice is a large word, but no

word can be large enough for that small moment. The only eloquence that fits is silence – which I will ask you to observe with me as I fulfil my gladly accepted duty and unveil this plaque.

Battersea Park, 1988

CATCHING UP

Like the short script for the BBC television programme about *Hamlet* reproduced in the previous section, the first two of these three articles hail from a time frame rather earlier than the one nominally set for this collection. But I am not putting them in just because I overlooked them last time. They were never overlooked: they were left out for a reason. The piece about photography included remarks about Janet Malcolm which a mutual friend told me had caused offence. If she had been offended, I didn't want to offend her again: but in the interim Malcolm (as an American magazine would refer to her) has proved herself tough enough to bear other people's embarrassment, so perhaps it's time for me to try proving that I am tough enough to bear hers. The piece on the House of Lords I left out before because I thought it made me sound servile to British institutions. By now I am convinced that any British institution offering a check or a balance to government power should be defended, whatever the risk to one's reputation. Besides, there are phrases in the piece that still strike me as the best way I could make that particular point. I like to think that true of any piece I write, of whatever brevity, even that of a caption. Over the years I have left a good proportion of my journalism uncollected, but I never wrote any of it with evanescence in mind: I abandoned a piece because of what it lacked in quality, not because of what its genre lacked in dignity. By other writers, books of collected casual pieces are the books I like best: in other words, I like the kind of writer who gets his gift into anything, and who, therefore, can never write anything so trivial that it does not bear reprinting. My own critics are fond of calling me the kind of egotist who would publish his laundry lists if he could get away with it. I have never found that gibe to have much force, because there are so many writers whose laundry lists I would like to read. The third piece, which I *did* overlook twenty-five years ago, is about a man who, as a matter of course, reprinted his every written utterance, and thank God he did. Beachcomber's books were like this one, at least in kind; so there can be nothing wrong with the kind, whatever might be lacking in the execution.

THE GENTLE SLOPE TO CASTALIA

The very first book illustrated with photographs, William Fox Talbot's *The Pencil of Nature* (1844), carried as an epigraph a quotation from Virgil. Talbot, who was a learned classicist as well as a chemist clever enough to invent photography, enlisted Virgil's aid in declaring how sweet it was to cross a mountain ridge unblemished by the wheel ruts of previous visitors, and thence descend the gentle slope to Castalia – a rural paradise complete with well-tended olive groves. The gentle slope turned out to be a precipice and Castalia is buried miles deep under photographs. A subsidiary avalanche, composed of books about photographs, is even now descending. In this brief survey I have selected with some rigour from the recent output, which has filled my office and chased me downstairs into the kitchen.

*

In her book *On Photography* (1977) Susan Sontag darkly warned the world that images are out to consume it. Books about images are presumably also in on the feast. Hers remains the best theoretical work to date, although competitors are appearing with startling frequency. Gisèle Freund's *Photography and Society*, now finally available in English, is half historical survey, half theoretical analysis. Her own experience as a celebrated photographer has obviously helped anchor speculation to reality. When the argument takes off, it takes off into a comfortingly recognizable brand of historical determinism. Thus it is made clear how the early portrait photographers served the needs of the bourgeoisie and wiped out the miniaturists who had done the same job for the aristocracy: hence the collapse of taste. Baudelaire, who hated the bourgeoisie, consequently hated photography too. These reflections come in handy when you are looking at the famous photograph of Baudelaire by Nadar. That baleful look must spring from resentment. Sontag makes greater play with such historical cruxes but Freund gives you more of the facts.

Janet Malcolm, the *New Yorker*'s photography critic, has produced a worthwhile compilation of her essays. She thinks 'discomfit' means 'make uncomfortable', but such lapses are rare. More high-flown than Freund, although less self-intoxicatingly so than Sontag, Malcolm is an excellent critic between gusts of aesthetic speculation. *Diana and Nikon* is grandly subtitled 'Essays on the Aesthetic of Photography'. Whether there is such a thing as an aesthetic of photography is a question which critics should try to keep open as long as possible, since that is one of the things that good criticism always does – i.e. stops aestheticians from forming a premature synthesis. In her essay on Richard Avedon, Malcolm assesses the April 1965 issue of *Harper's Bazaar*, the one edited by Avedon, as a 'self-indulgent mess'. But she insists on being charitable, against what she has already revealed to be her own better judgement, about his warts-foremost portraits of the mid-fifties. 'Like the death's-head at the feast in medieval iconography, these pictures come to tell us that the golden lads and lasses frolicking down the streets of Paris today will be horrible old people tomorrow . . . Avedon *means* to disturb and shock with these pictures, in the way that the young Rembrandt . . . the ageing Swift . . .'

Whatever its stature as aesthetics, this is low-grade criticism. Every artist who shoves something nasty in your face *means* to shock. When Rembrandt portrayed the decay of the flesh he was saying that ugliness, too, is a part of life, and even part of the beautiful. By using such a phrase as 'horrible old people' Malcolm unwittingly proves that she has caught something of Avedon's crassness, even while taking him to task. A photographer might be permitted to think in such coarse terms if he is inventive enough in his work, but it is a ruinous habit in a critic and can't be much of an advantage even to an aesthetician, who should be above making her older readers feel uncomfortable, or discomfited. *Cras mihi* – tomorrow it is my turn – remains a useful motto.

Malcolm calls photography the uppity housemaid of painting. Not a bad idea, but like her range of reference it shows an inclination to worry at the phantom problem of whether photography is an art or not. Sontag does better by calling photography a language: nobody wastes time trying to find out whether a language is an art. But Malcolm, between mandatory bouts of ratiocinative fever, stays cool enough to give you some idea of the thinner book she might have written – the one subtitled 'Critical Essays about Photography'. She shows herself capable of scepticism – a quality not to be confused with cynicism, especially in this field, where an initial enthusiasm at the sheer wealth of stimuli on offer can so easily switch to a bilious rejection of the whole farrago.

On the subject of Diane Arbus's supposedly revolting portraits of freaks and victims, Malcolm makes the penetrating remark that they are not really all that revolting after all – the reason for their popularity is that they are reassuringly in 'the composed, static style of the nineteenth century'. Such limiting judgements are more useful than dismissive ones, and more subversive too. Similarly, when she says that Edward Weston, far from being the 'straight' photographer he said he was, was simply copying new styles of painting instead of old ones, she isn't trying to destroy him – just to define him.

*

A vigorously interested but properly sceptical tone is the necessary corrective to the star system promoted by John Szarkowski. Operating from his command centre at New York's Museum of Modern Art, Szarkowski has conjured up from photography's short past more geniuses than the Renaissance ever knew. Szarkowski's passion would be infectious even if he lacked discrimination, but in fact he is a first-rate critic in detail and an admirably cogent thinker within his field. The Museum of Modern Art booklet *Looking at Photographs* (1973) continues to be the best possible short introduction to the entire topic. In it he draws the vital distinction between self-expression and documentary, and draws it at the moment when it is least obvious yet most apposite – with reference to a photograph by Atget of a vase at Versailles. Other photographers, according to Szarkowski, had been concerned either with describing the specific facts (documentation) or with exploiting their individual sensibilities (self-expression). Atget fused and transcended both approaches. Szarkowski's gift for argument manages to convince you that Atget's artistic personality is somehow present in a picture otherwise devoid of living human content. In an earlier Museum booklet, *The Photographer's Eye* (1966, reprinted this year), he declared himself aware that the 'fine art' and 'functional' traditions were intimately involved with each other – another vital critical precept.

So there is nothing simplistic about Szarkowski. It will be a rare aesthetician who matches his analytical capacity. There is not much wrong with his prose either, apart from his conviction that 'disinterested' means 'uninterested'. What disturbs you about his writings is how they make photography so overwhelmingly significant. For Szarkowski, photography is the biggest deal since the wheel. If he did not feel that way he would never have got so far as a curator and showman, but when the same fervour smites his readers they can be excused for succumbing to a mild panic. Surely photography isn't everything.

It isn't, but it isn't nothing either. One can be sceptical about just how great Szarkowski's great artists are, but there is no reason for deciding that they are anything less than a remarkable group of people. Just how remarkable is now being revealed by a swathe of plush monographs. The hard work of the archivists and curators is paying off in a big way. Only in a climate of acceptance could these sumptuously produced books come to exist. The late Nancy Newhall's *The Eloquent Light* is a new edition of her biography of Ansel Adams, first published by the Sierra Club in 1963. It traces Adams's career from 1902 up to 1938, by which time Alfred Stieglitz had given him – in 1936, to be precise – the one-man show that helped establish him as a master photographer.

The book has plates drawn from Adams's whole range, although the Yosemite photographs inevitably stand out. The text gives due regard to the emphasis he placed on cleanliness. The washed prints were tested for any lingering traces of hypo. Adams was not alone among the American photographers in taking himself so solemnly: with monk-like austerity they acted out the seriousness of their calling. That its seriousness was not yet unquestioned only made it the more necessary to keep a long face. In the case of Adams the results justified any amount of pious rhetoric about the Expanding Photographic Universe. Published last year, *Yosemite and the Range of Light* contains the finest fruits of Adams's long obsession with the Sierra Nevada. The quality of the prints is bewitching. They are so sharp you can taste the steel. Blacks, grays, and whites look as lustrous as the skin of a Siamese cat.

*

Walter Benjamin thought a work of art could have authenticity but a photograph could not. He said so in the famous essay whose title is usually translated as 'The Work of Art in the Age of Mechanical Reproduction', although really it should be translated as 'The Work of Art in the Age of its Mechanical Reproducibility', since Benjamin's point was that mankind had always produced everyday things in multiple copies but it was only lately that the work of art had become subject to the same rule. Since a given negative could yield any number of prints, Benjamin argued, to ask for an 'authentic' print made no sense ('*die Frage nach dem echten Abzug hat keinen Sinn*'). Sontag, who in other respects might have subjected Benjamin's great essay to a less awe-stricken scrutiny, realized that on this point at least the sage was exactly wrong. Negatives can be damaged, prints can be made from prints, paper and methods of reproduction can fall short of a photographer's wishes. Obviously some prints are more authentic than others and you can't have greater or lesser degrees of nothing. These prints of Adams's Yosemite photographs are so *echt* they sing. El Capitan looms through a winter sunrise. Half Dome shines clean as a hound's tooth under a thunderhead or fills with shadows as the moon, filled with shadows of its own, plugs a hole in the sheet steel sky.

Suppose Paul Strand had taken pictures of the same chunks of geology: could a layman, however knowledgeable, tell the difference? Even the most distinctive photographers tend to be defined more by subject matter than by style. If a photographer's any and every photograph were immediately identifiable as his he would probably be individual to the point of mania. Good photographs look better than bad photographs but don't often look all that much different from one another. Some of Paul Strand's photographs in *Time and New England*, a book devised in collaboration with the much-missed Nancy Newhall (she died in 1974), look as if Adams might have taken them, yet it is no reflection on either man. The book was first published in 1950 but is now redesigned, with the prints brought closer to the authentic state. Adams's senior by twelve years, Strand likewise profited from an association with Stieglitz. These connections of inspiration and patronage are very easy to be impressed by, but it is worth remembering that just because half the Florentine sculptors were all born on the same few hills did not make them blood brothers.

The life of art lies in what makes artists different from one another
– the individual creative personality. The main difference between a
clapboard church by Paul Strand and a clapboard house by Harry
Callahan is that in Strand's lens the church leans backward and in
Callahan's the house leans forward.

In *Brett Weston: Photographs From Five Decades* there is more
than enough clean-cut shapeliness to recall his father Edward's predi-
lection for 'the *thing itself*'. The air of dedication is once again
monastic. 'For Brett, the struggle has been a long, unhurried process
of refining an uncompromising, inborn vision. He did not acquire
it: it was simply granted to him, like grace.' There is no reason to
doubt the intensity of Brett's inborn vision. What niggles is the fact
that a beach photographed by Brett Weston and a beach photographed by Harry Callahan look like roughly similar stretches of the
same stuff – sand.

*

Water's Edge collects the best of Callahan's black and white Beach
Series (always capitalized) from 1941 until now. The light, the sand
patterns, the reeds, and the frail water could not be more delicately
caught. When they *are* more delicately caught, the result is the kind
of abstraction that leaves you striving to admire. But generally Callahan photographing is good at what Lichtenberg said was the most
important thing about thinking – keeping the right distance from
the subject. The text, a deeply rhythmless poetic concoction by A. R.
Ammons ('I allow myself eddies of meaning') is in the hallowed
tradition of overwriting for which, with his accompanying prose to
Walker Evans's photographs in *Let Us Now Praise Famous Men*, James
Agee unfortunately gave an eternal sanction. For crazy people, there
is a deluxe limited edition priced at $1,500. Presumably it is bound
in platinum. *Harry Callahan: Color* has some of the Beach Series in
colour and a lot more besides: clapboard houses, billboards, store
fronts and, most importantly, his wife Eleanor. Callahan composes
exceptionally pretty scenes but human beings keep stealing them.

The same applies to the old Czech master Sudek, who was born
in 1896 and is apparently still alive. Not much of his work has
been seen outside Czechoslovakia until now. Sonja Bullaty and Anna
Farova have compiled and introduced their monograph in a manner
befitting his unarguable stature. The amber haze of the early prints

proclaims his affinity with Steichen, whose symbolist nudes in *Steichen: The Master Prints 1895–1914* might have been signed by Sudek. The wily Czech's still lifes and surrealist fantasies are enough to keep aestheticians happily chatting, but once again the people, when they are allowed to appear, infallibly upstage the settings.

The same is doubly true for Lotte Jacobi, whose people are not, like Sudek's, anonymous. Jacobi was also born in 1896. Kelly Wise's book on her, called just *Lotte Jacobi*, was published in the US in 1978 but English readers might like to note that it has only lately succeeded in crossing the Atlantic. In New York for ten years after World War II Jacobi busied herself with abstract effects called 'photogenics'. Like all art inspired by its own technique, they dated instantly and are now of little interest. But her portraits, mainly taken in pre-war Germany, are of high value. The high value becomes especially high when the sitters are world famous, but there is no way around that. Weill, Lorre, Walter, Furtwängler, Piscator, Lang, Kraus, Planck, Zuckmayer, Grosz, and many more are all preserved in *echt* condition. She did a whole, fascinating sequence of Einstein portraits both in Germany and in American exile. There are also multiple portraits of Thomas Mann, Chagall, Frost, and Stieglitz. The cover girl is Lotte Lenya.

Jacobi also did a portrait of Moholy-Nagy. If Moholy-Nagy had done more portraits himself, Andreas Haus's book on him, *Moholy-Nagy: Photographs and Photograms*, might have been of more than historical interest. The volume is well kitted out for study by aestheticians, but even those up on Moholy-Nagy's theories of perception could well find that the photograms no longer thrill. Herr Haus speaks of Moholy-Nagy's 'attempt to solve his problems as a painter (the penetration of planes, the elimination of individual handwriting) by means of a new technique . . .' Unfortunately Moholy-Nagy's chief problem as a painter, shortage of talent, could not be solved by technical innovation, despite an abundant output of compensatory aesthetic sloganeering. Moholy-Nagy talked about 'the hygiene of the optical' and announced that 'everyone will be compelled to see what is optically true.' (I once heard Pierre Boulez, at a lunch thrown for him in London by my newspaper the *Observer*, promise that the general public would be made familiar with contemporary music 'by force'.) Moholy-Nagy's real contribution lay not in abstract doodling but in his knack for shooting reality from unexpected angles so as to reveal forms and textures previously unlooked for. Everybody has since appropriated these technical advances, with the result that most of his once startling photographs are no longer immediately identifiable as being by him. Such is the fate of the technical innovator.

*

But Moholy-Nagy's people are vivid enough. From a balcony in Dessau (datelined '1926–1928') a woman looks down at a pretty girl stretched smiling on a parapet. Moholy-Nagy was a tireless organizer of forms but the most interesting form, that of the human being, comes ready made. Cecil Beaton, to his credit, never doubted that his career as a photographer owed something to the human beings he was pointing his camera at. *Self-Portrait With Friends*, the selection from his diaries which appeared last year, now receives its necessary supplement in the form of *Beaton*, a collection of his best portrait photographs, edited by James Danziger. Raphael, Berenson was fond of saying, shows us the classicism of our yearnings. Beaton gave famous and fashionable people the look they would have liked to have. In many cases they had it already. Lady Oxford, photographed in 1927, may have been a battleaxe, but she was a regal battleaxe. Beaton wasn't a sentimentalist so much as a dandy who believed in glamour as a separate country. Until the fifties he was almost the only mainstream British photographer the young aspirants could look to. (Bill Brandt was a drop-out.) From the technical viewpoint he was awesomely capable – he snatched candids in Hollywood that look as uncluttered as the best official studio portraits.

Beyond technique he had a sense of occasion. At times this might have been indistinguishable from snobbery, but it served him better than the routine compulsion to record documentary truth. His book *New York* (1938) is painfully weak when it goes up to Harlem. ('These people are children.') In *Far East* (1945) he is plainly more interested in Imperial Delhi than in the air-raid casualties. In *Time Exposure* (1946) his 'Bomb Victim' is merely cute, whereas the portrait of John Gielgud 'in a Restoration role' slips straight into immortality with no waiting. These books and several more lie behind the present compilation, which loses little from being deprived of the original text. (The 'DeHavilland fighter, 1941' depicted on page 42 is, however, clearly a Spitfire, which was manufactured by Vickers Supermarine. How old is Mr Danziger? Eight?) Beaton was a social butterfly who wrote the higher gossip. But the circles he moved in provided him with human subjects who were, in many cases, works of art ready made. With Beaton's beautiful socialites, as with de Meyer's, it is hard to avoid the conclusion that they had no other reason for existence than getting into the picture. Beaton has, if anybody has, a clearly defined artistic personality. But once again the self-expression is largely defined by the field of documentation. His exquisite drawings, which he left like thank-you notes in the grand houses, are far more characteristic than his photographs.

*

Mainly by shading his eyes with a wide-brimmed hat and allowing his feet to take him in congenial directions, Beaton found the world seductive. He wasn't out to shape reality, even by photography, which he rated, perhaps jokingly, fifth among his interests. With Diana Vreeland seductiveness becomes Allure. In a folio called just that, Ms Vreeland collects some of her favourite twentieth-century photographs. Equipped with a stream of semi-consciousness text emanating from DV herself, the book (which I see the latest number of *Manhattan Catalogue* calls 'absolutely historic', not just historic) has been thrown together with such abandon that some of the captions have landed on the wrong photographs – in my copy, at least. The picture dubbed 'Baron de Meyer / *The New Hat Called Violette Worn by the Honorable Mrs. Reginald Fellowes – Alex, 1924*' should almost certainly be entitled 'Louise Dahl-Wolfe / *Balenciaga's white linen over-blouse, 1953*' and vice versa. In later copies, I understand, such anomalies have been put right. The model for the Balenciaga is, unless my eyes are giving out under the strain, Suzy Parker. Even at this late date, Ms Vreeland continues *Vogue's* queenly habit of always crediting the fashionable ladies but rarely the models. In effect this quirk has helped to glorify the photographers, who get kudos not only for the way they make the girl look but for the way she looks anyway.

The most striking pictures in Vreeland's book are by Anonymous, who snapped the British Royal women at George VI's funeral. By the time these prints, probably duped off other prints, have been blown up to fit the squash-court sized pages of *Allure*, there is not much left to say about authenticity. Yet aura – the many-layered immanence which Benjamin said photography deprived things of – is present in large amounts, possibly because Allure has been banished.

Not that it stays banished for long. On most of Vreeland's pages it seems fighting to get in somewhere. In the context of Vreeland's unbridled prose, Eva Perón becomes a figure of moral stature, since she cared how she looked to the bitter end. Vreeland is a place where appearance is everything. But the occasional big-name photographer manages to look timelessly unfussy. Some of the cleanest plates in *Allure's* pantheon are by George Hoyningen-Huene, this year the subject of a retrospective exhibition, called 'Eye for Elegance', at the International Center of Photography in New York. The catalogue gives a taste of his work, although really he is too protean to sample. Among other activities, he set the standard for pre-war French *Vogue's* studio photography and was colour consultant on some of the best-looking Hollywood films of the fifties and early sixties, including Cukor's wildly beautiful *Heller in Pink Tights*. No fashion photographer ever had a wider range. The shadows on his reclining swimsuit models are calculated to the centimetre, yet some of his celebrity portraits of the thirties look natural enough to have been done today. His 1934 Gary Cooper, for example, seems to be lit by nothing except sunlight. The profile is almost lost in the background and every skin blemish is left intact. Yet the result has aura to burn.

*

The Hollywood studio photographer retouched as a matter of course. In his splendidly produced *The Art of the Great Hollywood Portrait Photographers*, John Kobal gives us the rich benefit of his archival labours. Based in London, Kobal has built up a peerless collection of the original negatives. Kobal knows everything about how the studios marketed their property. Some studios assessed the daily output of their photographers by the pound. The stars were expected to cooperate and the smarter of them realized that it was in their interests to do so. Lombard, it seems, was particularly keen. Garbo was nervous, but Clarence Sinclair Bull never made the mistake of saying 'hold it' – he just lit her and waited. One key light, one top light, and a long lens parked some way off so she wouldn't notice. There are stories by and about, among others, Ruth Harriet Louise, Ernest Bachrach, Eugene Robert Richee, George Hurrell, and Lazlo Willinger. Sternberg knew exactly how he wanted Dietrich to look but otherwise it was a conspiracy between the studio and the photographer, with the star in on it if she was powerful enough. Before and after shots show how drastically Columbia rearranged the accoutrements of Rita Hayworth's face. One of the after shots, by A. L. 'Whitey' Schaefer, is surely an image for eternity.

But the studio photographers were not engaged in making something out of nothing, even though the lead used for retouching formed such a significant proportion of their daily poundage. The stars might have been helped to realize their ideal selves, but the ideal self was not, and could not be, too far divorced from the real appearance. When the silver transcontinental trains pulled in at Dearborn station in Chicago, a man called Len Lisovitch used to be lurking in wait. He was an amateur photographer who wanted the stars all to himself. Len collected, among others, Hedy Lamarr, Betty Grable, Merle Oberon and Greer Garson. His candids of Hedy Lamarr are not decisively less enchanting than the portraits turned out with such labour by Laszlo Willinger at MGM. Admittedly Lamarr had flawless skin and always photographed well as long as she was not allowed to become animated, but the point is hard to duck: the stars were already well on their way to being works of art before the hot lights touched them. They were simply beautiful human beings – if there is anything simple about that.

*

In *Mrs. David Bailey* – called, in the UK, *Trouble and Strife*, cockney rhyming slang for 'wife' – David Bailey celebrates the extraordinary beauty of his wife Marie Helvin. Bailey, Terence Donovan and Brian Duffey became such famous photographers in London during the sixties that they have been faced ever since with the requirement to astonish. This book is not wholly free from the strained compulsion to dazzle, but it is still Bailey's best effort since *Goodbye Baby and Amen*, mainly because Marie Helvin is so bliss-provokingly lovely that she takes the sting out of the naughtiest poses Bailey can think up. There is an admiring prefatory note by J. H. Lartigue, who would have done at least one thing Bailey hasn't – caught her smiling. *Avoir pour amour une femme aussi belle, jolie, charmante et troublante que Marie, quelle inspiration pour un artiste.* At eighty-four Lartigue still has an eye for a pretty foot.

Bailey has graciously allowed his model to retain her name. Helmut Newton takes that away and a lot more besides. *Special Collection 24 Photo Lithos* comprises big, slick prints of photographs you might have seen before in *White Women* (1976) and *Sleepless Nights* (1978). Rapturously introducing *Sleepless Nights*, Philippe Garner, billed as the photographic curator of London Sotheby's, unintentionally pinned Newton to the wall. 'There is, surely, an added spice in having the talent to present a subject as blatant as this in such a way that the spokespersons of a society which should, in theory, deplore such an image as shocking actually pat one on the back for taking it and reward one handsomely.' There was also a lot about Newton's alleged humour.

Mercifully his new book is deprived of textual accompaniment, leaving those who have a taste for these things free to indulge their fantasies of exhibitionism, bondage and flagellation. Apologists have explained that Newton loves women so much he wants to show how they retain their dignity no matter what you do to them, or pretend to do to them. So here they are in a variety of neck braces, trusses and plaster casts. For men who want to be in the saddle, there is a spurred and booted beauty wearing a saddle. Famous in the trade for his technical skill, Newton will take endless pains to find the right props and setting. I suppose he is trying to make us question our own desires, but I always find myself questioning his. It can be argued that Newton's sado-masochistic confections pale beside what can be found in hard-core pornography, yet the question still arises of why he thinks he is engaged in anything more exalted than a fashionable triteness already going out of date. He gives you the impression of somebody who has had his life changed by an Alice Cooper album. How his dogged prurience makes you long for Lartigue.

But what Newton does to girls is a sweet caress compared with what girls do to girls. *Women on Women* gave a broad hint at what was on the way. Women covered with cream, women with skulls in their twats, women flaunting six-foot styrofoam dicks, women solemnly feeling each other up in the back seats of limos. At first glance, Joyce Baronio's *42nd Street Studio*, with an introduction by Professor Linda Nochlin of CUNY, is the same scene, folio size. One's initial impulse, when faced with the spectacle of a naked girl attached by ropes to a blond stud in black boots plus obligatory whip, is to burst out yawning. But Baronio's pictures are laudable for their quality and most of the fantasies count as found objects. They litter the Times Square district where she works. She is performing a certain documentary service in recording them, even if you doubt the lasting value of her self-expression. For myself, I'm bound to say I'm at least half hooked, and would like to see what she does next. I don't *think* it's just because of the pretty girls, although I could certainly do without some of the guys, especially the one in the leather jockstrap and the hat.

*

A photographer who interests himself more in documentary than in self-expression is nowadays likely to remain anonymous until such time as his unassertive vision turns out to have been unique all along. For most photographers that time will never come no matter how arresting their photographs. *The Best of Photojournalism 5* enshrines some of the year's most riveting shots. You can flick through it and decide if reality is being consumed. I was particularly impressed by L. Roger Turner's three pictures of a Down's Syndrome boy hefting a bowling ball in the Special Olympics. Perhaps I am congratulating myself on my own compassion, which has in fact been reduced to a stock response by too many images. There is also a chance that my aesthetic sensibility is being blunted instead of sharpened when I admire Bill Wax's study of Chris Snode preparing to dive into a heated Florida pool on a cold winter's morning. Crucified in steam, Snode looks like a Duccio plus dry ice.

Eve Arnold's new book *In China* raises the question of veracity. Sontag argued persuasively that the beautifying power of photography derives from its weakness as a truth-teller. It is indeed true that a photograph can tell you something only if you already know something about its context, but the same applies to any other kind of signal. Here are some extremely pretty coloured photographs of China. They inform you of many facts, including the fact that there is at least one bald Buddhist monk still in business at the Cold Mountain monastery in Suchow. What they can't tell you is just how long those children singing in the classroom will be obliged to go on believing in the divinity of the man with his picture on the wall. The same kind of stricture, if it is one, applies to *Photographs for the Tsar*, which collects the astonishing pre-revolutionary coloured photographs by Sergei Prokudin-Gorskii, a forgotten pioneer now destined to be clamorously remembered.

Prokudin-Gorskii employed a triple-negative process of his own devising. Nicholas II commissioned him to perpetuate anything that took his fancy. The results fell short of those Eve Arnold is accustomed to obtaining but not by far. Prokudin-Gorskii was necessarily limited to photographing stationary objects but took care to pick the right ones. The book takes its place beside Chloe Obolensky's indispensable *The Russian Empire*, published last year.

Across the Rhine is the latest in the Time-Life corporation's admirable series based on its own World War II archive. Once again the text, contributed this time by Franklin M. Davis, Jr, but with the usual assistance from 'the editors of Time-Life books', is a sane corrective to the revisionist theories now rife among more exalted historians. The photographs do what photographs best can – they give you some idea of what the reality you already know something about was like in detail. Some of the pictures taken in the liberated concentration camps are included. Sontag tells us that her life was changed by seeing these very pictures – a moment in her book which I appreciated from the heart, since it was an extensive reading of the Nuremberg transcripts, with due attention to the horrific photographic evidence contained in Volume XXXI, that did more than anything else to shape my own view of life.

Sontag might agree that whatever else images had done to take the edge off reality, they rubbed her nose in it in that case. These photographs are hard to respond to adequately but then so might have been the reality. The brave documentary photographer Margaret Bourke-White, after taking her pictures in Buchenwald, told her editors that she would have to see the prints developed before she believed what she had witnessed. It is a point for an aesthetician to seize, but too much should not be made of it. She was speaking metaphorically. The thing had happened and she could tell that it had happened. Her photographs helped, however inadequately, to tell the world.

There is a case for photographing horrors, since not all torturers are as keen as Hitler's and Pol Pot's to keep their own pictorial record of what they get up to. Snapping celebrities with their pants down is harder to justify, but in his preface to *Private Pictures* Anthony Burgess does his best to convince us that the *paparazzi* are engaged in something valuable. From the photographs you can't find out much beyond a few variously startling physical facts about the firmness of Romy Schneider's behind, the pliancy of Elton John's wrist, and the magnitude of Giovanni Agnelli's virile member. It is also sensationally revealed that Orson Welles has a fat gut and Yul Brynner a bald head. Burgess is pretty scathing about Brigitte Bardot's breasts, but to me she looks in better shape than Burgess was when I last saw him.

Apparently Burgess shares the gutter press assumption that those who achieve fame should be made to suffer from it. But many of this book's victims are famous only as a side-effect of pursuing honourable careers. 'This book,' growls Burgess, 'in bringing stars down to the human level, is a kind of visual poem on the theme of expendability.' One night before a Cambridge Union debate I saw Burgess get angry because Glenda Jackson had not turned up to lead the opposing team. Burgess made it clear that to meet her ranked high among his reasons for being in attendance. Not even such unexpendable philosophers as Burgess are always entirely innocent of the star-fucking impulse. *Private Pictures* supplies additional evidence for the already well-documented theory that those who fuck the stars are the same people who enjoy sticking it to them.

The grinding triviality of the *paparazzi* retroactively makes the dedication of the documentary photographers sound less like solemnity and more like high seriousness. Karin Becker Ohrn's *Dorothea Lange and the Documentary Tradition* takes you back to the days of the Farm Security Administration, when a photographer could feel that she was helping to open the world's eyes. Lange believed that it took time for a photographer's personality to emerge. Some photographers can't wait that long, but even if the wrong people sometimes get famous it is generally true that only the right ones stay that way. *Dialogue with Photography*, edited by Paul Hill and Thomas Cooper, is an absorbing compilation of interviews with the big names, including Strand, Brassaï, Cartier-Bresson, Beaton, Lartigue and Kertész. The simplicity of true artistic absorption comes shining through even the murkiest rhetoric about Art. According to the late Minor White, Stieglitz asked him if he had ever been in love. When White said yes, Stieglitz told him he could be a photographer. Lartigue makes the same point. 'First, one must learn how to look, how to love.' It probably sounds better in French.

Brandt, the perpetual loner, is not present. On BBC radio recently he described how Cartier-Bresson, when they met in Paris in the fifties, wouldn't speak to him, because he had sinned against photographic purity by cropping the negative and using artificial light. At the time of writing, Brandt is all set to unleash on London an

exhibition of his recent work in which the girls are reportedly weighed
down with more chains and leather straps than Helmut Newton
ever dreamed of. Cartier-Bresson would doubtless not approve. The
photographers have always been quite capable of ideological warfare.
Ansel Adams said that Walker Evans's work gave him a hernia.

*

Peter Tausk's *Photography in the 20th Century* tells you how the
Western photographic tradition looks from Czechoslovakia, for whose
art and photography students this book was originally written. Tausk
has his nose pressed to the glass but is not unduly dazzled. He has a
useful way of pointing out that the reporters are as worthy of attention as the name photographers – the kind of thought which would
occur to you with special sharpness if you lived in a country where
there are no reporters. The best encyclopedia of the name photographers is still *The Magic Image* by Cecil Beaton and Gail Buckland
(1975). One had always suspected that Gail Buckland must have done
most of the work. The suspicion is confirmed by the high quality of
Fox Talbot and the Invention of Photography, the authorship of which
is claimed by her alone. Etymology, philology, mathematics, crystal-
lography – his interests were endless, and all pursued at the highest
level. On top of all that, he set the standards for the intelligent use
of his invention. His photograph of volumes from his own library is
a necessary reminder, bequeathed to us by the progenitor, that the
apparent divorce between word and image is really an indissoluble
marriage. One closes the book more astounded than ever at Talbot's
achievements. It was a genius who started it all.

Whether all those famous names that have cropped up since
should be thought of as geniuses is open to doubt. The Americans
are more vexed by such questions than the Europeans, who better
understand that some arts are minor and that it is more satisfactory
to be an accomplished practitioner of a minor art than a third-rate
exponent of a major one. Enjoying a less coherent social and intellectual life, the Americans have understandably either clung together
for warmth or been strident in isolation. The consequent rhetoric
should not too quickly be dismissed even when it is patent moon-
shine. The impure applied and minor arts are often accompanied by
dumb talk, off which it is easy for the critic to score points. He does
best, however, when addressing the thing itself. Photography, despite

the attendant cacophony of promotion, remains, after all, a miraculous event – almost as interesting, in fact, as Szarkowski says it is. Castalia still has its attractions. As for the higher thinker, he must sooner or later discover that the aesthetic of photography, like the aesthetic of the novel or the aesthetic of the ballet, is a snark. The best contribution a critic can make to aesthetics is to aim for consistency, argue closely, and be wary of big ideas.

Sontag's notion that images consume reality counts as a big idea. Intellectuals should speak for themselves in the first instance. Obviously images are not consuming *her* reality. So she must mean the rest of us. Nor was Benjamin being as penetrating as he sounded when he said that people flooded with images would not know how to read a book. My own children watch television for half a day at a stretch and still read more books than I did at their age. Benjamin thought of photography as one of the means by which fascism would allow the masses to express themselves without posing any threat to the social order. At that time everyone had a theory about the masses. Benjamin had already died his lonely death before it was generally realized that the masses do not exist. There are only people – so many of them that the aesthetician can be forgiven for finding their numbers meaningless. But the critic's job is to maintain what the best photographers have helped define – a discriminating eye.

New York Review of Books, 18 December, 1980

NOBLE TALKING HEADS

The first televising of the House of Lords, on 23 January, was, I found, a pleasant shock. It might well be that the other viewers consisted entirely of the unemployed, but I doubt if even the most bitter among them felt that time and money were being wasted. Helping to make the broadcast a surprise were one's expectations, which could not help but be dire.

Somehow the idea had got about that it was a lively moment in the House of Lords when Lord Hailsham bounced up and down on the Woolsack, and that in the normal course of business there was nothing to be heard from the buttoned red leather benches – pictures of these had been seen in the colour-supplements – except the death rattle of octogenarians. Things turned out to be not like that, either because they never had been or because they had been tarted up for the day. If the latter, it was a good argument in favour of televising Parliament.

The argument against was rehearsed at the eleventh hour by Lord Chalfont, talking to David Dimbleby on BBC 1. Lord Chalfont was against the televising of the House of Lords because he suspected that it was just a stratagem on the part of the broadcasters so that they could force the door of the House of Commons, after which the House of Lords, having served its purpose, would be once again plunged into obscurity. This sounded like a shrewd analysis. He was also against the televising because the peers would quickly become concerned with nothing else except fashioning an image, since television isn't interested in reasoned arguments, only in creating an impression. This sounded like a shrewd analysis only if you believed the premise, which I don't: television is just your eyes and ears on a stalk and doesn't like unreasoned arguments any better than you do. There is even a case for saying that it likes reasoned arguments better than radio, which won't tolerate dead air, whereas a pause on television makes you look as if you're thinking when you are. Television also makes you look as if you aren't thinking when you aren't, and thus helps to strip rhetoric of its binding energy. It is a bad medium for demagogues and offers its maximum excitement when one talking head is talking well. This is a hard point to prove, however: heads that talk well are in short supply.

Suddenly there they were, in abundance. The idea of starting off with Question Time was inspired, because the convention that a question must be kept short meant that a whole cast of characters were on their feet in the first hour, all choosing their words carefully so as to pack the most provocation into the briefest time. Probably they had rehearsed in front of the bathroom mirror, but it didn't matter. The level of language was high: that was what mattered. Would-be camera-hogs were steered back to the straight and narrow by a mass murmur of 'Too long'. Properly constructed sentences were to be heard, many of them with subordinate clauses. Contributions from Conservative, Labour and Alliance peers were all at the same respectable level of diction and articulacy, as if the English language were the common property of the British people, instead of, as in the House of Commons, something drawled by those who vote Conservative, bellowed by those who vote Labour, and spoken in recognizably human tones only by David Owen. Indeed the growing idea that Parliament might have to be dissolved and Dr Owen elected in its place will need to be revised, now that the House of Lords turns out to be full of people who are even better than he is at speaking as if you were listening. Some of them are a bit older than him, of course, although none of them actually died during Question Time. Lord Shinwell was seen to be sitting very still, but next time the camera came back to him he was sitting very still in a different position.

The reaction shot immediately showed its power. When the directors and vision mixers get more practice, the reaction shot will unquestionably become a principal feature, but even during this test run you found yourself listening harder when the face on screen was listening too. Whether Lord Hailsham was listening was hard to judge, because of his wig. All the other peers except the bishops were in street clothes: another expectation falsified. Despite having read quite a lot of journalism on the subject, I had somehow expected to see my noble lords in full drag. Doubtless they would have carried it off, but their looking ordinary made other conventions more immediately assimilable. The convention of calling your interlocutor 'my noble lord' or 'the noble baroness', for example, rapidly came to sound like ordinary courtesy, and one looked forward with regret to the next time the Speaker of the House of Commons would be obliged to eject Mr Dennis Skinner.

The Minister for the Arts, who is also the Chancellor of the Duchy of Lancaster, and who when neither of those things is the Earl of Gowrie, was referred to at all times as either 'my noble lord' or 'the noble Earl', or a combination of both. To be thus addressed is probably more comforting than otherwise, especially when your job, as far as the Upper House is concerned, hasn't got much else to offer except the obligation to field flak from above, below and all sides. During Question Time Lord Gowrie was asked to answer for the Government's economic policy, but because he was due to speak on that subject in the upcoming debate he staved off the question with a joke.

His jokes were no better than anybody else's. The House of Lords, like the House of Commons, seems to learn its humour in the Oxford and Cambridge Union debating chambers, where the audience will laugh at anything. An audience which will laugh at anything can teach you nothing about humour, which requires self-criticism. But when the peers stuck to questions and answers on serious points they were impressive, especially the women. Baroness Young almost got you convinced that the BBC's Overseas Broadcasting services, far from declining under this government, had actually flourished. In the reaction shots, however, the sadly shaking heads of her questioners showed you that something was up. Lord Whitelaw allowed the baroness to be questioned repeatedly, indeed repetitively, on the subject, so he was certainly not protecting her.

Lord Beswick opened the debate for Labour. He was no television star, but that was what made him a television star, and will eventually make them all television stars. He showed no sign of juicing his speech up for the camera or even the microphone. On the other hand, he showed every sign of speaking reasonably. His attack on government policy made sardonic use of the British Telecom flotation. Well-composed and ably enough delivered, his argument was hard to answer, as Lord Gowrie proved. My noble lord the noble Earl did his best to evoke a booming economy, but was hampered by lack of factual material. Baroness Seear, leader of the Liberal peers, made telling points which Lord Gowrie, seen in the reaction shots, either acknowledged for their skill or else simply agreed with. (Mrs Thatcher has probably already convened Lord Gowrie, the three other Cabinet nobles and every other Tory peer in order to tell them that it is no longer enough to be careful what they say. They must be careful what they think, and Lord Thorneycroft must not smile so much.) Making Baroness Seear's forensic sallies doubly impressive was the fact that they were spoken extempore. Again this was no television star, but most of television's female pitch-persons were going to sound pretty club-tongued by comparison. Imagine Esther Rantzen speaking for twenty minutes without notes.

The Bishop of Birmingham, Hugh Montefiore, fruitily delivered a maiden speech which took me back to Great St Mary's in Cambridge, where I listened to him earlier in his career. Familiarity bred indifference, but Lord Cledwyn, next up for Labour, offered what sounded like sincere compliments. Then Lord Stockton, after a commotion in the Strangers' Gallery which we were not allowed to watch, rose to offer insincere compliments. He too, he began, had 'recently passed through the ordeal of a maiden speech'. Everybody knew that his maiden speech had been a triumph. The sly old walrus was poor-mouthing himself again. But not as much, it turned out, as he was going to bad-mouth the government.

Lord Stockton's use of language verged on the exquisite ('this motion, drawn up in very wide, almost Pecksniffian terms'), but he was out for blood. Lord Gowrie was complimented on 'the very best defence of government I've ever heard made'. But this was a build-up for the let-down. Quickly it became clear that there could be no real defence of this government. In Stockton sixty-three years ago unemployment had been 29 per cent. What was unemployment in Stockon today? 28 per cent. 'A very sad end to one's life.'

He took no credit for the years in which he, in his earlier incarnation as Harold Macmillan, had told the people that they had never had it so good. The economy had been collapsing steadily since the First World War, and the Second World War had only appeared to shore it up. When the crash became obvious to all, the Labour Government had not known what to do. (As in a well-scripted movie, there was a reaction shot of Lord Wilson not reacting: giving points for liveliness, in fact, to Lord Shinwell. Whoever was on the buttons had a flying finger. When television is as well-directed as this, you're not only there, you're looking in the right place.)

'What is really happening,' Lord Stockton said, as if the whole crafty edifice of his oration were being made up on the spot, 'is that the third industrial revolution is on its way . . . and we're somehow out of it.' It was permissible to reflect that it isn't on its way, it's here, and we're not only out of it, we have little chance of getting back into it. But you had to allow him his measure of optimism, especially if it doubled the effect of his condemnation. And what he was condemning was Mrs Thatcher's government.

Mrs Thatcher will probably not be much concerned by the question of which it was that dealt her such a blow, an image of a shuffling old man or a real shuffling old man. She is doubtless sufficiently preoccupied by the likelihood that her back-benchers, should they be offered the same chance of television stardom, will show similar signs of independence. If her quondam image-expert Mr Cecil Parkinson has been consulted he will have had further implications to point out, among them being the possibility that unless the cameras are put into the House of Commons, or else removed from the House of Lords, then the Upper House will render the Lower House incredible. Augustus, reserving power for himself, lived modestly while allowing the senators all the glory. It didn't matter what they said because nobody could listen. But a national debating chamber to which the people can listen, and not only listen to but look at, becomes a power in itself.

After Lord Stockton sat down, Lord Taylor stood up to an emptying house, which was rather tough on the SDP. This, we were told, was how the benches normally looked. But the damage had been done, if damage it was. Back being interviewed on television that same night, Lord Chalfont explained how the cameras had made the whole thing histrionic. But he wore a Garrick Club tie to say so, and if television can't abide reasoned arguments, why was he arguing? Denis Healey, a realist, called Lord Stockton's speech 'a lulu', in the tones of one already planning a few lulus of his own.

London Review of Books, 7 February, 1985

BEACHCOMBER'S STUFF

Beachcomber: The Works of J. B. Morton **edited by Richard Ingrams, Muller**

To introduce and edit this hilarious selection from Beachcomber's outpourings has so obviously been a labour of love that it would be churlish to blame Richard Ingrams for the glaring fault of subtitling the book 'The Works of J. B. Morton'. In fact the volume is the merest chrestomathy, like Michael Frayn's pioneering effort ten years ago, although rather bigger and suitably adorned with some of the original illustrations by Nicolas Bentley. To capture the living heritage of Beachcomber's *Daily Express* column in a single book is an achievement not given to man, since an extraordinary proportion of the reams he wrote is still funny. There is no substitute for owning the original collections. *By the Way*, for example, contains the bulk of the column for the year 1930. There are more than 380 pages of text, with a laugh on almost every page. And *By the Way* is only one of many such compilations. Ingrams's book has a much larger format than those early – and much handier – volumes, but it doesn't begin to get it all together. Nevertheless it easily qualifies for the coveted spot alongside Frayn's *The Best of Beachcomber*, abiding the day when the maestro's own anthologies are reprinted as minor classics.

It is gratifying to see that the notoriously slapdash editor of *Private Eye* can concentrate when the occasion demands. His historical introduction – lavishly quoting Morton himself – is a searching effort, full of revealing things. Important to know, for instance, that Morton's conversion to Catholicism in 1922 took place in the aftermath of a war during which he saw far more than his share of the trenches and from which he was sent home shell-shocked. (He subsequently served in an Intelligence department called M.I.7b, which, as Frayn has noted, sounds exactly as if Beachcomber invented it.) Morton's aggressive, wine-worshipping religiosity – an obsession he shared with D. B. Wyndham Lewis, his close associate and similarly a disciple of Belloc – gains in interest when seen against a picture of European disintegration. It is a truism, but still true, that humour arises from pain.

The glories of the text defeat the designer's windy lay-out. Here are Mr Thake's Letters and the devastating poetic tribute to A. A. Milne, 'When We Were Very Silly'; 'Cads and Swine' and the adventures of Dr Strabismus (Whom God Preserve) of Utrecht; 'Big White Carstairs and the M'Babwa of M'Gonkawiwi' (but not the greatest of Carstairs's exploits, 'Trousers Over Africa' – which however you can get in Frayn's book); Thunderbolt Footle (the doomed pugilist managed by Scrubby Botulos) and half a dozen cases tried before Mr Justice Cocklecarrot, including the Case of the 12 Red-Bearded Dwarfs and several legal brushes with the Filthistan Trio; two stiff doses of Captain Foulenough and a long sample of 'Life at Boulton Wynfevers'; and, the pearl of the collection, the whole of 'Tibetan Moonflower', starring that Turandot-like oriental temptress, Dingi-Poos.

Let's see, what have I forgotten? Oh yes, 'The Saga of the *Saucy Mrs Flobster*' is here too – one of his maddest things. And there is a killing parody of John Buchan called 'The Queen of Minikoi'. And there are all the walk-on characters who turned up in story after story, like the singer Emilia Rustiguzzi and the chatelaine Stultitia, Lady Cabstanleigh: that airy profusion of magic names which came bubbling up inexhaustibly from Morton's slightly psycho talent. Evelyn Waugh spoke nothing but the truth when he said Beachcomber had 'the greatest comic fertility of any Englishman'.

Well, all that marvellous 'stuff' (Ingrams says that Morton calls his stuff 'stuff') is here, alive and kicking. Yet so much is missing. When I take the aforementioned *By the Way* down from the shelf (and I could just as easily take *Gallimaufry* or any of several others) I find Beachcomber's protean multiplicity made assimilable in a way no latter-day selection is ever likely to match. There are learned notes on setting Ronsard and Leconte de Lisle to music (did any other writer for the *Daily Express* ever allude to the *Song of Roland* or quote in Latin?) coupled with a typical counterfeit sea-shanty conveying his distaste for that tedious branch of folk art ('Blow the Man Up'). And here are Madame Sapphira's Sixty Superlative Mannequins, making, so far as I know, their one and only appearance. But the bright young thing Boubou Flaring was always coming back, as were the ballet-dancers Tumbleova and Trouserin. Here is the sole mention of 'Fluffy' Whackabath. And here, in all its ga-ga splendour, is *If So Be That*, one of Beachcomber's miniature serialized novels – a form conspicuously absent from Ingrams's book.

If So Be That, by Helpa Kitchen, is a romance of the Spanish-American War, which is why its opening chapter is set in Arabia and features the Sheik El Blista. A later chapter stars Okuno Pigiyama, Japanese Plenipotentiary Extraordinary with or without portfolio at the Court of Athens. ('But on the footplate of the Silver Monster, all unheeding, Ingeborg Maelstrom, the first Norwegian woman renegade politician to cross the Rockies, is braising carrots.') Frayn included *If So Be That* in *his* book, which is probably why Ingrams left it out, but how could that extraordinary tale *Hark Backward!* be ignored by both? Nowhere in all Beachcomber is there a mightier battle than the one fought out for the hand of Petunia Pewce between Captain 'Nark' Fiendish (a clear precursor of Foulenough) and the radiant and well-groomed Nigel Barriscale (triple blue and fourth in Archaeology), an Etonian dullard who converses entirely in permutations and combinations of 'Oh, I say' and 'Oh, I say, what?' (But he finally wins Petunia by donning skates and inscribing 'Play Up, You Fellows' on the ice in ancient Aramaic.)

Nigel Barriscale (whose epic climbing-party from Niederschwein to the peak of the Bumbelhorn included the mysterious Vivacity Dumpling) was merely the earliest of Beachcomber's researches into the psychology of the Upper-Class Twit. (He preceded *Monty Python* both in this and in his use of very long, extremely silly names – *vide* the full title of the Viscomte de Malsain-les-Odeurs-Subterrannées du Brebingotte Nonsanfichtre, which goes on for half a page – but then, he preceded everybody in everything.) His arch-conservatism was humanized by an irrepressible taste for anarchy, and indeed he was apt to rhapsodize seriously about the French revolutionary heroes. A nose for aristocratic cretinism led him onwards to invent one of his greatest characters, Big White Carstairs, but not even *that* ramrod-backed blockhead was his final word on the subject. The figure of the well-bred dumb-bell recrudesced to haunt his delicious fiction of World War II, *Geraldine Brazier, Belle of the Southern Command* – which is not in Frayn or Ingrams or anywhere I know of except an obscure anthology called *The Phoenix Book of Wit and Humour*, edited by Michael Barsley and published in 1949.

Geraldine Brazier (the loveliest WOOF in the British Army) is a German spy, but she is so beautiful that none of the male officers believe it, even when they catch her going through the safe. Neither Captain Roy Batter-Pudden nor Colonel Fritter can bring himself to condemn her, mainly because they are extremely stupid:

> 'That was not your mother,' said Colonel Fritter haughtily to Geraldine Brazier, as Captain Batter-Pudden and several officers dashed in pursuit of Ludwig von Rümpelgutz. But the girl was no whit abashed. 'Nein,' she said savagely, 'and I his daughter am not.'

Awkwardness with women is the norm in Beachcomber's ruling class. Awkwardness, and an utter deficiency of brains.

The old Beachcomber anthologies are getting harder and harder to find second-hand, and new readers have to start somewhere. Between this book and Frayn's they will get a good part of the message. No student of humour can do without a working knowledge of Beachcomber, but studiousness need not – and in this case could not – drive out enjoyment. Beachcomber hated (hates – he is still alive) the modern world, and there is about his work something of the frantic music of a death-dance buoyed up by the mutter of only half-forgotten guns. Wild liberty is the mark of his humour; not careless but carefree; as if the whole of his creative life had been a stolen evening. '*Ne vois tu que le jour se passe?*' writes Ronsard in one of Morton's favourite poems. '*Je ne vy point au lendemain.*' Believing that, Beachcomber could have done nothing. Instead, he did his 'stuff'.

New Statesman, 20 December, 1974

POSTCARDS FROM THE OLYMPICS

Apart from the programme note, these dispatches appeared in the *Independent* between 16 September and 2 October 2000, and were syndicated in the *Sydney Morning Herald* and the Melbourne *Age*.

A NOTE FROM THE OFFICIAL PROGRAMME
OF THE OPENING CEREMONY OF THE
SYDNEY OLYMPICS, 2000

Mount Olympus, meet Sydney harbour: you belong together. After a century of modern Olympiads, Sydney in the year 2000, even more than Melbourne in 1956, is the perfect place to put the games back in touch with ancient Greece. The reason, which at first hearing might sound like a paradox, is that Sydney is the last place in the world where the classical ideal of white-on-white, empty-eyed austerity can be achieved. But there is no paradox, because the classical ideal never had much to do with ancient Greece. The classical ideal was hatched two thousand years later, in the eighteenth century AD, when every piece of sculpted Greek marble that came under the scholarly magnifying glass had long since lost its paint. In ancient Greece the marble statues were painted in bright colours, and those vacantly staring eye sockets we see in the museums had jewels in them. Ancient Greece looked nothing like a cemetery. It looked like fun. When the ancient games were on, the air was hot, bright and vibrant with music, and sparkling water was never far away. Does that remind you of anything?

It reminds you of Sydney, which as long as it doesn't get too puffed up with seriousness is bound to stage the best modern games ever. Luckily, Sydney has never been a suitable place for sustained solemnity. I can remember how in my childhood the local population would manage to stay solemn for the first half of Anzac Day, and then the joy of life once again took over. Shutting the pubs at six o'clock in the evening, our wowser authorities did their grim best to keep the joy confined, but it would always burst out, even before the postwar migrants gave us interesting things to eat and drink. We

used to do pretty well even with the uninteresting things: prawns
wrapped in newspaper and a few beers, with the odd Lamington for
a touch of luxury. Nowadays you hear a lot about what an unsophisti-
cated life we used to lead, and in many ways that was true: but it
was a blessed life too, fed with fruit, bathed in sunlight, and full of
playful energy. A lot more energy went into play than into work, but
that was inevitable. Too many of the best things in life were free.
Hence the fact, much complained of by those who cared for our
cultural welfare, that sport counted for more than art. Art was something you had to work at shut away. Sport, even if you were slogging
to be a champion, could be pursued out there in the open air, the
sole difference between you and one of those ancient Greeks being
that you were only practically naked, instead of naked.

Australians worshipped sports champions as a way of giving
thanks for the land we lived in. In a vociferously egalitarian culture,
to praise the tall poppy was an activity rarely well received even by
the poppy, which sensibly feared for its vulnerable stem. Even today,
Australians can feel uncomfortable about singling themselves out: it
might be taken for conceit. But our athletes were assumed to be
personally no more ambitious than Phar Lap, who ran fast because
it was in his nature, having been born under the Southern Cross.
Yes, our medal-winning swimmers were remarkable, but weren't we
all remarkable swimmers? At the baths, the champion was just the
one who charged up and down the pool all day while we hung
around the sandpit with the girls. We all thought of ourselves as
sports experts simply for having been born here. We could talk about
the finer points of a sport as if it were an art.

Looking back on it, I can't see that we were wrong. Pundits who
bewailed Australia's philistinism were missing the point. Culture was
not to be had by elevating our pretensions, but by broadening our
range of spontaneous enjoyment. And that was exactly how it happened. Music had always been a natural form of Australian
expression. Long before the First Fleet arrived, there had been music
in the air. And any singing teacher will tell you that merely to grow
up speaking with an Australian accent equals ten years of free lessons
in how to place the centre of the voice up there where it belongs,
just behind the nose. Back before World War I, the Australian
Impressionists had already proved that their country was a natural
open-air studio. Literature was longer on the way because it had

further to come: requiring more thought, it was more easily discouraged, and only in recent years have our writers begun to carry themselves with the confidence of our painters and musicians – which is to say, with the same confidence as our athletes, who have always wanted to take on the world, and always known that there is nothing incongruous in such a wish.

There ought to be, of course: though a big country on the map, we are a small one by population. But history doesn't work that way. Most of the nations big enough to do even better than Australia in the Olympics of the last century would have given, at the end of it, an awful lot to have been called back and asked to start again. We, too, had to fight to stay alive, but our social fabric stayed in one piece, and with the help of many who escaped from less lucky places it grew to maturity in a way that has made us the envy of the world – a nation where all the creative possibilities of life can flourish at once, and so reveal themselves to be more complementary than opposed. There never was a real opposition between sports and arts; there only appeared to be; and now we can see for a fact how they join up. All we have to do is look at these buildings and their natural setting, and look forward to the voices of the children's choirs. The Sydney Olympics are already an aesthetic event before a single starting pistol is fired. If the ancient Greeks could have seen this, they would have said: yes, that's it. *That's* the classical ideal. You've got it right at last.

1. CARRY THAT TORCH

Just after lunch on Tuesday I left a London that was running out of petrol and on Wednesday evening I arrived in a Sydney that had everything, up to and including the Olympic Games. The contrast was stunning. Prosperity, energy and sheer friendliness flooded the atmosphere even at the airport, where I was busted for drugs in the nicest possible way. In the customs hall a sniffer dog took an interest in one of my bags. Interest escalated into a passionate relationship. While the mutt was humping my holdall, its handler, a dedicated but charming young lady with freckles, regretfully insisted that she had to frisk me. Jet lag was joined by trepidation: what if some pharmacist for the Chinese swimming team had disguised himself as a baggage-handler at Bangkok and planted a gallon jug of human growth hormone in my spare underwear?

Barely had half my intimate garments been unloaded on the examination table before it transpired that the canine narc had been turned on by a box of chocolates I was bringing in for my mother. I should have guessed. Even when of German extraction, an Australian dog can only be a hedonist, and Sydney was out to prove that it can do hedonism better than any other city on earth or die trying.

If that sounds like a contradiction in terms then it fits Australia's collective state of mind as the games get under way. Never in the world was there such a degree of national well-being plagued with so much insecurity, although it's a fair bet that most of the paranoia is generated by the press rather than the people. For the media and the intelligentsia – two categories which in Australia share the one mind to an extent rare in the civilized world – there is a nagging, never-ending doubt about whether Australia has yet taken its rightful place as a Mature Nation. Will the Sydney Olympics finally work the trick? Or will we screw the whole thing up?

Among ordinary people the same intensity of soul-searching is hard to detect. They just get on with enjoying the good life, on the sensible assumption that the rest of the world must be doing pretty well if it's got anything better than this. A lot of the ordinary people were there among the milling foreign visitors as I arrived downtown in a cab driven by a Lebanese who had found the way with remarkably little trouble for someone who had immigrated the previous week. Squadrons of local roller-bladers in kangaroo-eared helmets zoomed politely through strolling swarms of guests joining one jam-packed pavement bar to another. Australians from out of town were easily identifiable, especially if they were wrinklies. A wrinkly is anyone my age or even older. Wrinklies often still wear the Akubra hat of legend. There were wrinkly married couples in the full kit of Akubra, many-pocketed leisure suit and bulging backpack, except that the whole ensemble was coloured Olympic blue. When there are wrinklies in the street at night, it means everybody is in the street at night. Ancient cries of 'No worries' echoed under the awnings, even as the fiendish music of the young blasted out of the bars.

A wrinkly myself and creased with it, I checked into the Went-worth. My usual drum is the Regent, but it was full of the International Olympic Committee, an outfit famous for living high on hot money. The Wentworth was packed out with a guest list that pays its own way and helps pay for the games at the same time – the executives of the giant electronics conglomerate Panasonic. The foyer was alive with Japanese executives in impeccably tailored suits, giving each other the cool nod that nowadays serves as shorthand for the formal bow. In my travelling kit of M&S black T-shirt stained with airline food, black jeans with Lycra content and twenty-four-hour stubble, I felt lucky that my room hadn't been cancelled. Born and raised in an era without air conditioning, I opened my bedroom window to let in the warm Pacific night and crashed out to the sound of happy laughter coming up from the street in twenty languages, some of them spoken in countries where life is a lot less attractive. 'I know why they're laughing,' was my fading thought. 'They can't believe this is real.'

I woke to a late morning of perfect sunlight and ambled down to Circular Quay to take breakfast at Rossini's, my favourite snackeria on earth. For years it has been my custom to sit out in the sun at Rossini's for a slow latte and cinnamon toast. The bridge soars on the left, the Opera House ruffles its wings on the right, and the office workers pile off the ferries as I relax with the morning papers. This time I had to queue up for a table. The whole of the quay was one big multilingual *paseo* of quietly ecstatic world citizens. The newspapers, when I finally got a seat, revealed that they, too, had caught the mood. Their big question now was who would be chosen to run the last few yards of the torch relay and light the cauldron at the opening ceremony. Dawn Fraser? Don Bradman? Phar Lap? On most mornings of the previous six months, their big question had been whether the games would sink to destruction under a growing load of drug scandals, corruption and administrative incompetence, thereby further delaying Australia's pain-racked ascent to its rightful place among the world's mature nations. If experience had not taught me better I would have expected to arrive in a city with the same festive atmosphere as Sodom and Gomorrah on the morning after a wrathful God spat the dummy.

Certainly the press had not been deprived of grist to its mill. Two of Australia's members of the IOC had performed less than brilliantly. Both ex-athletes of distinction, they had fallen prey to the Olympic Movement's time-dishonoured habit of smoothing its way with fat from the pork barrel. Phil Coles had copped some heavily discounted holidays, during which his wife had adorned herself with jewellery of unexplained provenance. The depredation had amounted to only a few thousand Australian dollars – barely a small van-load of peanuts when you factor in the current exchange rate – but it had been enough to obliterate the kudos Phil had coming to him for doing more than anyone else to snare the games for Sydney. Phil is a simple soul whose true stamping ground is the sand in front of the surf club, but perhaps he should have known better. And Kevan Gosper, a more sophisticated spirit, should definitely have known better: when it was suggested that his little daughter might like to run the first leg of the torch relay in place of the Aussie Greek girl who had been scheduled for the task, he should have said no. On the other hand, his explanation – 'My fatherly pride simply clouded my judgement' – should have been held sufficient. For the Australian press that had already called him a 'reptile', his tardy but remorseful *mea culpa* was merely a further sign of arrogance. He went on to be inundated with the sort of abuse that Vyshinsky, during the Moscow show trials in 1938, used to unload on Trotskyite wreckers and other tools of imperialism who seemed to think that abject self-accusation could mitigate their perfidy.

The outfit running the Sydney Olympics is called SOCOG, pursuant to the standard Australian journalistic delusion that acronyms make prose easier to read. SOCOG's initial issue of tickets was a SNAFU, and it was assumed from then on that All Fucked Up would be Situation Normal. The organizers have hence had to operate in a media climate by which everything they do right is their merest duty, while everything they do wrong is a calamity hindering Australia from its rightful place among mature nations. There were also suggestions that Aboriginal leaders might, or even should, bring the whole thing to a halt with flaming spears, if an overdose of performance-enhancing drugs had not already propelled a majority of the world's athletes raving into Sydney harbour to drown bloodily among man-eating sharks trained on a diet of triathletes. No worries? Nothing but.

But at Rossini's I concluded that the press, at the eleventh hour, had caught up with the crowds around me. In both senses of the last word, 'She'll be right, sport' was the phrase that fitted. Hard-bitten journos had put off the burden of Australia's global destiny and begun to exult. Some of the exultation might be as debilitating as the previous angst. Legitimate national pride is easily infected by nationalist fervour, especially when it comes to medal prospects. Australia has always punched a ton above its weight in that department, but success can breed hubris. With feet longer than my legs and the facial profile of a racing yacht's keel turned on end, Ian Thorpe is a mighty swimmer, but the expectations heaped upon him could add up to a haversack full of lead. Cathy Freeman has been hiding out all year from a double pressure: some of the Aboriginal activists didn't want her to run at all (conniving at the fake prestige of racist Australia, etc.), while many who wish her well imbue her inevitable victory with a mountain of symbolic significance (incarnating the multicultural unity of mature Australia, etc.). There is much less press about her French rival Marie-José Pérec, who is not only physically bigger but on several occasions, notably the last Olympics in Atlanta, has run faster. If Cathy comes second, the press who have badgered her will bear a heavy responsibility, but you can bet that most of it will be transferred to her.

Still, you can't blame the media for being fascinated; and stuff about national prestige was nothing but true when it came to the torch relay, which had been a triumph, an example to the watching world, and huge fun. The thing had fulminated its way all over Australia by now. It had been carried by celebrities, poets, artists, palsied kids who had to be carried themselves, and representatives of every known ethnic group including, bizarrely, Crown Prince Albert of Monaco. That night it was due to be carried past Circular Quay, where the crowds would be colossal. There was small chance of seeing anything at ground level. Spotting the Paragon hotel, a classic two-storey sandstone edifice that was already old when I waddled past it as a tot on the great day my mother took me on the ferry to the zoo, I made my plans. That second storey was the secret.

That night I was in an upstairs pub room looking down into the tumultuous crowd. What I had failed to calculate was that part of the tumultuous crowd would be in the room with me. The joint was jumping with the young and beautiful. Jammed between two scintillating lovelies called Claire and Polly, each of whom had at least four boyfriends standing behind us, I had an upper circle seat for the triumphal march from *Aida* revamped as a musical comedy. The progress of the torch in our direction was visible in detail on a giant television screen hanging from the Cahill expressway on the far side of the plaza. The screen relayed images from cameras all over the sky. Media helicopters thwacked overhead, weaving to avoid a giant dirigible marked 'G'DAY'. As they dodged the diridge, they were getting pictures of heaven on earth. At the Opera House Olivia Newton-John, radiant in her flour-bag jogging whites, passed the torch to the even lovelier Pat Rafter, his darling knees dimpling in the photo-flash. While the boyfriends blew satirical raspberries, piercingly audible even through the uproar, Claire and Polly passed out screaming. They screamed 'Nice pants!' and 'Call it off, we've had enough!' Shouting was the only way to communicate basic information. At that moment the Olympic rings lit up on the bridge and fireworks erupted from the pylons at each end. One of the boyfriends, a pug-faced wag called Nugget, yelled 'And we *live* here!'

It was the right thing to yell. The bunch around me were all in the professions: architecture, law, finance. They had all been at university together. When they were born, the Melbourne Olympics were already more than twenty years ago. This was their time, their city and, I had to admit, their country. Their combination of boundless energy, unbridled humour and fundamental gentleness would be the best guarantee for preserving the future that was already here. As the torch went by, they assured me it was a fake and made sure I noted that down. They were referring to the hallowed tradition by which a hoax torch always precedes the real one. It first happened when the torch went through Sydney on its way to Melbourne in 1956. The Lord Mayor of Sydney was presented with a flaming plum-pudding tin on a stick, fell for it, and launched into his official spiel. In the laughter that followed him for the rest of his life, his only consolation was that nobody ever did that to Hitler.

The big day dawned cool and cloudy. Out at Homebush Bay the Olympic stadia still looked good under a darker sky as the itinerant population roamed, schmoozed, kibitzed and rehearsed. The great thing, for which the officials have received insufficient credit, is that it all got built in good time. The main stadium's 1,500 eco-friendly dunnies have thrilled the nation. Earlier in the year I had flown in to host a black-tie fundraiser for the Australian Olympic team and had been massively impressed. But did I really want to watch the opening ceremony from a box full of blasé journos sneaking sideways looks at the size of each other's modems? Or did I want to watch it in the city, surrounded by the best party on the planet? It was no contest. The real story was in the streets. My Croatian cab driver found the Harbour Bridge at only his second try.

Watching the show on the giant screens in the city there must have been a million people. A lot of them were at Circular Quay and in Martin Place, my two choices of al fresco venue. To get a view I had to play the wrinkly line for all it was worth. By a long mile it was the best show of its kind I have ever seen, perhaps the first great choreographic work of the new century. To know the whole world would see it brought tears of pride to my tiny eyes. It was a triumph for its impresario, Ric Birch. At the handover in Atlanta, he sent in a team of bike-riding inflatable kangaroos and earned an undeserved reputation for naffness with the Australian media, worried that he might have damaged our rating as an incipient mature nation. But with this effort he proved himself the Diaghilev of the Southern hemisphere. The aerial reef ballet staged in imaginary water was a miracle. My favourite bit was the fluttering swarm of jellyfish. The whole lyrical synthesis of the Aboriginal dreamtime and the modern age was an unrelenting wow. At Circular Quay thousands of people were agog, as if an autistic Almighty had used human mouths endlessly to inscribe the letter O. The Tap Dogs extravaganza went down especially well in Martin Place, where the boys got exuberant. There being no more room on the ground, they started to climb anything vertical, including tall women. One boy got all the way to the top of a flagpole. The cheers were deafening. He was part of the show. Everybody was.

The pop anthems were uniformly dire, and the Olympic Committee top dog Juan Antonio Samaranch spoke English in a way that made you wonder if his Spanish was any better, but nothing could dent the show's integrity. Asking Australia's Olympic women to share the final lap of the torch was the right thing at long last, because the women's vote lies at the heart of our democracy. All in all it was life that was celebrated, and not mere health. (In that respect, choosing the wheelchair-bound Betty Cuthbert to carry the torch into the stadium was a masterstroke.) As for asking Cathy Freeman to light the cauldron, well, it might do as much to inspire her as to weigh her down, and anyway she is a brave girl who feels free to choose, so she must have chosen this. But the best thing about the whole spectacle was that its precision wasn't military. When Nietzsche addressed the problem of whether there could be a work of art without an artist, the first example he came up with was the human body, and the second was the officer corps of the Prussian army. The idea caught on strong in Germany, where the Berlin Olympics in 1936 sealed the deadly conjunction between athletics and squad drill. (By no coincidence, the man in charge, Edgar Feuchtanger, turned up again as the commander of the 21st Panzer Division at Caen.) Filmed by Leni Riefenstahl, the Nazi dream of beautiful bodies on the march had a long and sinister influence, but Sydney buried its last remains. At Birch's invitation I wrote the programme note, so you must allow for a vested interest: but I guessed the show would be a bobby-dazzler and I was right. What I didn't guess was that it would be so beautiful, a work of art. The sport will be hard-pressed to match it.

In Martin Place there were a lot of broken beer bottles by the time I left, but as far as I could see nobody was getting hurt. It was sad to think that an equivalent concentration of young people in

Britain would have been hard to trust. I can remember when the Australians were the hoons and the British behaved. The world has turned back to front: but when you think about it, the world does that all the time.

2. THORPIE, HOOGIE AND THE GOLDEN LOLLY

As was only appropriate following a quasi-religious experience, on the day after the opening ceremony of the Olympic Games the morning sky over Sydney was a silk sheet dyed blue by Fra Angelico. It was a blaze of glory marred only by the tubbily lurking presence of the G'day airship, the dirigibledoo. The media helicopters would appear again a bit later. At the moment they were sleeping it off with rotors limp. After a party that had lasted until nearly dawn, Sydney's collective hangover should have screamed to heaven, but all you could see on the milling multicultural faces was uncomplicated bliss.

Down at Rossini's on Circular Quay I substituted an iced coffee for my usual latte in an effort to offset the heat poured forth by Australia's newspapers, which after months of preaching imminent doom were now all vying for the title of the biggest fan of the Sydney Olympics on the face of the earth. They had plenty of competition. Real, ticket-buying, fare-paying fans from all over the planet were parading past the ferry wharves shoulder to shoulder, or backpack to backpack: a slow-motion stampede in trainer shoes. Right past my table shuffled a platoon of Japanese softball supporters who were actually *holding* fans: white fans with little red rising suns. They were fans with fans. From the Netherlands, fans in studiously comical hats went by uttering the strange word 'Hoogenband', doubtless the Dutch way of saying 'G'day'. But the papers weren't just full of the sensational previous night. They were predicting a series of aureate tomorrows, which would all belong to Thorpie.

You can forget about that 'Thorpedo' stuff. That was just the strained coinage of an overtaxed feature writer. To the Australian public, Ian Thorpe is automatically known as Thorpie. At the age of seventeen, he has acquired the honorific diminutive, Australia's hallowed masonic sign of universal spiritual adoption. Cathy Freeman, of course, was born with it, handily attached to her first name. But for the next week, until the swimming was over, Thorpie would outrank even Cathy. The papers assured us that Thorpie, already an icon, was about to ascend to the empyrean with his huge feet dripping chlorinated tears of molten gold, or words to that effect.

They were right, which must have been a big relief to them, because too many of their entrail readings, most of which portended an apocalypse for Australia's place among mature nations, had already needed to be modified in the light of reality. A bussing disaster on the Atlanta scale had been gleefully forecast, and indeed, on the eve of the opening, a female bus driver had failed to find the Olympic Park at Homebush Bay, broken down sobbing at the wheel, and required counselling. But now the buses were running like trains. The reported hillocks of unsold tickets were shrinking by the hour. An Aboriginal leader who had previously hinted that the city might be reduced to steaming ashes of protest was now on record as having found the reconciliation theme of the opening ceremony a gesture sufficient to stave off mass destruction. The sharks that were scheduled to pick off the triathletes as they desperately flailed through the harbour (veteran sharks with yellow noses and swastikas on their tail fins, hungry for one more victory) had failed to show up.

With so little going wrong, there had to be a story in something going right, and Thorpie was the something. During the morning, his heat in the 400m freestyle filled the seats of the colossal Aquatic Centre, and during the afternoon his majestic win held the whole of Australia spellbound in the street, like the Melbourne Cup in the days when most of Australia's TV sets were still in the windows of the appliance stores. 'We have witnessed the birth of a legend!' screamed a commentator. Filling the screen, Prime Minister John Howard's radiantly ordinary face broke into a smile, as if his were the legend to whose birth we were bearing witness. In the streets of downtown Sydney, viewers numberless as the dust and high on Thorpomania took a moment off to convey their appreciation of the Prime Minister's beauty. By the pure-hearted, affection could be detected in the storm of ritualized abuse. He will never be called Howardie, but unless he makes the mistake of slapping his beloved value-added tax on baby food he should come out of these Olympics

smelling like a nasturtium. All he has to do is stand next to Thorpie
as often as possible and think tall.

Piling nirvana on Elysium, Thorpie that night swam the fourth
leg of the 4×100m relay and managed to beat out the Americans by
the length of his arm – which is about the length of your kitchen,
but still looked pretty close. Close was far enough. The invincible
Yanks had been vinced in their fave event! 'Ian Thorpe has shown us
Aussie pride, Aussie glory and Aussie spirit!' Either it was a different
commentator or the same one had gone up an octave. At Circular
Quay young people were sitting on each other's shoulders in groups
of three like dancing totem poles. It was only the start of the party.
As midnight approached, young people did Circus Oz acrobatics over
the crowd, furthering the new Australian tendency, so prominent
in the opening ceremony, for taking to the air as if it were water.
Wearing a little frock consisting mainly of its fringe, a sinuous girl
twisted in a red ribbon high above our heads. When she momentarily
returned to earth for a quick swig I joined her in her tent for purposes
of research. It turned out she was an exotic dancer who had spent
several years in an English circus before coming home. 'I wouldn't
have wanted to miss this. What about Thorpie?'

There weren't many wrinklies at the quay that night, but out at
the Olympic Park next day they were there in force. In fact a lot of
them *were* the force: many of the countless volunteer officials would
look like bus-pass material if it weren't for their sprightly white bush
hats, kaleidoscopic shirts, and the smile induced by saying 'Thorpie'
repeatedly. 'What about Thorpie?' I was asked by a woman who
had been there when Murray Rose swam to a pile of gold in the
Melbourne Olympics in 1956. 'Never seen anything like him.' Since
she *had* seen something like him, this was a pretty good measure
of the hold he had taken on the public imagination. It wasn't just
the media talking.

On the TV screens another story temporarily leapt to prominence:
the Romanian weightlifters had been busted for dope and were on
their way home. In the press pavilion there was a wonderful rumour
about why Channel 7, which has the games locked up – I have to
tread carefully here, because Channel 7 transmits my programmes in
Australia: great channel, terrific taste – strangely failed to screen their
much heralded and potentially immortal images of Greg Norman
carrying the torch over the Harbour Bridge. Just for that one crucial

job, they had deployed a brand-new self-propelled gyro-stabilized camera with inertial navigation system, but its operator had forgotten to put in the tape. A suddenly chastened Channel 7 had asked its frozen-out rival Channel 9 whether they would care to loan their footage if they just happened to have any. Channel 9 opened all its phones so that the entire staff could give a two-word answer in unison. Apparently the camera operator was already at the bottom of the harbour, lashed to the camera.

This was all very fascinating but it wasn't long before 'Thorpie' was once again the only word heard, except of course for the joke-hatted Dutch male fans who kept saying 'Hoogenband' when attempting to introduce themselves to an Australian female cop of outstanding beauty and size of gun. Australia finally found out what the word meant when Hoogenband broke the world record in his 200 m semi-final. Thorpe broke his personal best in his own semi, but a pb is not the same as a wr. The final would be next day. Could Thorpe be beaten? Don't be ridiculous.

Next day the image of Australia's new hero was already on the stamps, giving many a wag the chance to announce his intention of licking Thorpie. That Thorpie might be licked by Hoogenband was beyond contemplation. Thorpie, it was explained, had a strong finish that would annul Hoogenband's undoubtedly high velocity in the initial stages. But there was a whole day to get through before the race at night, with nothing to distract Thorpie-worshippers except a hundred other Olympic events, some of them quite interesting even though taking place on dry land.

There was news from the weightlifting. Either the dope-fiend Romanians had got all the way to Bucharest and back again in a few hours or they had never left the village. The latter proved to be true. Indeed they were still lifting weights, after paying a fine of 91,000 Australian dollars for the privilege. Would they have paid this fine if they were not guilty, and should they be lifting weights if they were? It was a mystery. So was the habit of Korean archery fans of chanting loud slogans at the very moment when the tensely concentrating Korean archer was due to let loose. Why were they doing that? Were they trying to kill a judge? And why was their archer not called Park? All their baseball players were.

If you didn't have 91,000 dollars for a fresh supply of dope, the beach volleyball was the most effective time-killer. Here, at last, was a case of the press and the protesters having successfully predicted a catastrophe. The stadium on Bondi beach had been designed so that nobody inside it could see the beach, and was so vast that nobody outside it could see the beach either. Those inside suffered the additional insult of being subjected to the volleyball, an event whose already perfect stupidity was abetted by boom-box music and a screaming commentary. Many of the female competitors were very pretty, an effect aided by their attire, which tended towards a vanishing point between their inner thighs. The TV cameras behaved reasonably well, closing in for the butt shot only with the excuse that the girls made finger signals behind their backs. What the signals meant remained a puzzle, especially after they were explained by barely coherent experts, but one of them seemed to indicate that the competitor's costume, to the detriment of her manoeuvrability, would shortly disappear altogether unless extracted by a gynaecologist.

The anxious evening was ushered in by vox-pops focused on the race. Suddenly elevated to the status of prime interviewees, the joke-hatted Dutch fans were saying stuff like 'Hoogenband's goana beat your Ion Torp.' The idea was still a gag but only just, because when Hoogenband stood beside Thorpe on the blocks he looked just as big, had the same-sized feet and seemed no more overawed than a naval shell being loaded into a gun. What happened next was an education for everyone concerned except him, the Dutch fans in the hats, and all the girls in Holland, for whom the wonder boy is an Apollo propelled through a lake of champagne by the aching force of their desire.

Right to the end the Aussie commentators were still talking about Thorpe's unbeatable finish, but Hoogenband had burned it off with his unbeatable start, and in the end it was he who stood on the golden lolly. In Australia when I was young, sweets were called lollies. The medal podiums on the Sydney pool deck look like big lollies. Thorpe had already stood on the golden lolly twice, but this time it was Hoogenband's turn, and Thorpie stood on the silver.

Thorpie took it well, kept his poise, and on the next night came out of the call room undaunted to lead the Australian world record-breaking 4×200 m relay victory. But his biggest victory was to stay in one piece on the night Australia found out he was mortal. He already knew it. The mature nation has produced a mature young man: a good sign. At Circular Quay, for the first time, there were people who left the party early, but they'd be back the next night. I heard one of them say 'Hoogie was too good.' Pieter van den Hoogenband had become Hoogie. There could be no better way for Australia to take over the world.

3. PRELUDE TO CATHY

With Cathy Freeman yet to run, the first week of the Sydney Olympics would still have been a dreamtime for Australia even without the sparkling results from the big billabong. Blessed by heavenly weather, clever organization and twenty million people ready to party it up for two and a half weeks solid if they absolutely had to, the games were a hit. But it was a bonus that the Aussie swimmers had made an initial assault which left even the Americans flabbergasted.

It was too good to last. In fact if it *had* lasted it would have been bad, because it would have meant that nobody else had bothered learning to swim. They had, however: and especially the Dutch, who had come out of nowhere – i.e. the Netherlands – to remind even Ian Thorpe that majestic young men with unfeasibly large feet had been born elsewhere on the planet at about the same time as he was. *Primus inter pares* among these was Pieter van den Hoogenband. When Hoogie touched out Thorpie over 200m, Australia woke up. The continuous party was still on for young and old, as they say locally, but the bodies under the tables and draped over the banisters were suddenly galvanized again and staring at the TV screens, where Hoogie's face was all too frequently to be seen, unabashed by his own temerity and handsome beyond belief.

Most Australians have never seen David Ginola, but if, by some trick of instantaneous teleportation, he had appeared in his underpants in downtown Sydney, the young women would have run over him like small trucks to grab a piece of the preposterously handsome Hoogie. Still smiling like Julia Roberts being awarded an Oscar in her bathtub, the next night Hoogie took out the 100m three places ahead of Australia's Michael Klim, whose mere appearance – shaven head, vulpine smile, the eyes of a cashiered SMERSH officer pledged to wreak vengeance with a stolen atomic bomb – can usually be relied on to drain the opposition's will to live.

Australia's darling, the kanga-cuddling Susie O'Neill, unexpectedly took out the 200m freestyle, but equally unexpectedly swam second in her fave event, the 200m butterfly, beaten by America's wonderfully named Misty Hyman, who sounded like a doubtful virgin from mythology but responded to the Aussie cheers for Susie by going faster herself. The Americans loved the idea of so much attention being focused on swimming. In the USA hardly anybody cares. In Australia hardly anybody doesn't. Misty, already equipped with the honorific diminutive, joined Hoogie on the short roster of aquatic adoptees. It helped that she looked like a bit of a kanga-hugger herself.

American back-stroker Lenny Krayzelburg was harder to adore. He psyched our boys out in the preliminary races by leaving off his cap and bodysuit and swimming in nothing but hip-slinger trunkettes, in the same way that snow-bums wear street clothes to make you feel like an idiot for buying all that expensive gear. But in the finals, decently dressed, he was so good that he earned from the Australian crowd the rarely awarded supplementary diminutive, given to the second name of an adoptee who already has one on the first. He was not only Lenny, he was Krazy. (There is an Australian girl diver called Loudy Torky, but she was probably born that way, unless her real name is Loud Talk.)

The Italians were also doing indecently well. Their multi-purpose star swimmer Massimiliano Rosolino was assigned the name of Massie. Diana Mocanu of Romania won two back-stroke golds and will henceforth be known as Mockie. How did the Romanians afford a swimming pool? Even the Swedes were featuring. Did they have any warm water in Sweden? And who was this guy from Iceland? In the glaring advent of all these new stellar personalities, Thorpie's refulgence was threatened with eclipse.

He had, however, won three gold medals, with possible others in the offing if his respiratory infection got no worse or media pressure did not get him down. In this latter respect he is better off than his senior compatriot Shane Gould, probably the greatest swimmer of either sex there has ever been. At Munich in 1972 she won three gold medals but at least five had been expected, so one of the Aussie papers ran the delicately judged headline SHANE FAILS. (Shane dropped right out of civilization after that, but recently resurfaced as the author a fascinating book called *Tumble Turns*, which proves that

her outlandish athletic gifts were matched all along by an unusual
purity of spirit.) The Aussie press, perhaps having learned a thing or
two in the interim, handled Thorpie more gently. But what would
the world press think? Thorpe had been built up as a global figure.
Would he be torn down on the same scale?

As I took a sunlit late breakfast of latte and panzerotto down at
Rossini's on Circular Quay, it was a relief to find that Japan's great
newspaper *Asahi Shimbun* was a model of common sense on the
subject. In the sports section they had a prominent article on Thorpie
complete with photograph. My Japanese is no longer what it was
when I was studying it every day, but I think I got the drift, feeling
my way in by looking for the transcribed foreign names. In Japanese,
alien loan-words are registered in the *katakana* phonetic alphabet,
and are always a good place to start unpacking a sentence. In this
case the job was less easy than usual. Van den Hoogenband came out
as Fuanden Hohenbato. Actually, after I checked it out with a couple
of Dutch fans in yellow hats – riding on the crest of Hoogie's success,
they are all accustomed by now to being interviewed on a continuous
basis – this turned out to be pretty close: the only thing wrong was
the final 'o', which had to be there because the only consonant that
can end a Japanese word is 'n'.

But the *katakana* transcription of 'Thorpe' was necessarily a bit
of a shambles, because there is nothing the Japanese can do with the
'th' sound, which is not in their syllabary. So 'Ian' comes out all right
but 'Thorpe' comes out as Sopu. The text, though, was up-beat. If it
spent a lot of time probing the psychological equilibrium of Sopu's
mother under the tremendous pressure that was clearly being at least
partly applied by the Japanese reporter trying to climb through her
front window, the sensible conclusion was reached that Sopu had a
big future to go with his bag of gold medals. Particular praise was
lavished on the staunchness with which Sopu had led Osotoraria to
victory in the 4×200m relay. (It is quite likely, incidentally, that the
Australians will end up speaking a version of English which sounds
more like Japanese English than British English: witness the growing
Aussie habit, already universal among the younger generation, of
expanding a terminal 'r' into a complete syllable, as in 'One, two,
three, for-wa.')

At this stage, for all of us blow-in journos writing colour pieces
to an easy schedule, it looked like a smooth cruise up to the next big

story, starring Cathy Freeman of Australia and Marie-José Pérec of France – both black, both beautiful, but only one of them with all her marbles. Since her victory in Atlanta, Pérec had established an almost unbroken track record as a no-show, but this time she was here. It was going to happen. Meanwhile the atmospherics were practically fighting to get into the laptop: all you had to do was stick your head out of the window. Australia stood revealed not only as a sporting nation, but as a sportsmanlike one, which is an even better thing. Out at the trap-shooting, the Australian Russell Mark came second to the Briton Richard Faulds. Markie reproved certain elements in the crowd for cheering when his opponent missed, and praised him when he took the gold. 'Great shot, great champion. Better man won.'

At Circular Quay and in Martin Place, certain elements in the crowd had been booing German cyclists as they flashed across the giant screen like furious lizards riding pairs of joke dark glasses. German fans had packed up their camp kitchens and moved out, perhaps in the direction of Germany. These developments were duly deplored by the television commentators. The certain elements, it was concluded, were a small minority. There seemed no reason to dispute this conclusion. Tolerance and generosity were universally apparent. Evidence of this was the adulation heaped on Eric Moussambani of Equatorial Guinea, the man who swam alone in his 100m heat and still didn't qualify for anything except artificial respiration. An aquatic version of Eddie the Eagle, Moussie woke up to find himself admired for his grit – which, indeed, he might as well have been swimming in when it came to speed, although he would have found it harder to sink so effectively. There were suggestions that Eric was being mobbed by sponsors who wanted to sign him up to endorse their products: life rafts, water pumps, rescue equipment.

Even greater evidence of magnanimity was the public response to Prime Minister John Howard's remarkable propensity for appearing in the background of any event, no matter how obscure. In Australia, members of the moneyed élite are known as silvertails. These, naturally enough, were to be seen at all the glamorous events, and necessarily Howard was to be seen along with them, but he was also there for the shooting, the shuttlecock, the hockey and the kayaks. As the tuneful but tongue-twisting national anthem 'Advance Australia Fair' was played to mark the winning of yet another gold medal,

Howard's lips moved as if he knew the words. Judging from these labial modifications, he could even articulate the impossible line 'Our land abounds in nature's gifts', a collection of impacted vocables which has reduced professional singers to spitting on the conductor. Howard is a man devoid of style – as opposed to Paul Keating, who was eventually, and fatally, perceived as having too much of it – but he looks like emerging from these games as one of nature's gifts himself, with a personal beauty which, although perhaps not rich, is certainly rare.

From the official sales points, ticket queues stretched for city blocks. People were ready to settle for anything: team skittles, formation pottery, three-day shirt-ironing. They would even settle for weightlifting, which was very generous of them, because drugs had made it a farce. Bulgaria's minuscule lifter Ivan Ivanov, not to be confused with Russia's gymnast Ivan Ivankov, was stripped of his gold medal, which was handed to the Chinese runner-up – an act of faith, when you considered the number of Chinese weightlifters who had got no further that Beijing airport, owing to their perceived dependency on the same joy-juice that had energized Ivan. There was more farce when two criminals escaped from Silverwater prison and hijacked a van full of Korean officials, who apparently thought it was part of the arrangements. But nothing could wreck the mood: so much was thrilling, and some of it was beautiful. In the men's gymnastics, Alexei Nemov was an almost poignant reminder of how powerful the old Soviet Union used to be when its tanks could still get to any rebellious East European capital city in a matter of hours. His flips and loops above the high bar, which he seemed to use as a mere reference point, were so enthralling you had no time to wonder just how far he would bury himself into the floor if he missed. Even if Cathy and Marie-José never ran their race, there was so much to remember.

Nobody should have been surprised at what happened next. Perhaps the sunlight and the bonhomie had dulled our senses. Anyway, Pérec left the starting blocks a few days early and headed for Singapore, where her bad choice of boyfriend monstered a cameraman. After eleven hours of being questioned, the happy couple left for France, doubtless to rob a bank or burn down a hospital. Back in Australia, the media went nuts. A spokesperson for Pérec's chief sponsor, Reebok, foolishly neglected to claim that Pérec would never have made it to the airport in such a short time if she had been wearing Nike.

The one who wears Nike is Cathy Freeman. Whether Cathy will now win in a walk is a nice question. It should be noted that she still has plenty of rivals left who won't be walking, they'll be running. An Olympics event is a competition, not a photo opportunity. There are at least four women entered for the event who share Cathy's happy knack of running 400m in 49 seconds and a bit, and they won't be carrying her burden. I don't want to add to it by what I write – these despatches are appearing in two of the biggest Australian papers a day later – but I'm bound to say that Australia wants an awful lot from her, and we have only her supernatural self-control to thank that she didn't catch the next plane after Pérec's.

There is a fountain in Singapore's Changi airport that Cathy could have soaked her head in while she wondered how she got into this. It would have been the second soaking in a week. At the opening ceremony she stood in a waterfall while ringed with fire: a great moment for Reconciliation, but from the athletics viewpoint not quite as good as being tucked up in bed watching television while Evonne Goolagong did the same job. Evonne was the first Aboriginal athlete to astonish the world. She was the one who started the breakout, when the danger was still too much real hatred rather than too much glib love. She was never in the Olympic Games but that was only because the Olympics had no tennis at the time. She was, and is, a true, fully realized champion. Cathy is not that yet, and to fulfil her destiny she now finds herself obliged to fight her way not only through fire and water, but through yet another, uncommonly colossal, media *tsunami* – the current vogue-word for what used to be a tohu-bohu or a brouhaha.

In those circumstances, my own time over 400m is twelve minutes. If Cathy does better than that, she will be doing all right. Last night she strolled to the front in her first heat, which looked encouraging. But at the very moment when Australia shows signs of actually believing in itself as a mature nation (and it was only the belief that was lacking, never the maturity) it is a damned pity to see it missing the point about the crime against the Aboriginals. The crime is more insidious than we think, just as the only valid expiation is more elusive. The crime is to demand of one person that she represent a people, and the expiation is to respect her individual rights. But Cathy Freeman knows that, and has decided to go through with it. Perhaps Marie-José knew it too, and decided otherwise. We might have been too hard on her. She might be another example of the imperial aftermath working itself out, and not so well.

4. SECOND WEEK IN SYDNEY

As the swimming handed over to track and field, after a week of Olympics euphoria Australia faced the arrival of the reality principle, in the form of black athletes and white moths. The swimming ended on an Aussie high when neurotic new boy Grant Hackett and bemedalled veteran Kieren Perkins fought it out to be first over 1,500 m, with the rest of the world nowhere. At Darling Harbour, one of the many open-air TV mega-venues, a crowd stacked up to the freeways cheered a win-win contest for the Aussies. Children with face and hair dyed green and gold looked as if they had been dipped in duckweed and dusted with wattle. When they rinsed off their make-up, it would surely be in the training pool at the beginning of their own careers: a purification before battle, as with the Greeks, the Romans and the Zulus, if any of those warlike peoples had a swimming squad.

From the hysterical media coverage and the heady week of parties in the streets you would have thought that the Yank swimmers had been well and truly stuffed by the home team. The medal tallies, of course, said otherwise. The USA had dominated as usual, and in its privileged second spot Australia had come close to being upstaged by the Dutch. But it didn't feel that way. It felt like power, as if a selectively benevolent deity, leaning down in a blaze of sunlight, had dipped his finger into the wet heart of a single city and beatified a continent.

Then the sky darkened, and the moths came. They did not stay long, because the rain came after them, but they stayed long enough to remind the citizens of Sydney of what it really means to be outnumbered. As the athletes ran their first races in Stadium Australia, the moths swarmed suicidally around the light-towers like a particularly brainless blizzard. Suddenly I remembered when I had seen them before. Forty years ago, after an indeterminate evening of heavy petting with some luckless girlfriend on the North Shore,

I had been hobbling back to town over the walkway of the Harbour
Bridge when the air, with terrifying abruptness, came alive. Seemingly
within seconds, the annual spring migration of the Bogong moths
had settled on the bridge, turning it into an enormous fluffy souvenir.
There were billions of the things.

And now, just as suddenly, there were the black athletes, and they
were all from somewhere else. Except for Cathy Freeman, we didn't
have any of our own who could get near them. The Americans were
in the vanguard of the invasion, and this time there was no blinking
the fact. Blinking was all we had time to do as Marion Jones zipped
through her 100m qualifying heat dressed in a full-length sweatsuit.
It was clear that she could have done the same in a cocktail frock
and high heels, although she did us the honour of partly disrobing
when she ran for the medal. Winning over the same distance, Maurice
Greene wore gold-soled shoes, and it was obvious that if the shoes
had been solid gold with a hat to match he would still have finished
first. With their souvenir value of a hundred thousand dollars each,
it was generous of Greene to throw one of the shoes into the crowd,
and prudent of him to retain the other: he could limp all the way to
the bank. The red-haired boy from Wagga Wagga who caught the
shoe will be lucky to make as much in his life as Greene makes in a
month. And these were the *repressed* people of America.

Could our Cathy, representing the repressed people of Australia,
keep up with this display of muscle? Ever since World War II, Australia, haunted by the spectacle of American abundance, has had to
console itself with the thought that its own abundance is more justly
distributed, yielding a better life. But then these super-cool black
Yanks turn up in their designer shades and investment footwear,
flanked by their agents, accountants, chiropractors and manicurists.
They tour town in rented Ferraris. They make our television
interviewers sound inarticulate. It was good to hear that NBC's
transmission of the Olympics to the US had been a ratings disaster.

In the light of this satisfactory fact, the Australian coverage on
Channel 7 seemed not so bad: and indeed it wasn't, if you accepted
the requirement that any event with an Aussie in it had to be covered,
even at the cost of cutting away from something more thrilling. In
this regard, a notable victim was Britain's authentically heroic Steve
Redgrave, whose victorious coxless four was seen crossing the line,
but whose appearance on the dais to receive his fifth gold medal in

as many Olympiads was not featured. Having survived the ravages of time, he had succumbed to a television producer with an itchy trigger finger. You would have thought he rated a short interview, if only for old time's sake. After all, he wasn't an American. Whatever happened to Bundles for Britain?

Naoko Takahashi wasn't American either, but there was no ignoring her. Not only did she win the women's marathon with puff to spare, she was so cute that the cameras misted over as they tracked her through the streets of a smitten city. Sydney had once been attacked by Japanese midget submarines but this was different. Though Naoko was tiny too, she was armed with nothing but the unquenchable conviction that her *netsuke* dimensions were some kind of an advantage instead of a handicap. Cheer-squads of Japanese fans injured their lungs on the sidelines as she came pattering up the last hill and on into the roaring stadium, where she circulated like a pet mouse which had been sent into the Colosseum to make up for a shortage of lions.

Next day's Japanese newspapers were evidence of what Japan's women have done for themselves and their country in the long years that the ashes have taken to cool after the war the men started. *Yomiuri Shimbun* had her breaking the tape on the back page (i.e. the front page) while in the front of the paper (i.e. the back) there was a two-page spread full of nothing but her. In a culture where even the empress must devote her efforts to ensuring that she does not appear taller than her husband, the new *marason* winner is part of a feminist breakthrough that makes ours look like a walkover. In the light of that fact, the pictures were historic. Here she was in close-up, her teensy teeth taking a bite out of a medal the size of a *vermeille* mill wheel; and here she was again, hugging the runner-up. Snuggling up to the *gaijin*! It was a new world.

Nor, you can bet, will her endorsements be just for noodles. Look forward to the Sony Takahashi compact sound system, the Mitsubishi Marason miniature sports car, and any number of tie-ups with Panasonic. In my hotel, the Panasonic executives were still arriving and leaving by the bus-load every day. Their top man, Matsushita-*san* himself, the venerable *daimyo* of Japanese electronics, had already been and gone, bowed in and out by platoons of suits, but his fine nose for a market would already be on the case. Panasonic didn't back the Olympics by accident. When I stepped into an elevator full

of people wearing Panasonic ponchos, they were discussing Taka-
hashi-*san* in terms they usually reserve for Elle McPherson. Helping
to sponsor the games had been worth it to them anyway, but here
was a bonus.

But if Takahashi-*san* meant a lot to Japan, Cathy Freeman meant
everything to Australia. Right through the weekend, the television
channels ran special Cathy programmes. As her big Monday dawned
cool and wet, the papers were special Cathy issues. It was universally
assumed that Australia's future as a mature nation would be secured
by her victory. Few and brave they were who dared to suggest that
the possibility of her losing could not be ruled out, in view of the
presence on the track of several other athletes all faster over 400m
than the average journalist.

For the beleaguered minority who had retained their sanity, there
was solace to be gleaned by the information – only fleetingly mentioned in the media – that Cathy herself had not read a newspaper
in months. Her final would not happen until after eight in the
evening. It was a long day's journey into night. I spent half of the day
at the diving pool, watching incredible things, and the other half in
one of the crowded downtown bars, watching even more incredible
things – TV commentators pushing themselves to the edge of desperation as they cranked up the tension with a gigantically clumsy verbal
winch.

By this time the whole city had turned into a huge network of
viewing parlours. One of the best was the foyer of the Qantas
building, but you had to pretend to be a pilot to get in. Qantas staff
were in there with glasses of wine. Circular Quay, however, was still
the prime spot. In about half a square mile of usually open space,
there was absolutely nowhere to sit down unless you had arrived
before nightfall, but the giant screens had the whole story. Out at
the track, Cathy peeled off her outer tracksuit to reveal an inner
running suit, a sort of Green Hornet ensemble that would be hard
to explain away if she fizzled. 'In many ways,' bellowed a commentator, 'her fate may be decided in the next few minutes.' The same
words were probably the last that Mary Queen of Scots ever heard.

Her fate wasn't decided, of course, although it might well have
been had she lost. But she won, with that long, lovely stride that puts
Puck's girdle around the earth; and she will now be able, from a
position of strength, to get on with the difficult business of controlling

her own life when everyone she meets wants a piece of it. Blessed with the uncommon gift of public privacy, she will probably cope. Her post-race interview was perfect. 'Something like this happening to a little girl like me!' It was exactly the right thing to say, as a whole nation congratulated itself on its faith, love and maturity.

But Reconciliation will be harder than that. As Cathy (not our Cathy: her Cathy) is all too aware, there are thousands of Aboriginals who can't run, and now they have nowhere to hide either. Mature, multicultural Australia's one and only recalcitrant minority is likely to go on being buffeted by two contradictory paternalistic exhortations: 'Stay as sweet as you are' and 'See what you can do if you try?' Both are patronizing, and it is a nice question which is the more mischievous.

Just as we were soothing our collectively inflamed liberal conscience with the prospect of Cathy taking her place among the international community of super-cool black athletes, Marion Jones turned out to have a problem, in the shape of C. J. Hunter, her other half, or other eleven twelfths. The shape of C. J. Hunter takes a box of pencils and a large sheet of paper to describe. Let's just say that he is a shot-putter who looks as if he could put a London bus on the roof of your house. The news came through that he had withdrawn from the games not because of a torn meniscus, as he claimed, but because of the presence in his body of about a thousand times the permitted level of an anabolic steroid. There was no reason, we were told, to suppose that Marion Jones had known about this.

The assurances seemed reasonable. Crouching in her corner of the bedroom while C. J. Hunter fills the rest of it, she could hardly be expected to keep tabs on what every area of his body is up to. But looking at Marion's tearful smile, it was hard to quell awful memories of Flo-Jo in her final phase. Would there be no end to the drug thing? No, because there is no end to the big money. It was almost enough to make you long for an end to the Olympics. But not quite: in Sydney, nothing could do that.

5. OLYMPIC CRESCENDO

To prove that God is not mocked, for a day or two it rained on the Sydney Olympics, and there was a sense of divine retribution for too much profane enjoyment. Drugs were threatening to spoil the party. Everyone agreed that it was the best party ever, but worshippers of the golden calf thought the same. Then Moses made them melt it down and drink it.

C. J. Hunter, the mountainous shot-putting husband of American star sprinter Marion Jones, called a press conference to explain how an infantry division's lifetime supply of anabolic steroids had got into him by accident. To help defend his innocence, he was attended by Johnny Cochran, the very mouthpiece who had shown us how the Los Angeles police framed O. J. Simpson, and who would soon, presumably, show us how the International Olympic Committee had backed up a tanker of nandrolone to C. J.'s condo and transferred its contents to his sleeping form by intravenous injection at dead of night.

As the stunned Australian press looked on, it became apparent that C. J. Hunter and Johnny Cochran were made for each other. C. J. burst into tears, Johnny railed against injustice, and the combined effect was enough to persuade you that the Olympic movement was so far gone into pharmaceutical hell that there was nothing to do except pour concrete over the whole deal, surround it with a barbed-wire fence, and put up signs warning children that if they played there they would have to be hunted down and shot.

As if things weren't dismal enough, Romania's teeny-bopper gymnast Andreea Raducan was stripped of her gold medal for swallowing a cough drop prescribed by her team physician, the aptly named Dr Dill. This seemed unfair until her appeal to a higher authority was rejected with draconian hauteur. 'The anti-doping code,' droned a man with an all-purpose international accent, 'must be enforced without compromise.' Andreea, it was explained, was so tiny that a single one of Dr Dill's pills was enough to multiply her muscle-tone like a Benzedrine inhaler up the nose of a performing flea.

'I don't make nothing wrong,' wailed Andreea, touchingly missing the point. It not only sounded unfair, it *was* unfair, and in that fact lay salvation. Sydney would be the games where the drug thing hit the wall, no matter what the cost. A few Bulgarian kayak paddlers who had tested positive might still be paddling their kayaks, but apparently there were technical reasons for that. (Perhaps they had put on so much heft that they could not be removed from their kayaks without surgery.) On the whole, however, this was a story of the rules being the rules. As Wittgenstein said just after he hit Bertrand Russell over the head with a billiard cue, a game consists of the rules by which it is played. No rules, no game. Drugs were out.

Sex, however, was still in, and it helped to save the day. In many minds an evil comparable with drugs, sex was everywhere in the Sydney Olympics, in the form of delectable bodies sketchily attired. Not all of these were female, but the ones most likely to arouse ire mainly were. I myself had been guilty of looking upon the female beach volleyballers with more attention than their diffident skills warranted. The Brazilians, especially, were too much, brushing the sand from their lightly tanned flanks as if aware that every grain of it was reluctant to leave. As they skipped, bounced, dived and tumbled without ever adopting an ungainly pose, I thought I recognized one of them from the Oba Oba club in Rio, but it's twenty years since I've been there. Perhaps it was her mother into whose spangled G-string I tucked a ten-dollar bill after a samba routine that left every man in the room with his head in his hands, weeping softly for the evanescence of human life.

In the Kuwaiti version of the Olympic television transmission, the female beach volleyballers did not appear at all. The Kuwaiti television authorities, after studying the videotape with care, had decided that the dress code drove a coach and horses through the Koran. When the Kuwaiti female beach volleyballers take the field at the next Olympics, they will be wearing the full, theologically approved kit. Nothing will be visible except their eyes. Concealment should be a great aid to tactics: try guessing where a Kuwaiti female beach volleyballer is going to hit it next.

Meanwhile the heavily breathing Kuwaiti television authorities and I were on a certain loser. Female beach volleyball, although an abject failure on the mental level, was a raging success in terms of base desire. The Australian team, not just because they won the gold medal but because they were so easy on the eye, had the crowds around Sydney's giant TV screens yelling in orgiastic self-congratulation. They made Sydney's women feel beautiful.

Sydney's women *are* beautiful. It can be fatal to say so, because feminist orthodoxy rules Australia the way Torquemada used to rule Toledo, but to dodge the facts you would have to tape your eyes shut and walk with a white stick. The ethnic blender that has been humming away ever since World War II has produced varieties of comeliness to boggle the Australian male mind. Unfortunately for the varieties, the Australian male mind has been slow to respond to this plenitude. It is said that the women of Saigon lost the Americans the Vietnam War, because their loveliness made the grunts think twice about putting their lives on the line. The women of Sydney, had they been present at the time, would have sufficed to get the Hundred Years War restricted to three weeks and the Thirty Years War called off altogether. Why do the men of Sydney not fall on them like satyrs?

There are several theories. One theory says that many of the more attractive men have eyes only for each other, and that the rest are subdued by political correctness. Whatever the reason, the fact remains that the influx of international male visitors has brought Sydney's females something they are not used to: appreciation. They are looked at in the street; softly whistled at; engaged in conversation. They are not sure they like it. They are not sure they don't. Away from the pool, an Australian male swimmer is not necessarily a model of sophistication. An Italian male swimmer, on the other hand, could be a model for Armani. He wants to discuss the book you are reading. You forgive him for the way he touches your wrist while he admires the nail-polish that none of the local boys have ever noticed. Perhaps the Olympics should always be held here.

Square men of Sydney will undoubtedly retaliate by upping the ante of their amatory commitment. The air is charged with pheromones as never before, and even in daytime the giant screens of downtown work like the walls of an enormous discotheque, pumping out images of physical allure. In Stadium Australia, while Cathy Freeman's elegant legs were in the very act of propelling her to glory, Australia's star female pole-vaulter was hauling herself skyward to a silver medal. An exalted blonde goddess whose ten-foot pole looks like the one she wouldn't touch you with, she bears the nowadays typical Australian name of Tatiana Grigorieva.

Tatiana and her husband (equally gorgeous, and also an Olympic pole-vaulter) have made a new life here, far from the tragic confusions of their background. Your heart would be melted by Tatiana's early struggles if her beauty had not already broken it. Tatiana, or Tattie as she is fated to be called, has already posed naked for an upmarket glossy. For purposes of research I tried to buy a copy, but was told that it had sold out instantly, mainly to men my age who spoke out of the side of their mouths. I would hate to believe that the pictures were any more arousing than the effect she generates when she launches herself upside down towards the bar that topples at a touch.

In the slow-motion television image of her silver-winning jump, which days later is still being played over and over, she stays up there for an age, sidling over the bar and seeming to whisper to it on the way, as if promising to give it a kiss if it behaves. Would I were that bar, thinks many a poor swain, that she might misjudge her jump and fall with me in her embrace, e'en into yon soft bag. From young men with tinnies in their hands, a concerted, lyrical groan goes up. Australian masculinity is on its way back. In so many ways these games have expanded the national consciousness – or perhaps they have just given it an opportunity to express itself.

Australia has been promised by Tatiana's management team that she will become a catwalk model. Fashion industry experts say that not many pole-vaulters have made the transition to catwalk model, but it can't be as hard as making the transition from catwalk model to pole-vaulter. Naomi Campbell is built along the right lines. She might care to give it a try. She could keep the judges waiting until they go to sleep, and then just walk under the bar and lie down.

Beauty becomes more beautiful when it does something, and also more bearable; in line with the principle that sex, when sublimated into aesthetics, is purged of longing. The thought crossed my mind when Marion Jones crossed the finishing line to win her second gold medal, for the 200m sprint. Shedding tears for C. J. Hunter, she looked as if he had just sat on her, but in full flight she was a glorious thing to see. She is a big girl – sprinters of either sex are nearly always big – but has the air of having been scaled up from something smaller while retaining its fine proportions, in the same way that the Boeing 747 reminds you of the F-86 Sabre.

Like everyone in Sydney I have become a one-man kangaroo court on the matter of drug-enhanced sporting performance, because when *all* the competitors are suspect you have to make up your mind somehow or stop watching. I go by appearances. On Thursday night, after four days of deliberation, I finally found Marion not guilty. She was just too feminine. In certain aspects, notably in the area of the gluteus maximus, she tends towards the chunky, but not in the way that Flo-Jo did in her second phase, when she had biceps on her jawline like Arnold Schwarzenegger.

Since Flo-Jo was never busted except by an early death, you will note that I find her guilty by the same method that I find Marion innocent, but you have to draw the line somewhere, and I draw the line where women start turning into men. If that's their object, it's their business; but as a side-effect of ambition it seems unfortunate, and to force them into it is surely a crime. By that criterion, the news that a whole generation of East German women athletes and swimmers had been doped to the eyeballs was the least surprising news ever published. Now that doping is associated with the big money attendant on success, it should not be forgotten that it started in the East, as a weapon in the battle for national prestige. Actually the big money was operating there, too. If the athletes refused to roll their sleeves up for the needle they were thrown off the team and back into everyday life, where there was no access to the special stores that spelt the difference between a life worth living and mere existence. The welfare of their families was on the block. It was hard to say no. But the men who made them say yes were criminals, and it is hard to accept that some of those men are walking free while an itsy-bitsy sprite like Andreea Raducan weeps for the medal she lost for a cough-drop.

In the middle of the week the sun had fought the rain, but on Friday it was no contest. The same bright sky that lit the beginning of the games was back to light its three-day climax, which would culminate in a closing ceremony tipped to be the most exciting thing the world had seen since the opening ceremony. The crowds that had retreated to the bars and cafés now filled the streets again, and once again the pixilated children out of a Max Reinhardt production of *A Midsummer Night's Dream* were everywhere, their green and gold heads popping out from windows, from behind trees, from above the rails of ferries. It seemed a silly time to be indoors, but that was where the diving was, and of all the aesthetic pleasures of the games there was nothing to touch the diving.

A lot of it hit the giant screens, because Australia did well for once in the only department of aquatic sport where success has traditionally proved elusive. One of our female synchro divers was the very girl whose name had caught my attention ten days before: Loudy Torky. It turned out that she had been born in Palestine. Once again Australia had profited from upheaval elsewhere in the world. Palestine had Yasser Arafat, and we had Loudy Torky. It could have gone the other way. Yasser Arafat could easily be imagined as an Australian diver, doing his famous two and a half forward somersaults with triple hand grenades. But such considerations shrank to insignificance beside the achievements of China's great female diver Fu Mingxia. At the age of twenty-two she was in her third Olympics, and dominating the scene with imperial assurance.

Fu Mingxia is the woman that Madame Mao would have liked to have been, but Madame Mao had no talent. China is still a monster, and there can be no doubt that the thirty-seven athletes who were withdrawn before the games were doped in the first place as a matter of policy. But China has come on, and the clearest proof is that Fu Mingxia can practise her art unhindered. Madame Mao would have killed her. The commissar mentality hates talent with a passion, and Fu Mingxia has so much talent that it hurts.

Apart from her dignity, she is nothing special in repose, but in motion it is a different matter: sex, having risen to the aesthetic, takes off into the realm of the spirit. From the qualifying rounds all the way through to the final, every tower dive she did was like a falling ballet solo, as if Altynai Asylmuratova had thrown herself out of a window for doomed love. Coming down from ten metres with your knickers in a twist, if you hit the water with your hands even a tiny bit apart you might as well have run head first into the side of a house. The moment of impact is called the entry. With Fu Mingxia, the entry made the sound of ripped silk. She was adorable, and it was strange to think that she will never endorse anything, and that her gold medals will be the only valuable objects she will ever own. Unless, of course, China, like Australia, becomes a mature nation.

6. OLYMPICS FINALE

As the games of the XXVIIth Olympiad ran out of events, the Olympic Village joined the party that had been raging all over Sydney since the torch arrived. Athletes with nothing left to do were whooping it up into the wee hours: a blast for them, but bad news for the marathon runners whose upcoming ordeal would be the prelude to the much-anticipated closing ceremony. Sole competitor in the first marathon in history, Pheidippides had been obliged to run the distance without benefit of sponsorship from a shoe manufacturer, but at least he got some kip the night before.

Press speculation was rife about how impresario Ric Birch could stage a finale that would top his overture, the opening ceremony that had stunned the world and given Australia confidence in its new position as a mature nation. Some of the other mature nations had already brought their teams home. When their empty chalets were entered to be cleaned, all too many of them turned out to be littered with syringes. Where the Bulgarians had been, the cleaners had to back out and wait for the army: there were needles in there like the floor of a pine forest after a tornado.

But the drug thing, like the bad weather, was by now a back number. Think-piece journalists raided the thesaurus to describe the sky: azure, cerulean, Arcadian, Poussinesque. This, surely, was Eden, and minus the serpent. The Germans and the Israelis remembered Munich, but if any terrorists were going to raise their balaclava-clad heads in Sydney, it was getting late. Either they hadn't come or they had gone native – dumped the AK-47s and gone into business selling Semtex to the female discus throwers, who put it on their muesli.

When you considered that the Australian press, during the run-up to the Olympics, greeted their advent as if an invasion force of Martian troop-transports had entered the earth's atmosphere, the papers had done pretty well. Their praise for Australia's champions might have bordered on the hagiographic, but the athletes of other nations got frequent mentions, and the photo spreads looked as if the United Nations had been reconstituted as a beauty contest. On television, Australia's Channel 7 at least did better than America's NBC, which was faced with the awful knowledge that it had paid more than a billion dollars for a ratings clunker, and would have done better putting its money into *Battlefield Earth.*

Channel 7 had no problems with the time difference or the receptivity of its audience. Apart from its gift for the ill-chosen word, its only but insoluble problem was with the events, which if they are to be covered fairly on screen must interrupt each other continually, thus guaranteeing that any given viewer, umpteen times a day, will be hauled away from something interesting to something soporific. By the final weekend the traffic in visual narcotics had thinned out, but there was still enough yawn-material available to ensure that anything gripping could be cut away from at the crucial moment.

Thrilling bike races through the crowded streets were interrupted by the thousandth transmission of the same commercial for Australian Mutual Provident, an organization which is apparently dedicated to arranging for its subscribers a visit from their future selves, who will assure them that they were right to dream of that little house on the hill, because the time would come when they would magically be able to buy it, owing to the inspired assistance of Australian Mutual Provident. Watching transfixed, as a man will when he meets a funnelweb spider on his way to the wood-pile, on several occasions I was visited by my own future self, who assured me that the time would come when the migraine induced by too many screenings of a transcendentally dumb commercial would melt away, after I had entered the headquarters of Australian Mutual Provident, tied up its executive in charge of advertising, and burned the place down.

'The right to dream' was a media buzz phrase throughout the Olympics, hanging around like a blowfly at the barbie. Reserving to myself the right to dream of kicking the set in, I took solace in the thought of the imminent return to the bike race, but instead the screen was filled with a man in a top hat riding a horse walking sideways, or six canoes with twelve men in them crossing the middle distance at a not very surprising rate. Channel 7 had a cable TV subsidiary, but on that one you were likely to be confronted with a couple of small boxers in headgear the size of sofas hanging on to each other as if they had finally realized that a slow foxtrot felt better than getting hit.

Boxing has no place in the Olympics, not because it damages the brain – if you want to see a damaged brain, take a look at a Taiwanese judo competitor who thought he had devoted his life to an intricate Oriental art form until a 400lb Norwegian fell on him – but because you can get it better elsewhere. The same applies to tennis and football. I would have said that the same applied to basketball, in which America's dream team – a bunch of subluminary pros playing an exhibition tournament for charity – had been declared invincible. But by behaving as if their supremacy were beyond challenge, they made themselves so obnoxious that when the Lithuanians almost beat them the whole of Sydney went mad with joy around the giant TV screens.

In the whole of the games I saw no event more riveting. In the velodrome there had been an event called the Madison in which about a dozen teams tangled in a flat-out dogfight while the spectators, including myself, struggled for breath to yell with. When the British team crashed I had to prise somebody's hands from my throat but found it easier after I realized they were mine. I had also developed an unexpected passion for Australia's women's hockey team, the Hockeyroos. Men's hockey still strikes me as something a dweeb does to get out of playing rugby, but women's hockey is a different matter, or anyway it is when the Hockeyroos play it. They also attain a surprising level of pulchritude for women who could take your head off with a stick.

On top of all that, as the linkmen say, there had been the last rounds of the men's platform diving. Every man in the final could do the inward three and a half that Greg Louganis had astonished the world with only two Olympiads ago. With everyone diving to the same stratospheric standard, the medals were decided by the pointing of the toe, the shape of the haircut, the flaring of the nostrils. You have to see a dive like that go wrong before you can grasp what's involved. Not all that long ago a diver got killed doing the inward three and a half. I watched the whole final as if Damocles beneath the sword were dancing like Fred Astaire. But not even that could touch the excitement of seeing Lithuania come within ten seconds of stuffing it to the dream team.

Despite what you may have heard, Australia's spirit of all-embracing Olympic tolerance does not exclude the world's only remaining superpower. But the Yanks are not always able to unpack the semantic content of a friendly heckle. It is a fallacy that Americans are without irony; but they do tend to take words at their face value; and it is misleading enough to do that with British English, while to do it with Australian English makes misapprehension a certainty.

Particularly when it comes to humour, Australian English is a richly ambiguous poetic phenomenon which must be interpreted for tone. When T. S. Eliot said 'We had the experience but missed the meaning' he could have been speaking for American basketballers who switched Channel 7 on late at night and found themselves watching *The Dream*, the hit media experience of the Sydney Olympics. Hosted by two wits calling themselves H.G. and Roy, *The Dream* celebrated the Olympic ideal by inserting a pointed stick up its crazy date.

The Crazy Date was H.G. and Roy's name for a certain legs-apart manoeuvre performed by gymnasts in the floor exercises and on the pommel-horse. The term depended for its evocative power on your being able to deduce, if you hailed from elsewhere, that a specific item of human anatomy was being referred to. You had to remember that the Australian scatological vocabulary is precisely visual.

H.G. and Roy did a short stretch on British television at one stage, but they are too fond of lingering improvisation to get going in a tight slot. (They would pounce on that statement: they are very rude.) The two-hour expanse of *The Dream* was ideal for them. They had space to do their thing, and so did their unofficial Olympic mascot, Fatso the Fat-Arsed Wombat. Fatso did his thing in the form of Olympic gold medals expelled majestically from his fundament as he wandered in graphic form across the bottom of the screen. Billie-Jean King, incidentally, was one American who got the point of *The Dream* exactly. She came on the show to read the news, and looked more than ever the way she always did at Wimbledon – like the brightest girl at the ball.

Though the mass media had not been as triumphantly awful as the occasion might have invited, the truly heartening coverage was in the Australian ethnic press. If you were looking for the Mature Nation, there it was. Admittedly the satellite digest edition of *Bild* had two screaming pages about how Germany's long-jump champion Heike Dreschler had seen off Marion Jones. The main piece was headlined *Der Sprung in die Unsterblichkeit* the jump to immortality. It featured a Junoesque picture of Heike in mid-*Sprung*, looking like a wet dream by Arno Brecker. There was no mention that Heike began her career in the old East Germany, the needle park of the Warsaw Pact. All this was pretty chauvinistic, not to say *völkisch*, but if you looked at Australia's home-grown German weekly *Die Woche in Australien* you got a different slant. They were telling two stories at once: one about the Fatherland, and one about Australia. Germany's obscure slalom canoeist Thomas Schmidt was congratulated for having propelled himself into the top rank (*Unbekannter Schmidt paddelt sich in die Elite*), but the main story was a hymn to Australia's heroes: Cathy, Thorpie *und so weiter*.

It was the same with all the other examples of the ethnic press I could lay my hands on. *El Espanol*, which caters for the Hispano-American community, lauded Milton Wynants of Uruguay for his silver in the cycling and was moved by the humility of *este excelente pedalista*. And *Edinenie* ('Unification') praised Svetlana Khorkina for not letting her disaster in the vault stop her going on to win an individual gold medal. 'Not what the Russian Princess of Gymnastics had dreamed of, but all the same . . .' The word for 'dream' is particularly beautiful in Russian and so, of course, is Svetlana. There was a picture of her with her tongue sticking out, but she was doing it beautifully. The same paper, a few days before, had gone appropriately batso for Tatiana Grigorieva, now an Australian; but what impressed me was the connection with the homeland. This was the eternal Russia, the one that had been remorselessly assaulted for seventy long years by its own government: and now it was here.

They were all here, and in that lay the jest. As the other big Spanish-language paper *Extra Informativo* said in its front-page story headed (you guessed it) 'THE RIGHT TO DREAM', Australia is a country of the evolved world, *el mundo evolucionado*. From the political viewpoint, all that stuff about Australia's delayed ascendancy to the status of a mature nation is an insult to millions of innocent dead. One of the oldest, most stable and productive democracies in existence, Australia was a mature nation when Russia, Italy, Germany, China and Japan were in the grip of madness. What happened to the Aboriginals was no bush picnic, but their sufferings are further trivialized when Australia is portrayed as a racist country, as too many of Australia's subsidized intellectuals are fond of doing. The

question of Australia's institutional racism was settled at the Melbourne Olympics in 1956. There was no Olympic Village to speak of
and the citizens were invited to accept the visiting athletes into their
houses. A full two-thirds of those who offered their hospitality asked
for coloured guests, and the more coloured the better. After that, the
White Australia policy had no chance of survival: and anyway, it had
always been based on the fear that non-Caucasian immigrants, far
from being inferior, might work too hard and do too well.

When the marathon finally got going on the last day, there they
were again, working too hard and doing too well. In a light wind
that made the harbour glitter like a tray of crushed ice, three men as
black as Egypt's night were cheered to the echo through streets whose
every shop window held more wealth than the annual crop yield of
the countries they came from. There was even a cheer for John
Brown, the lone Brit who came fourth, although the television producer managed not to show him crossing the finishing line. Luckily
the handling of the Olympics had outstripped the coverage, just as
it had outstripped all expectation.

My viewing point for the closing ceremony was down at Circular
Quay. On the second floor of the Paragon hotel I found my chosen
window seat already occupied by my young friends from the torch
relay, Polly, Claire and Nugget the pug-faced wag. Polly and Claire
were dressed to kill. As I complimented them on their shoes, Nugget
poured a litre of lager on mine, probably by accident. Communication
was by sign language. There were millions of people waiting for the
showdown and quite a few of them were in the room with us.

I could see the images on the giant screen but couldn't hear much,
which was probably a mercy. In the winged words of Juan Antonio
Samaranch, what I can say? It off got to a start bad, with a vestal
virgin routine scored by Vangelis that boded ill for Athens. The
virgins wore Fortuny-style pleated gowns that stirred listlessly in the
breeze, almost as if something were about to happen. Then one of
the virgins slowly lifted a wreath. Nugget said they were the only
virgins in Australia.

When the Aussies came on, things picked up, although the local
pop music is more derivative than it thinks, especially when it has a
statement to make. Sub-Springsteens and semi-Stones assured the
Aboriginals that salvation was at hand. No doubt Cathy Freeman was
relieved to hear this. Kylie Minogue, arriving on the wings of a thong,

turned the night around, although her Abba song 'Dancing Queen' was a sop to the gays that they scarcely needed, because the Mardi Gras was in control out there like martial law. The *Strictly Ballroom* routines made you want to join in and thousands of the athletes did. Some of the floats were quite good, but not the ones bearing Paul Hogan and Elle McPherson. Hogan rode on an Akubra hat and Elle on a giant camera. Neither star had been given anything to do. At least Greg Norman hit a golf ball. In keeping with his nickname, Greg emerged from a great white shark. The relatives of two people who had been eaten by great white sharks off the coast of South Australia during the previous week were probably not watching.

I thought the Aboriginal ensemble Yothu Yindi was the best thing, but really it was no occasion for critical analysis. The maturity that Australia is right to be nervous about is cultural maturity, which can't be had by wishing, but only through achievement – through creativity in all walks of life, from high art down to the small change of civil discourse. In that respect, the inspired contribution of the 45,000 white-hatted volunteer workers, many of them older than I am, was perhaps the most original feature of the whole jamboree. They were all charmingly helpful and some of them were outright funny. The visitors loved them. Small groups of Chinese would follow them around, confident that they were going somewhere interesting.

*

The Sydney Olympics, by synthesizing and highlighting what we already possessed, put us on our own map. We were already on everyone else's, as a destination, a refuge, an ideal and (whisper it) a dream. The opening ceremony brought Australia together. The closing ceremony might have tried to show a united world, but it would have mocked the global tragedies that have given Australia its unique life and have made it the good place where all the earth's agonies come to be assuaged, the last garden. The full story is too terrible to be told in a night. Better to let your hair down, and to camp it up.

The Olympics began with Cleopatra's arrival in Rome, and they ended with Elizabeth Taylor's departure for the airport. Next day I did the same. I have done so many times, but never with such regret.